RIO GRANDE

~

Rio

AUSTIN  UNIVERSITY OF TEXAS PRESS

Grande

Edited and with a Text by JAN REID

*Publication of this book
was aided by the generous support
of the University of Texas Press
Advisory Council.*

Compilation copyright © 2004 by Jan Reid
All rights reserved
Printed in China
First edition, 2004

Requests for permission to reproduce material from this work should be sent to
Permissions, University of Texas Press, P.O. Box 7819, Austin, TX 78713-7819.

∞ The paper used in this book meets the minimum requirements of ANSI/NISO Z39.48-1992 (R1997)
(Permanence of Paper).

Library of Congress Cataloging-in-Publication Data
Rio Grande / edited and with a text by Jan Reid.
    p.   cm.
ISBN 0-292-70601-4 ((cl.) : alk. paper)
1. Rio Grande—Description and travel. 2. Rio Grande Valley—Description and travel.
3. Rio Grande—Pictorial works. 4. Rio Grande Valley—Pictorial works.
5. Rio Grande—Literary collections. 6. Rio Grande Valley—Literary collections. I. Reid, Jan.
F392.R5R56 2004
917.64′4—dc22   2004002629

FRONTISPIECE: LAURA GILPIN

EARL NOTTINGHAM

"Rio Grande at Noon, Rio Grande at Midnight"

Water has no memory; that is why it is so clear
RAMON GOMEZ DE LA SERNA

~

Ramon, the water here forgets nothing
a brown syrup of grease and ash that cleaves

at rust canyons, caustic black cough of coal
from smokestacks extending river from razor wire

to sky. We have seen the devil and he is
a cartographer—rivers as wells, the Styx

wrapped seven times around his realm; ashamed,
the Border Patrol resigns, gathers cactus

flowers for their lovers—love songs all evening
spill from round-mouthed guitars like lava, like melting

snow—a river knows its source . . . Tell us
what is enough love and what is more

than enough, and what it is to dream as rivers
dream—to not just swim but to be the ocean.

CHRISTOPHER CESSAC,
from *Republic Sublime*

CONTENTS

W. D. SMITHERS

PROLOGUE

SIXTEENTH-CENTURY SPANIARDS called the stream Río de las Palmas. At first they knew only the river's mouth and its lush delta. Framed by beaches and dunes of blond sand, the broad bright forest of Sabal palm trees around the river's mouth was a landmark for navigators of the Gulf of Mexico. Those being a lonely and anxious few. In 1527, 194 Spanish explorers marooned by a failed expedition in Florida sailed west from Tampa Bay in five barges, hoping their crossing of the gulf would deliver them to the River of Palms and more Spaniards they might find there. Desperation had driven them to the attempt: scores of men had died of disease, starvation, and attacks by Indians, and the Spaniards had eaten all their horses. They caulked and tarred the barges with gummy exudates of palmetto and pine, twisted their rope and rigging from the manes and tails of the dead horses, tore off and stitched together their ragged shirts for sails. An officer named Alvar Núñez Cabeza de Vaca reflected on their chances at the outset. "We resumed our voyage," he would write, "coasting toward the River of Palms, our hunger and thirst growing daily more intense because our scant provisions were nearly exhausted and the water-bottles we had made had rotted."

They tried to keep in sight the coast's barrier islands, sand peninsulas, and mangrove thickets, putting in for rest in the sheltered bays. But after several days the mighty outwash of the Mississippi River spewed the flotilla far out into the gulf, and then in those fragile crafts they ran afoul of a hurricane, which drowned many and crashed a few ashore on Galveston Island, which they named Malhado, the "Island of Doom." Only six of them ever saw other Spaniards again.

Cabeza de Vaca set out on a six-thousand-mile odyssey, at times as a slave of Indians, then as a shaman drawing on prayer and necessity that he could be a faith healer, and ultimately as a trader of copper, turquoise, deer hearts. The survival of Cabeza de Vaca and his few companions was a magnificent feat of endurance, achieved on no more than the strength of wits and prayer, a sheer refusal to give up. Legend has it that Cabeza de Vaca plunged through thorny canyon lands and crossed the glistening jewel of Rio Grande tributaries, the Devils River. Many days later, the wanderers found the first real village beside the river, which ran between stark unwooded mountains—probably the future settlement of El Paso. Aborigines cultivated beans, squash, and corn along the river. Replenished and encouraged, Cabeza de Vaca and his companions roved onward in distance the Indians measured by *jornadas*—treks between the semipermanent tribal *rancherías*. The walk carried them several days along the Rio Grande's bottoms of cottonwood and willow, switch grass and cane; they crossed the wide, chest-deep stream in today's southern New Mexico. The Europeans came upon a tribe of planters and bison hunters—"Cow People"—who received them with prescient misgivings and stressed the harsh difficulties before them, whether they stayed near the river or braved a desert crossing. The only things they would find that were halfway edible were juniper berries.

Did Cabeza de Vaca sense that the river he camped beside was the Río de las Palmas his companions had died trying to find? There is no hint that he made that geographical connection. He just had faith that if he kept walking and, basically, rounding back to the left, he would someday encounter Spaniards. Cabeza de Vaca explored enough desert, shortgrass plain, and juniper-studded hills that he ardently believed the stories of Cíbola, the fabulous Indian cities of gold and plantations of cotton that had been founded on the plains, it was said, by seven fugitive bishops. (Fugitives from where, one has to wonder, and whose authority?) At least Cabeza de Vaca relayed the stories of Cíbola as if he believed them—at the end of his long walk he dazzled countrymen with tales of arrowheads made of emeralds. Of course, he hadn't brought any specimens along. This phantom civilization, which the Spaniards hoped would rival the riches surrendered to the crown by the Aztecs and Incas, was always just a little farther on, a few more horizons north or west. Knowing they were not the ones who would find it, Cabeza de Vaca and his companions circled southward through the country of the Gila River and the Chiricahua Mountains; they eventually began to hear from the Indians tales of men who were Christians. Near the northernmost settlement of Spanish empire, Culiacán, New Galicia (which is today the Mexican state of Sinaloa), they found these Christians terrorizing the Indians as slave hunters. The year was 1537.

Cabeza de Vaca must have thought many times in that decade that his luck had run out, that this was his destiny, the place where he would die. He came to love the vast country whose gateway was the Rio Grande and many of the peoples he encountered there. He helped indigenous Americans fend off slave traders from rival tribes, and he wanted to leave all of them peace, priests, and plenty. Conquer them, yes, but make their lives better. As a leader of subsequent expeditions in South America, the conquistador punished Spaniards who had come across the ocean to loot and rape—also ordered his men to carry his bed through a jungle. They mutinied and sent him back across the Atlantic in chains. After so many brushes with death in a place almost as foreign as the moon, he nonetheless came to his end amid his family, a pensioner honored in his country. He died in 1557 at about age 67.

Cabeza de Vaca was a survivor in another important way. Men named Dorantes and Castillo and another known only as "the Negro" lived to tell much the same story. But Cabeza de Vaca had the talent and foresight to put it down on paper—to write about it—and as a result their wild experience has lived on under his signature. *La Relación* (*The Relation*, or his account) was first published in 1542; seven years later he retitled a second edition *Naufragios* (*Shipwrecks*), which seems to imply an impish sense of humor. Cabeza de Vaca wrote a longer chronicle about his time in South America, but the first one became an ageless book of travel and adventure. For Europeans it provided the first vivid glimpse of a wilderness that would be called Texas, and of a river that one country severed from Spain would call Rio Bravo and that another country severed from Mexico would call the Rio Grande. For the people who came to call themselves Texans, his book was the foundation of a literary heritage. Cabeza de Vaca was not the best-educated survivor of that shipwreck—nor was he the only one to put thoughts and quill to paper—but he wrote with subtle, instinctive flair. "Eating the dogs," he began one chapter, "seemed to give us strength enough to go forward; so commending ourselves to the guidance of God our Lord, we took leave of our hosts, who pointed out the way to others nearby who spoke their language." *La Relación* is a work of art. And from it has flowed a shared literature of Mexico and the United States.

~

AT 1,885 MILES, the Rio Grande ranks twentieth in length among the earth's rivers, yet it has only two major tributaries. The river that Cabeza de Vaca knew as Río de las Palmas has gone by many names, a number of them lovely: Mets'ichi Chena and P'osoge and Paslápane ("big river" in languages of native peoples), Río Caudaloso ("carrying much water" in Spanish), Río de la Nuestra Señora ("river of our lady"), Río Turbio ("muddy" or "turbulent"), Río Guadalquivir, Río de la Concepción, Río de la Buenaventura del Norte, Tiguex River, River of May, Grand River, Río del Norte, Río del Norte y Nuevo México, Río Bravo del Norte, Río Grande del Norte. The river's distinctiveness is captured by the two names that have endured: Mexico's Río Bravo ("angry river" or "fierce river") and the United States' Rio Grande ("great river"). If not for the happenstance of politics, war, and history, it might have attained the name recognition of, say, the Brazos. It was a long river on the Indian frontier. But it became an international boundary—"the Border"—a heavy burden for any river to bear. Particularly one that runs through such dry country.

The story of the Rio Grande of course precedes the coming of Europeans. The river was born through eons of clash and shove of rock and lava and ice, its secrets known by beings that communicate by sniff and howl and rattle, its legends and fables and gods celebrated and passed down through the ages by oral storytellers. The Rio Pecos, which heads in the stunning Sangre de Cristos, may have been the first stream to force its way to the sea, followed by the Río Conchos, which is born in the Sierra Madres Occidental; flattened on maps, the Conchos's tributaries look like the root system of a large old tree. In the river's northernmost reach, the continent's divide sends the runoff and snowmelt racing from the San Juan Mountains. In these mountains, glaciers once crunched and moved rock, melted, and filled basins until one by one they broke through the dams and flowed without ceasing to the Gulf of Mexico.

One cave farther downriver has evidence of human occupation going back fifteen to twenty thousand years. Canyons in the upper Rio Grande have sustained tribes at least twelve thousand years. The cave-dwelling Sandia culture gave way to the Clovis mammoth hunters and Folsom bison hunters and Archaic peoples who learned to grow corn and the Basketmakers who trained dogs to help them hunt. The Anasazi learned to make ceramic pottery, and they used timber for ladders and supports in their construction that evolved from cave dwellings to pueblos; they advanced from spears to bows and arrows and established that turkeys were fine to eat and, perhaps, easier to hunt than large mammals. The Anasazi flourished and then abruptly vanished, giving way to several pueblo-dwelling peoples who enjoyed a sort of golden age along the Rio Grande while Crusaders and Muslims were fighting over another desert's Holy Land. But the pueblo dwellers were always being marauded by nomads. And then in 1540, to their utter stupefaction, they were attacked by Spaniards under the command of Francisco Vásquez de Coronado, whose greed for the mythical Cíbola was whetted by the briefings of Cabeza de Vaca.

Within the Spanish empire, the making of a *mestizo* culture was by then well under way; a granddaughter of Hernán Cortéz and great-granddaughter of the Aztec emperor Moctezuma II married a rich Basque named Juan de Oñate, who in 1598 claimed "all the kingdoms and provinces of New Mexico" for the Crown. As governor, Oñate made the tribes of the upper Pecos and Rio Grande submit to an Act of Obedience and Homage. The Pueblos endured the rule of soldiers and priests until 1680, when Apaches and Navajos joined them in rage and rebellion, killing 413 missionaries and colonists and sending the rest in pell-mell flight down the Rio Grande. Though the Spaniards soon returned and crushed the puebloan revolt, many refugees of that fighting chose not to take any more chances upriver. Their adobe settlement was named El Paso del Norte, but its soil and riverbank was that of Ciudad Juárez, not the city that Texans today call El Paso. The settlers did not build and till north of the river for another two hundred years.

~

FOR ALMOST FIVE CENTURIES—a blink of an eye in many civilizations; a long time in one forced with some difficulty on the watershed of the Rio Bravo or Rio Grande— the river has mystified and inspired humans to write about it and make its images and moods linger through (what is for me) the alchemy of photography. Artful painters have also been drawn to the river, composing on rock walls ages before anyone knew of canvas; and writers of poetry, drama, screenplays, and songs, not just fiction and nonfiction prose. The decision to limit the scope and modes of artistic expression in this book was mine alone—a matter of what I'm comfortable with. Though the focus of their reflections and narratives may range far back in time, most of the writers featured in this story of a river are contemporaries of mine. The photographs, like the prose, seek a balance of historic and contemporary. To my eye, presentations of color and black-and-white photographs within the same book detract from each other. The subtlety and starkness of the river and terrain invites black-and-white imagery. Early photographers who did not have

W. D. SMITHERS

the option of color are an important part of this book's scheme, and some of the most superb contemporary photographers of the Rio Grande work only in color. I salute those latter artists with regrets.

This is a book about the river. The border—and the immigration and contraband and music and food and sixteen-wheelers; all the tragedy and richness of its wildly varied culture—are closely related themes, but they are secondary. The other thing I wanted to do in selecting these pictures and pieces of writing was to set the bar high. I was not surprised by the wealth of talent and work I had to choose from, but I was startled by the cheerfulness and eagerness of so many artists, or their estates and archivists, to lend these voices and visions to the undertaking. The magic of the Rio Grande far exceeds its natural beauty and the power of its commerce. A friend who was instrumental in bringing this book to the page discovered that since 1890 at least ninety-seven movies have been made with titles that include the words "Rio Grande." This story of the Rio Grande is meant to be impressionistic and accumulative, not definitive. While gathering material, I was twice challenged by men of gifts and discernment (moviemakers) to identify a single story which crystallized and summed up everything one ought to know about the river. The dominant political issues nowadays are the regional and international strife over its water and the U.S. government's decision that the river and all other borders of its sovereignty are the new frontier of a war against terrorism in the Middle East. Beyond that, all I could reply was: "You got me." The Rio Grande's narrative is like the silt of its bottomlands and delta—a complex layering of many locales and traditions. The river belongs to two countries, and as a consequence it is protected and managed by neither. It is a broken river now, overused and abused and in peril. Yet still it glows, emerald-like, in a collective imagination. And that mystique is its best hope for salvation.

~

ON A WARM JULY AFTERNOON in 2002 I was going to see the river's mouth for the first time. The centuries of clearing for farms and communities have today reduced the Sabal palms known by Cabeza de Vaca to one last stand in a small Audubon preserve outside Brownsville, and a withering drought had this summer left most of the wetlands as dry as chalk. In years of good rain the lowlands along the Rio Grande would be marshes teeming with shellfish and minnows hunted by ibises and herons, stepping sprightly in the brine. But now as I rode eastward on Highway 4, the most striking features out ahead were airborne white swirls of sand and salt. Freshwater inflow is an estuary's lifeblood, but these days the Rio

Grande has little of that to give. Symptomatic of its biological illness were crusts of salt that lined the banks for hundreds of yards; they resembled icy slush. The once-sprawling river delta had been reduced to a nearly barren, eroded strip of earth. Across South Bay, which is the lower end of Laguna Madre, I could make out in the haze a few buildings in Port Isabel. My guide remarked that some residents of Port Isabel were having trouble breathing—there was so much windblown grit in the air.

The guide was a pleasant man named Gilberto Rodriguez. He grew up on a farm in the Valley, spent some years working as an investigator for law firms, and now roamed the lower Rio Grande as a watermaster specialist for the Texas Commission on Environmental Quality. In layman's terms, Rodriguez was an unarmed water cop; he spent much of his time checking pump gauges on the Texas side, making sure none of its farmers were drawing more water than they were allowed. For many Rio Grande Valley residents, the mere inference of such cheating sparked outrage, and Rodriguez told me there had been times when he feared violence. "The hotter the water," he reflected, "the more hostile people become."

He was not referring to water temperature. Valley growers were livid over what they believed was Mexican theft of Rio Grande water in the northern state of Chihuahua. In the United States we learn that the Rio Grande begins with snow-melt and rapids in the Rockies of Colorado and New Mexico and then the river marks the plains with graceful lines of cottonwood and willow as it winds south-ward and claims its legacy as the Texas-Mexico border. Among geologists and geographers, especially of U.S. education and persuasion, that is gospel. Other experts on the river have long contended that the genuine stream of origin is Mexico's Río Conchos. Whatever the technicalities and truth of that science of water and gravity and elevation, these days dams in New Mexico, the thirsty and sprawling border cities of El Paso and Juárez, and giant tangles of salt cedar strangle the Rio Grande's flow by the time it enters Texas. In undisputed fact, if not in science, the river's headwater is now the Río Conchos, which begins high in the Mexican cordilleras, crosses a forbidding pan of Chihuahuan Desert, and revives the parent stream at Presidio and Ojinaga, the storied La Junta above Big Bend.

By terms of a 1944 treaty, two-thirds of the Conchos's flow belongs to Mexico; the remaining third is supposed to be released to the United States. Yet how ex-actly does one possess a river? In the 1990s Mexico began to amass a huge "water debt." Instead of regularly releasing Río Conchos water downstream, managers in Chihuahua stored it in reservoirs for the use of its towns and for irrigating farms. Texas farmers believed that their way of life was being sold down the river—or up the river—and in their confusion and exasperation they were infuriated by the tepid support of the U.S. government. Because of Mexico's water debt, the growers calculated the loss to their fields at about 489 billion gallons of water and warned that the Valley economy could collapse. Their anger had embroiled Mexican president Vicente Fox in a domestic furor that could only sour his once-bright relations with his American counterpart, George W. Bush. Invoking the rhetoric of America's war on terrorism, Texas agriculture commissioner Susan Combs—an ambitious Republican politician and one of the farmers' key supporters—branded Chihuahua "a rogue state." But the farmers' ire was aimed not only at Mexico. The conflict had embarrassed Texas governor Rick Perry and the hugely popular (at least in Texas) President Bush.

A dwindling supply of water was an issue for all Texans—no less for those in the rain-soaked forests and coastlands whose plenty was eyed enviously by Houston, Dallas, San Antonio, and other cities. But few Texans raised as desperate a fuss as Rio Grande Valley farmers. For a decade they had suffered a dry spell rivaling the legendary drought of the forties and fifties that had turned most of Texas into a federal disaster area. Because the groundwater is brackish, the Valley could get no help from its underlying aquifers; the Rio Grande carried all the water there was. Every drop of Conchos water was vital to the farmers, but that spigot had been all but turned off.

Nowhere was this more apparent than at the mouth of the Rio Grande, which was further depleted and consumed by spongy mats of hyacinth and hydrilla. At the terminus of Highway 4, Gilberto Rodriguez and I jostled from pavement to loose sand. It was a pretty day at the beach. The white-capped waves were a bright dark blue, and squadrons of brown pelicans folded their wings and smacked beak-first into the surf, trying to catch dinner. Boca Chica, which means "small mouth," had none of the glitz of nearby South Padre Island, but families were out fishing, splashing, building sand castles. Ahead, a portable light tower had been erected. That landmark, Rodriguez told me, was Mexico. Parked on the beach, hood pointed toward the surf, was a green-and-white SUV marked "U.S. Border Patrol." For hours on end two agents sat and stared at beachcombers and the gulf. They returned our nods as we passed, but their expressions were not particularly friendly.

The agents represented the increased vigilance that had come to America since terrorists crashed airplanes into the World Trade Center, the Pentagon, and the Pennsylvania countryside. The pressure of Mexican and other Latin American immigrants on communities and institutions north of the Rio Grande was hardly new. During the Second World War, Texas was excused from the regulations of a federal program that brought in Mexican farm laborers because its own system of making that arrangement was so deeply ingrained. Yet generations later, members

JAMES EVANS

of the Texas congressional delegation were instrumental in pushing through a wholesale revision of immigration laws in 1996 that turned away virtually all Latin Americans. They continued to pour across the border illegally.

But the tenor now was quite different. The discord was no longer driven by jealousy over jobs and trade and resentment at the cost of educating and providing health care and social services to illegal aliens, known more politely as undocumented workers. America's policy makers perceived a nation living in fear and resentment of just about all foreigners except the British. Many decades had passed since Juan Cortina and Pancho Villa flouted U.S. power and killed gringos on American soil. But once again, American might was being employed to make the Rio Grande a barricade, not an inconvenience.

Citizens of all nations could now legally cross the border only at official ports of entry. The closest one to Boca Chica was a bridge across the Rio Grande between Brownsville and Matamoros. If any of those beachgoers, Rodriguez, or I strayed past the line marked by the portable light tower, U.S. agents would arrest us when we tried to come back across the sand.

Which added to the surreal aura; for it was all sand. The spot was not unlike other strips of sand and shell that the tide and currents lay out in the gulf's endless construction of beaches becoming dunes becoming barrier islands. The difference was that this sandbar had obliterated a natural frontier between nations and left the celebrated Rio Grande a tepid, stagnant shallow. It had too little push to cross the sandbar and reach the ocean.

Rodriguez and I got out of his pickup and walked. The border was further marked by a couple of barrels and a stretch of sagging, yellow plastic construction fence. Beyond the plastic fence I watched some Mexican boys skimming a pool with fishing nets. One stood in the middle of the great river about a quarter of a mile inland, and the water came no higher than his knees.

"I have not brought you to the mouth of the river," Rodriguez said with a slight smile. "I have brought you to the end of the river."

PART 1

Río del

I HAVE A FRIEND WHOSE FATHER once announced they were going to see the very beginnings of the Rio Grande. In the San Juan Mountains of southwestern Colorado, the man and the boy set out on mules, the most reliable transportation in such country, for mules are patient climbers and incredibly sure of foot. The father soon rued the day, though, for the weather turned on them and they rode into a snowstorm. The clouds at last relented, and they came upon a broad, rolling tundra surrounded by blunt rock mountains that look like Brazil nuts stood on end. The summits of the mountains approach 14,000 feet. The tundra beneath the San Juan Dome was thrust into being by volcanic forces. In the brief summers the ground under the golden tundra is soggy and it seeps, forming rivulets and brooks that become the three main headwater creeks. Glaciers once crunched, then pulled back from, this terrain; a few feet below the surface, a sheet of ice permanently resides. During the winter, temperatures plunge to 60 degrees below zero Fahrenheit and the winds reach gale force. And yet, incredibly, abandoned mines are scattered up in here. If the riders had reached the top of Stony Pass they would have looked toward the Pacific from the Continental Divide. But the father clamped his jaws and told the boy to turn his mule around. They made that ride sixty years ago, and no feature of Stony Pass has changed much since. For the man from Texas, a businessman and city dweller, the voyage was pretty quickly a pain in the ass. But he believed it was a rite of passage, an essential part of his son's education. My friend still feels the sting of that snow and hears the creak of the mule's saddle; no memory of his dad is stronger.

~

THE CREEKS CONVERGE within timber. The newborn Rio Grande splashes over rocks and is pooled up amid an aspen grove by stubborn beaver. Paleo-Indians, the first humans in North America, hunted in these highlands when the glaciers were still active. In recent times they were the domain of the Utes and their intrusive archenemies, the Comanches. The Utes roved far back in the canyons in search of game during the warm months and camped in the sheltered valleys during the snows. The Spaniards did not arrive until 1779, when a Nuevo Mexico governor named Juan de Anza led a punitive expedition against a Comanche chief named Green Horn—he took his name from the unusual feature of a buffalo skullcap he used for a helmet, and believed that its magic made him invincible. In the course of proving otherwise, the Spaniards realized for the first time that the river's origin lay in the San Juan Mountains. They had presumed it flowed from somewhere in the Arctic.

Having conquered and claimed the high country, the Spaniards left it alone. It began to be settled during the middle 1800s. Mexicans came from the south, and norteamericanos came over and through the Colorado ranges. Kit Carson's father-in-law was farming at

Wagon Wheel Gap by 1840. A few years later some gold deposits were found in the San Juan Mountains, and U.S. soldiers forced the Utes, led by their legendary chief Ouray, into the Four Corners nexus of Colorado, New Mexico, Arizona, and Utah. The gold discoveries led to more finds of high-grade silver, great quantities of silver. Suddenly 10,000 people were living in tents and rough log cabins and clapboard hovels—places called Jimtown, Stringtown, Amethyst. Riches were humped out of mines named Holy Moses and Last Chance. Saloon proprietors included Bat Masterson and Bob Ford, the assassin of Jesse James. Tourists came by train to fish, drink, and gamble. A railroad reached Willow Creek Canyon in 1891, and within its imposing rock walls Jimtown coalesced into Creede. Be-

LAURA GILPIN

cause of its superior ore grade, Rio Grande silver was sought and sold even through the resounding market bust of 1893. In the early years of the twentieth century, some farmers from the San Luis Valley packed in tools and supplies on mules and built a pile of rocks and earth and named it Farmer's Union Dam. The obstructed stream behind it became the Rio Grande Reservoir. They wanted to check the river's floods, and even at 9,000 feet and in that climate they were trying to irrigate, to capture water at its highest point and let gravity and plenty do the rest. The money crop was hay for the miners' and townfolks' horses and mules.

For fifty miles below the dam, the river runs narrow and fast between mountain and forest wilderness—it is a consummate trout stream. The upper Rio Grande habitat is calculated to support 1,300 fish per mile. Below those rapids the river broadens out in the lush but unspectacular San Luis Valley. It was the first of the bowls that filled up with water and pressed against its rim until at last the earth and rocks yielded and freed the river to go off in search of an ocean, gravity and slope dictating the Atlantic. The alluvial soil in the San Luis Valley is wonderfully fertile. Among the farmers and merchants who immigrated to the Rio Grande headwaters were a contingent of Mormons. They complained of religious persecution in New Mexico and Utah, but had only gratitude for the Hispanic Catholics who lived in a villita called Los Cerritos; they helped the newcomers survive a first hard winter.

On the short Rio Grande tributary called the Conejos, near the New Mexico border, the Mormons founded Manassa. The hamlet's Old Testament namesake was Manasseh, a son of Joseph and patriarch of a chief tribe of Israel. From here came Jack Dempsey, the valley's most famous native son. Born in a Manassa log cabin in 1895, Dempsey began his career in the saloons of mining towns. Known in those days as "Kid Blackie," Dempsey may have fought up to a hundred bouts on the sawdust floors of barrooms before he had an official pro fight. His career was rescued from that obscurity by a manager named Jack "Doc" Kearns. The popular novelist Jack London must have loved their story. As a Washington teenager Kearns had stowed away on a freighter and run off to the Yukon goldfields. He came back broke and worked as a ranch hand and a smuggler of Chinese immigrants. Kearns fought professionally out of Billings, Montana, until he had to go to prison over a street brawl. On his release he moved into managing and promoting fighters in Spokane and San Francisco. Kearns claimed that he met Dempsey when the youngster came to his aid in a bar fight in 1917. Just two years later, Kearns positioned Dempsey, now billed as "the Manassa Mauler," to challenge and batter senseless the heavyweight world champion, Jess Willard. For one title defense Kearns delivered Dempsey a $300,000 purse that bankrupted the town of Shelby, Montana.

Kearns parted ways with Dempsey (allegedly over the champion's new movie-star wife, Estelle Taylor) before his classic losing bouts with Gene Tunney in 1926 and 1927. Kearns remained a flamboyant power in boxing until his death in 1963. Dempsey settled into being a restaurateur and celebrity in New York City; he lived almost to age ninety, an American hero of the stature of Babe Ruth.

Today, the Colorado reaches of the Rio Grande are dominated by the redolence of irrigated hayfields and alfalfa, though the farmers have diversified, sowing potatoes, sugar beets, and vegetables. The last silver mine in the Rio Grande uplands closed in 1985. Creede is the only town left in Mineral County, which has a year-round population of 850. Apart from agriculture, tourism drives the economy: whitewater rafters, skiers, backpackers, trail riders, and anglers. They fish for trout and other cold-water species; many are fly-fishing purists, but below the clear and fast-running stretches, anglers who are not too proud to use a worm have learned that brown trout especially are curious travelers and like the cloudy waters stirred up by irrigation gates. For favorite clients, guides tie a fly called the Eisenhower. The World War II general and 1950s president loved to get away and throw out his line in the Rio Grande.

~

AS THE RIVER COMES DOWN into New Mexico it gouges some of the most spectacular landmarks on the continent. Rapids crash and hurl spray at the bottom of an astounding split in the earth; many of the cliffs are so sheer that the stream is almost always cloaked in shade. The effect of the chasm is made more shocking by the contrast of the utterly flat, gold and bluish plain that extends right to the brink. It's possible to imagine that on a dark night you could just walk off into a very long fall. A few miles from Taos is the U.S. Highway 64 bridge, more than a third of a mile across. More breathtaking, say those who've seen it, is the base of the Rio Grande Gorge. One long stretch of rapids is almost impossible to raft. People who crave and train constantly for such adventure are forced to give up and lug their rafts and kayaks up the switchbacks of the precipice. Even the experts fear this Rio Grande.

Downstream, the river slows, building some modest floodplains, and the canyons grow more hospitable. Here the puebloan tribes had water and good soil for their corn, squash, and beans, and the cliffs were an inverted sort of fortress, offering protection from nomadic predators. Near Santa Fe, an exemplary ruin of cliff dwellings in a handsome setting has been preserved and named for an archaeologist and ethnologist, Adolph Bandelier. He was a conscientious scholar and scientist but also a priggish gentleman. His journals of the 1880s and a 1916 novel drawn from his observations, *The Delight Makers,* are full of suggestions that the libidinous behavior of the Indians kept his nose out of joint.

Nearby is Los Alamos, whose name today conjures not the river's cottonwoods but the secret compound where nuclear physicists were sent to ensure that the United States triumphed in World War II. New Mexico brims with that mixture of the ancient and the future, neither quite known. The Spaniards made the puebloan peoples submit with brutality and relative ease, but the country they occupied was deceptive and dangerous. The scouts of the Basque scion Juan de Oñate named its principal river Río Bravo del Norte—allegedly intending its meaning to be the "wild" river of the north—when a spring 1598 flood drowned two of their horses. A month later, Oñate almost led his expedition to doom by trying to cross an ancestral valley of the river—the waterless wasteland that would be named Jornada del Muerto, Dead Man's March. In the 1670s the desert took that name: a German who was about to be tried for witchcraft and treason broke out of a Spanish jail with the help of an Indian and tried to escape his pursuers. Near the only spring the soldiers found the German sorcerer's dead roan horse. Nearby they found his blue trousers and fur-lined jacket. Farther on yet they found hair and bones that had been tasted by scavengers. The presumption was that the Indian had murdered him. Two hundred seventy years later—during the U.S. military command of Dwight Eisenhower—the desiccated river valley would gain another grim distinction. It was the test site for the first explosion of an atomic bomb.

~

AFTER THE COMING OF THE SPANIARDS, history's most important bend of the river was the Treaty of Guadalupe Hidalgo, which ended the U.S.-Mexican War in 1848. Mexico had lost its war with rebellious Texas in 1836 but refused to recognize the infant republic, and in any case maintained that Texas's border lay farther north, on the Nueces River. But after American troops had overrun Mexico, sacked the capital, and imposed martial law, Mexican negotiators did not bargain from a position of great strength. The diplomats retreated to Guadalupe Hidalgo, which was then a small town outside Mexico City; it has since been swallowed by the suburbs. The Treaty of Guadalupe Hidalgo established the Rio Grande as the U.S.-Mexico border from its mouth to the thirty-second parallel, then west to the Pacific. Mexico watched Texas's annexation become final and also lost all, or parts of, land that became California, New Mexico, Nevada, Utah, Arizona, Colorado, and Wyoming—half its territory. The United States at last controlled the breadth of North America. The young empire could now look abroad to advance its notions of Manifest Destiny. The bitterness and resentment that were planted in the Mexican psyche simmer to this day.

The change in sovereignty quickly transformed the upper Rio Grande. The young state of Colorado, with backing from English investors, seized on the potential of Rio Grande agriculture and diverted the river and put it to use in the San Luis Valley. Farmers in New Mexico Territory scrambled to catch up. By 1896, between 350 million and 500 million gallons of water a year were being lavished on farms in Colorado and New Mexico. The farmers rationalized that they irrigated only when the river was running high with snowmelt and monsoon freshets, and maintained in any case that the water was theirs even if the river went bone-dry downstream. Mexican growers each year saw a decrease in water reaching the El Paso Valley through a channel called Acequia Madre, Mother Ditch. Fields withered and orchards died, and Juárez faced a shortage of drinking water.

In 1897 another British-financed company, headed by a physician in Las Cruces, announced plans to build a dam near a big barren clod called Elephant Butte, 125 miles north of El Paso. The speculators promised flood control and more orderly distribution of water, but Mexicans around Juárez cried that they would be dried up. Boosters in El Paso claimed that a more rightful place for such a dam was on the outskirts of their city. The U.S. secretary of the interior embargoed construction of the dam. Congress held hearings. A lawsuit reached the U.S. Supreme Court, which bounced it back to a lower court. The matter remained unresolved for seven years.

Finally, an irrigation congress convened in El Paso in 1904. Every party to the dispute had a defensible legal claim. The feuding parties were getting nowhere one day as a man named R. F. Burges watched in boredom and annoyance. Burges had been sharing with a friend, Julius Frakauer, an idea that the U.S. should guarantee delivery of 60,000 acre-feet of water a year to the Mother Ditch; in return, Mexico would drop all claims against the U.S. "Put it to a motion," said Frakauer. "They won't know if you're a delegate or not."

Burges raised his hand, and suddenly a stunning compromise was reached: the United States would build the dam at Elephant Butte. An El Paso newspaper correspondent described the scene: "As one man, the five Mexican delegates arose and bowed, giving their consent in this manner . . . L. Bradford Prince, former Governor of New Mexico, was presiding. He said he believed this was a happy solution to the matter, put it to a vote, and the convention adopted it unanimously."

Sixty thousand acre-feet of water was in most years a minute fraction of what would be available to users in the United States. Gringos in El Paso and points upstream would share up to twelve times more than the Mexicans. Was Mexico steamrolled again by U.S. power? Was there a covert payoff? Or did the Mexican officials just perceive self-interest in the dam—believe it was the best deal they could get? Perhaps they thought the fields, orchards, and vineyards of Juárez would be salvaged, and flow from the Río Conchos and lesser tributaries would be enough to support Mexico's towns and farms on the lower Río Bravo. The thinking behind their concession is veiled in a dense murk of years, pride, and diplomacy. Whatever the explanation, the new treaty was ratified by the countries in 1907, and the dam was completed in 1916. "The Great Elephant Butte Reclamation Project" was hailed as a vital step in realizing America's dream of making its arid West bloom. Elephant Butte severed Texas from the snowmelt stream. The river of legend and myth was cut in two.

PAUL HORGAN

from *Great River* (1955)

THE MOUNTAIN SYSTEM of the northern Rio Grande was a vast, secret world. Wandering Indians there made shrines of twig and feather and bone, and went their ways. Close to the high clouds that made their rivers, the inhuman peaks doubled the roar of thunder, or hissed with sheets of rain, or abided in massive silence. Below them lay every variation of park and meadow and lost lake; gashed canyon and rocky roomlike penetralia in the stupendous temples of the high wilderness. Along hidden watercourses and in little cupped lakes lived and worked the family of a small creature destined to be the cause of great change in the human life of the river during the early nineteenth century. It was the beaver.

In still pool or mild current the beaver made his house of mud and twig. Its doorway was underwater. The occupants dived to enter it and came up beyond into the dry shelter of their lodge that they had built of sticks and mud, where their food was stored and where they were safe from animal predators. The backwater before the den had to be three feet deep, and if this did not exist naturally, the beavers built dams to collect it. They chose a tree by the edge. Sitting upright, they chewed away bark in a belt, eating of it now and then from their paws. Down to bare wood, they gnawed away until the tree was ready to fall. Often it fell into water where it would make a stout beginning for a dam. Working in concert they brought from nearby woods bundles of stick and bush and starting out from the bank began to shore up their barrier. They dived to the bottom of the water and brought up loads of mud. This was plaster. With their broad tails they trowelled mud over the laid timbers, layer upon layer, always extending the reach of the dam until it touched the opposite limit of the course or cove where they worked. At times they paused to play, racing each other in the water, diving, and loudly slapping the water with their tails.

When house and dam were finished, it was time to lay up provisions within against winter when there would be no green sprouts of willow and cottonwood and fresh grass to eat in season. The beaver clan went foraging, often far inland from their water, in search of bark. The best bark was on the smaller branches high out of reach. The beavers brought down the tree, and then stripped the tender young bark off the branches laid low. They cut the bark into three-foot strips, pulled them to their water, and there floated them to the lodge. They made little signs to guide them as they went—mounds of twig and earth which they impregnated with castoreum, a musk secreted by the animal itself, that attracted their sense of smell and reassuringly meant *beaver* and told them where the road lay. Once in the lodge and eating, they were neat and fastidious. They took out through the doorway all the refuse of a meal and threw it into the current. Drifting away, it lodged downcurrent out of their way—bits of gnawed stick and knotty branch and hard root.

In the spring came the young. Leaving the mother during gestation, the male went traveling, often far away to other water, where he swam and frolicked, ate tender greens at the bank, and did not return home until the offspring were born. Then he took them in charge, trained them in work, and in the late summer led them out to forage before the sharp frosts and the thickening of their fur against the cold. Every-where in the secret lakes and along the tributaries and in the quieter passages of the river this lively cycle was continued by beavers in incalculable thousands, and wher-ever mountain and water met, evidences of it were scattered and lodged undisturbed—until the last Spanish and the first Mexican years of the Rio Grande.

For by then the beaver's fur was in great demand for the making of men's hats. The hatters of London and Paris, Boston and Philadelphia consumed great cargoes of beaver pelt, and the fur trade moved westward out of St. Louis over the American continent to Astoria and the northern Rockies. While Stephen Austin was complet-ing his organized arrangements with the new government of Mexico to bring new settlers from the east nearer to the lower Rio Grande, the river's upper reaches knew

ARTIE LIMMER

from another sort of growing infiltration by men who whether they came alone, or with a few companions, or many, still came without formal approval by the Mexican government, and with no resounding program of colonial loyalty or pious hope.

They came to take beaver in the mountain waters, in spring and autumn up north, or all through the winter in New Mexico if the season was mild. Many of them were French Canadians; the rest were from anywhere in the United States, though mostly from the frontier settlements. They outfitted themselves in St. Louis, and remembering what was commonly known as the Pike's reports, crossed the plains and entered the mountains by the hundreds in the 1820s. Among their number were men who made the first trails beyond the prairies, that led overland so early as 1826, to the Pacific. Jedediah Smith, Charles Beaubien, the Roubidoux brothers, Céran St. Vrain, Bill Williams, the youthful runaway Kit Carson for whose return a reward of one cent was posted by the employer to whom he was apprenticed—such men went to the mountains after beaver skins to sell off for a few dollars a pound, and all unwitting showed the way across the continent.

The movement had already had its pioneer in James Purcell, the Kentuckian, who had been detained at Santa Fe in 1805 under the Spanish governor. Others entering New Mexico from the plains were arrested, marched down the Rio Grande to El Paso and the prisons of Chihuahua in 1812, after confiscation of their goods, and were not released until the freeing of Mexico in 1821. Another party of trappers were taken by the provincial Spanish government in 1817, jailed in irons for forty-eight days at Santa Fe, and were finally released after being stripped of thirty thousand dollars' worth of furs and supplies. Such actions by the government were meant to protect the trapping industry already worked on a small scale by the Mexicans of the valley. Regulations declared that only permanent residents might hunt beaver. They were required to buy a hunting license, their number in any party was carefully fixed and recorded, and so were the length of time to be spent and the weapons to be used—traps, firearms, or snares. If the early American trappers could not buy official licenses, they soon found ways to get around the law. "The North Americans began to corrupt the New Mexicans," noted a Santa Fe lawyer, "by purchasing their licenses from them," and so risked arrest.

But still the trappers came, and against other hazards. The greatest of these were the roving Indians on the prairies and the eastern upsweeps of the Rocky Mountains. For an Indian hunter could read the menace that came with the white hunter; and he moved with every savagery to defend his hunting grounds. The trapper retaliated. He fought the Indian with Indian ways, and took scalps, and burned teepee villages, and abducted women, and pressed westward. He fought distance, hunger, and thirst, and if he was unwary enough to be bitten by a rattlesnake, he cauterized the wound by burning a thick patch of gunpowder in it. Once in the mountains he met his second greatest adversary in great numbers. This was the great grizzly bear, who was curious, fearless, and gifted with a massive ursine intelligence. With lumbering speed the grizzlies could travel forty miles between dawn and dark through mountains. It was not unusual for trappers to kill five or six in a day, or to see fifty or sixty, and one hunter declared that one day he saw two hundred and twenty of them. The grizzly towered above a man. His forepaws were eight or nine inches wide, and his claws six inches long. He weighed from fifteen to eighteen hundred pounds. His embrace was certain death. So steadily did he smell and find the trappers that in a few decades by their guns his kind was made almost extinct.

The earthen village of Rancho de Taos near the Rio Grande was the northern town nearest the beaver waters of the mountains, and there came the mountain men to organize their supplies for the trapping seasons. They found some men of Rancho de Taos already, though to a limited degree, followed the trapper's life. Seeing how swarthy they were, the newcomers thought they must be of mixed Negro and Indian blood. It was astonishing how primitive were the ways of life in Taos—the farmers used only oxen in cultivating their fields, and a miserable plow made of a Y-shaped branch from a tree, with an iron head to its end that turned the earth. Hoes, axes, and other tools were old-fashioned. There were no sawmills: no mechanical ingenuity to speed up work; and—what was oddest to the squinting and raring trappers from the East—the people seemed to have no desire for such means to change their slow, simple ways.

The mountain men entered at Taos their first experience of the Mexican government. Taos was the seat of the northernmost customshouse of Mexico. As the trappers brought little to declare in goods for sale, they were evidently allowed to go about their preparations for departure into the mountains. They bought what flour and produce they could, and recruited an occasional Taoseño to join their parties, and made ready their equipment. In the far northern Rockies the trapping parties were often large, numbering from fifty to a hundred men. Most of these were camp personnel who maintained a base for the trappers and hunters who went forward into the wilderness. The "Frenchmen" from Canada sometimes kept Indian wives, and established in the mountains a semipermanent household with rude domestic amenities. Other parties were smaller, and instead of working for the great fur companies as contract employees, went their ways alone, as "free" trappers. Those who descended on the Rio Grande's northern reaches were more often than not in small units of a dozen, or three or four, or even a single man, who meant to take their furs and sell them to the highest bidder at the season's end. But all the trappers shared aspects of costume, equipment, and even character, many of which grew from the tradition of the forest frontiersman of the late eighteenth century.

The mountain man was almost Indian-colored from exposure to the weather. His hair hung upon his shoulders. He was bearded. Next to his skin he wore a red flannel loincloth. His outer clothes were of buckskin, fringed at all the seams. The jacket sometimes reached to the knee over tight, wrinkled leggings. His feet were covered by moccasins made of deer or buffalo leather. Around his waist was a leather belt into which he thrust his flintlock pistols, his knife for skinning or scalping, and his shingling hatchet. Over one shoulder hung his bullet pouch, and over the other his powder horn. To their baldrics were attached his bullet mould, ball screw, wiper, and an awl for working leather. When he moved he shimmered with fringe and rang and clacked with accoutrements of metal and wood. The most important of these were his traps, of which he carried five or six, and his firearm with its slender separate crutch of hardwood. It was always a rifle—never a shotgun, which he scorned as an effete fowling piece. Made in the gun works of the brothers Jacob and Samuel Hawken, of St. Louis, the rifle had two locks for which he kept about him a hundred flints, twenty-five pounds of powder and several pounds of lead. The barrel, thirty-six inches long, was made by hand of soft iron. The recoil from its blast shocked into a hardwood stock beautifully turned and slender. Peering vividly out from under his low-crowned hat of rough wool, he was an American original, as hard as the hardest thing that could happen to him, short of death.

Alone, or with a companion or a small party, he packed his supplies on two horses and, riding a third, left Taos for the mountains and other trapping parties. For nobody could stake a claim on hunting country, and every trapper party competed against every other. He did his best to keep his movement and direction secret, to throw others off the trail, and find the wildest country where he would be most free from rivalry. Following the groin of foothills, the mountain men came among high slopes and rocky screens. If two worked as a pair, they sought for a concealed place where they could make camp and tether their horses, near beaver water. There they built a shelter, and if their goal was a mountain lake, or a slow passage of stream, they set to work hacking out a cottonwood canoe. In natural forest paths they looked for the little musky mounds that marked beaver trails. They searched currents for the drift of gnawed beaver sticks. Every such sign took them closer to their prey. When they were sure they had found its little world, at evening under the pure suspended light of mountain skies they silently coasted along the shores of quiet water to set their traps.

They laid each trap two or three inches underwater on the slope of the shore, and, a little removed, they fixed a pole in deep mud and chained the trap to it. They stripped a twig of its bark and dipped one end into a supply of castoreum, the beaver's secretion that would be his bait. They fastened the twig between the open jaws of the trap leaving the musky end four inches above water. The beaver in the nighttime was drawn to it by scent. He raised his muzzle to inhale, his hindquarters went lower in the water, and the trap seized him. He threw himself into deeper water; but the trap held him, and the pole held the trap, and presently he began to drown. In the high, still daybreak, the trappers coasted by their traps again in the canoe, and took up their catch.

Working a rocky stream from the bank the trappers lodged the trap and its chained pole in the current, where the beaver found the scent. In his struggles he might drag the trap and pole to shore, where his burden became entangled in "thickets of brook willows," and held him till found. Sometimes he struggled to deeper midstream water, where the pole floated as a marker; and then the trappers putting off their buckskins which if saturated would dry slowly and then be hard as wood, went naked and shivering into the cold mountain stream to swim for their take. And some parties rafted down the whole length of the river in New Mexico, all the way to El Paso. Their method astonished the New Mexicans, to whom it seemed suspect because it was new. Was it proper to use a new kind of trap, and float noiselessly to a beaver site, taking their catch by surprise, and spend the night in midstream with the raft moored to trees on each bank to be out of the reach of wild animals? And at the end of the journey, to sell the timbers for a good price at El Paso where wood was so scarce, take up the catch and vanish overland eastward without reporting to the government? The New Mexicans frowned at such ingenuity, energy, and novelty.

When in the mountains they had exhausted a beaver site the trappers moved on to another. With their traps over their shoulders they forded streams amidst floating ice; or with their traps hanging down their backs they scaled and descended the hard ridges between watercourses where the harder the country the better the chance that no others had come there before them. The trap weighed about five pounds, and its chain was about five feet long. A full-grown beaver weighed between thirty and forty pounds. The catch was an awkward burden to carry back to camp for skinning. Removing the pelt from the animal, the trappers attached it on a frame of sprung willow withes to dry. The flesh they cooked by hanging it before a fire from a thong. The carcass turned by its own weight, roasting evenly. The broad, flat tail they liked best of all. They cut it off, skinned it, toasted it at the end of a stick, and ate it with relish, as a relief from the usual hunter's diet of deer, elk, antelope, bear, lynx, or buffalo meat, or buffalo marrowbones, or buffalo blood drunk spurting and warm from the throat of a newly killed specimen.

All through the winter-fast months the mountain men worked, obedient to animal laws and themselves almost animal in their isolation, freedom, and harmony with the wilderness. Their peltries were cached and the piles grew, in the end to be baled with rawhide thongs. A trapper took in a good season about four hundred pounds of beaver skins. Sometimes his cache was invaded and destroyed by prowling animals, or stolen by mountain Indians; and then his months of hardship went for nothing. But if he kept his pile, he was ready to come out of the boxed mountains whose cool winds brushing all day over high-tilled meadows carried the scent of wild flowers down the open slopes where he descended with his haul. At five dollars a pound it would bring him two thousand dollars in the market.

But once again in Taos, he might then meet trouble with the Mexican authorities. Now that he had his cargo, they showed an interest in him. If he was unlucky, they questioned him, examined his bales, and invoking regulations that nobody mentioned when he started out months before, confiscated his whole catch. If he resisted he was taken to Santa Fe and jailed, with official talk about the Mexican decree of 1824 that prohibited trapping by foreigners in the Mexican territory. Since there were no public warehouses hunters could only store their catches in towns by making deals with local citizens for storage space on private premises. If a Mexican citizen gave protection to a foreign trapper he was in danger from his own government. At Peña Blanca on the Rio Grande in 1827 one Luís María Cabeza de Vaca hid in his house the "contraband" of beaver skins left there for safe keeping by a trapper named Young. From Santa Fe a corporal and eight soldiers of the presidial company came to seize it. Cabeza de Vaca resisted them, firing upon them in protection of his home. The soldiers returned the fire and killed him. The official report of the affair stated that "the deceased died while defending a violation of the . . . rights of the Nation," and asked exoneration for the corporal and his squad.

But local officials might be bribed, and a license trumped up, and the catch restored to the trapper. In any case, after his mountain months, he was ready to burst his bonds of solitude, and he did so with raw delight. All his general passion and violence that his mountain work required him to suppress while moving lithe and crafty after watchful creatures now broke free in the clay village where he returned among men and women. He had a frosty look of filth all over him. His hair was knotted and his beard was a catch-all for the refuse of months. His clothes reeked like his body. His mouth was dry with one kind of thirst and his flesh on fire with another. If the one tavern in the town was full, he went to a house and asked for a corner of the packed mud floor where he could throw his gear, and was granted it. The family knew what he came to seek with his comrades. The women took kettles out of doors and built fires around them to heat water. When it was hot they brought it in, and found him waiting in his crusted skin sitting in a wooden tub. The women poured the water over him. He thrashed. He was as hairy as an animal and as unmindedly lustful. The water hit him and he gave the recognized cry of the mountain man—"Wagh!"—a grunt, a warning, and a boast. Bathing as violently as he did all other acts, he began again to know his forgotten satisfactions. As he emerged with wet light running on his skin, white everywhere but on his face and hands whose weather could not wash off, he was a new man.

The whiskey of Taos—they called it "lightning"—now warmed him within. He drank until he had fire under his scowl. The women did what they could to improve his clothes. He rattled his money and they made him a supper that burned him inside with chiles and spices. Early in the evening he stamped his way to the tavern in the plaza where a fandango was about to start. All benches and tables were pushed back against the walls of the large room. Tin lanterns pierced with little nail holes in a design hung from the raw beams of the ceiling. Two fiddlers, a guitarist, and a flutist began to make up the music together. They played popular ballads—the same ones that a slower tempo also served for accompaniments to the Mass and to processions. As the crowd grew the room was hazed with blue cigarette smoke from the mouths of men and women alike. The women were powdered till their faces looked like pale lavender. They clustered together at one side of the room. From the other the men came and took them somewhat as cocks took hens—a dusty pounce met by a bridling glare, and then an impassive harmony between the sexes suggesting absentminded enjoyment. Lacking milled lumber the floor was a hard and polished cake of earth. The couples moved with expressionless faces—all but the mountain man. His heels made muffled thunder on the ground. The Mexican dances were set pieces, with evolutions and patterns. He did not heed them. He threw himself in baleful joy through whatever movements occurred to him, "Wagh!" The lightning jug went around. The music scratched and squealed. The windows of the tavern hall were like lanterns in the pure darkness below Taos Mountain. When the fandango was over, all went home. The mountain man took a woman from the hall to her house. At rut like a big, fanged mountain cat—"W-a-a-a-gh!"—he spent the night with her to nobody's surprise or censure; and, as one such man said, he had no reason afterward to bring "charges of severity" against her.

Presently he traveled to a trading post on the prairies, or to St. Louis, to sell his catch. In the frontier cities of the United States he was a prodigal spender, uneasy in their relatively ordered society, loose as it was compared to life in older and more easterly places. When the season rolled around again, he was off again to his lost lakes and rivers where obscurely content he felt most like the self he imagined until it came true.

For over three decades the trapping trade flourished. At its height the annual shipment of beaver skins from Abiquiu on the Chama and Taos on the Rio Grande was worth two hundred thousand dollars. But in the 1830s the market for beaver began to break, for the China trade out of England and New England was growing, and the clipper ships were bringing silk in great quantities to the manufacturing cities of the world. Fashion changed. Silk was offered for hats instead of fur; and the change brought the decline and almost the virtual abolishment of the Rocky Mountain fur trade. The trapper was cast adrift to find new work. He could abide it only in the land of his hardy prowess, and there he found it, whether he joined the overland commercial caravans as a wagon hand, or the American Army's later surveying expeditions as a guide, or amazingly settled on river land as a farmer. He knew the craft of the wilderness and he made its first trails for the westering white man. Some of the earliest venturers in the Mexico trade were trappers; and as the trade continued to grow and establish its bases ever farther west, the trappers met it with their wares; and what had been a memorized path became a visible road; and along it moved another of the unofficial invasions of the Mexican Rio Grande that could only end by changing nations. The first sustained effort toward that end was made by the individual trapper. His greatest power to achieve it lay in his individualism. Where the Mexican was hedged by governmental authority, the trapper made his own. Where the Mexican was formal, he was wild. Where the one was indolent, the other was consumed by a fanatical driving impulse. The invasion, unorganized as it was, commercial in purpose, wild and free in its individuals, seemed to express some secret personal motive beyond the material. The trappers forecast a new, wild strain of human society to come to the northern river.

LAURA GILPIN

TONY HILLERMAN

from *New Mexico, Rio Grande and Other Essays* (1992)

IF YOU STAND ON THE WORN PLANK FLOOR of the Lobatos Bridge just north of the New Mexico border, the only visible reminders of the tribes that once controlled the valley to the north are their sacred mountains. To the west, overlooking the Conejos River, is the cinder cone the maps call Ute Mountain, where the shamans of the tribe communed with their God. Directly upriver to the north looms Mount Blanca, one of the six sacred mountains of Navajo mythology. The Navajos call it Naajini (White Shell Mountain). It was built by First Man and First Woman, who spread a blanket of white shell on the earth and piled upon it soil carried up from the dim, subterranean Third World. On top of this, more white shell was spread, and Dawn Boy, one of the Holy People of the Navajos, entered the mountain to guard Dinetah (the Land of the People) from the east. Dawn Boy still lives there, watched over forever by Shash, the magic bear. But the people he was to guard are gone. The Rio Grande must pour through its great lava gorge into the Española Valley before it finds Indians who make it a part of their mythology and float the spirits of their dead upon its waters.

The line between the Rio Grande of the San Luis Valley and the Rio Grande below is appropriately abrupt and dramatic. It is formed by the Taos Plateau—a layer of volcanic basalt and ash up to a quarter mile deep through which the river has sliced the great zigzag canyon called the Rio Grande Gorge.

Lobatos Bridge is at the very end of the San Luis. The flat croplands are gone now, and the land beside the river rises in gentle mounds—the time-worn flanks of old, and minor, volcanic eruptions. It isn't flat enough here to irrigate, and it's too dry for trees—a sagebrush climate. The river lies in long, almost motionless pools in a shallow, gently sloping valley. The canyon develops a caprock rim only a few hundred yards above the bridge. As far as you can see downstream, this rim rises no more than fifty feet. But this is the beginning. At this lonely bridge, that brotherhood which finds its thrills testing courage and skill against stone and fast water begins one of America's most challenging runs.

The American River Touring Association rates rivers on a scale similar to that used by mountain climbers to classify peaks and cliffs. The scale runs from an easy I to VI. The first twenty-four miles below Lobatos—from the bridge to Lee's Trail—is rated II. That means one with a rubber raft and "intermediate" experience can safely run it. Beyond Lee's Trail, the river becomes Class VI, which translates to "utmost difficulty—near limit of navigability"—a stretch of water that should be attempted only by a team of experts taking every precaution. Michael Jenkinson, author of *Wild Rivers of America*, calls the stretch between Lee's Trail and the point where the Red River pours into the Rio Grande "pure nightmare." In that scant twelve miles, the river squanders 650 feet of its altitude. It's a thunderous passage, even at low water, with the river roaring through a convoluted series of chutes and rapids, breaking into plumes of spray on house-sized boulders, and slamming into the slick, blank wall of its canyon. Experts have made it through this slot in low-water seasons. But a team of professional river guides who tried it in the spring of 1970 gave up and climbed out after covering less than five miles in four dangerous and exhausting days. In relation to the vast sweep of geologic history, the gorge is new, formed in the last half million years—the last tick of cosmic time. The river cut through this fifty-mile volcanic block like a hot wire sinking into a cake of ice, and not enough centuries have passed for wind, rain, and gravity to soften the effect. The walls are sheer, the canyon narrow, and at places it is almost a thousand feet from rim to river.

For one approaching the Rio Grande across the Sunshine Valley north of Taos, this phenomenon can produce an eerie effect. Nothing on this plateau suggests the nearness of a river. Sagebrush, chamisa, and grama grass stretch unbroken toward the western horizon. But as you near the rim of the still-invisible gorge, you become aware of a sound. You seem to hear it through the soles of your feet—a muted subterranean thunder as if Mother Earth herself were murmuring in her eternal sleep. The sound, of course, is the booming of cataracts—tons of water pounding over basalt boulders.

Down among those water-slick boulders there is no surcease from sound. From Lee's Trail, about a dozen miles south of the Colorado border, to the confluence of the Red River, the Rio Grande is a bedlam of boiling rapids. The fishermen who are lured into this noisy world can reach the upper end of this strip with a 220-foot descent from the rim. Twelve miles downstream at the La Junta campground, it takes a vertical climb of more than eight hundred feet to reach earth's surface again. The trail is good, zigzagging safely up the cliff. But, safe or not, the effect is much like getting to the eightieth floor of a skyscraper without using the elevator.

Among a small fraternity of fiercely ardent New Mexico and Colorado trout fishermen, this sunken piece of river is known as "The Box." The pools they prefer are reached neither by Lee's nor La Junta trails. There are other ways down, rough and chancy, by which those agile, strong-lunged, brave, and fanatic enough can lower themselves by dawn's light to a favorite pool and escape from the depth at sundown. The reward for this is a chance to catch German brown trout of trophy size (this piece of river is often called the best brown trout fishing in America), lunker rainbows, and odd as it sounds, northern pike. The pike have appeared only recently. It's speculated that they made their way downstream from some Colorado lake and reproduced in the cold, oxygen-rich water of the deep canyon.

There is another reward not measurable in pounds and inches. A day spent at the bottom is a day spent in a world which has nothing to do with civilization. The sun reaches the river only as it passes overhead at midday. The cliffs cut off everything, making the horizon a thin strip of blue overhead. The thunder of water echoes from the basalt walls and engulfs you. With all this, there is the spicing of risk. The Rio Grande here demands respect. When the current is up, losing your footing on spray-slick stone can be lethal. Even a sprained ankle requires a complicated and time-consuming team rescue effort. I recall four such rescue missions in the past five years (a drowned rafter, a dead fisherman, and two who survived). In a society which has slain all its dragons, this noisy stretch of water serves a sort of primal purpose. The angler who emerges on the rim at sunset with the voice of the river shouting far below him tends to feel he has tested more than his fishing skill.

ANSEL ADAMS

WILLIAM LOGAN

"The Old Meat Hunter" (1972)

"AS YOU KNOW," says the old Meat Hunter, "the Sangre de Cristo is steeped in legend and tradition, not the least of which is that there are some beautiful native trout in those environs.

"And what is known as the New Mexican Approach to Running of Waters, with modifications of the well-known Rio Grande Gorge Gouge, is practiced with both stealth and ordinary furtiveness, with some of its finer points being handed down by word-of-mouth through the generations."

I admonish the old Meat Hunter, "You do not say?"

"Yes," the old Meat Hunter avers. "Another name for this system, though you do not hear it mentioned often these days, is the Irrigation Ditch Delight.

"I tell you, any time mankind tinkers with his waters and runs it willy nilly around the country in ditches by opening little gates and what have you, you will sometimes find trout, especially browns, who are great travelers and sightseers, in places which to you seem unlikely but very natural if you turn your mind on it a little bit.

"You may, for instance, believe that the celebrated Taos Lightning is a drink or Thunderbolt, but, no. Taos Lightning is nothing more than a local allusion to the Sangre de Cristo Stream Trout Technique.

"I know that by now I have you sitting on the edge of your chair just waiting to be let in on this little secret and some of its ramifications, are you not?

"That is what's wrong with some of you fancy fellows, for you have neither patience to savor your thoughts in your mind nor the common sense to apply even the least amount of imagination, I tell you.

"Just the other day I picked my way through what pretended to be a learned discourse on how to take them from the muddy streams and found, as I expected, not the slightest honorary mention of the New Mexican Approach to Running Waters.

"But since you are my friend and have now sat so patiently here today, let us discuss the elementary equipment that is needed for the Sangre de Cristo Trout Technique.

"Your ordinary willow whip or limber shoot will do, though I myself in this modern day used a cheap glass flyrod. It should not be too short or sporting but a rod of some length which can be poked in the little places, whether they be found in rocks or thickets.

"Now from this pole you dangle a line 36 inches or not more than about 40 inches at the most, with just a little bit of lead stuck on it about eight inches above the hook.

"You need not use very fine line for this, for some use regular cord, and your ordinary little hook will serve you well. Now let us say a man with a field of onions or drying up crops of any kind places a call of water and that on a Sunday morning they open the gates on a reservoir for him.

"This will make your ordinary little brook rise fast and change its color to a cloudy brown, and it is at such times that your Sangre de Cristo Trout Technique is a godsend.

"The worms you should use should not be very large, though they do not need to be especially lively. Simply run the little hook through the ring of the worm and poke the pole through the gaps in the trees and shady places in the holes; let it all drop in and hang there.

"In a few moments you are likely to be rewarded with a determined tug, though do not be too hasty but allow the worm to be chewed firmly. And lift away, my boy, and haul them flopping in a sort of overhand and freestyle way to where you can pounce on them."

LAURA GILPIN

JOHN NICHOLS

from *The Milagro Beanfield War* (1974)

JOE MONDRAGÓN WAS THIRTY-SIX YEARS OLD and for a long time he had held no steady job. He had a wife, Nancy, and three children, and his own house, which he had built with his own hands, a small tight adobe that required mudding every two or three autumns.

Joe was always hard up, always hustling to make a buck. Over the years he had learned how to do almost any job. He knew everything about building houses, he knew how to mix mud and straw just right to make strong adobes that would not crumble. Though unlicensed, he could steal and lay his own plumbing, do all the electric fixtures in a house, and hire five peons at slave wages to install a septic tank that would not overflow until the day after Joe died or left town. Given half the necessary equipment, he could dig a well, and he understood everything there was to understand about pumps. He could tear down a useless tractor and piece it together again so niftily it would plow like balls of fire for at least a week before blowing up and maiming its driver; and he could disk and seed a field well and irrigate it properly. "Hell," Joe liked to brag, "I can grow sweet corn just by using my own spit and a little ant piss!" He could raise (or rustle) sheep and cattle, and hogs, too, and slaughter and butcher them all. And if you asked him to, he could geld a pony or castrate a pig with the same kind of delicate authoritative finesse Michelangelo must have used carving his Pietà.

Joe had his own workshop crammed full of tools he had begged, borrowed, stolen, or bought from various friends, enemies, and employers down through the years. In that shop he sometimes made skinning knives out of cracked buzz saw blades, and sold them to hunters in the fall for five or six bucks. At the drop of a five-dollar bill he could also fashion an ornate Persian wine goblet from an old quart pop bottle. Then again, if the need arose and the money to pay for it was resting lightly on his main workbench like an open-winged butterfly taking five, Joe probably *could* have invented the world's tiniest dart gun, to be used by scientists for crippling, but not killing, mosquitoes. Just to survive there had to be almost nothing Joe couldn't or would not at least try to do.

The Mondragón house was surrounded by junk, by old engines, by parts of motors, by automobile guts, refrigerator wiring, tractor innards. One shed was filled with wringer washing machines, and when Joe had the time he puttered over them until they were "running" again; then he tried—and often managed—to sell them . . . with pumps that went on the fritz (or wringer gears that nearly stripped themselves) ten minutes after Joe's three-month warranty (in writing) expired. This presented no problem, however, because for a very small consideration Joe was more than willing to fix whatever broke in whatever he had sold you.

In a sense, Joe was kept perpetually busy performing minor miracles for what usually amounted to a less-than-peanuts remuneration. Still, when something, when anything was wrong in town, when a pump was frozen or a cow was sick or the outhouse had blown down, the call went out for Joe Mondragón, who would defy rain, hail, blizzards, tornadoes, and earthquakes, in order to skid his pickup with the four bald retreads and no spare to a stop in your front yard and have the thing or the animal or whatever it was temporarily patched up and functioning again. Reeking of energy like an oversexed tomcat, Joe was always charging hell-bent for election around town in his old yellow pickup, like as not with a beer clutched tightly in one fist— arrogant little Joe Mondragón, come to fix your trouble and claim your two bits, who didn't take no shit from nobody.

But he was tired, Joe had to admit that. He was tired, like most of his neighbors were tired, from trying to earn a living off the land in a country where the govern-

RUSSELL LEE

ment systematically gathered up the souls of little ranchers and used them to light its cigars. Joe was tired of spending twenty-eight hours a day like a chicken-thieving mongrel backed up against the barn wall, neck hairs bristling, teeth bared, knowing that in the end he was probably going to get his head blown off anyway. He was tired of meeting each spring with the prospect of having to become a migrant and head north to the lettuce and potato fields in Colorado where a man groveled under the blazing sun ten hours a day for one fucking dollar an hour. He was tired, too, of each year somehow losing a few cows off the permits he had to graze them on the government's National Forest land, and he was tired of the way permit fees were always being hiked, driving himself and his kind not only batty, but also out of business. And he was damn fed up with having to buy a license to hunt deer on land that had belonged to Grandfather Mondragón and his cronies, but which now resided in the hip pockets of either Smokey the Bear, the state, or the local malevolent despot, Ladd Devine the Third.

Usually, in fact, Joe did not buy a license to hunt deer in the mountains surrounding his hometown. Along with most everybody else in Milagro, he figured the dates of a hunting season were so much bullshit. If he hankered for meat, Joe simply greased up his .30-06, hopped into the pickup, and went looking for it. Once a Forest Service vindido, Carl Abeyta, had caught Joe with a dead deer, a huge electric lamp, no license, and out of season to boot, and it cost Joe a hundred dollars plus a week in the Chamisa County Jail. In jail he half-starved to death and was pistol-whipped almost unconscious by a county jailer, Todd McNunn, for trying to escape by battering a hole in the cheap cinderblock wall with his head.

Joe had been in jail numerous times, usually just for a few hours, for being drunk, for fighting, for borrowing (and consuming) Devine Company sheep, and each time it had cost him fifteen or twenty-five dollars, and usually he had been manhandled, too. The corrections personnel laughed when they clobbered Joe because he was funny, being so small and ferocious, weighing only about a hundred and twenty-five pounds, kicking and hitting, trying to murder them when he was drunk, and when he was sober, too. Sometimes they tried to hold him off a little for sport, but Joe was too dangerous, being the kind of person—like the heralded Cleofes Apodaca of yore— who would have slugged a bishop. So they tended to belt him hard right off the bat and then let him lie. Joe had lost a few teeth in that jail, and his nose had been operated on by police fists, clubs, and pistol butts so as to conform to the prevalent local profile. Outside the jail Joe had broken fingers on both his hands hitting people or horses or doors or other such things. "I ain't afraid of nothing," he bragged, and thought he could prove it, although when he said that his wife Nancy hooted derisively: "Oh no, that's right, you're not afraid of *any*thing."

But Joe was tired of the fighting. Tired of it because in the end he never surfaced holding anything more potent than a pair of treys. In the end he just had his ass kicked from the corral to next Sunday, and nothing ever changed. In the end half his gardens and half his fields shriveled in a drought, even though Indian Creek practically formed a swimming pool in his living-room. In fact, Milagro itself was half a ghost town, and all the old west side beanfields were barren; because over thirty-five years ago, during some complicated legal and political maneuverings known as the 1935 Interstate Water Compact, much of Milagro's Indian Creek water had been reallocated to big-time farmers down in the southeast portion of the state or in Texas, leaving folks like Joe Mondragón high and much too dry.

This situation had caused a deep, long-smoldering, and fairly universal resentment, but nobody, least of all Joe Mondragón, had ever been able to figure out how to bring water back to that deserted west side land, most of which, by now, belonged to Ladd Devine the Third and his motley assortment of dyspeptic vultures, who (not surprisingly, now that they owned it) *had* figured out a way to make the west side green again.

But then one day Joe suddenly decided to irrigate the little field in *front* of his dead parents' decaying west side home (which Joe still owned—in itself a miracle) and grow himself some beans. It was that simple. And yet irrigating that field was an act as irrevocable as Hitler's invasion of Poland, Castro's voyage on the *Granma* or the assassination of Archduke Ferdinand, because it was certain to catalyze tensions which had been building for years, certain to precipitate a war.

And, like any war, this one also had roots that traveled deeply into the past.

For several hundred years, and until quite recently, Milagro had been a sheep town. Nearly all the fathers of Joe Mondragón's generation had been sheepmen. There was no man, however, and there had been no men for more than a hundred years, perhaps, who had truly made a living off sheep; the basic reason for this being that Milagro was a company town, and almost every herder, simply in order to survive as a sheepman, had been connected to the Ladd Devine Sheep Company. And being a sheepman connected to the Devine Company was like trying to raise mutton in a tank full of sharks, barracudas, and piranha fish.

For this, the people of the Miracle Valley had the U.S. Government to thank. Because almost from the moment it was drawn up and signed in 1848, the Treaty of Guadalupe Hidalgo, which not only ended the war between the United States and Mexico, but also supposedly guaranteed to the Spanish-surnamed southwestern peoples their communal grazing lands, was repeatedly broken. Shortly after the war, in fact, the U.S. Congress effectively outlawed their communal property, passing vast acreages into the public domain, tracts which then suddenly wound up in the hands of large American ranching enterprises like the Devine Company. Later, during Teddy Roosevelt's era, much remaining communal territory was designated National Forest in which a rancher could only run his animals providing he had the money, and political pull to obtain grazing permits.

Hence, soon after the 1848 war, most local ranchers found themselves up to their elbows in sheep with no place to graze them. In due course, the small operators were wiped out either from lack of access to grazing land or from trying to compete with the large companies that now dominated the public domain and Forest Service preserves. The sheepmen who survived did so only by becoming indentured servants to the large companies that controlled the range and the grazing permit system.

In Milagro this meant that since the last quarter of the nineteenth century most sheep ranchers had been serfs of the Devine Company, which, during the seventies and eighties, in one of those democratic and manifestly destined sleights of Horatio Alger's hand (involving a genteel and self-righteous sort of grand larceny, bribery, nepotism, murder, mayhem, and general all-around and all-American nefarious skulduggery), had managed to own outright, or secure the grazing rights to, all the property on the Jorge Sandoval Land Grant in Chamisa County.

At the end of each year since this takeover, every sheepman, woman, and child in Milagro had discovered themselves heavily in debt to the Devine Company. In fact, after an average of ten years under the sheep company's tutelage, just about every man, including men like Joe Mondragón's father, Esequiel, had owed the rest of whatever resources he might accumulate in his lifetime to whichever Ladd Devine happened to be sitting on the family nest egg at that particular moment.

Of course, the Ladd Devine Company had not only been interested in land and sheep and its company (now Nick Rael's) store. It owned controlling interests in both the First National Bank of Chamisaville and its Doña Luz branch. The Dancing Trout Dude Ranch and Health Spa had been operating on the Devine estate up in Milagro Canyon ever since the early twenties. When the Pilar Café was constructed across from the company store in 1949, it was a Devine operation. And when, more recently, the Enchanted Land Motel was built on the north-south highway to handle the new breed of pudgy tourists, who simpered by in their baroque apartment houses on wheels, it was a Devine-financed and Devine-controlled operation.

To be truthful, the Devine Company, which had gotten fat on sheep, was not dealing in wool anymore. The company had much more interest in a project called the Indian Creek Dam, a structure—to be located in Milagro Canyon—that was considered the essential cornerstone of a Devine development endeavor known as the Miracle Valley Recreation Area. A dam in Milagro Canyon had been the dream of both Ladd Devine, Senior and the present caudillo, Ladd Devine the Third, who took over the Devine operation when his grandfather (who was eighty-nine at the time) was caught alone and on horseback up beyond the Little Baldy and Bear Lakes in an early autumn snowstorm back in 1958. Ladd Devine the Second, a profligate and playboy who married five times, put a bullet in one ear and out the other on the Italian Riviera at the age of thirty-nine, thus accounting for Ladd Devine the Third's early ascendancy to the throne.

The Ladd Devine Company had started drawing up plans for the recreation development about the same time people were losing their water rights and beginning a wholesale exodus from the hapless west side. The original Ladd Devine had not objected much to the unfair 1935 water compact shenanigans, which somewhat damaged his sheep operations by driving many of his herders elsewhere, because he was too busy buying up those herders' momentarily worthless land at bargain-basement prices. In this way, during the years immediately following World War II, when the water compact really began to be enforced, almost all the abandoned and apparently worthless land on the west side passed into Devine hands.

And now—*Qué milagro!*—the Indian Creek Dam was conveniently going to restore water rights to the west side so Ladd Devine the Third could bless the few surviving small farmers of Milagro with a ritzy subdivision molded around an exotic and very green golf course.

The dam would be built across Indian Creek at the mouth of Milagro Canyon, establishing a mile-and-a-half-long lake whose easternmost shore would extend up to within hailing distance of the Dancing Trout's main lodge. And the dam—or paying for it, that is—would be made possible by creating a conservancy district whose boundaries, for taxation purposes, would incorporate almost all the town's largely destitute citizens.

Wherein lay a rather profound rub.

At least one person understood this rub. Hence, right after Ladd Devine the Third announced plans for the Miracle Valley Recreation Area (which would include the Indian Creek Reservoir, the Miracle Valley Estates and Golf Course, and the Miracle Mountain Ski Valley) by erecting an elaborate wooden sign on the north-south highway just below town, the old bartender at the Frontier, Tranquilino Jeantete, began telling anybody who would listen:

"You watch. The conservancy district and the dam is a dirty trick. Like the 1935 water compact, it's one more way to steal our houses and our land. We'll be paying the taxes for Ladd Devine's lake. And when we can't pay our conservancy assessments, they'll take our land and give it to Devine. And that fucking Zopilote will sit up there on his throne in his fucking castle putting pennies on our eyes as they carry us to the camposanto, one by one."

But most farmers, completely baffled by the complexity of a conservancy district, did not know what to do. Should they hire a lawyer and fight the vulture? Or should they just sit tight and let this terrible thing happen the way terrible things had been happening now ever since the 1848 war, trusting that, like Amarante Córdova, they could somehow, miraculously, survive?

In the end, after much talk and many heated arguments the people shrugged, laughing uneasily and a little ashamedly. "That conservancy district and that dam," they philosophized, "will be as hard to live with as Pacheco's Pig."

Pacheco being an enormous, shifty-eyed, hysterically lonely man who—in the time-honored tradition of Cleofes Apodaca and Padre Sinkovich—had been losing his marbles at a vertiginous rate ever since his wife died six years ago, and who owned one of the world's most ornery sows, an animal he could never keep penned. For years it had been a regular thing in Milagro to see unsteady, mammoth Seferino Pacheco staggering across fields or splashing through puddles in the dirt roadways, searching for his recalcitrant porker, which was usually inhaling a neighbor's garden or devouring somebody's chickens. Pacheco was forever knocking on front doors and back doors and outhouse doors asking after his sow. And people were forever shouting at, and shooting at, and throwing rocks at Pacheco's gargantuan, voracious animal. Yet for a long time the pig had led a charmed life, nonchalantly absorbing high-powered lead lumps in its thick haunches, or else—it being also a rather swift pig—escaping on the run unscathed. "Maybe that marrana carries a chunk of oshá in her cunt that protects her from poisonous people," Onofre Martínez once giggled. And because the pig, with Pacheco gimping crazily after it, had become such a familiar sight all over town, sayings had grown out of the situation. Such as: "He's more trouble than Pacheco's pig." Or: "She's got an appetite like Pacheco's pig." And again: "It's as indestructible as Pacheco's pig."

And of course: "That conservancy district and that dam will be as hard to live with as Pacheco's pig."

Which is about where things stood when Joe Mondragón suddenly tugged on his irrigation boots, flung a shovel into his pickup, and drove over to his parents' crumbling farmhouse and small dead front field in the west side ghost town. Joe spent about an hour chopping weeds in the long unused Roybal ditch, and then, after digging a small feeder trench from Indian Creek into the ditch, he opened the Roybal ditch headgate at the other end so water could flow onto that fallow land.

After that Joe stood on the ditch bank smoking a cigarette. It was a soft and misty early spring morning; trees had only just begun to leaf out. Fields across the highway were still brown, and snow lay hip deep in the Midnight Mountains. Milagro itself was almost hidden in a lax bluish gauze of piñon smoke coming from all the fireplaces and cook stoves of its old adobe houses.

Last night, Joe recalled, the first moths had begun bapping their powdery wings against his kitchen windows; today water skeeters floated on the surface into his field, frantically skittering their legs.

The Trailways bus, with its lights still on, pulled off the highway to discharge and pick up a passenger. And the water just kept gurgling into that field, sending ants scurrying for their lives, while Joe puffed a cigarette, on one of the quietest lavender mornings of this particular spring.

~

ABOUT FIFTEEN AND A HALF MINUTES after Joe Mondragón first diverted water from Indian Creek into his parents' old beanfield, most of Milagro knew what he had done. Fifteen and a half minutes being as long as it took immortal, ninety-three-year-old Amarante Córdova to travel from a point on the Milagro-Garcia highway spur next to Joe's outlaw beanfield to the Frontier Bar across the highway, catty-corner to Rael's General Store.

Back in 1914 Amarante had been Milagro's first sheriff. And he still wore the star from that time pinned to the lapel of the three-piece woolen suit he had been wearing, summer and winter, for the last thirty years. The only person still inhabiting the west side ghost town, Amarante lived there on various welfare allotments (and occasional doles from Sally, the letter-writing Doña Luz daughter) in an eight-room adobe farmhouse whose roof had caved into seven of the eight rooms. Until the year before Jorge from Australia keeled over with his mouth full of candied sweet potato, Amarante had gotten around in a 1946 Dodge pickup. But one summer day he steered it off the gorge road on a return trip from a wood run to Conejos Junction, was somehow thrown clear onto a ledge, and from that spectacular vantage point he watched his rattletrap do a swan dive into the Rio Grande eight hundred feet below. Since that day Amarante had been on foot, and also since that day, come rain or come shine, he'd walked the mile from his crumbling adobe to town and back again, babbling to himself all the way and occasionally lubricating his tongue with a shot of rotgut from the half-pint bottle that was a permanent fixture in his right-hand baggy suit pocket.

On this particular day, as soon as Amarante had safely landed his crippled frame on a stool in the huge empty Frontier Bar and fixed a baleful bloodshot eye on the owner, eighty-eight-year-old Tranquilino Jeantete, he said in Spanish (he did not speak English, or read or write in either language):

"José Mondragón is irrigating his old man's beanfield over there on the west side."

Tranquilino turned up his hearing aid, and, after fumbling in his pockets for a pair of glasses, he perched the cracked lenses on his nose, muttering, "Eh?"

"José Mondragón is irrigating his old man's beanfield over there on the west side."

Tranquilino still couldn't hear too well, so he muttered "Eh?" again. Neither man's pronunciation was very good: they had six teeth between them.

Ambrosio Romero, a burly carpenter who worked at the Doña Luz mine, sauntered through the door for his morning constitutional just as Amarante repeated: "José Mondragón is irrigating his old man's beanfield over there on the west side."

Ambrosio said, "Come again? When are you gonna learn how to talk, cousin? Why don't you go down to the capital and buy some wooden teeth? Say that once more."

With a sigh, Amarante lisped, "José Mondragón is irrigating his old man's beanfield over there on the west side."

"*Ai, Chihuahua!*" Ambrosio made his usual morning gesture to Tranquilino Jeantete, who slid a glass across the shiny bar, selected a bottle, and poured to where Ambrosio indicated stop with his finger.

In silence the miner belted down the liquor, then belched, his eyes starting to water, and as he left he remarked: "What does that little jerk want to do, cause a lot of trouble?"

Ambrosio went directly from the bar to Rael's store where he bought some Hostess

ANSEL ADAMS

Twinkies for a mid-morning snack at the mine, and also casually mentioned to Nick Rael, "I hear José Mondragón is irrigating over on the other side of the highway."

Nick's instinctive reaction to this news was, "What's that little son of a bitch looking for, a kick in the head?"

Four men and two women in Rael's store heard this exchange. They were Gomersindo Uyba, an ancient ex-sheepman who would, for a dollar, chauffeur anybody without wheels down to the Doña Luz Piggly Wiggly to do their shopping; Tobias Arguello, a one-time bean farmer who had sold all his land to Ladd Devine the Third in order to send his two sons to the state university (one had dropped out to become an army man; the other had been drafted and killed in Vietnam); Teofila Chacón, the mother of thirteen kids, all living, and at present the evening barmaid at the Frontier; Onofre Martínez, a one-armed ex-sheepman who was known as the Staurolite Baron and also as the father of Bruno Martinez, a state cop; and Ruby Archuleta, a lovely middle-aged woman who owned and operated a body shop and plumbing business just off the north-south highway between Milagro and Doña Luz in the Strawberry Mesa area.

These six people scattered like quail hit by buckshot. And by noon, many citizens engaged in various local enterprises were talking excitedly to each other about how feisty little Joe Mondragón had gone and diverted the water illegally into his parents' no-account beanfield.

And, by and large, the townspeople had three immediate reactions to the news.

The first: "*Ai, Chihuahua!*"

The second: "What does that obnoxious little runt want to cause trouble for?"

And the third: "I'm not saying it's good or bad, smart or stupid, I'm not saying if I'm for or against. Let's just wait and see what develops."

At two that afternoon an informal meeting convened in Rael's General Store. Attending this meeting were the Milagro sheriff; an asthmatic real estate agent named Bud Gleason; Eusebio Lavadie, the great-great-great-grandnephew of Carlos the ringside-seat millionaire, and the town's only rich Chicano rancher; the storekeeper, Nick Rael; two commissioners and a mayordomo of the Acequia Madre del Sur—Meliton Mondragón, Filiberto Vigil, and Vincent Torres; and the town's mayor, Sammy Cantú.

The sheriff, forty-three-year-old Bernabé Montoya, had held his job now for nine and a half years. All four of his election victories had come by three votes—27 to 24—over the Republican candidate, Pancho Armijo. Bernabé was an absentminded, rarely nasty, always bumbling, also occasionally very sensitive man who dealt mostly with drunks, with some animal rustling, with about five fatal car accidents a year, and with approximately seven knifings and shootings per annum. He also reluctantly assisted the state police, once in the spring and again in the fall, during their raids on the Strawberry Mesa Evening Star hippie commune, during which raids they confiscated maybe five hundred marijuana plants that later mysteriously turned up in the pockets of Chamisaville Junior High School kids. Bernabé had arrested Joe Mondragón a dozen times, and had personally driven him down to the Chamisa County Jail twice. In earlier times Joe and Bernabé had run together, and the sheriff still admired his former pal's spunk, even though Joe was a constant hassle to the lawman's job—a troublemaker, a fuse that was always, unpredictably, burning.

Bernabé had gloomily called this meeting because he sensed a serious threat in Joe's beanfield. He had understood, as soon as he heard about the illegal irrigation, that you could not just waltz over and kick out Joe's headgate or post a sign ordering him to cease and desist. Because that fucking beanfield was an instant and potentially explosive symbol which no doubt had already captured the imaginations of a few disgruntled fanatics, and the only surprise about the whole affair, as Bernabé saw it, was, how come nobody had thought of it sooner?

"So I don't really know what to do," he told the gathering. "That's how come I called this meeting."

Eusebio Lavadie said, "What he's doing is illegal, isn't it illegal? Arrest him. Put him in jail. Throw away the key. Who's the mayordomo on that ditch?"

Vincent Torres, a meek, self-effacing old man, raised his hand.

"Well, you go talk to him," Lavadie huffed. "Tell him to cut out the crap or some of us will get together and break his fingers. Or shoot his horses. I don't see what all the fuss is about."

A commissioner for the Acequia Madre, Filiberto Vigil, said, "Don't be a pendejo, Mr. Lavadie."

The other commissioner, Meliton Mondragón, added, "What kind of harm does anybody think this really might do, anyway?"

"It's a bad precedent," Lavadie said. "This could steamroll into something as unmanageable as Pacheco's pig. Any fool can see that."

"Are you calling *me* a pendejo?" Meliton Mondragón asked.

"Not you personally, no. Of course not. But it's obvious the question isn't whether to let this go on or not. The only question is, how do we stop it?"

There was silence. Nobody had a suggestion.

At length, Bernabé Montoya said, "If I go over and tell him to stop he'll tell me to shove a chili or something you know where. If I go over to arrest him he'll try to kick me in the balls. And anyway, I don't know what the water law is, I don't even know what to arrest him for or charge him with or how I could hold him. I know as soon as we fined him, or he got out of the Chamisa V. jail, he'd go irrigating that field again.

It seems to me it's more up to the water users, to the ditch commissioners and the ditch bosses here, to stop him."

"Well, have them talk to him, then," Bud Gleason said. "How's that sound to you boys?"

It didn't sound that good to the boys. The two commissioners and the mayordomo shrugged, remaining self-consciously silent.

"For crissakes!" Lavadie suddenly exploded. "What a bunch of gutless wonders we got in this room! If you all are too chicken to do it, I'll go talk to that little bastard myself. There's no room in a town like ours for this kind of outrageous lawlessness—"

Five minutes later Lavadie's four-wheel-drive pickup lurched into Joe Mondragón's yard, scattering chickens and a few flea-bitten hounds.

A cigarette lodged toughly between his lips, Joe emerged from his shop tinkering busily with a crowbar.

"Howdy, cousin," Lavadie said.

Joe nodded, eyes crinkled against the cigarette smoke. Nancy opened the front door and stood there, flanked by two big-eyed kids.

"I came over to talk to you about that field you're irrigating on the other side of the highway," Lavadie said.

"What interest you got in that beanfield?" Joe asked.

"I figure what's bad for this town, whatever stirs up unnecessary trouble, is bad for all of us, qué no?"

Joe shrugged, inhaled, exhaled, and replaced the cigarette Bogey-like between his lips.

"I just came from a meeting we had over in Nick's store," Lavadie said. "We decided that since it's illegal to irrigate those west side fields, we ought to tell you to quit fucking around over there."

Joe delicately flicked the head off a small sunflower with the crowbar.

"Well—?" Lavadie said.

"Well, what?"

"What's your answer to that?"

Joe shrugged again. "Who says it's me irrigating over there?"

"I guess a little birdie told somebody," Lavadie grunted sarcastically.

"Hmm," Joe commented.

"So what's your answer?" Lavadie demanded.

Joe spit the cigarette butt from his lips and, swinging the crowbar like a baseball bat, expertly caught the butt, lining it across the yard at his antagonist, missing him only by inches. "Maybe you better quit fucking around over *here*."

PART 2

Desert

THE VOLCANIC FORCES that thrust the San Juan Mountains into being created another cordillera, the Sangre de Cristo Mountains, and between their valleys and gorges course the headwaters of the Rio Grande. The rock faces of pink and cream seem to have inspired the evocative name, Blood of Christ. As the Rio Grande is settling down from its race through the Taos Gorge, to the east is born another clear-running stream, the Rio Pecos. Down through New Mexico and desert West Texas, the Rio Grande and its long Pecos tributary flow along almost parallel paths. The Pecos is heir to its own outsized history, legends, and myths. Pueblo roomblocks of stone and mortar date back in the Pecos highlands to about A.D. 1300. These first builders on the Pecos were pushed out by Querechos and Teyas, tribes that were likely of the same stock as the Apaches. In 1541, when Francisco Vásquez de Coronado followed the black magician and probable Shawnee called Turk on the wild goose chase for Grand Quivira, the most golden chimera on the plains, the Spaniards encountered the Pecos puebloans and blasted them in one battle with arquebuses and protocannons. But when winter forced Coronado to halt the expedition, he negotiated a truce at Pecos and sent a Franciscan friar to the pueblo as his emissary in the spring. The Pecos Indians saw the numbers and force of Juan de Oñate's expedition in 1599 and surrendered without a fight. Except for the Taos rebellion of 1680, which began as a tax revolt and erupted in bloodshed and sent the Spaniards galloping toward the new town of El Paso, the worldwide Franciscan Order imposed its will on the Rio Grande and Pecos highlands until Mexico overthrew the Spanish colonialists in 1821. The Franciscans were quietly withdrawn. But by then, the Pecos pueblo was being abandoned anyway.

New Mexico became a profoundly different place after the U.S.-Mexican War and the Treaty of Guadalupe Hidalgo. In the 1860s the *norteamericanos* forced the Navajos out of their homeland mountains in northwest New Mexico and in a disastrous episode almost starved them at a squalid reservation on a sun-baked bend of the Pecos called Bosque Redondo. The place soon adopted the name of its army stockade, Fort Sumner. At the end of the War between the States, Texas cowboys rounded up longhorn cattle that had gone unsold to the Confederacy and were being butchered as food for hogs; at great risk to their investment and their lives, some drovers took the shortest and quickest route through the Indian Territory to markets in Kansas. From the Palo Pinto country on the Brazos River, Charles Goodnight and Oliver Loving blazed their trails to the west, following the Pecos course in order to dodge Comanches and Kiowas on plains to the east and Apaches in the Guadalupe Mountains and other highlands to the west. Loving died in 1867 from gangrene and other complications of an arrow wound suffered on the Pecos. Goodnight took his friend and partner all the way back to Texas to bury him. The story of Goodnight and Loving would inspire Larry McMurtry's epic novel of the Old West, *Lonesome Dove*. The real-life Goodnight and another Texan, John Chisum, built New Mexico ranches and sold their beef to army quartermasters, many of them corrupt, who were charged with feeding the troops and reservation Indians. In rangeland near Fort Sumner, Chisum gave work to a bucktoothed drifter and horse thief who somehow struck the spark of worldwide fancy in the guise of Billy the Kid.

The Pecos flows through desert in southeast New Mexico and West Texas, picking up sediments of salt and trace metals that make the water hard to swallow, at best. The Pecos country in Texas has been known for the flavor of its cantaloupes and now sustains commercial vineyards—the white wine is better than the red—but the most notorious facet of its character comes from the time of the cowboys and Indians. Near the boundary of present-day Pecos and Crane counties was a fording spot called Horsehead Crossing. It was on the Comanche Trail that raiders followed from the buffalo plains to Mexico; Goodnight, Loving, and other Texas drovers knew and used it well. Goodnight's biographer, J. Evetts Haley, passed on a description of Horsehead Crossing in the book, attributing it to a famed Texas ranger and Indian fighter: "The origin of the name is befogged in legend, but according to old Rip Ford, returning Comanches drove so hard from the last water hole, sixty miles beyond the Pecos, that their thirsty horses sometimes drank their death of the Pecos brine. From the great numbers of skulls lying about, and others stuck in mesquites to mark the crossing, the place derived its name."

John Chisum was party to the bizarre and vicious Lincoln County War, a feud that sent a fugitive Billy the Kid into the Texas Panhandle, where he womanized and danced for a few months in the newborn town of Tascosa. The Kid and his pals went back to New Mexico with large numbers of horses and cattle that belonged to the Texas ranchers. Among them was Goodnight, who had claimed Palo Duro Canyon as a new home place after the defeat of the Comanches and Kiowas. Goodnight and other Texas cattle growers financed and recruited the posse that hounded Billy the Kid to his probable grave in New Mexico Territory. The Kid waited until it was too late to accept an amnesty offer from the territorial governor and novelist, Lew Wallace. Working with a certain resentment of the Texans but glad to take their money was the newly elected Lincoln County sheriff, Pat Garrett. A failed buffalo hunter and sometime bartender, Garrett took credit for slipping out of a peach orchard and killing the Kid, who had been his friend, inside a Fort Sumner house one night in 1881. The New Mexico watershed of the Pecos is still known, without apparent fondness, as Little Texas. And in Santa Fe the non-Hispanic political power bloc has long been derided as the Cowboys.

～

TODAY WATER IS THE DOMINANT POLITICAL ISSUE in New Mexico. The evidence of its scarcity and hold on the country is especially dramatic when viewed from the air. During the day, from an airplane one sees two lines of green bordered and divided by the desert's

grayish brown. At night two glittering lines of lights are divided and bordered by dark-
ness. Southward on the Rio Grande the lights intensify and broaden in the vicinities of
Taos, Santa Fe, Albuquerque, Las Cruces; in the valley of the Pecos glow Las Vegas, Roswell,
Carlsbad. The settlement of New Mexico was made possible by its two oasis streams.

Seventy years ago large parts of the West dried up and blew away, and now frightful
drought was reviving memories of the Dust Bowl. Ski resorts were going broke. On the Rio
Grande, 2002 was said to be the most damaging single drought year of record. Above the
headwaters, a large forest fire that year coated the soil with fine black ash; when monsoons from the Pacific at last pushed a few summer storms across the mountains, the runoff filled the Rio Grande with ash and dead fish, most of them young brown trout. City
government in Santa Fe imposed unprecedented water-use restrictions on its industries

LAURA GILPIN

and homes. That June some friends and I had flown into Albuquerque and met Steve Harris, who had driven down from Taos to join us. A river guide, Harris had been a founder of the storied Far-Flung Adventures, which was based for many years in Big Bend. He now booked whitewater tours out of Taos and directed a prominent nonprofit organization called Rio Grande Restoration. The summer monsoons had begun; as we made our way down Interstate 25, which follows the river valley through the state, low clouds obscured the mountains and bestowed periodic rain showers.

Harris mused as we rode along: "Somebody once said that the Rio Grande is in perpetual drought, occasionally mitigated by periods of abundance. Eight inches of rainfall a year is normal. Yet when a period of abundance comes along we act like it's going to last forever."

A bluff and a levee within Albuquerque have made the river behave. Irrigation ditches and drains hold development at bay and allow a green belt to wind through the city. But the appearance is deceptive. Compounding problems of the drought, the city and much of the upper river's watershed were embroiled in a fight over an endangered species called the silvery minnow. "The dams that have been built on the Rio Grande have punished the habitat of several indigenous aquatic species," Harris was saying. "Fish like the silvery minnow evolved in a river system that was broad and sandy and slow. When you put a reservoir across the river you stop the flow of sediment. And then when you release that clean, clear water that humans love out of a reservoir, it stirs up the sediments below the dam, holds them in suspension, and takes them on off downstream."

So a fish that by name never outgrows its appearance as a minnow is threatened with extinction. "So *what*?" many people would bellow with indignation, especially out west. But if U.S. Fish and Wildlife and local governments did not try to stave off the silvery minnow's extinction, the failure violated a federal law that has held up under every court challenge and was signed by Richard Nixon and reauthorized by Ronald Reagan—heroes of a broad constituency that tends to loathe the Endangered Species Act. Environmentalists have learned in recent decades that they can use the Endangered Species Act and the courts to impose standards of stewardship that would never be supported by Congress. The complex and contradictory fight goes on and on. The critters themselves have become pawns.

Just downstream from Albuquerque is the Isleta pueblo where Coronado's Spaniards once marched up in their coats and hats of iron and proclaimed the Indians subjects of some king. From the interstate the pueblo hardly looks like a typical American Indian reservation. In "the long ago"—perhaps the fifteenth century—tribal tradition has it that drought forced these people out of the west and into the Rio Grande flood plain. Today the Isleta pueblo has scores of thousands of acres of bottomland under cultivation, but the moneymaker for the tribe is an expanse of tract housing—bedroom-community real estate made available to the commuters of Albuquerque. The Isleta pueblo kept the legal right to manage its water, which complicates the task of Albuquerque planners and the Middle Rio Grande Conservancy District.

Near a village called San Acacia, we stood on levees that had channeled the Rio Grande away from its historic meanders. Cooper's hawks boosted themselves off the dam and cruised low in search of unwary fish. A man in a conservation district pickup, whom Harris identified as a "ditch rider," came along and gave us a close look. On the levee was a blunt hand-painted warning that the river was not as tame as it looked: "Today my next of kin were notified that while I was fishing in the river, I had been pulled under the water by the run-off current. Rescue teams are looking for my body."

"The river valley is six to twenty miles across," Harris told us, "and the river channel would occupy different parts of the valley according to whether it had flooded recently or not. So what you had was a riparian forest. There were copses of cottonwoods and willow and oxbow lakes, pothole lakes, little remnants of the river on that flood plain. Today, because of the dams and some of the other alterations we've made, the river is confined within its channel."

Around the town of Socorro a stretch of river valley and forest becomes marshes that are a federal wildlife preserve called Bosque del Apache. In the fall it is one of North America's finest viewing sites for geese, cranes, ducks, hawks, hummingbirds—countless species of migratory fowl. But where those wetlands play out, the Rio Grande commences a long broadening into a reservoir. Hidden by a cordillera to the east is the ancient Rio Grande that lost its way, the fierce desert and nuclear-contaminated test site called Dead Man's March. Near its southern end is Truth or Consequences, a town that changed its former name, Hot Springs, in honor of a 1950s television game show. On the outskirts of Truth or Consequences is the dam of Elephant Butte. The dam has the imposing lines and scale of that bygone era of public works when the federal government threw itself into altering river courses with the optimism and grandiosity reserved in later times for building interstate highways and propelling astronauts into outer space, but behind the Elephant Butte dam was, I thought, about the ugliest lake I'd ever seen.

No trees grew on the shores, the campgrounds and picnic tables were deserted, and only a few fishing boats were scattered about. Between the opaque blue water and slopes of maroon rock and soil was a strip of ground that looked bleached.

"People call it the Bathtub Ring," Harris chuckled. He said the dark ground marked Elephant Butte's historic water line; the pale strip below gauged the recent years of too little rain. "They built it to hold 2.2 million acre-feet. It's filled up and gone over the spillway a few times. But after they built it, the first thing they got was thirty years of extraordinary drought."

A dry cycle of climate and a reservoir reflecting the priorities of a bygone era are not the only things that have siphoned water from the Rio Grande. Tamarisk, or the misnamed salt cedar (it does carry salt, but is not cedar), was brought from North Africa and Central Asia to the American plains in the nineteenth century to help stabilize riverbanks. With lacey, light green foliage and a frail lavender bloom, a single tamarisk is not unattractive. But brakes of the pest brush are taking over the Rio Grande and many other rivers in the West. "They use twice as much water as the native willow and cottonwood," Harris said. "Between Socorro and Elephant Butte"—about sixty miles—"a hundred thousand acre-feet of water is just swallowed by the salt cedar." They spread thickly and far from a river's bank; into their tangle of roots, once-flowing streams have just disappeared. Prolific tangles of the brush block the waterways and, when there has been some rain, they create surreal marshes in desert terrain. Salt cedar has consumed much of the Rio Grande between El Paso and Big Bend.

The river valley we passed was marked by cottonwoods, tamarisk that had been up-rooted and piled for burning, and dark green irrigated fields of alfalfa. Gazing at mesas to the west and a shallow tributary set running by the monsoons in a broad and usually dry bed, Harris told us that beyond them lay the sprawling ranch of the conservationist and media mogul Ted Turner. It struck me that Turner bore a distinct resemblance to Pat Garrett. I idly wondered what those two would have had to say to each other. Garrett was an ardent hustler. Working with a drunken newspaperman, he went broke self-publishing a book of braggadocio climaxed by his tale of killing Billy the Kid. On the basis of his fame, Garrett gambled again with a mule-punishing scam called the Pecos Valley Land and Ditch Company. In those days before Elephant Butte and the other dams, it was the biggest earth-moving operation the territory had ever seen. He boasted that as a master irrigator he knew the secret of making water run uphill. He went broke again, continuing to blame his choice of partners, so he returned to the muscle trade—helping break a strike of cowboys who wanted to form a labor union in the Texas Panhandle.

In 1896 Garrett crossed paths with Tex Rickard, the legendary boxing promoter. Rickard's premier accomplishment may have been promoting that heavyweight title fight between Bob Fitzsimmons and Frank Maher. Boxing had been outlawed in Texas and New Mexico, and Mexico sent in troops to keep the match from being held in Juárez. Rickard investigated the possibility of holding it onboard a ship in the Gulf of Mexico—a prospect of challenging footwork for the fighters. Dusting off the law west of the Pecos, Rickard persuaded Langtry's Judge Roy Bean to let him put on the show on a sandbar island in the Rio Grande, and security for the bout was provided by Pat Garrett. It was a short night's work—Fitzsimmons knocked out the challenger in the first round.

For a time Garrett found steady work on the federal payroll. But before President Theodore Roosevelt approved the appointment in 1901, he required Garrett to read aloud and sign a pledge: "I, the undersigned Patrick F. Garrett hereby give my word of honor, that if I am appointed Collector of Customs at El Paso, Texas, I will totally abstain from the use of intoxicating liquors during my term of office."

Garrett's great loves were a daughter, who was blind, and a hard-won ranch outside Las Cruces, where he advertised himself as a breeder of racehorses. In 1908 he was trying to pay his taxes and get out of debt by leasing his grazing rights to a reputed hit man called Deacon Jim who was driving a cattle herd out of Mexico. But Garrett already had a tenant with 1,800 goats on his place, and the man refused to yield the lease. Garrett and the tenant met one day in their buggies and set out to resolve the matter. Garrett was a tall man whom local Latinos called Juan Largo, Long John, due to the length of his legs. Though he was fifty-eight, he was still prone to fistfights and carried a shotgun under his wagon seat; he had clearly been trying to intimidate the goat herder. On a lonesome dirt road Garrett was unbuttoning his fly to relieve his bladder when some pistoleer shot him in the back of the head. The goat herder stood trial for it and was acquitted. Garrett's murder was never solved. The Old West couldn't help but die hard.

~

AS WE CAME INTO TEXAS and the suburbs of El Paso, my gaze fell on a vast feedlot. In the summer heat, cattle stood in undeviating rows, jaws busy in the grain troughs, as a system of showerheads dispersed a fine spray over them to keep them cooled off. Sunlight caught the mist and refracted a rainbow across the herd. I wondered at the water bill for that. We left the interstate and followed a road that took us into an industrial strip divided by the Rio Grande from the slums of Ciudad Juárez. The Hacienda Café overlooks the river. We were reading historic markers on the lot when the owner, Chip John, walked outside to greet us. He wore a cowboy hat, big belt buckle, and sharp-toed boots. "This is where it happened," he announced proudly. "Don Juan de Oñate came across the river right here in 1598. There were soldiers and priests, a hundred thirty families, seven thousand head of livestock. The first horses ever seen in Texas. They had a thousand sheep. I never would've thought about it, sheep. I guess they brought them along to eat."

One might visualize another scene on that part of the Rio Grande in 1911—Francisco Madero's revolutionaries camped on the riverbank across from the old El Paso smelter. A few weeks later, when Mexico's revolutionary war began, El Pasoans climbed on their roofs and observed the military debut of Pancho Villa.

The 1944 U.S.-Mexico Treaty for Utilization of the Colorado and Tijuana Rivers and of the Rio Grande does not leap to the fore of popular imagination in quite the same way. But it was one of the most important milestones in the relations of Mexico and the United States. The pact changed the name of the governing authority to the International Boundary and Water Commission (IBWC), and it was supposed to make up for the truncation of the Rio Grande. Except in severe droughts, Mexico would release an annual average of

350,000 acre-feet from the Río Conchos to the Rio Grande. Mexico was entitled to keep at least 700,000 acre-feet a year. The Amistad and Falcón reservoirs would be built downstream to store water and check floods.

The Pass of the North is a great turnstile of immigration and trade. Generations of Latinos, especially those from Mexico and Central America, speak of El Paso as Europeans speak of Ellis Island. Here their families cast their lots with another nation, started anew. But not all the people swarming to Juárez long for work on the other side. Immigration, legal and illegal, is too hard; they don't want to be cut off from their villages and clans; all they want are jobs in foreign-owned maquiladoras, which in 1998 paid workers an average wage of $1.32 an hour. Two centuries ago the Santa Fe Trail sent the caravans of freighters through the pass to the markets of Chihuahua. A century ago Americans sold guns in El Paso to the revolutionary followers of Madero and Villa. Today drug barons sit in sprawling living rooms in Juárez and laugh at the surveillance gadgets and "intelligence" of the DEA command center in El Paso. The slums of both cities are a festering sore of street crime. A horrific murder spree in Juárez has claimed the lives of hundreds of women. The mountain pass and fertile valley where Cabeza de Vaca once walked and Juan de Oñate claimed all the northern lands for God and a king have begotten an urban train wreck.

El Paso is "a non-attainment area" under the federal Clean Air Act, with pulmonary consequences that fall heaviest on children and the elderly; but what can the technology-driven Environmental Protection Agency do when much of this smog is caused by poor people in Juárez burning tires for heat? A decade ago, in a much-publicized report the Texas attorney general and local health officials revealed that rates of hepatitis, tuberculosis, and dysentery in El Paso County were running three to five times the national average. Residents of one colonia—an unincorporated subdivision—stored all their drinking water in 55-gallon drums; seventy percent of those barrels were labeled as used containers of toxic chemicals.

The commonality of all these people is the Río Bravo, the Rio Grande. Average rainfall here is just eight inches a year. Aquifers were supposed to help meet the water needs, but that was before the population exploded to two million; now the Bolson Aquifer, the main source of groundwater for El Paso and Juárez, is expected to dry up by 2030. Thirty percent of Juarez's drinking water is believed to be lost by leaking mains and pipes. In recent years wealthy Texas water investors—some call them hustlers—have been buying up rights to groundwater and proposing to pipe it across the desert to El Paso. But neither the Texas city nor its Mexican counterpart has any credible answers to the long-term problem of water supply. The solution is sure not the Rio Grande.

Just upriver from the Hacienda Café, the river's bend toward the Oñate crossing is dominated by a large complex, the century-old Asarco copper smelter. Its American owners closed the smelter in 1999, citing low copper prices, but Texas water quality regulators and the Environmental Protection Agency had beleaguered them with repeated assertions of contamination. The day my friends and I arrived, El Paso evening newscasts blared a story that the EPA had found that much of the soil around the smelter, which is near the downtown business district, contained high levels of lead and arsenic. Lawns in a prominent middle-class neighborhood would have to be dug up and trucked away in the emergency cleanup, and the groundwater was believed to be endangered. But beneath Asarco's cracked windows, dormant smokestack, and concertina wire, we watched boys from Juárez swimming happily in the river.

~

THE INTERNATIONAL BOUNDARY AND WATER COMMISSION is housed in a small office building on El Paso's west side. The next morning I met a polite and soft-spoken IBWC official named Bob Ybarra. In our federal government, the IBWC occupies a tertiary tier of the State Department, but all public policies and pronouncements are carefully coordinated with the Juárez-based counterpart, the Comisión Internacional de Limites y Aguas (CILA). "Our high point," Ybarra reminisced, "was the Chamizal Convention of 1963. The river always meandered back and forth in El Paso and Juárez. It affected hundreds of acres. Every time we had a flood the river course would change, and there would be a big dispute over which country and landowners had legal right to the property. John F. Kennedy came here and promised to resolve the situation. The solution was to make the river channel permanent. For 4.4 miles," Ybarra said with a smile, "we set the border in concrete."

With a stately sort of measure, all formal agreements of the IBWC and CILA are called minutes. Minute Number 258, channelization of the Tijuana River. Minute Number 290, construction of a new bridge in El Paso. And so on—up to 306, 307, and 308, the recent minutes dealing with the release of Río Conchos water to the Rio Grande and the debt of water that Mexico owes the United States. Those agreements have shed unprecedented and unwanted light on the little-known commission.

IBWC literature stresses environmental protection along the border. But in Ybarra's intricate rundown of his agency's history and responsibilities, he made no mention of these cities' biggest news of the day: heavy-metal contamination spreading from a smelter on a bank of the Rio Grande. Nor did he mention any other environmental matter. In fairness, not all the problems of the Rio Grande have been created by politics and men in the last century and a half. Coronado himself was flabbergasted when he saw that the river he had followed and camped beside abruptly vanished below the stark mountain pass. But the first death of the Rio Grande is no longer seasonal. Water released downstream from El Paso and Juárez is mostly treated affluent. And then the tamarisk stakes its claim. Ensnarled by salt cedar, a 216-mile stretch of the Rio Grande from Fort Quitman to Presidio has been reduced to a trickle. The stretch is known as the Forgotten River.

JOSIAH GREGG

from *Commerce of the Prairies* (1844)

WE WERE STILL SOME SIXTY MILES above Paso del Norte, but the balance of the road now led down the river valley or over the low bordering hills. During our journey between this and El Paso we passed the ruins of several settlements, which had formerly been the seats of opulence and prosperity, but which have since been abandoned in consequence of the marauding incursions of the Apaches.

On the 12th of September we reached the usual ford of the Rio del Norte, six miles above El Paso; but the river being somewhat flushed we found it impossible to cross over with our wagons. The reader will no doubt be surprised to learn that there is not a single ferry on this "Great River of the North" till we approach the mouth. But how do people cross it? Why, during three-fourths of the year it is everywhere fordable, and when the freshet season comes on, each has to remain on his own side or swim, for canoes even are very rare. But as we could neither swim our wagons and merchandise, nor very comfortably wait for the falling of the waters, our only alternative was to unload the vehicles, and ferry the goods over in a little "dug out" about thirty feet long and two feet wide, of which we were fortunate enough to obtain possession.

We succeeded in finding a place shallow enough to haul our empty wagons across: but for this good fortune we should have been under the necessity of taking them to pieces (as I had before done), and of ferrying them on the "small craft" before mentioned. Half of a wagon may thus be crossed at a time, by carefully balancing it upon the canoe, yet there is of course no little danger of capsizing during the passage.

This river even when fordable often occasions a great deal of trouble, being, like the Arkansas, embarrassed with many quicksand mires. In some places, if a wagon is permitted to stop in the river but for a moment, it sinks to the very body. Instances have occurred when it became necessary, not only to drag out the mules by the ears and to carry out the loading package by package, but to haul out the wagon piece by piece—wheel by wheel.

On the 14th we made our entrance into the town of El Paso del Norte, which is the northernmost settlement in the department of Chihuahua. Here our cargo had to be examined by a stern, surly officer, who, it was feared, would lay an embargo on our goods upon the slightest appearance of irregularity in our papers; but notwithstanding our gloomy forebodings, we passed the ordeal without any difficulty.

The valley of El Paso is supposed to contain a population of about four thousand inhabitants, scattered over the western bottom of the Rio del Norte to the length of ten or twelve miles. These settlements are so thickly interspersed with vineyards, orchards, and cornfields, as to present more the appearance of a series of plantations than of a town: in fact, only a small portion at the head of the valley, where the *plaza pública* and parochial church are located, would seem to merit this title. Two or three miles above the plaza there is a dam of stone and brush across the river, the purpose of which is to turn the current into a dike or canal, which conveys nearly half the water of the stream, during a low stage, through this well-cultivated valley, for the irrigation of the soil. Here we were regaled with the finest fruits of the season: the grapes especially were of the most exquisite flavor. From these the inhabitants manufacture a very pleasant wine, somewhat resembling Malaga. A species of *aguardiente* (brandy) is also distilled from the same fruit, which, although weak, is of very agreeable flavor. These liquors are known among Americans as "Pass wine" and "Pass whiskey," and constitute a profitable article of trade, supplying the markets of Chihuahua and New Mexico.

ROBERT BOSWELL

from *American Owned Love* (1999)

DENNY'S OLD BUICK SEDAN was parked halfway into the street, the back tire in the gutter while the front angled out into the driving lane. Gay couldn't tell the color in the near dark, but she guessed blue. The air still felt wet but not cool, the horizon light despite the late hour.

Denny opened the passenger door for her. "It may be a mess," he said, not so much an apology as a warning.

"That's where I live." She pointed to her dark, tree-infested yard. "So you'll know."

"Okay," he said, staring. "Looks haunted—the yard anyway." He ducked down to peer through the wall of leafy limbs. "The house looks sort of . . . pink." He straightened and turned to her. "Bad light," he said.

"No, it's pink," she said. "I always wanted a pink house."

"Hmm," he said, rounding the car. "What else have you always wanted?"

A good question, she thought, and one she had no intention of answering. The front seat had been badly reupholstered in white vinyl and was darkening from human wear. She thought for a moment of her failed bananas. Gum wrappers littered the floorboard, and wads of silver filled the open ashtray.

"I chew gum," he said, climbing in, "especially when I drive." He started the Buick and shifted into gear, easing out into the street. "What is there to do in Persimmon besides—"

"I can't stay out late," she said. "I have to see someone at eleven. I'll need to be home by ten-thirty."

"Okay." He glanced at his watch as he drove. "We've got an hour or so." He had shoved his sleeves up and rested an elbow out the window. "I don't know my way around yet. What—"

"Let's go swimming," she said.

He eyed her suspiciously and slowed the car as they approached the intersection. A huge yellow bulldozer was stationed on the corner like a sentry. "Swimming?"

"I know a good place," she said. "Nearby."

He pursed his lips and nodded, staring out the windshield at the highway. "Okay," he said. "Show me." He flicked a finger in either direction. "Which way?"

"You're not a mindless jock, are you?" she asked him.

"No," he said. "Although I had ambitions for a while. Which way do I turn?"

She pointed left, and he hit the turn signal. "Have you got anything in here that could pass for bobby pins?" she asked him. "I don't want to get my hair wet." The glove box held a bundle of maps, a jumbo pack of sugarless gum, and a pocketknife. She took a rubber band from the stack of maps.

"Help yourself." He edged the car forward to see past the giant bulldozer. "You want your gum?" she asked him.

"Not this second."

"Quit smoking?"

He shook his head. "I just like gum."

The river's deepest spot, about a mile downriver from her house, was at the Apuro ledge, halfway through town. A man had taken Gay swimming there one drunken night a decade ago, and she had been back every year since then.

"We're still in the city," Denny pointed out, slowing the Buick as he surveyed the area. "It's not entirely dark yet, and I don't have a bathing suit."

"Trust me," she said. "Park in front of that brown house."

"I hardly know you," he added with annoyance, but he parked the Buick as she directed, the front bumper grazing the ugly paneled wall of the cheap frame house. He's a lousy parker, she thought, and wondered how that would show itself in bed.

She had discovered that driving habits often revealed sexual traits. There were times that the life she had constructed made her feel merely sleazy. She felt almost obligated to be promiscuous. But she liked the idea of seeing another man just before she and her husband celebrated their wedding anniversary. Her husband would appreciate it, too—the spirited defiance of convention.

She circled the Buick and opened his door. His dubious expression reminded her of the limits of cynical men. "Just don't get me fired before my first day," he said, but he climbed from the car willingly and took her hand before she could tell him to.

A stand of mulberry trees bordered the opposite side of the two-lane highway. "It'll be dark in another five minutes," she said, although in the shade of the trees it

LAURA GILPIN

was already dark. A wall of high cane separated the trees from the river, and she pulled him into the green, leafy thicket, pushing the pliant cane to one side and then the other, working their way to the water. "See," she said, tugging him onto a secluded spit of sand. The river, still brown from the rain, rolled leisurely past. It would not turn black for another three hours.

Gay stepped out of her skirt. "We're completely protected." She hung the skirt on a cane stalk.

"So," Denny said, slipping off his shoes while he watched her undress. "What is it you do here? For a living?"

"I work at a company that transports cars to dealers," she told him, unsnapping her bra. She stepped out of her panties, and hung her underwear beside her skirt and blouse. She folded her arms but didn't try to hide her breasts. She liked the way he looked at her. She wished she had a cigarette to pose as a nude Statue of Liberty. Real liberties often required nudity. "*Apuro* means 'deep water,'" she said. "You swim, don't you?"

He nodded. "Yeah, I swim."

"Don't dive. It's too shallow on this side to dive." She stepped off the short ledge into the water, waded in a few feet, then crouched down. "There's a space here where cars on the road can spot us." She turned from the road to look at him. "Wait until there aren't any headlights."

He had a nice body and wore boxer shorts, which she preferred. His stomach was not so firm that he might be a bodybuilder. She didn't like bodybuilders. He snapped the elastic band of his shorts. "You're going to watch these come off?" he asked.

"You watched me," she said.

"That I did," he said, slipping them down. . . . "No laughing," he said.

They crouched together in the murky water, watching headlights approach. A spray of light illuminated the water, coming so near them that Denny leaned away from it.

"We're safe here," Gay said. "We just have to be patient." Her chest was so inflated with the hilarity of the situation, she felt she could float across the river, cutting through the water like the ornamental prow of a ship. Two more cars came and went before she pushed off and began swimming. Denny followed, splashing a good deal more than she. "You come here a lot?" he asked, the strain of the swim in his voice, almost a bleat.

"Not that often," she said. "I like to swim."

"I can see that," he said.

"It gets deep here," she warned as they neared the far side of the river. She swam ahead to the bank and stopped there, treading water.

He collided with her. "Where we going?"

"We're here," she said. "Look."

Peering through the limbs of the scrubby bushes that lined the bank, they could make out several adobe houses built at odd angles to one another, a peculiar quality of light in their windows, the mud nest of wasps beneath the eaves of the nearest dwelling.

"Is this some kind of suburb?" Denny asked.

"You're breathing awfully heavy," Gay said. "Is it from swimming or bumping into me?"

"I said I could swim, I didn't say I was a good swimmer."

"Here." She reached for the branch of a gray tree whose limbs fanned out across the river. "Hold on."

He dangled by one arm from the branch, wiping water from his face with his free hand. "I feel like a monkey." He nodded toward the houses. "Why are the lights so weird?"

"No electricity. I don't know whether they're gas lamps or—"

"What is this we're looking at? This isn't Mexico, is it? We're not on the border."

"Not Mexico," she said. "The Rio Grande doesn't become the border for another thirty miles. This is Apuro. The local colonia. Weren't you listening during dinner? The boonies. The shantytown. The wrong side of the tracks—only the tracks, in this case, is the river."

"They don't look like shanties. They look like pretty solid houses."

"Adobe shanties. No running water, no electricity, no sewer."

"No sewer?"

"I don't know," she said, inhaling through her nose, the water brackish but not really foul. "That's what I've heard, but I don't smell anything."

"They must have some kind of pipes, then," he said. "So this swim was inspired by that clown Morrison?" He paused, waiting, she could tell, for her to disagree. "Hate the thought of that," he went on. "There must be sewer pipes. You're romanticizing the place."

"Maybe, but—" A voice came from inside the nearest house. Another voice answered in Spanish. She put her lips close to his ear and whispered, "Could you understand that?"

He shook his head, water flying from his hair, his cheek brushing against hers. "Why are we spying on these people?"

"Because I like to," she said. "Because they're across the river and there's no bridge. Because they speak another language. Because we're naked and they're lit by fire."

WILLIAM LANGEWIESCHE

from *Cutting for Sign* (1995)

THE BOUNDARY HAS A KEEPER. His name is Narendra Gunaji, and I spent a morning with him in El Paso, Texas. Gunaji is a trim, white-haired man with a severe disposition and the accent of his native India. He is an American success story—an immigrant with a Ph.D. and a ten-page resumé. For twenty-eight years he taught civil engineering at New Mexico State University in Las Cruces, where he also dabbled in Republican politics. In 1987 Ronald Reagan appointed him to head the U.S. section of the International Boundary and Water Commission. His Mexican counterpart, Arturo Herrera Solis, is based across the Rio Grande, in Ciudad Juárez. Together the two men manage the physical boundary—the markers and waterflows—along the 1,951 miles from the Pacific to the Gulf of Mexico. It is not a small task. Gunaji has 270 people working under him. When I got to the offices in El Paso, I heard a lot of "Yessir, Commissioner." Gunaji seemed to relish it. He gave the day's orders easily, with his arms folded. Then he took me for a ride along the boundary in the back of an official minivan, chauffeured by two assistants. One carried a cellular telephone.

The twin cities of El Paso and Juárez, with a combined population of two million, mark the midpoint of the border. This is where the Rio Grande, having flowed south from its origin in the Rockies, snakes through a gap in the desert mountains and turns southeast. It is also where the two halves of the boundary join: to the west the line runs crisply across the deserts; to the east it rides a more ambiguous midchannel course through the curves of the Rio Grande. For an engineer, these are two very different sorts of boundaries. The spot where they meet is a short drive from Gunaji's office, on the outskirts of the city. To get there, we crossed a rickety single-lane bridge and followed a gravel road along the Rio Grande. Boundary Monument No. 1 is an eleven-foot masonry obelisk in a postage-stamp park. There is no fence, since Mexicans crossing illegally into El Paso find the downtown more convenient. Gunaji encouraged me to stand with one foot in each country.

As an airplane flies, we were 645 miles from the Gulf of Mexico. Through innumerable meanders and one huge S-turn, the Rio Grande doubles that distance to 1,254 miles. Little of the water flowing by Monument No. 1 actually gets through; it is dammed and diverted for irrigation, and replaced by other waters that are dammed and diverted in turn. Nonetheless, you can imagine floating the eastern boundary in a boat. Allowing time to sleep and discounting delays in the two big reservoirs, it would take about a month. There are no dangerous rapids, but you would run the risks of sunburn, sewage, and occasional sniper fire.

At Monument No. 1 we were closer to the Pacific—only 585 air miles away. But even across dry land, the boundary follows an indirect route, totaling 698 miles. You could walk it in about a month, mostly through wilderness, without the slightest chance of getting lost. Gunaji's predecessors have erected several hundred obelisks of iron and masonry. The westernmost obelisk, Monument No. 258, is made of marble and is sometimes described as "historic" because it was the first one built, in 1849.

In El Paso the desert was growing hot. Gunaji wore a jacket and tie and sunglasses. He had begun to sweat and was tiring of my questions about dry land. The five-year surveys have become routine. The obelisks are like geologic features. The intermediate concrete posts are more vulnerable, but when one is knocked down, it simply gets replaced. What else is there to discuss? There is no glory in monuments. Gunaji wanted to move on to the Rio Grande.

I persisted. "What about graffiti?"

"Graffiti is everywhere. It's probably on the moon."

"It doesn't bother you?"

He smiled thinly. "I have a plan to keep the markers clean. I want to put up signs saying Please Perform Graffiti and Pornography Here. As Good Americans."

Gunaji himself is a good American. He told me his story after we climbed back into the air-conditioned van. He was raised in India in a family that was poor, lettered, and anti-British. His father, a lawyer active in the Indian National Congress, studied the American civil rights movement and wrote a book about Booker T. Washington. His older sister, jailed by the British and later called a freedom fighter, was married in a ceremony performed by Mahatma Gandhi. Young Gunaji was a patriot, but ambitious too. He graduated in engineering from the University of Poona, got a small job with the city of Bombay, and saved his rupees to buy a ticket out. There was no question where he would go.

El Paso is a strip city spreading along a freeway. Juárez is a slum. As the Rio Grande flows between them, it is hemmed in by twin levees, which are the domain of government. Gunaji had us driven downriver along the northern one, and sat with the pride of a proprietor in the back of the van. He was in an expansive mood. On the opposite shore the tin and scrapwood shantytowns sprawled over low hills. The Juárez slums are as bad as others along the border. They are as bad as the slums of Bombay. I wondered if they reminded Gunaji of his past. A gully spewed black water into the river. Tainted upstream by agricultural runoff, the Rio Grande swallowed the filth easily. A family bathed among the bushes. The men had stripped down to their shorts; out of modesty the women had kept their dresses on. They stood in the water and watched us pass, a world away. Ahead, the bridges between Juárez and El Paso spanned the river. A rowboat heavy with passengers nosed against the U.S. shore, bypassing immigration formalities. One woman couldn't climb the steep embankment. Others, who had already made it to the top, went back down to help.

The young Gunaji had no one to help him. He got a student visa, came to New York by ship, took a train to Madison, Wisconsin, and started graduate studies on his last twelve dollars. He worked as a dishwasher and soda jerk, lived upstairs, got a scholarship and eventually a doctorate, fell in love with an American, married her, had five children, became a professor and ultimately a consultant. He said without irony, "I stand as an example that the American dream is still alive."

Other examples stood outside. Sealed in the van, we crept through a crowd on the levee. Perhaps a hundred people waited there, getting their bearings and watching for the Border Patrol. Though the levee is technically U.S. territory, in practice it is neutral soil, since retreat to the river is easy. The crowd was mostly local—unemployed Juárez youths without border-crossing cards going to El Paso for the day. A few, however, were greater travelers. They had come from the interior of Mexico, or from Central or South America, and they were going farther than El Paso. They carried suitcases and scurried away from the van. The locals were not so shy. Recognizing the boundary commission seal on the door, they tapped on the roof, peered through the windows, smirked, and joked. They begged cigarettes, which we did not have. Boys stood in the van's way nonchalantly, showing off for girls. Gunaji's assistants exchanged long-suffering looks.

Gunaji seemed oblivious. He spoke about his decision to become an American citizen. His older sister objected, but he had prepared an argument for her. "I told her, 'I'm going to serve India by staying out of India.'"

I interrupted him. "Doesn't it seem odd, if you think back, to find yourself managing this boundary?" I gestured toward the crowd.

He looked annoyed. "In the United States I have always tried to participate in the workings of government. I served on the Las Cruces City Council. Now I serve as commissioner. I am happy such an honor has been bestowed upon my family. A nation needs its boundaries, no?"

I nodded yes. You need a *them* to have an *us*.

We drove downriver to the Free Bridge, so called because no tolls are charged. The Free Bridge belongs to the boundary commission. It spans the Rio Grande at a patch of riverland named the Chamizal, after the desert grass *chamizo* that once grew there. The Chamizal is Mexican territory that was lopped off and delivered to the United States in 1864 by a southward shift of the river. This event kicked off a century of squabbling. The remedy, finally agreed upon in 1963, was radical surgery: 4.3 miles of new concrete riverbed were laid and the Free Bridge was built. On December 13, 1968, Lyndon Johnson came to town, met Mexican President Diaz Ordaz at the border, and diverted the Rio Grande into its new course. Mexico walked away with a net gain of 437.18 acres. On the U.S. side, Johnson has still not been forgiven. The problem is, one nation's gain is another's loss. And the boundary commission is guilty by association.

I learned this within minutes of landing at the El Paso airport, having mentioned to a pilot that I had come to visit the commission. "Those sons-a-bitches," he said. "They're the ones who gave away Texas."

He assumed I shared his sentiment, since I, too, had lived in Texas and had flown the border as an air-taxi pilot. He was less open-minded about Gunaji, whom he had seen on television. He said, "Who the hell is that guy? I can't even understand when he speaks English."

It was not a good week for Gunaji. We stood in the shade of the Free Bridge and watched workmen drilling into the concrete. The bridge was rotting. It was built by the Mexicans, of substandard materials, long before Gunaji's time, but it was his problem now. He had ordered emergency shoring. Yesterday he had banned the truckers who haul cargo to and from the *maquiladoras,* the big American assembly plants in Juárez. Hundreds of these drivers make short runs across the border with Mexican rigs loaded to 100,000 pounds. The Free Bridge is their cheapest and most convenient route. Gunaji had forced them twenty miles downriver to the toll bridge at Zaragosa. People were outraged because, after all, the Free Bridge had not yet collapsed. The American managers of the *maquiladoras* threatened to go to Washington over Gunaji's head. There was talk of conspiracy and corruption. There was talk of violence. Now Gunaji stood under the bridge with his arms folded, looking alone and defiant. Watching him, I thought I understood the severity of his mood. He was an engineer trying to do his job. Other boundary engineers have certainly been allowed to do theirs.

The remaking of the Rio Grande at the Chamizal was not the first operation of its kind. In the 1930s the boundary commission rectified the river downstream from El Paso. Rectified means this: the meanders were cut off, the river was straightened and run between levees, and the length of the boundary from El Paso to Fort Quitman was shortened from 155 to 86 miles. The two countries ex-changed 6,920 acres of land in equal amounts, and none of Texas was lost. Here and there the commission has rectified the Rio Grande all the way to the Gulf of Mexico.

But rivers make old-fashioned, troublesome boundaries. One problem lies beyond Fort Quitman, where the rectification ends and the Rio Grande resumes its natural course between faulted mountains. For 198 miles downriver, past Candelaria to the confluence of the Conchos, the Rio Grande braids through jungles of salt cedar. Salt cedar is not a native plant. It is a bush or small tree, a tamarisk brought to North America from the Mediterranean in 1852, sold in California as an ornamental, and planted in New Mexico to control erosion. By the end of the century it had infested riverbanks through the desert and beyond. It is estimated now that 1.5 million acres of salt cedar grow in the American west. The seeds drift in the wind and when they land on moist sand, they plunge taproots thirty feet deep into the permanent water that lies below riverbeds. The taproots make salt cedar resistant to drought and flood, the on-again, off-again condition of desert rivers, and allow the plant to dominate the less robust native species. The domination is not all bad: salt cedar provide an ideal habitat for birds and other creatures. However, by clogging established channels, it also forces floodwaters to spread farther and encourages rivers to braid. Braiding is the untidy process by which a current laden with sand and silt restlessly builds bars, then divides around them. It is a particular problem on the Rio Grande because it makes the location of the channel, and therefore of the boundary, impossible to establish. The imprecision bothers surveyors, if not the residents.

In the 1970s the commission decided on an engineering solution: for these 198 miles the river would be made to follow the boundary. The two countries agreed. The commission filed environmental-impact statements, compromised with conservationists, promised to "enhance wildlife," and in 1980 unleashed the bulldozers. The work continues today, shared by the two countries. The channel is being "restored" to an angled cross-section six feet deep, sixteen feet wide at the bottom, and thirty-eight feet wide at the top. A V-shape is the most efficient design because it minimizes evaporation and encourages the scouring action of a fast, smooth flow. Floodways fifty-six feet wide are being scraped through the salt cedar along both banks.

Nellie Howard, an old woman who lives in Candelaria, was not impressed. She said, "When they channelized the Rio Grande, they forgot it was a river and tried to give us a ditch. Come the first rain, the water went everywhere." Soon after work was completed in Candelaria, thunderstorms burst on the mountains and filled the creek beds with torrents for two days. The Rio Grande went wild and returned nearly to its natural state. Nellie Howard smiled and said, "Those engineers came down here pretending to know everything. We tried to tell them, but they wouldn't listen. The river reminded them who's really in charge."

Gunaji himself must wonder. One warm spring day I accompanied him on a working tour of the banks downriver from Candelaria. Our guide was the boundary commission's local engineer, a burly man named John. He drove us in a Ford Bronco along a recently repaired dike, past fields of blue wildflowers. Gunaji was in another of his expansive moods and sat with his arm over the seat back. He said, "What are these flowers, John?"

"Weeds, Commissioner."

"They may be weeds, John, but they bring color to the country, John."

"Yessir, Commissioner."

Later Gunaji seemed to remember his mission. He turned to me with a frown and said, "You see all this vegetation? We need to mitigate this vegetation."

I asked why.

He said, "It impedes the water."

And the water impedes the boundary commission. The project is years behind schedule. There have been difficulties with earth-moving equipment and international coordination. Floods have washed away the floodways. And salt cedar, which can grow nine feet a year, spreads as fast as it can be cleared. From the air the river looks like it has always looked. The conservationists must be pleased. They agreed to a compromise, but this is better because the river itself is fighting back.

The engineers, however, show no signs of fatigue. They are armed with a 1970 treaty that resolved all pending boundary disputes, reaffirmed the channel as the dividing line, and forbade any further misbehavior by the water. The Rio Grande has become boundary first and river second. And time is on the side of government.

CHARLES BOWDEN

from *Down by the River* (2002)

SAL HAS A BROTHER AND TWO SISTERS, and when he is a child the family lives in the lower valley of El Paso near the oil refinery.

The father works driving a government bus full of workers to White Sands Missile Range just north of El Paso in New Mexico. He also cuts meat, a traditional skill in the Martínez clan. In El Paso, relatives market their own brand of pork skins. The father is often gone during the week and leaves his wife a simple instruction: tell the children I will deal with any failures in their conduct when I return. Sal's mother tends her brood and her church, holds down a job also, and so the family thrives. He is the quiet boy, sometimes prone to stuttering, the kid who seldom says anything and stands on the edge of things. His mother never spanks him, not once.

The thing that sticks in his mind is Sunday and Sunday is always blue. His dad and older brother would be off for softball, and Sal just didn't like being in the park while the men played and drank beer. His mother and sisters would be off to visit her people. He'd be home alone, left with his chessboard, and that made Sunday something to dread, made it the blue day when even the smallness of his normal El Paso closed in yet more and seemed to choke him. His body becomes rigid as he remembers those Sundays.

Though he is not large at 165 pounds, he excels at football and in high school makes all-city as defensive halfback. His life is odd jobs and football. He is spooked by women and does not have a girlfriend until the last month of his senior year. In his studies, he has a knack for math, scores very high on the SATs, and his high school counselor points him toward a career in accounting. Sal looks into that field and learns that accountants have a very high suicide rate. He decides to study criminal justice. He hangs out with buddies, has a few beers after the big game but never touches marijuana, not even when he goes to those heavy metal concerts.

His grades are good and he gets into college at Sam Houston in Richland. But after a year of odd jobs and a full class load, he is sinking financially and returns home to attend the University of Texas at El Paso, sometimes called Taco Tech. He washes dishes, bags groceries, buses tables, and graduates in law enforcement in May of 1984. He has a degree and no job and so he continues bagging groceries.

One day he helps a lady to her car and she gives him a 10-cent tip. He's working in his own neighborhood and he realizes there is no money and the tip is all the woman can spare and this is going to be it, degree or no degree, unless he does something. By January 1985, he has offers from military intelligence, the El Paso police department, and the Texas highway patrol. He speaks Spanish, he fulfills a quota in the era of minority recruitment, and he's got those grades. The highway patrol academy lasts eighteen weeks. They instantly cut his hair off and Sal loves every minute of the training. There are about 120 in his class but only eighty-four make the cut and get the badge and the gun.

By the summer of 1985, Sal Martínez is a trooper with the big hat, the Magnum on his hip, and his own new turf, Floresville. He is the law for a town of six thousand and he relishes entering cafés and having everyone fall silent as he walks past.

He is twenty-two years old, out cruising in his squad car, and there is an accident, busted metal, broken glass, people reeling with injuries, blood streaming, and Sal rolls up and gets out of the car with that big hat and he takes control, he calms the panic, gives the orders, has the power. And this sense of control, this force flowing from him, gives him self-confidence for the first time in his life. He thinks: I can do this. He is the man.

He accepts a transfer to El Paso because he has friends working for the big DEA intelligence center there, EPIC. After two years he jumps to U.S. Customs—better pay, better pension, and best of all they teach him how to fly a plane. He flies along the border for eight or nine months looking for smugglers and then, suddenly, his ticket is punched. DEA wants him and he starts at $36,000 a year in May 1991.

Their academy lasts thirteen weeks. He grows comfortable with a machine gun at his shoulder. They teach him various scenarios for a life underground, a rich background in role playing. He takes to this part of the life.

Law enforcement feeds off snitches and cops generally lean on informants to make their cases. DEA often raises this game to a different level. They become the informant. They go into the room and walk the talk and talk the talk and the talk is bad shit. They live the life, the hair long, that earring, the clothes, the tricked-out pickup, the stance. And this can last an hour, or a day, or weeks. Don't tell the wife, don't discuss it with friends. Everyone armed, talking that shit, the rich border Spanish studded with English words, a language almost choking on slang, talking bad, dirty, talking big, making the deal, being a heavy guy, and drinking, so much drinking but somehow staying alert. Angling for the buy, the money on the table, the dope right there, angling for that moment of truth and this trust has grown like a weed, been nurtured for hours, days, weeks, months, been handled tenderly so that the forbidden ground of budding friendship is reached and then when it is kickback time, when everyone feels safe, then the betrayal, the gun at the head, the handcuffs, the ride to jail and long mandatory sentences falling down and sending everyone away for decades until they cannot even remember their youth, can barely recall that time when they trusted and relaxed.

He's good at this jive. He loves making buys, talking up the dude, going to the deal, then taking him down. Once, God he smiles at the memory, once he did a twelve-ounce heroin deal in four minutes flat from the first hello to the cuffs.

Then comes the next step, across the river and into Mexico. Move this south, move it just a little ways across that bridge into Juárez and suddenly there is no real backup, the Mexican cops working with DEA, well, everyone knows they are on the pad to the cartel. And the room is electric now, there is no call to make, no place to run, now the acting had better be good, be better than good, be the performance of a lifetime, this is the place where people disappear all the time, hundreds of people, poof! gone just like that, vanished into vapor. Or bodies turn up, their hands and ankles tied, holes in their heads, signs of attention dancing on the bodies, marks where an ice pick has been shoved in again and again, a custom called bone tickling. Or the genitals have been severed and shoved into the mouth. Or a vat of acid has devoured all the flesh. Or a dose of milk, quicklime, has been dolloped on the hide. Or the body has been tossed onto a stack of mesquite and burned like a roast. Or the grave has been dug and the person tossed in alive. Or the body is left on a public street, hands and ankles tied, bullets in the brain, and graced with a bow of yellow ribbon, a gift to the authorities from the people who despise the authorities.

Sal Martínez loves this part of the work, loves the culture of the DEA. The rush flooding him from pretending, from being in control, from being the only one who really knows what is going on.

DAGOBERTO GILB

from *The Last Known Residence of Mickey Acuña* (1994)

MAYBE IT WAS BECAUSE of that western novel he'd been reading, where rock-hard Jake spurred his sorrel around chasing the Apaches who'd stolen off with his unflawed vision of love in body and spirit, a rich and beautiful Mexican woman named Consuela—not spelled Consuelo like people in Mexico commonly and on this side too named their daughters, beautiful or not—whose father wasn't as stolid in his manliness as Jake was. Anyway, the effect of the book, as Mickey broke out of the double doors of the Y, as he chanced coming out of hiding for a walk in the air, was that his eyes were on the Old West: Those Paseños in the cowboy hats looked like the real thing to him, and the paved streets and poured sidewalks took on a much more recent occupation, like an affectation, a clean shirt for Sunday, a sprucing-up despite all the dirt stain under the nails, when the boots had been shined many times instead of being replaced. The mountains on either side of the river, like certain kinds of haircuts, gave a lot of it away—raw brown, bare of civilization, their vegetation thorny and hard. Beer bottles shattered at the edges of the sidewalks and in the gutters, glittering the dirt alleys, colored an attitude that held the territory. Mickey didn't

64 hear any hooves but felt they'd come beating up any minute. Nothing attached to the soil seemed bolted on. Not this old asphalt with all its cracks that these modern cars used, even less so the squat buildings thrown up without any attempt to be more than what they were—four walls, brick mortar, glass, enclosures for the necessities of a trader's commerce. They could not cover all that loose dust underneath, which above ground blew into the eyes to brand its reality. Mickey's mind saw lots of animals—horses, mules, donkeys—and not the automobiles or trucks or buses. As honest as bleached blond hair on a dark Mexican woman, El Paso's truth was not beauty-parlored well enough, couldn't even be ignored completely by driving on the concrete overpasses or the many-laned highway at its center, though maybe enough for those whose foot pressed hard into their Americanized dreams.

Mickey stopped at the San Jacinto Plaza, which was a peaceful place to rest despite the whiny blow of buses and hollow thud of jackhammers surrounding it, despite the harsh voice of God communing through the inspired, head-shaking man in a white guayabera on stage who pounded out Old Testament fear and wrath. Mickey ignored these warnings and brushed off a spot on the iron bench, the relief on it of cherubic English farmers sowing, then reaping, under a pleasant sun—cotton and chile grew by the river, and the wind now had soured even more. Near Mickey a wino, clods of dust clinging to his matted hair, his beard streaked gray and tangled, stretched out on his linen of cardboard and newspaper, teddy-bearing a very old and wrinkled brown paper sack, and battled to tuck himself in. He muttered to himself and everyone else

RUSSELL LEE

about the difficulty of that until the bulls showed up to spare him his complaints, one of them ending a striped blue-gray pant leg on the bench and leaning both forearms onto his knee, shoulders still square, directing him to a bedroom somewhere else. The wino landed on the floppy soles of his shoes and scraped them across one of the cement paths slicing through the plaza. God's voice had stilled while his brown-skinned angels, these young, sweet-eyed girls in white matching chiffon dresses, passed Mickey the literature about eternal damnation and hell.

Merciful angels. What Mickey needed were more mature angels to cheer him up. He looked around. A group of gray-haired locals with straw western hats made in Mexico like themselves sat over there peacefully, wordless, in dull though neat and cared-for clothes, not too far from a bench where their Anglo counterparts—theirs were new beige Stetsons—found the time to share words with a black tramp about Jim Crow laws and those times past. Where chopping through were the hurried secretaries in their high heels and sticky hairdos, and businessmen in sports coats and pressed slacks and those snappy briefcases. And beyond them, where women with black hair and brown hair and even red hair, those women who cleaned the rich people's houses, waited at a wooden bus-stop bench. Where Mickey saw one woman, one young woman whose hair wasn't red, it was dark copper, and it was so pretty, mercilessly pretty, devilishly beautiful.

The way Mickey told this one was that he first had to slip in closer to her, close enough to see how exactly she suited the picture of the woman just for him, close enough to make certain she was no apparition. Among the maids, she didn't wear a uniform. She was simply there for him, a message of hope from the gentle God Mickey remembered to love whenever his heart beat so excitedly.

Mickey walked right up to her, in front of all of them, two benches lined and loaded with chubby middle-aged ladies—except her, of course—waiting on the red bus home to Juárez.

"Con su permiso," Mickey said with his best manners, "but may I have a few moments with you to introduce myself?" His announcement startled all the women on the benches. Mickey, too, as a matter of fact, even though once upon a time he was sure he was good at these things. The less-mature ladies wanted to check him out real well before they giggled into their hands, while the two more elderly women next to Mickey's Consuela tried to be more discreet, holding their chins and eyes down as though they weren't so actively curious.

"Maybe I could walk you home," he said, suddenly self-conscious and self-critical. Was he too direct, acting like he was in a bar? Or maybe too sappy, like he was in a church? At some moments he did feel he was a bum, and she was laughing at him. "If you don't mind the long walk across?"

One of the ladies beside her gave some eye and head movement and a few words Mickey could hear—"Talk to him."

And then she got up. And Mickey was confirmed in his belief in the goodness of this world. He felt true and honest, so satisfied he was sure this was an example of how everything else might fall into place too.

Together they strolled away from the bus benches. Mickey, nervous, struggled to work past first lines. Lately he'd been feeling unskilled in some things; he was also reminded, fumbling in a pants pocket, that he was on the starvation plan and possessed only a few dollars and assorted bits of change. He was virtually broke.

"Mickey Acuña," he said, reaching out his hand. She said her name was Ema Quintero. They shook hands tenderly, like kids. Or maybe just like Cowboy Jake did at the beginning with his lovely Consuela. The way Mickey would tell it, it was love for both of them.

~

THE TWO OF THEM TURNED onto El Paso Street and continued to exchange the basics with each other about what each liked to do—music, dancing, movies, eating—and Mickey lobbed the usual to win her through accounts of his wild days in California, which everybody who'd never lived anywhere else but Juárez especially wanted to hear about, even if it were bullshit. He seemed to succeed at making an impression on her that he was ready to settle down and find the right occupation since he'd already experienced so much, the right place to live since he'd been so many places, and the right woman since he had, he more than hinted, sowed so many seeds.

Mickey was good, good enough to convince himself, and so his mind narrated the story and description. With Ema at his side—sometimes he rested his hand, gentlemanly, on the small of her back as they walked—El Paso Street, where he'd spent some dive evenings at the Grand, was picturesque, a setting from that western novel. Or better yet a movie. It was an old days street where walking started up an old days-style romance. Here they were, this young couple. Mickey, down on his luck, in danger, suffering through his hard times, but ready to reform. Ema, a poor girl born on the poor side of the river. And the two of them walking forward, through the town of old, passing dark-lit bars without stools, poolrooms whose clicking never stopped, pawnshops advertising themselves with blaring norteña sound, all-night restaurants featuring everyday menudo, champurrado, or café con leche, and used-clothes stores where plump, faceless, and stooped-over women sorted and sorted through the crumpled piles, searching, their kids and grandkids running into each other everywhere and all around them, never quiet, in a high pitch of innocent happiness. And look: The colors were village Mexican—black, red, green, blue, yellow, as bright and uncomplicated as a thin crayon box, as true love. The old street, the architecture on it as cowboy western as a John Wayne set, jumped to life with so many human mysteries—cowboy hats, baseball caps, bonnets, scarves, and watchmans, boots and sandals, jeans and long skirts and khakis and shawls. And the young couple, in love, drenched with this joy of being alive, walking hand in hand like nobody ever had before.

So what if it were only Mickey's view, his lonely delusion, his crush, his infatuation? He didn't believe that, and it worked just the same as mutual love anyway. What man wouldn't love Ema's hair, and even if it were dyed that color, why question her? Who wouldn't love her eyes, wouldn't want to kiss her skin? They were together, walking, it was undeniable evidence, and like a first date, Mickey paid the bridge toll.

They paced side by side, up then down the concrete international bridge, over the river whose banks were cement, where young boys, like skid marks against its gray embankments, screamed for pennies or pesos or better yet pesetas, while their sisters on the walkways pleaded, supplicant and sad, for the same coins, wearing clothes and faces and arms that reached out, whose chapped, cupped palms were no less blackened and unwashed than their brothers below them.

Avenida Juárez, the main tourist street in the city, was hollering with hawkers and vendors. Mickey and Ema didn't spend too much time with them or their blankets or paintings or jewelry or ceramics or tacos or liquidadas—Ema worried so much about what the time was that Mickey, relieved, understood he didn't even have to offer to take her to the Kentucky Club for a drink or to Villa Espanola for steak tampiqueño, and so he gambled for the good impression, he bluffed, asked if she wanted to go— and scored. They compared los discos as they passed them—which were the best for drinks, which for dancing—and Mickey learned that she hadn't been to any of them. She could say only what she'd heard. She was not a fast American girl, looking for the quick boyfriend, he would say. She was real, he would say.

Sure of himself, Mickey wanted to show off. When they came upon the blind, legless singer playing this giant guitar, howling out his verses of love and bravery, he insisted they listen. He clinked half his coins into the poor man's rusted coffee can. The singer sang more heartily in gratitude, and Mickey's arm went around Ema's waist. He gave dimes to the barefoot and shirtless brother and sister who approached them with the moping faces and weak voices, and he pulled Ema, tight next to him, squeezed. He gave the rest, nineteen cents, to a Tarahumara Indian woman with long, braided hair, admired openly her hand-woven poncho of so many colors, complimented her on her serene, tiny baby wrapped in a blanket like a doll. The mother's face was tan triste y sincera, so sad and sincere, he told Ema quietly, that whether he believed her story of woe or not, she deserved the money. And then Mickey kissed Ema on the lips.

Mickey felt sincere too, and he wanted Ema to know he intended to be serious about her. He asked her to go out with him tonight, or tomorrow, told her he'd take her to the nicest places, here or on the other side if she could, anywhere she wanted.

She looked up at him with those eyes whose beauty was matched only by her hair, like a sunset, and she blushed. Mickey was so hopeful!

The couple turned off this main street right after 16 de Septiembre, and walked, this way and that, a few blocks more. Ema worried about Mickey going to her home, but he told her he didn't mind where she lived, missing the point of her concern. They finally stopped at a small, nameless calle so narrow that the cars parked there—not many—dripped oil on the sidewalk so that moving ones could fit down the middle. It was a paved street, though with brown, dusty potholes that had been sinking for many years. The houses on the block were short and very small, built close together. Each had a cemented patio, about as wide as the sidewalk, and most were enclosed with decorative wrought-iron fences, some painted pink or baby blue, most black. It probably was a quality development out in the suburbs not that many years ago. Ema's house was originally painted white, but had become shady, like muddy desert sand. The plaster under it seemed about as solid. Once plants decorated the inside of the pots on the patio. In a couple of them a dried vine or stump survived, while what remained in the others was parched dirt, cracked like broken stone.

Mickey kissed Ema outside her house. Such a kiss! He could tell you about this kiss. It was like no other. It was body and soul, almost better than making love. Maybe, he'd say, it was better.

Ema's mother yelled. She was mad.

Mickey waited, still content, on the other side of the iron gate for Ema to come back, or to invite him in. He would save her from here. He would take her away. He knew how some people thought. How this was a beautiful little Mexican neighborhood, postcard quaint. It was easy for rich people to romanticize someone else's poverty, to make colorful the bottle caps in the street, or a banged-up '58 Ford pickup with only a windshield, the piles of bald tires and rusted chrome bumpers in the front yard of Ema's neighbor's, to forget that the squealing laughter of those dusty, barefoot children running past was only a fragment of their ongoing lives, a tourist's snapshot of the culture. Then just as suddenly Mickey became mad at himself for feeling the opposite, for owning presumptions, for having an opinion at all, for judging one way or another, him or her or them or them. Mickey was tired of himself, was worried. Mickey loved Ema, and Ema loved Mickey. He was sure of it. He was confused. Even if he could persuade Ema, anyone, how he used to be or how it would be, he still was broke.

Mickey didn't have to pause on that too long. Behind him Ema and her mother were arguing beneath the rounded arch of the front door, which had opened. Her mother did the majority of the loud talking, and it was often with the word no, a syllable that traveled, unobstructed, clearly, into the path of his hearing. Ema looked over at him one brief time, forlorn, as her mother blasted her. And then the door closed, firm and secure.

EARL NOTTINGHAM

CECILIA BALLÍ

"Ciudad de la Muerte" (2003)

BACK BEFORE THERE WERE CUSTOMS checkpoints and border guards, before nations and national sovereignty, the Rio Grande sliced through a cluster of desert mountains and created a valley that would in time birth one of the most densely populated border regions in the world. Today, the cities of Ciudad Juárez and El Paso stare at each other across an international line. Their relationship is defined by both allegiances and antagonisms; some days they feel they are one and the same, while others they sit in silence, refusing to speak. But for the past ten years, they have shared a common mystery. Neither side fully understands how it is that Juárez became such a dangerous place for women to live. Today it is a city where females disappear silently, every day, and then reappear in desolate corners—their bones exposed in the blazing sun, their skin black and dry as cardboard.

In February 1996 a seventeen-year-old girl named María Guadalupe del Río Vázquez went shopping in downtown Juárez and vanished into thin air. Days later, her body was found in the desolate mountains of the Chihuahuan Desert—raped, strangled, her left breast mutilated. As girls continued to disappear, residents of the city formed bands and scoured the mountains for more bodies. The state police picked up the corpses—seventeen in all, an epidemic of murder—and quickly scurried away, leaving behind clothing, locks of hair, shoes curled like orange peels. The girls' hands were bound with their own shoelaces. All of the victims resembled each other: pretty, slim, medium to dark skin, long, straight dark hair. In a country that privileges men, whiteness, and wealth, these victims were female, brown, and poor. In a city that resents immigration and anything else from central and southern Mexico, these young women who had come to the northern border hoping to find work were social outcasts, strangers without names—especially now that they lay in silence in the sand, looking just like the ones before and the ones who would follow.

The deaths in the mountainous desert region known as Lomas de Poleo confirmed the worst fears of the women of Juárez: that something sinister had overcome their city. Beginning in 1993, there had been an unusual number of news reports in Juárez about the abduction and murder of women, an anomaly in Mexico. The grisly discoveries in the desert signaled that the worst crime wave in modern Mexican history had entered a new and more intense phase. Today, the toll of women who have been murdered in the past ten years is more than three hundred, staining the reputation of the country's fourth-largest city worldwide. Some of the women were murdered by their husbands and boyfriends. Other killings seemed to be random acts of violence. Around a third of the victims, however, were teenage girls whose deaths appear to be tied to a cryptic and chilling kind of serial killing. The crime is indisputably solvable: Evidence has been scattered like bread crumbs all over the crime scenes, but the state authorities have jailed no one who truly seems responsible. Be it incompetence or a cover-up, the lack of credible prosecution in these cases is perhaps the most blatant—certainly the most baffling—illustration of the nearly flawless record of impunity that characterizes the Mexican justice system.

Who would commit such crimes? Juárez brims with rumor and suspicion. A serial killer with government protection is an obvious possibility. The indifference of the authorities charged with investigating the murders has focused suspicion on themselves. Maybe it's the Juárez police, some people say—they drive those white pickups with the campers, where they could easily hide a rotting body or a pile of bones, and they're always prowling around the shantytown of Anapra, on the edge of the desert, peering out their windows. The Chihuahua state police zoom about in sleek, unmarked SUVs capable of navigating the rugged desert terrain. Federal investigators have speculated that fourteen of the killings might be linked to an organ-smuggling ring, though forensics experts dismiss that theory.

Or maybe it's the drug dealers. The desert is, after all, their country, a frontier on the fringe of globalization. Between dips in the mountains, you can glimpse El Paso to the north, its downtown towers gleaming like teeth. In Lomas de Poleo there is only the sand and the desert scrub and a sea of trash—empty jugs, shabby toys, broken toilets, an unwound cassette of English lessons, plastic bags clinging to the brush like confetti. A frail man picks his way through a dumpster, and an occasional small truck rattles off into the distance. They say that at night, this becomes the realm of gang members and drug runners, an army of men hauling their illicit goods into the United States. Rumor has it that if you wander far enough into the disorienting maze of primitive roads that have been scratched out of the sand, you will come upon a crude runway and a marvelous ranch with a swimming pool. If anybody sees you there, you should say you got lost and quickly turn around.

The obvious questions—who, why, how—remain unanswered. The abductions occur in mysterious moments, in quick, ghastly twists of fate that nobody seems—or at least wants to admit—to have witnessed. Most recently, they have transpired in the heart of the city in broad daylight. Some people believe the girls are taken by force, while others think it is more likely that the victims are lured by a seemingly innocent offer. A few mothers have said that their daughters disappeared a day or two after being approached about a job. Only one thing can be said with certainty, and it's that in Juárez, Mexico, even the surreal is possible.

The sun shimmers over downtown Juárez like white linen, but I have learned to march down its streets staring at the ground or ahead with icy, distant eyes. To do anything else is to acknowledge the lusty stares from men of all ages who stand at the corners of the city's busy thoroughfares waiting for nothing. So begins the taunting. A skinny man with red eyes lets out a slow whistle through clenched teeth. Two young boys look at me, look at each other, and nod with a dirty grin. From among a group of men huddled on the steps of a shop, one calls out, *"¡Una como esa!"*—I'll take one like her!—and the rest burst out laughing, their mustaches spreading gleefully across their faces as they watch me walk by. This is everywhere in urban Mexico, I remind myself. But knowing what I do about the fate of women in Juárez, their glares begin to feel more predatory. I watch my feet skitter on the pavement and, with every step, wish I could shed these hips, this chest, this hair. To walk downtown Juárez is to know and deeply regret that you are a young woman.

Juárez, however, is a city of young women. They run its shops and keep its hundreds of factories humming. In 1964 the United States terminated the Bracero guest-worker program with Mexico and deported many of its laborers, dumping thousands of men along the Mexican side of the border. In an effort to reemploy them, the Mexican government launched the Border Industrialization Program, which prodded American manufacturers to assemble their products in northern Mexico using cheap labor. The plan succeeded, but its main beneficiaries turned out to be the women, who, it was determined, made better workers for the new factories, or maquiladoras, because of their presumed superior manual dexterity. Word spread throughout Mexico that thousands of assembly-line jobs were cropping up in Juárez, and the nation's north quickly became the emblem of modernity and economic opportunity. In the seventies, factory-sponsored buses rumbled into the heartland and along the coasts and returned with thousands of hungry laborers. Among them were many single women with children in tow, who, aside from landing their own jobs in the *maquilas*, were soon staffing the throngs of stores and restaurants that proliferated to satisfy the new consumerism of Juárez's once cash-strapped population.

And so, if the working women of this border city had once earned reputations as prostitutes or bartenders, they now earned paychecks as factory workers, saleswomen, police officers, teachers—a few even as managers and engineers in the concrete tilt-ups that were constructed all around town to house around four hundred maquiladoras. For anywhere from $4 to $7 a day, they assembled automotive parts and electronic components and made clothing. Of the girls who couldn't afford to go to college—which is to say, the vast majority—some took computer classes, where they learned to use Microsoft Word and Excel hoping to become secretaries and administrative assistants. Juárez is a city that places a high premium on knowing how to use computers and speak English. Even in its most impoverished desert neighborhood, a collection of impromptu homes stitched together from wood pallets, mattresses, cardboard boxes, and baling wire, I saw a tiny brick shack with a dozen mismatched chairs planted outside and a hand-painted sign that promised "*Clases de inglés.*"

ALAN POGUE

But the migration was too fast, too disorganized. The population shot up to an estimated 1.5 million. Gone was the charm Juárez had possessed in the thirties, when its valley bore succulent grapes, or in the forties, when the music of Glenn Miller and Agustín Lara never stopped playing on Juárez Avenue, even as its neighboring country went to war. It was one of Mexico's biggest blunders to have planted its largest industrial experiment in the desert, in a city separated from the rest of the country not only symbolically, by its distinctly North American feel, but also physically, by the stunning but unforgiving Juárez Mountains. Cardboard shanties began to dot the landscape. Sewage spilled onto the streets. Power lines reproduced like parasites. Today, radio talk-show hosts ramble on about the ways in which immigrants ruined their beautiful community. I asked a well-bred young man what he thought were the virtues of his hometown, and despite a genuine effort, all he could name were the swank, cavernous clubs where the rich kids spend their weekends consuming alcohol by the bottle.

Even as the maquiladoras have begun relocating to China, the reputation of Juárez as a city of opportunity lingers in impoverished rural Mexico. Inside the city, however, Mexico's economic vulnerability is exposed like raw flesh. The city is filled with broken people who crack with the most innocent of questions. I met a woman from Zacatecas who lives in Anapra with her husband and three daughters in a minuscule house that they built out of wood pallets and thatched with black roofing material. They possess one bed, no refrigerator, and a tin washtub for bathing. State officials offered them this free sliver of land, but the sliver is in the desert mountains, where life is not "beautiful," as the woman's brother had sent word home; it's shivery cold and always covered in a thin film of orange dirt. When I asked her how she liked living in this colonia along the city's northwestern frontier, the woman's smile quivered and a puddle of tears dribbled to her chin.

Still, the worst part about Juárez, she told me, is the threat of violence that hangs over the sprawling city like a veil of terror. Just a short distance from her home, the bodies of girls who resemble her own sixteen-year-old Ana have appeared in the desert. Lured to their deaths—perhaps by promises of a job—they lie abandoned like the heaps of trash that fleck this interminable sea of sand.

~

"DISCULPE, SEÑORITA . . ." I turned around toward the male voice behind me and saw a dark-skinned, round-faced man in his thirties striding in my direction with a large basket of candies wedged between his neck and shoulder. He was heavyset and was clad in light-brown slacks, a white, long-sleeved shirt with blue pinstripes, and a green windbreaker.

It was lunchtime, and I had walked out of a restaurant to return a call to a source on my cell phone, leaving behind three journalists with whom I'd been roaming the city. Diana Washington Valdez, an *El Paso Times* reporter who has been chronicling the Juárez women's deaths for years, had thought I should meet an attorney who is defending one of the government's scapegoats for the murders. But when we rattled the wrought-iron gates of his office, there was no reply. We decided to wait at a small restaurant next door, and since a peal of music was issuing from a nearby television, I went outside to return the call. After I finished, I dialed my sister's number.

He looked rather humble, and this, I thought, was confirmed by the apologetic smile he wore, as if he hated to intrude for something as mundane as the time or directions to a street. I half-smiled at him. "Hold on," I told my sister. I was about to save him the trouble by telling him that I was not from around here when he spoke again.

"Are you looking for work?"

~

JOURNALISTS AND ACTIVISTS and sociologists trying to explain the loss of hundreds of women have constructed a common narrative. Their story suggests that when the immigrants came to Juárez from the countryside, they brought along traditional Mexican ideas about gender. Women were to stay home, obey their husbands, and raise their children. But when wives and girlfriends and daughters began earning their own paychecks, they tasted a new independence and savored it. They bought nice things for themselves, went dancing, decided when bad relationships needed ending. In many cases, because unemployment rates for men were so high, the women even took on the role of breadwinner in their families. The men saw their masculinity challenged and lashed out. Their resentment, uncontained by weakened religious and community bonds, turned violent, into a rage that manifested itself in the ruthless killing of women. This story has become so popular that when I interviewed the director of the Juárez Association of Maquiladoras, he recited it for me as though he were delivering a pitch at a business convention.

Yet the violence in Juárez—against men as well as women—is at its barest a criminal act that results directly from the lack of rule of law in the Mexican justice system. Killers know that the odds are overwhelming that they can get away with murder. Nationally, only two in every one hundred crimes are ever solved, including cases that are closed by throwing a scapegoat in jail. There are no jury trials, and it is easy to influence a judge with money. If not one of the Juárez girls' cases has been properly resolved in ten years, only two explanations exist: Law enforcement is inept or corrupt. Most people believe both are true.

"I got to witness the inefficiency," says Oscar Maynez, the chief of forensics in Juárez from 1999 to 2002. Maynez has followed the cases of the murdered women of Juárez from the beginning. In 1993, as an instructor at the state police academy, he was skimming criminal files to use in his class when something disturbing grabbed his attention: In three separate cases, three young women had been raped and strangled. Fearing that a serial killer might be on the loose, he created a psychological profile of the killer. When he approached his superiors with the report, however, every one of them, including the Juárez police chief and the deputy attorney general in the state capital, dismissed its importance.

Maynez left his job a year later to pursue a master's degree in Washington, D.C. When he returned to reorganize the state crime lab in 1999, he was greeted by a growing pile of women's remains along with case records and forensic evidence, all of it hopelessly confused. Though some of the bodies still had vital clues embedded, the lab had never done any follow-up on those that had appeared between 1993 and 1999, including DNA analyses of the rapists' semen. Maynez was certain now—and the thought enraged him—that either a serial killer or a well-funded criminal ring was systematically targeting Juárez's youngest and poorest women. And yet, six years after his initial findings, neither the local nor the state authorities had made an effort to pursue an investigation according to the profile he had offered them.

In early November 2001, eight female bodies were discovered in a cotton field across a busy street from the maquiladora association's offices. Five of them had been dumped in an old sewage canal, the other three in an irrigation ditch. Most indicated a similar modus operandi: hands bound, apparently raped and strangled. Two days after the first corpses were found, Maynez and his crew began their investigation, dusting for evidence with tiny paintbrushes. As they did so, a man drove up in a bulldozer, saying that he had been ordered by the attorney general's office to dig up the area in search of more bodies. Maynez sent him off to work elsewhere, preserving the crime scene.

Just a few days later, the police presented an edited videotape confession of two bus drivers who said they had killed the women, naming each of the eight. It seemed strange that the murderers would know the complete names of their victims—middle names, maternal and paternal names. When the accused were admitted to the city jail, it became obvious that they had been forced to confess, for they showed multiple signs of torture, including electrical burns on their genitals. The cost of defending them turned out to be high. In February 2002, one of the two lawyers who was representing the drivers was shot and killed by state police officers as he drove his car; they say they mistook him for a fugitive. (An investigation was conducted, but the officers were never charged.) And a few days after the national human rights commission agreed to hear the drivers' cases, one of them mysteriously died in custody while undergoing an unauthorized surgery based on forged documents for a hernia that he had developed from the torture.

To date, eighteen people have been arrested in connection with the murders, including an Egyptian chemist named Abdel Latif Sharif Sharif, who arrived in Juárez by way of the United States, where he had lived for 25 years. He had accumulated two convictions for sexual battery in Florida. Sharif, who has been jailed in Mexico since October 1995, was accused by Chihuahua state prosecutors of several of the Juárez murders but convicted of only one. Though the conviction was overturned in 2000, a state judge ruled in favor of the prosecution's appeal, and Sharif remains imprisoned in Chihuahua City.

Judging from the lack of evidence, none of those eighteen individuals has been justly charged or convicted. The biggest testament to this is the fact that the murders continue unabated. At a press conference in jail in 1998, Sharif divulged information he had received from a police officer who claimed that the person behind the killings was Armando Martínez, the adopted son of a prominent Juárez bar owner. Sharif's source, Victor Valenzuela Rivera, said that he had overheard Martínez bragging about the murders at the Safari Club, one of his father's bars and a place frequented by police officers and *narcotraficantes*. Valenzuela insisted that Martínez, who also goes by Alejandro Maynez, had said he was being protected by government officials and the police and that he had talked about his involvement in the trafficking of drugs and jewelry. The following year, Valenzuela repeated this account before several federal legislators and reporters; again, there were bloody repercussions. After Irene Blanco, the woman who had defended Sharif in court, demanded that the press investigate the allegations against Martínez, her son was shot and nearly killed by unknown assailants. The police say the shooting was drug-related, while others say the crime was committed by the officers themselves. Martínez's whereabouts are unknown.

Valenzuela's testimony was not the only suggestion that the murders might be linked to the drug world. In 1996 a group of civilians searching for women's remains in Lomas de Poleo came upon a wooden shack, and inside of it, an eerie sight: red and white votive candles, female garments, traces of fresh blood, and a wooden panel with detailed sketches. On one side of the panel was a drawing of a scorpion—a symbol of the Juárez cartel—as well as depictions of three unclothed women with long hair and a fourth who lay on the floor, eyes closed, looking sad. A handful of soldiers peered out from behind what looked like marijuana plants, and at the top there was an ace of spades. The other side showed similar sketches: two unclothed women with their legs spread, an ace of clubs, and a male figure that looked like a gang member in a trench coat and hat. The panel was handed over to Victoria Caraveo, a women's activist, who turned it in to state authorities. Though the incident was reported by the Mexican papers, today government officials refuse to acknowledge that the panel ever existed.

As Oscar Maynez sees it, the problem with the Mexican justice system begins with "a complete absence of scruples among the people at the top." The criminologist says that workers in the state crime lab merely sign death certificates. In the case of the eight girls' bodies discovered in 2001, Maynez told the *El Paso Times*: "We were asked to plant evidence against two bus drivers who were charged with the murders." Though the drivers were prosecuted, their evidence file remained empty. Frustrated, Maynez resigned in January 2002.

The federal government hasn't done much to solve the Juárez murders, either. Some of Chihuahua's top leaders a decade ago now sit in the highest ranks of President Vicente Fox's administration. In December 2001 federal legislators formed a committee to investigate the issue; no report has been released. The bad blood between political parties and the long history of turf wars between state and federal law enforcement groups have prevented any sort of interagency cooperation, a key to solving difficult crimes in the United States. Activists in Juárez and El Paso believe that the only way to solve the murders is for Mexican federal officials to invite the American FBI to investigate, but historically, neither side has seemed eager for this to occur. Nationalism runs high in Mexico, and the country's leaders do not want Americans meddling in their affairs. In El Paso, officials like outgoing mayor Ray Caballero hesitate to offend their peers in Chihuahua. Caballero, who has had little to say publicly about the murdered women, said to me: "For me to come out and make one pronouncement does not solve the problem."

Perhaps circumstances are changing. This spring his office announced the creation of a hotline that will allow people in Juárez to report information to the El Paso police, who will then turn it over to investigators in Chihuahua. In late April, two deputies of the Mexican federal attorney general asked the FBI to collaborate with them on their investigations of the Juárez murder cases and the Juárez drug cartel. FBI agents have also been training Mexican prosecutors and detectives in Juárez and El Paso. And, with women's rights groups in Juárez watching warily, in July 2003 Mexico's secretary of the interior announced a broad security plan to put 2000 local, state, and federal cops on the city's streets.

~

"ARE YOU LOOKING FOR WORK?" My heart stopped. I knew that line, I knew it immediately. My eyes, frozen, terrified, locked onto his.

"N-n-n-o," I believe I stuttered, but the man spoke again: "Where are you from?" His eyes crawled down my body and back up to my face. I was wearing black leather boots, a black turtleneck, and fitted blue jeans—the last pair of clean pants I had managed to dig out of my suitcase that morning. And I regretted it immediately, because they might have been appropriate for trekking in mountains but not, I realized now, for walking the downtown streets of Juárez, where the men stare. My heart began to pound furiously. Only then did I notice that as I had talked on the phone, I had absentmindedly paced half a block away from the restaurant's door. At that moment there was nobody within sight, not a single officer from the police station next door. I tried to envision the scenarios, tried to imagine some chance of safety. Would he ask me to follow him somewhere? Would someone drive up out of nowhere and force me into a vehicle? Did I have control of the situation or did he? If I darted toward the restaurant door, would I startle him, causing him to reach over and grab me? If I screamed, would my sister, who was now dangling by my thigh on the other end of a cell phone—listening, I hoped desperately, to this conversation—be able to help? Would Diana and the others inside the restaurant hear me over the music? If I was not able to escape, how much would I have to suffer before they killed me? Was this it? Had I really—and the brief thought of this made me sad—gambled it all for a story?

For a few infinite seconds, nothing, and everything, was possible. But as my heart began to slow down and my mind sped up, I thought of another possibility.

"I'm from El Paso," I said.

~

IRMA MONRREAL LIVES in a dust-tinged neighborhood known as Los Aztecas. The streets are unpaved and lined with tiny cement homes that peek out from behind clumsy cinder-block walls. Her home on Calle Grulla, which she bought on credit for $1,000, originally consisted of one room in which she slept with seven children, but her eldest sons constructed another two rooms. Like so many immigrants in Juárez, Irma had hopped on a train and headed to the border with visions of prosperity flitting about in her head. In the fields of her state of Zacatecas, she had earned $3 a day hoeing beans and chiles. The big talk those days was of the factories in Juárez, where one could make nearly three times as much money. Since she and her husband had separated and her two eldest boys, who were thirteen and fourteen years old, would soon be needing jobs, she moved to Juárez and altered her sons' birth certificates so that they could immediately begin working in the maquiladoras.

Though Irma had a bundle of children to care for, she was closest to her third-youngest, Esmeralda, a blithe girl with a broad, round face and an unflinchingly optimistic vision of life. At fifteen, she had completed middle school and was determined to keep studying so that someday she might work in a big place—like the airport, she told her mother—and make lots of money. She was an excellent typist. She didn't date or spend much time with friends, but she was extremely close to her little sister Zulema, who was four years younger. The two pretended that they were television stars or models, and on special occasions they attended Mass and treated themselves to lunch. When nighttime set in, they dreamed in bunk beds.

The only thing Esmeralda desired even more than an education was to have a quinceañera and to wear, like every other girl in Juárez who turns fifteen, a white gown to her rite-of-passage ceremony. Her mother, who earns about $30 a week at a plastics factory, was saving up what she could to pay for the party, but Esmeralda felt the urge to pitch in. When an acquaintance asked Irma if she could borrow her teenage daughter to help around the house, Esmeralda pleaded with her hesitant mother to say yes, promising that she would work only up until the December 15 celebration.

A week went by, and Esmeralda was excited, chatty. One evening she confided to her mom that a young man who was a few years older than she and who worked at the print shop where she had ordered her invitations had asked her out to lunch. She seemed deeply flattered that someone would notice her, but Irma admonished her not to take any offers from strangers. Her daughter promised that she wouldn't. A second week passed. Esmeralda would finish working at about four o'clock and head straight home, arriving well before Irma departed for her overnight shift at the maquiladora.

But a few days later, something went terribly wrong. At four-thirty, there was no sign of Esmeralda. Then it was five o'clock. Then six. At ten minutes to seven, Irma was forced to leave for work, but she asked her other children to watch for their sister. In the factory, she punched her time card and began talking to God silently.

The night dragged. When her shift was finally over, at seven in the morning, Irma rushed home to see her daughter's face, but her world imploded when her children opened the door: *Esmeralda no llegó.* The girl had vanished.

During the following ten days, Irma sometimes wondered whether her mind hadn't just taken a crazy turn. How could this be real? At night, she was overwhelmed with terror as she speculated where the girl might be, what she might be going through at that very moment. To lose a family member and not know what has happened to her is to live an existential anguish of believing fiercely, and at the same time losing all notion of truth. I spoke with a psychologist at a Juárez women's crisis center who said that she finds it almost impossible to help the relatives of disappeared people heal because they are unable to discount either possibility that their abducted family member is dead or alive. In El Paso I met Jaime Hervella, a Juárez native who runs a small accounting and consulting business as well as an organization for relatives of the disappeared on both sides of the border. "It's the worst of tragedies," he said, motioning with his wax-like hands over a cluttered desk. Then his bifocals fogged up, and he wept suddenly. "I just can't handle talking to the little old women, the mothers. Morning comes and they implore God, the Virgin, the man who drives the dump truck. Nighttime falls and they are still asking themselves, 'Where could my child be?'

And the hours pass in this way, and the sun begins to disappear."

As she scavenged her memory for clues, Irma recalled the young man who had invited her daughter to lunch and immediately sent her son to look for him. But the owner of the print shop said he'd left his job. He refused to give any more information. After several visits herself, Irma finally persuaded the shop owner's son to tell her where their former employee lived. She found the little house, but it was locked; she banged on the door, the windows, screaming loudly in case her daughter was inside, listening. Esmeralda had told her mother that the young man had asked her for her schedule and that he had wanted to know whether her mom always walked her home from work. As Irma circled the house, the man arrived. She explained who she was and asked if he knew anything about her daughter, but he brushed her away, saying that he was married.

A few days later, a co-worker at the maquiladora asked Irma if she'd heard the news: Eight bodies had been found in a couple of ditches at the intersection of Ejército Nacional and Paseo de la Victoria. Could one of them be Esmeralda?

Next came the phone call from the state prosecutor's office, asking her to identify the body. At the morgue, however, Irma was told it was too gruesome to view. She would have to obtain signed permission from the prosecutor's office. They offered to bring out the blouse that was on the corpse when it was found, and Irma's heart collapsed when she glimpsed the speckled yellow, pink, orange, and white. It was the blouse that Esmeralda's older sister Cecilia had sent from Colorado, where she had moved to be with her husband. Yet there was still that lingering doubt, so Irma requested the permit to see the body. Fearing the shock would be too great for their mother to bear, her two eldest sons insisted on identifying it themselves.

When they arrived home from the morgue, they were silent, their heads hung low.

"So?" Irma asked anxiously. "Was it your sister?"

But the response was hesitant, brittle: "We don't know."

"What do you mean, you don't know?!"

"It's just that . . . she doesn't have a face."

The words shattered like crystal on the cement floor. "But what about her hair—was it her hair?!"

"It's just that she doesn't have any hair," the sons replied, grief-stricken. "She doesn't have any ears. She doesn't have anything."

The corpse presumed to be Esmeralda's was one of the three found on November 6, a day before the other five were discovered a short distance away. All of the bodies were partially or wholly unclothed, some with their hands tied. But unlike the other girls, most of whom had been reduced to mere skeletal remains, Esmeralda's state of decomposition was particularly grisly and perplexing. She was missing most of the flesh from her collarbone up to her face. The authorities suggested that the rats in the fields had had their share, but Irma noted—and Oscar Maynez, the chief of forensics, concurred—that it would have made more sense for them to take the meatier parts of her body. The mystery deepened when the forensic workers took hair and blood from Esmeralda's mother and father and sent them to a laboratory in Mexico City, along with DNA samples from four other bodies and from the parents who had identified their clothing. The results came back without a match. This opened up two possibilities: Either the samples had been grossly contaminated or, even more eerily, the murderers were switching clothes with other, as yet unfound, victims.

"Why?" Irma cried out as I sat with her one wintry afternoon in her tidy home, which is crammed with curly-haired dolls and deflated balloons and stuffed animals her daughter had collected—the last traces of happiness left in her little house. "Do they want to drive me crazy or something? Is it her or isn't it?" In a silver picture frame atop a brown armoire, Esmeralda sat squeezed into a strapless red top, her shoulder-length hair dyed a blondish brown. She was laughing irresistibly, cracking up, but across from the photo, Irma slumped in her chair in blue sweats and a denim shirt, her body heaving uncontrollably as I listened, speechless. "Why does God let the evil ones take the good ones away? Why the poor, if we don't harm anybody? Nobody can imagine what this trauma is like. I go to work and I don't know if my children are going to be safe when I return. It's a terror that's lived day by day, hour by hour."

Like numerous stories I'd heard from other victims' families, Irma's included the lament that her family has fallen apart as her children struggle to confront the tragedy of losing their sister and try to assign blame. Unable to channel their newfound hate, they have begun hating each other. Her eldest sons have stopped talking to her. Zulema, who refuses to sleep in her bunk bed now, attempted to kill herself and her eight-year-old brother with tranquilizers a doctor had prescribed for Irma. Defeated, the woman spoke with the shame of a child who has discovered that she has made an irrevocably wrong choice. She wished, with all her might, that she had never made that fateful decision to come to Juárez. "They've destroyed my life," she said with vacant eyes and a flat voice, once she had regained her composure. "I don't believe in anything anymore. There is a saying that one comes here in search of a better life, but those are nothing but illusions."

Irma eventually claimed the body, she says, so that she would "have somewhere to cry." Instead of determining whether more lab work needed to be done, the authorities instantly handed it over. They never interrogated the suspicious young man Irma had reported, and they ruled that the cause of the young woman's death was "undetermined" even though it seemed apparent that she had been strangled. On November 16, Irma buried the corpse, using the quinceañera savings to pay for the $600 coffin.

"SOY DE EL PASO," I said to the man outside the restaurant. I held my breath. I remembered what Diana had told me when we first met to talk about the story: "They know who to leave alone. They leave the Americans alone. They leave the rich girls alone, because there might be trouble. The other girls? A dime a dozen." And yes, his interest faded instantly.

"I'm sorry," he said, still bearing his apologetic smile, though somewhat more sheepishly. "I—I just saw you holding that piece of paper so I thought maybe you were looking for a job. Sorry." He turned around and began to walk away.

"Why?" I called out nervously. "Do you know of a job?"

He turned around and stared at me. "I hire girls to work at a grocery store," he said. His eyebrows furrowed. "Where are you from?"

Shaking my head, I stammered, "Oh, no—I'm from El Paso. My friends are waiting for me inside this restaurant."

I brushed past him in a hurry, skipping up the restaurant's steps and to the table where the rest of the group was finishing their meal. Diana was gone. I took my seat and noticed that my legs and hands were trembling violently.

"You'll never guess what happened to me," I said in a shaky voice. The others fell silent and looked at me curiously. "I just got offered a job."

As the words spilled, one of the group nodded slowly. "You fit the profile," she said. When I described the man to her, she said that he had walked into the restaurant earlier, while I was on the phone. He had chatted with the woman who was cooking, taken some food, and left.

I jumped from my chair and stepped over to the counter. "Excuse me, señora," I said to the woman at the grill. "Do you know the man who just came in a few minutes ago?"

"Not very well," she replied. "At night he guards the lawyer's office next door and by day he sells candies on the street." At that moment, something blocked the light from the doorway. I turned around and found myself face to face with the same man from outside, this time without his basket.

He looked nervous. "Let me buy you a Coke," he offered.

"No, thanks," I replied firmly. I asked him, "Do you really have a store?"

But he ignored my question. "You're a journalist," he said, "aren't you?"

I turned toward my table, confused, then back into his intense gaze. "I—I'm here with some journalist friends," I stammered.

"No," he said forcefully, "but *you're* a journalist, aren't you?" It was obvious that he knew.

"Well, yes, but I'm just here accompanying my friends, who are working on a story."

His tone softened. "Come on, let's sit down. Let me buy you a drink. En confianza." *You can trust me.*

"No," I repeated, "I'm with my friends and we're leaving." I walked back to the table. Diana had returned, unaware of what had transpired. Later, I would learn that she had gone to the lawyer's office, encountered the candy vendor, and told him she was with a group of journalists who wanted to see his boss. But with the man standing there, all I wanted to do was get away. We all gathered our belongings and hurried toward the door.

"The lawyer says he'll be here tomorrow, if you want to see him," we heard him call out to us. I never turned back.

That night, safe in El Paso, I stared at the ceiling in the darkness of my hotel room and replayed the afternoon's events over and over. My family had worried when I told them that I was going to write about the women of Juárez, even after I assured them that plenty of other journalists had done so safely. But *you*, they shot back, as if I'd missed the most obvious point, *you* look just like those girls. I thought of how much care I had taken not to go to Juárez alone, even if it had meant sacrificing my journalistic independence. And yet, in that one brief instant when I had let my guard down, I had been approached by someone mysterious. I will never know for sure if that was it—if, as I have told colleagues I felt at that moment, I really touched the story, my own life colliding with those of the girls whose lives I had been hoping to preserve. What I do know is this: that I felt my heart beat the way they must have felt theirs beat, too.

As I thought this, warm tears spilled down the sides of my face and trickled into my ears. And I realized that I was crying not for myself, but for the women of Juárez—for the girls who had died and for the mothers who survived them. They say that whenever a new body is found, every grieving mother relives her pain. I was crying for the girls who had stayed on the other side of the border. For the ones who couldn't leave their reflections on paper and run far, far away, as I was going to do. I cried because I realized how easy it would have been to believe the man who approached me; because I understood that the girls were not naive, or careless, or as a former attorney general of Chihuahua once said, asking for it. They were simply women—poor women, brown women, fighters, dreamers. And they weren't even dreaming of all that much, by our standards: a secretarial job, a bedroom set, a new fifteenth-birthday party. A little chance to live.

I cried because of the absurdity of it all, because it was possible for a life to be worth less than a brief taste of power. I cried thinking of how we had failed them.

PART 3

Junta

THE CONCHOS is an amazingly resourceful river. A sprawling network of tributaries delineates canyons in the Sierra Madre Occidental range of the northern Mexico states of Durango and Chihuahua. When the Conchos comes together and flows as one it first turns north, then makes its way across or around hundreds of miles of creosote bush wasteland and five cordilleras in its push toward its mouth and an exotic locale called La Junta de los Dos Ríos. The headwaters of the Conchos are home to Tarahumara, Pima, Yaqui, and several other indigenous tribes. To survive, many of the northern Mexico Indians have come down from their tribal highlands and found work in mines of coal, copper, and for a while, gold and silver. Chihuahua is renowned throughout Mexico for vast ranches and the quality of its beef; the state's unofficial symbol is a straw cowboy hat. But the Conchos country also attracted a large contingent of Mennonites of German-American and other ancestries who immigrated to Mexico with hopes of an agrarian utopia. The upland Conchos valley has been farmed and irrigated since the seventeenth century.

In 2000, when I had traveled in the Conchos watershed on another writing project, the vistas had been sand-colored and desolate. The most striking signs of activity were towering dust devils that roamed about. (The Comanches, who often raided in this part of Mexico, believed they were ghosts.) But in the summer of 2002, a few weeks before my trip to the mouth of the Rio Grande, I found that the short-grass range and sparsely wooded peaks had greened up spectacularly. The annual monsoons—fragrant showers moved east by fronts off the Pacific—had come a few weeks early, and the rain kept up. I had been riding south from El Paso through Chihuahua City, and on one stretch of toll road my party's car passed a high-sided truck loaded so extravagantly with fresh hay that it looked like a McDonald's carton stuffed with French fries.

A young Austin woman named Karen Chapman, who worked for the Environmental Defense Fund, had made the trip to help us with introductions and translation. "Chihuahua had three years of crippling drought in the mid-nineties," she told me. "Authorities held water back on the Conchos when the weather improved in 1997, allowing farmers to irrigate more and try to recoup their losses. The 1944 treaty says that the U.S. is entitled to 350,000 acre-feet a year from the Conchos, but that's an average, measured in five-year cycles. The Mexicans thought they could make it up. Then it stopped raining again, especially in 2001. Now they've come to the end of the line, Mexico has an enormous water debt, and they're going to have to figure out a way to pay it. The mess was inevitable, because of the way water is managed—or not managed—in both countries."

The streets of a pleasant small town named Delicias were full of storm water when we arrived. People looked happy walking in the rain. The next morning in a spare downtown office we met Ricardo Valdez, the district chief of the Comisión Nacional de Agua (CNA), the national water commission. "In Mexico all water belongs to the federal government." Valdez began to explain the fundamental differences between the two countries' water traditions and law. Texas, for example, subscribes to the Rule of Capture, born of medieval England, which holds that any water that flows across or wells up on land is an individual property right, neighbors be damned. In contrast, with quasi-governmental authority and great political power, irrigation districts in Mexico apportion water privileges to landowners. Valdez said, "The district in Delicias has 800,000 hectares"—about 200,000 acres— "that are irrigable, but realistically only forty or fifty percent of those qualify. We have problems with salinity, and this drought has been severe. We try to increase efficiency by lining the irrigation canals and leveling the fields, but that costs money. And water is just one element in the production chain. With free trade, we have to compete in the global market. Many hectares have been taken out of production."

Later in the morning, employees of the CNA took us to the Madero reservoir in the hills above Delicias. Our guide told us that the small lake had risen about 25 feet since the summer rains began. Still, he claimed, Madero stood at just 34 percent capacity, and other Conchos reservoirs were doing no better. In Texas, agriculture commissioner Susan Combs had spent much of the year offering satellite photographs as proof the Chihuahuans had been hoarding water and turning the countryside green all through the alleged drought. She claimed the Mexicans rushed into production crops that required great amounts of water, and that they opened their gates and just flooded the fields, an obsolete, wasteful way to irrigate.

I know little about farming and less about reading satellite photographs. But I had seen the Madero lake two years earlier, and the water level then was far higher than what I saw now, even after all the rain and 25-foot rise.

However, around Delicias I encountered lush pecan orchards and fields of tomatoes, chiles, onions, cotton, and the thirsty alfalfa. The area's alfalfa growers were guaranteed a market by a huge nearby dairy farm. Our CNA guide took us to a farm where peacocks strolled the grounds and workers were sorting garlic in a barn thick with the smell. The head of the 300-acre family farm was away on an errand; his daughter walked out from the office. About thirty, Rosa María Ruiz was shy but confident. She listed the crops and their acreage with precision and pride. Chapman asked her if she had heard much discussion of Mexico's water debt and the dispute with farmers in Texas. "We're all aware of it," Ruiz said. "But it's too complex. Nobody is paying much attention to it."

One of the major complexities at play was Mexican electoral politics. Not until 1929, twelve years after the Mexican Revolution ended, was order fully restored by the oligarchy of generals and plutocrats that would come to be known as the Partido Revolucionario Institucional (PRI). The PRI was rewarded with overwhelming support from the electorate for seventy-one years. The conservative, business-oriented Partido Acción Nacional (PAN) first gained footing by winning local and state races in Chihuahua in the 1970s. But in the 2000 national election the nation's pundits were predicting a challenge to PRI from the left when Vicente Fox, a rancher, Coca-Cola magnate, and governor in Guanajuato, expanded the PAN base and sent a thunderbolt through the nation by winning the Mexican presidency. Fox had a longstanding friendship, from the time they were governors, with President George W. Bush. Mexican people were giddy with the prospect of real change, and relations with the United States had seldom been so cordial. Fox was invited to address the U.S. Congress, and the tall, striking man made a speech in English that went over quite well.

Main streets in Mexican towns sported large banners, a Fox initiative, that read "Bienvenidos Paisanos." Literally "welcome cousins," the reference was to Mexicans who went north to the United States to work, often permanently. Come home now and then, the Fox campaign was saying: don't let the family ties lapse, we are one people. While trying to deliver the reforms and economic recovery he had promised his country, Fox wanted to advance trade with the United States and win concessions on immigration. But the lovefest was complicated by the September 11, 2001, terrorist attacks in New York and Washington, their effect on border security policies, and the Bush ultimatum that all allies follow his military lead. The last thing either administration wanted or needed now was a nasty fight over the Rio Grande.

EARL NOTTINGHAM

If the Mexican federal government owned all the water, Texas farmers and politicians argued, why didn't it just do the right thing and honor the 1944 treaty? Fox administration diplomats replied that they *were* honoring the treaty, and in any case, the situation was not so simple. Just as the PRI was being routed and kicked out of power in Mexico City, it had figured out how to beat PAN and win again in Chihuahua. The northern state's governor, Patricio Martínez, had challenged drug lords and survived the bullet of an assassin they sent after him. He had a populist streak and oratorical flair, and the way to cultivate and flaunt support in Chihuahua, he seemed to figure, was not to roll over for a bunch of Texans. Besides, why make things easy for a president from PAN? Fox was limited to a single six-year term as president, and someone had to emerge as PRI's candidate in the national election of 2006. Why not a charismatic governor with a history of standing up to the United States? "Neither war nor boycott nor discord is going to put one more liter of water in the valley of the Río Bravo," Martínez said in one speech. "The sky is denying us all."

A close political ally of the Chihuahuan governor was Rogelio Bejarno, head of Delicias's irrigation district. Seated behind a large desk in his downtown office, Bejarno was a tanned and broad-shouldered man with rugged features and a movie star's smile. "Farmers are worried about the price of pecans falling from twenty pesos to eight," said the grower, rancher, and former mayor of Delicias. "A bale of cotton is worth half as much as it was two years ago. Who wants to farm anyway? Our people are independent and isolated. To them, a treaty is not important. It doesn't matter what it says on paper—if water doesn't exist, you can't deliver it. There shouldn't be any basis for anger. All of us use the same water. All of us breathe the same air. All of us live on the same land."

Bejarno told us bluntly that all these *norteamericano* questions about the Conchos had begun to bore him. "It does not bother me a bit if Texans are upset," he said. "Our people have suffered. They've had to reduce planting. Here, if the land is not productive and people don't use their irrigation rights, they lose the water. It's reassigned. Many have given up."

"What happens to them?" I asked.

Bejarno tilted his head and smiled. "They sell their land and go work in Texas."

~

BETWEEN CHIHUAHUA CITY and Ojinaga, where the Conchos joins the Rio Grande, is a hundred miles of highway through almost empty country. Here Pancho Villa rode to fame during the Mexican Revolution. Villa was a bully and alleged rapist and reputed butcher of stolen beef. He was a horseman credited with making innovative use of railroads a stratagem of lightning warfare. Americans were captivated by him at first. The old cynic and satirist Ambrose Bierce wandered off in search of Villa's romance with history and probably was murdered—he simply vanished. John Reed, the Oregon-born reporter who now

EARL NOTTINGHAM

lies buried as a hero of the communist revolution in the Kremlin (and was played by War-ren Beatty in the 1981 movie *Reds*) got his start as a war correspondent and radical sympa-thizer covering Villa's campaigns. American moviemakers negotiated a deal to film Villa's battles. But the charm wore off fast. Feeling himself betrayed by the United States, Villa and his horsemen sacked a lightly defended garrison and the village of Columbus, New Mexico, in 1916, killing eighteen people. In what was later interpreted as a useful field exercise for America's entry into World War I, U.S. army general John J. Pershing and troops who included Lieutenant George Patton invaded Chihuahua and chased Villa's guerrillas in an unsuccessful punitive expedition. American civilians were urged to clear out of Big Bend.

The farmland marked by the Conchos's cottonwoods and willows scarcely resembled the acreage we had seen around Delicias. The people in this part of Chihuahua are very poor. On a dirt road beside a fast-running irrigation canal we had paused beside the home of people who stopped planting cornfields long ago. They opened the gates now to make mud. The man and woman appeared to be in their seventies, and in the unbroken sun-shine they spent their days crafting adobe bricks. Not far from the Texas border, the most forbidding cordillera in the Río Conchos's path is the Sierra Grande. Unable to find a way between bristling rock mountains, the Conchos over the ages has dug down through them, creating a chasm, Cañon del Pegus, that is as awesome as any in Big Bend. As we came off that massif, we were abruptly reminded of both the region's history and its contemporary affairs. A squad of Mexican soldiers was stuck out there on a 105-degree day with nothing but a scrap of tarp hung between tent poles for shade. We had dropped off Karen Chapman at the airport in Chihuahua City. Four men who could charitably be called middle aged, we thought we hardly fit the profiles of drug smugglers or gunrunners or terrorists, but at the checkpoint a sergeant barked and ordered us out of the car. The United States had asked for heightened Mexican surveillance of the border since the attacks of September 11. The mestizo youngster was just following orders. But his eyes were cold, and as he yanked back seats and flung open suitcases, he was careless with the muzzle of his slung M-16. He let us go with a mutter and a jerk of his chin.

The new day on the Texas-Mexico border is most evident in one of its emptiest stretches. The bridge between Ojinaga and Presidio is an official port of entry, the only legal crossing of the Rio Grande between El Paso and Del Rio. Federal agencies with border authority were being merged into the new Department of Homeland Security, and local officers were eager to demonstrate their vigilance. At the bridge a U.S. customs official routinely asked if we were U.S. citizens, then asked to see the papers of our rental car. He rebuked the driver for trying to take a car rented in Mexico into the United States. My friend ex-plained what we were doing and where we were going and said that insurance and rental company policies had made it advisable to rent the car in Juárez. Making a loop in our travels, he planned to drop off the car on his way to the El Paso airport. The man said that regulations required that we drive the car back to Juárez if we couldn't drop it off in Ojinaga. He glanced at the town and a smile tugged at his mouth as he said this. Finally he whacked the papers on his palm, handed them back, and stepped aside, letting us know that as a countryman he was doing us a huge favor by waving us through.

Presidio has gained quaint notoriety and name recognition by consistently reporting the hottest temperatures in the country. "Today in Presidio, Texas . . ." TV meteorologists love to say. As tracked by the office of Texas agriculture commissioner Susan Combs, one infuriating thing after another happens around La Junta. Some Mexican farmer puts an illegal irrigation pipe in the Rio Grande. The Conchos runs so feebly one month that other Mexicans dam and divert it just by piling some rocks across the stream.

The river bottom around La Junta has been coveted and cultivated farmland for millennia. These days the two rivers are channeled together through a system of levees. The contrast is startling. The water of the Conchos is a pretty green and has some clarity—the Rio Grande is brown and opaque. The indispensability of the Conchos could not be more tangible. Upstream, toward El Paso, is the so-called Forgotten River; on a tour of the levees and metering stations, I asked John Lee, a longtime regional director of the IBWC, why the Rio Grande ran so muddy. "That's salt," he answered. "Ninety percent of the salinity comes from the salt cedar. Those things take in three hundred to five hundred gallons of water a day, and what they put back in the river is brine. People call the river coming out of the Conchos 'sweet water'—say it 'sweetens the river.'" To Lee that was an engineering term, not just a metaphor. "For some reason," he explained, "salt cedar has never spread up the Conchos. We'd better hope to god it never does."

~

LA JUNTA DE LOS DOS RÍOS has another intriguing name: El Columpio del Diablo, the Devil's Swing. The tradition that the locale is bewitched goes far back in the lore of Indians. One legend is that Cabeza de Vaca and "the Negro" in his company spent nights among the indigenous people and left women pregnant with the first children born to a strange mix of colors. After the coming of the priests, the namesake tale proposed that Satan rode an iron ball that swung across the river from the Texas side and landed in Ojinaga—and that the scrape and dent of his landing could always be found by those who knew how to look. A subsequent story had Pancho Villa buying his bullets at La Junta from a U.S. merchant who smuggled them across the river. In the late 1940s, perhaps, came the drug lords, whose legacy of shootouts, riches, and Robin Hood-like toleration in Ojinaga have inspired *corridos* and made a strong impression on U.S. law enforcement. In the early days the "mules"

EARL NOTTINGHAM

of the drug traffic actually had long ears and hooves, but the trade broadened from marijuana to heroin and cocaine, and control passed among men named Manuel Carrasco, Martín "El Shorty" López, and—the most notorious one north of the river—Pablo Acosta. Born a U.S. citizen, Acosta was for many years a close friend of Mimi Webb Miller, a blonde ex-debutante from Dallas and relative of Texas U.S. senator John Tower. Webb remains a well-known character in the Big Bend country. But Acosta's luck ran out in 1987 when Mexican *federales* gained permission from the FBI to utilize U.S. airspace and, with a supporting crew of FBI agents, flew helicopter gunships into Santa Elena canyon and machine-gunned the drug baron, his *compañeros*, and his hideout into oblivion.

Eighteen miles downstream from La Junta is the hamlet of Redford. A book-filled house on the highway is the home of a perennially outraged man named Enrique Madrid. A University of Texas graduate, an accomplished historian, and an archaeological steward, Madrid has been waging an unending war of pride against the slander of his neighbors and community. He is angriest about the fatal shooting in 1997 of an eighteen-year-old goat herder, Ezequiel Hernandez, Jr., by U.S. marines sent to the border as part of the war on drugs. But the coals of Madrid's outrage are forever being stoked. Mexican children of families on the other side had long come across the river and attended school in Redford—having no school of their own. From the river crossing they followed a well-worn path up the bank. After the terrorist attacks of September 11, all federal agencies were under pressure to do something. One day the IBWC sent out a truck and dumped a load of boulders on the Mexican children's path, trying to make it impassable. The kids just climbed over the rocks, but to Madrid it was one more insult and proof of the U.S. militarization of the border.

"There were fourteen Indian pueblos around La Junta," Madrid said one night in his home, his eyes flashing. "They built sophisticated weirs on the river that let them irrigate. We've been here twelve thousand years. In our hearts there is no border. It does not exist. Our soul is not divided—it's the land that's divided. After the marines killed that boy, that innocent American citizen, they told Congress that Redford is filled with unfriendly people, that seventy-five percent of them are involved in drug trafficking. A hundred people live here! Seventy-five of us are smuggling drugs? Now we're terrorists on top of being drug traffickers."

He brandished a newspaper story about the border illustrated by a photo of a U.S. officer in camouflage grease paint and black attire, aiming an assault rifle at the camera. "What business do they have pointing combat weapons at my face?" Madrid thundered. "Who is that supposed to frighten? Who is that supposed to comfort?"

OTIS AULTMAN

JOHN GRAVES

"Big River" (1982)

WHILE RAFTING NOT LONG AGO down part of the Rio Grande in the Big Bend, I learned with a shade of disappointment that the blackish, dense, fluted, and sculptured material forming the superb high walls of Mariscal Canyon consists of Lower Cretaceous limestone partially metamorphosed toward marble by ancient heat and pressure. Not being a devout or even passably competent geological type, I don't ordinarily get emotional about the composition of rocks. But a good many years before, I had canoed happily and ignorantly in that region with some others mainly as happy and ignorant as myself along a stretch of the Conchos in Chihuahua to where it joins the Rio Grande at Presidio in the Big Bend, and when passing through other fine canyons sliced out of that same stone we had airily classed it as basalt. This was because it was dark and hard and sometimes shiny, but even more, I suspect, because "basalt" as a word rang richly in our ears, sounding igneous and exotically different from the prosaic limestones and sandstones and shales we were used to in our more easterly and sedimentary native habitat.

The friend who provided this mild disillusionment, Jim Bones, does not see the Lower Cretaceous as undramatic at all, and of course it isn't, not in a haunting, otherworldly place like Mariscal Canyon. The Rio Grande, all 1885 miles of it plus some tributaries, is "his" river in a mental way that I understand, having felt thus myself in my time about a couple of other streams. The feeling comes not from deeds of title but from knowledge and caring, and it gives every stone and thorny bush and biting bug and cry in the night its full significance in the riverine scheme of things. Through informed awareness, friend Bones possesses the Rio Grande where it begins in the snowy Colorado Rockies, and where it courses clear and cold and copious through the mountain valleys and high cool deserts of the ancient Pueblo country of northern New Mexico, and in the hotter arid places south of there to El Paso and beyond, where it is often reduced to a trickle or no flow at all by irrigation, evaporation, and absorption in the spongy desert soils and is replenished only when the Conchos, and later other tributaries, enter it far downstream. I think it's most especially and belovedly his in the Big Bend, where we were taking that raft trip, a stark, lovely, forbidding jumble of deserts and canyons and crags in far West Texas. But his claim extends on past where the canyons end, or are drowned, in the upper waters of huge Lake Amistad near Del Rio, and includes the less scenic but powerfully historic final reaches where it runs through brushy rolling lands past old towns and battlefields to the tropically lush Lower Valley, discharging itself at last into the blue Gulf just beyond the pale clean sands of Padre Island.

~

INSOFAR AS MOST NATIVES of this state feel proprietary about the Rio Grande, it is probably in terms of this final stretch below Del Rio. Not only is that the part they see most often but it is also an international boundary imbued with the fascinated feeling that all such boundaries generate—a feeling, illusory perhaps, of distinct languages and distinct cultures and distinct breeds of people facing one another across a mere stream, or fence, or arbitrary line traversing hill and dale. Moreover, the South Texas part of the Rio Grande has had strong bearing on the flavor and direction of Texas' past, as it still has on its present and thus is "our" river in a basic way.

Myself, I first knew the Big River there when young, seeing it most often as a tawny flow beneath international bridges when I crossed them. Sometimes I was with college friends on feckless weekend or vacation forays that didn't usually get past the stubby towns at the south ends of the bridges, with their promise of adventure that seldom materialized, though I guess we thought it did. Short of cash in those Depression times, we subsisted on things like street-stand goat tripe tacos at 3 cents a throw, found lodgings with corn shuck mattresses, haggled in markets over the price of straw sombreros and other gewgaws, emerged somehow unscathed late at night from side-street cantinas whose habitues sat around drinking very cheap fire-water and thinking up new reasons for detesting gringos, scouted the Boys Town *zona* and on rare occasions did something about it but more often were scared off by impecuniousness or thoughts of disease and mayhem.

The Rio Grande was there, sluggish and turbid most of the time, but I don't recall thinking about it much as a river, as water, except when I envisioned, as I always did when first sighting it and often do to this day, little midnight groups of brown men wading through it up to their breasts or necks and holding bundles aloft. For wetbacks were very much with us even then, and I had worked with them on country jobs in summer and felt the pull of their language and of their grave, gentle ways. One midnight during those years in fact, I got a wet back and other parts myself when we waded out to an appointment in the river's shallow channel near a ruined bridge somewhere, meeting a furtive fellow with an ocelot kitten in a box, unacceptable at customs, for which my college roommate handed over $6.

Just outside the more garish Gomorrahs' commerce and fleshly joys, though, lay the real border country, a belt of dry, scrub-clad, thorny, and inhospitable land on both sides of the river, which had very little to do with fleeting weekend pleasures but held some fine, tough, laconic ranch people, white and brown, as well as a great deal of tangled history splattered with an astounding quantity of blood. Coahuiltecan indigenes, Spaniards, Mexicans, Comanches, Apaches, Anglo-Texans, Confederates, Yankees, and other breeds had overlapped and mingled there, and while the results had been sometimes beneficent (all readers of Webb and Dobie know, for instance, that Americans learned basic ranching and cowboy skills from Mexicans in those parts, and from there carried them up the length of the West), more often they appear to have been disastrous, if often romantic in a murderous way. I know these awarenesses have faded now, as possibly they should have, but for young Texans of my generation there were dozens of borderland names of violent places and people that rang like bells in the mind and stirred you when you went there. Roma, Mier, Camargo. Resaca de la Palma . . . Cheno Cortinas, Tom Green, McNelly and his Rangers, Zachary Taylor, Pancho Villa . . . but let them rest.

Some of us went hunting from time to time in the brushlands north of the river, for quail or dove or deer, and lucky ones got an occasional look at unchanged, almost biblical old Mexican places to the south, where practically everything was still held together with rawhide, plows were of wood and drawn by oxen, women carried water in clay vessels on their heads, and long-stirruped, casual, superbly balanced horsemen used plaited hide reatas on scrub Longhorn cattle among the mesquites.

Life both human and wild was most abundant near water, and dense spiny tangles of brush near the river in its lowest part teemed with tropical beasts and birds unknown north of there. Most of that riverside thorn woodland is gone now, cleared away for irrigated farms and orchards, and with it have gone many of the creatures, including those cats—ocelot, jaguarundi—that still occurred there in my youth. Poking about with a field glass and a stock of curiosity, though, you can still find remnant thickets and in them, at the right times, chachalacas and groove-billed anis and a number of other bird species not seen elsewhere in this nation. You may find remnant shards of history too, enigmatic for the most part. Following some strange bird's call, I once stumbled over the ruins of a thick-walled stone house where generations must have led quiet, useful, rawhide lives and where something (Indians, pestilence, outlaws, armies, flood, fire, drouth, what?) had brought it all to an end, and came afterward to a clearing where a small Mexican graveyard lay, fenced with hewn weathered slabs of mesquite, fragrant with that same tree's bloom, and loud with the cucurucu of white-winged doves and the hum of yellow bees hived within a nineteenth-century patriarch's cracked white limestone tomb.

~

MANY PEOPLE FEEL vaguely and benevolently possessive toward one or another river or just toward rivers in general as is pleasantly manifested in the uproar that pollution, proposals for big dams, and other threats to the well-being of running waters can sometimes awaken these days. Fewer are stirred to emphatic and particular claims of property rights such as good Jim Bones exercises in relation to the Rio Grande, which may be well for the public's general peace of mind. It is a stout urge when it hits you, and giving in to it whole hog does not always lead to ecstasy.

For one thing, other people, troublesome as always, seldom cede you the rights of ownership; louts instead catch your fish, shoot canoes down your rapids, ogle your scenery, shatter your quietnesses with portable radios, strew your sandbars with beer cans and orange peels and busted minnow buckets, and wash their sweaty torsos in the rippling, living waters you have claimed as your own. Worse, acting as individuals or corporations or bureaucracies, they may foul your river with sewage or poisons, grab part of its flow for irrigation and give back only a shrunken muddy surplus, or impound it in reservoirs that change forever the age-old manner of its functioning, if indeed they don't dam your own stretch and wipe it out of existence. In short, if you wax too possessive toward a river you stand a good chance of ending up permanently enraged.

For another thing, a river is a complex entity, and instead of possessing it you may turn out to be possessed, even obsessed. This holds true even if you limit your interest to one facet of the river's possibilities, as did Robert T. Hill, who mapped the Big Bend Rio Grande in 1899, battering his way through its unknown canyons with his crew in three cumbersome wooden boats, passionately in love with the river's geography and the magnificent jagged terrain that had produced it but contemptuous of the desert with its "spiteful, repulsive vegetation" and in general of people stupid enough to choose life in such surroundings. Equally obsessive is the fascination of local historians with local streams, the loyalty of anglers to known pools and riffles, or the single-addicted river runners in their kayaks and canoes and rafts. On the Rio Grande and elsewhere these last are a numerous breed with whom I feel much kinship, even if they're sometimes jealous and authoritative enough within their watery domains; that a birdwatching, rather wide-ranging friend of mine says they remind her of a certain aggressive African species of river duck that takes a linear segment of stream for its own and assaults any living thing that comes there.

But broader river obsession may be worse. It derives from having a slant of mind that needs to know how things work, and it doesn't lead to easy answers. For a river does not work by just running handsomely through its allotted landscape but rather, with its network of tributary streams, as the drainage system of a wide basin within which lie a variety of terrains and minerals and climates, all of which have bearing on what the river itself is like, as do most human activities within that basin. It works too as a small stir in water's eternal global restlessness, which not only is vital to most of Earth's protoplasm, including our own, but also, in conjunction with crustal upheavals and subsidences, plays a main part in shaping the planet's surface. Whether as pounding rain and hail, mountain-gnawing frost, erosive runoff from downpours and melting snow, floods laying down gravel, and silt in bottomlands and deltas, seeping underground flow, or invading seas that drop their vast thick loads of lime and clay and arid sand and then recede, water is primary in texturing the land. Most of visible Texas, we know, has been deposited and carved by such action, and it will keep on being thus deposited and carved and changed even if, as seems most likely, our own sort of protoplasm does not survive its brief blink of geological time to witness and study the process.

Tricked into such bottomless and somber realms of inquiry by what may have started out as simple lyric appreciation of a quantity of pretty water flowing downhill in a channel, the possessor of a river, Adam-like, has lost his innocence: It's unlikely that thereafter he'll look at his river, or any other, and be able merely to note (as he still will note, however, if he ever did) what birds flit in the willows and what green tongue of current might hold feeding fish and what jumble of boulders would need some fancy paddle work if one were navigating where the water churns loud among them. He'll be queasy about the river's well-being even when it looks fine and will find himself pondering in addition where it winds from and why and how; what all its tributaries are like along with the country they drain, what sort of life various kinds of people have managed to shape in those places, how they've rubbed on one another and on the river system, and all such manner of things. He has diluted his pleasure based on wonder by turning it into a quest for knowledge, and such a quest once started seldom has an end.

Pleasure based on wonder is pretty nice stuff, though, and I find with gratification that in relation to waters like the Rio Grande, together with the Conchos, Pecos, Devil's, and San Juan rivers that feed it, I can still keep a little wonder going. I am not inwardly compelled to learn all I can about them, even though I do feel a sort of ownership in certain spots and areas and stretches along them that I've known passingly or fairly well.

One such place is the mountain country of northern New Mexico, which holds the snowy sources of the Pecos and lies not far below the high part of Colorado where the Rio Grande is born. Most of us, I believe, think of rivers as arising in mountain wilderness and flowing down through more wilderness to find civilization in lowlands and near the sea. But while there is some fine wild scenic ruggedness in that section, the Big River itself has contact with civilized folk almost from the very start, being used for irrigation within a few miles of its source near Creede and then dropping down to lands where Pueblo Indians maintained a big level of culture for many centuries before Spaniards arrived to take things over. But Pueblos and Latins shaped rather tranquil and graceful lives there, bloodied a bit at times by conflict between them and by jealous incursions of Navahos and Apaches, and outland gringos in later years have sought to take that tranquillity unto themselves, some times shattering it in the attempt.

That presence of appreciative and often quite literate outsiders in Santa Fe and Taos and other favored spots has produced a good many expert interpreters of the region, and I am in no sense one of them. But I learned to fish for trout there long ago, after the Second War, and once spent an agreeably lonesome six months in a cabin on a creek flowing to the Pecos, a high, fresh, sparsely peopled place. Some-times I sought larger quarry in the Pecos, or I would drive to the Rio Grande itself, below where it left its gorge near Taos. I remember wading and fishing on a quiet evening there when caddis flies were thick on the water and above it, and trout were striking on them from below while bats and violet-green swallows devoured them in the air, swooping of times beneath my elbow as I cast.

There is no fishing like that in the river's flat hot desert reaches lower down in New Mexico where the desert air and soils work their subtractive magic on its snow-fed flow, the land where in Spanish days difficult trails coming up through El Paso connected New Mexican colonials tenuously with their parent civilization far to the south, and names like Jornada del Muerto, "dead man's march," testify to the perils that were found there. Nor is there any real sport fishing where the Rio Grande becomes a real river again down in the Big Bend, though I remember we took much tackle with us on that cheerfully ignorant expedition to the Conchos one spring nearly two decades ago.

If I wanted to be contrary in a picayune sort of way, I might argue that we actually made that trip on the Rio Grande itself, for a number of respectable authorities— among them intrepid, wooden-boat-encumbered, canyon-surveying, desert-hating Robert T. Hill—have maintained that the Conchos is the mother stem of the Rio Grande system because of the immensely greater volume of water it brings to the confluence at Ojinaga-Presidio, the place early Spaniards had named Junta de los Rios.

We made an effort to learn what we could about the Conchos beforehand, but that turned out to be very little. All we were able to glean came from a couple of sketchy maps, and in gladsome consequence, whether or not we were the first to paddle all the way down the last 130 miles of the Conchos (or whatever it was; I've still never seen a decent map on which close measurements could be made), we were at least able to believe that we were the first—latter-day incarnations of Meriwether Lewis and John Wesley Powell, with maybe a touch of French-Canadian coureurs de bois and for that matter Robert T. Hill. This was, I admit, maybe a rather boyish feeling for six grown men in three aluminum canoes to have, but it was a fine one nonetheless and was enhanced rather than dashed by vague, rather gleeful accounts from Mexican customs officials of an enormous deadly waterfall—or was it several— somewhere in the depths of the Conchos canyons.

In any event, we found enough river adventure to keep that feeling alive, along with some awesome and spectacular places in whose like I had not been before. Places that were twilit in midafternoon, the sky a thin bright slit hundreds or some- times thousands of feet overhead, with perhaps a golden eagle or falcon momentarily silhouetted against it, and the only sounds, down where we were, a faint murmur of potent water against carved canyon walls and nearly always the muted hollow twitter of cliff swallows whose mud nests adorned those walls, with now and then the distant down-laughing note of a canyon wren, a raven's croak, the rap of someone's paddle against a gunwale. We had upsets in rapids here and there, a few portages where nerve failed us or good sense didn't, and always the pit-of-the-stomach wonder about that big waterfall. Villagers we met along the way made it sound like a huge bathtub drain down which canoes would be inexorably sucked.

These people on the whole turned out to be among the most receptive and lik- able I've ever found on trips to Mexico, curious but not nosy about what we were doing and wanting to help to the extent that the intensely parochial tenor of their lives and their ken permitted. Their presence made the trip much different from the wilderness jaunt we'd envisioned, but it was still wilderness in a way because they were there so organically, a part of the river's fauna.

Even back in the wilds of the canyons and the rough hilly desert, where there would be coyote and javelina and mountain lion tracks in sand by the water in the mornings, we found a few human beings, most of them outlaws of a hardworking amiable sort. These were sturdy souls engaged in harvesting candelilla, a low, many-fingered spurge plant of the region, and rendering out its industrially useful wax by boiling the stuff in iron vats set up in secret places along the river. They were outlaws because in a poor region of a poor country the candelilla trade was fairly profitable, and the government sought to restrict its harvest to favored licensees. They had the dash and certitude and color that being outside the law can give, together with the courtesy and aplomb that being country Mexican practically always does, and also more knowledge of the region than their kinsmen in the pueblos.

We found five raffish-looking friendly outlaws at their wax camp in a pile of boulders one morning, and they had the enlightenment we craved. Yes, said their mustachioed, bold-eyed leader, the waterfall lay only three or four kilometers down-stream, and it was very frankly, my friend, an unholy son of a bitch, a place where the river ran between and beneath stones much bigger than houses and no boat could possibly pass. And so, quite exactly, it turned out to be, except that beside the falls—a huge long cascade down through a rockslide, really—we found a couple of other affable wax-camp types tending catfish lines, who for a few pesos each helped us mightily with a tough portage over boulders and chasms and reduced to two or three hours what could have been a day's work.

I'm told there are big modern dams on the Conchos now, with good new roads running near the river and the pueblos, but they say also that despite that kind of change the *candelilleros* are still functioning and still being kept on the dodge, not only in their native land but in ours too, since "wax weed" abounds in Big Bend National Park, and park personnel with a quite commendable ecological viewpoint try constantly to prevent its harvest. Myself, I'd hate having to persecute such noble criminals as those, but on the other hand their lives are no doubt made richer and fuller and more vibrant by that sustained matching of wits.

~

FEW OF THEM are simmering spurge beside the Rio Grande itself these days, however, even those who gather plants in the park. On that recent four-day raft trip through several canyons, we saw only some flood-silted remains of disused boilers and their stone fire pits on the Mexican side, which, should they endure, will in time, I guess, take on an archeological aura of the sort that attaches to the area's old Indian caves, petroglyphs, walls of melted adobe and tumbled stone with bloody tales behind them, mine shafts, and ruined riverbank hot-spring spas where once travelers came from far and wide to achieve a cure, it is said, for gonorrhea and other rooted ills.

The problem is not so much an excess of law enforcement, it seems, as a lack of privacy, for no self-respecting outlaw would want to carry on his operations in the public gaze. And the public gaze is what the Rio Grande's shoreline gets a great deal of these days in the Big Bend, which until the thirties and later was the river's true wilderness section, a hostile, difficult, beautiful place where no one went from outside without compelling reason. Establishment of the national park and the building of access roads not only have changed that state of things but have just about turned it around. Now, from the point where river canyons begin, well upriver from the park's western boundary, to far beyond its eastern one where they disappear in Lake Amistad, the Rio Grande's course has been intricately charted, its navigational hazards analyzed and rated on an established white-water scale of one to six, its features of interest noted and described in maps and booklets available to those who want to run any or all of the canyons in canoes, rubber rafts, kayaks, or for that matter shallow-draft jet motorboats. And on days when the river is right, neither so low as to make travel hard nor so high as to make it dangerous, anywhere from scores to hundreds of healthy outdoor Americans are likely to be doing so.

A lot of river is there, of course—about 235 miles in the part most commonly used—with a good many put-in and take-out points, so that few stretches are more than occasionally what could be called crowded, unless perhaps by a Robert T. Hill or a wax-camp operator. Moreover, the people who go there to float, whether in pairs or small groups or sizable commercial flotillas of rafts maneuvered by skillful guides, are for the most part the kind who go to see the river and the country for what they are, since fishing in the alkaline, usually turbid water is poor except for catfish caught on bait, and there are no standard American-garish attractions along the way, or even any standard American comforts beyond some showers and flush toilets at Rio Grande Village, where a good many canyon trips end. It is not, in other words, a suitable or comfortable place for large, loud, pleasure-bent groups of sightseers and revelers of the kind so often found amid the fleshpots of the Lower Valley, and there are no such around. Outside of some members of the jet-boat set, who seem always to be at the point of getting themselves banned by park authorities but never quite achieve that desirable status, most of the Big Bend's boat folk are clearly good, quiet, interested sorts, often gifted with wilderness skills and sensitivities and knowledge and no more anxious to disrupt others' enjoyment of the river than they are to have their own disrupted.

For the more solitary-minded among them, though, having others there at all does diminish what they came for. Treasuring wildness, they have journeyed there to be alone with it, either individually or with four or five friends at most, because being alone with wildness is what wildness is all about. And the presence of other people, even or maybe especially other people who treasure it too, is a diminution of wildness and a diminution of the aloneness they seek. Crowds are not needed to achieve the diminution; it resides in the knowledge that on any given day you are most likely going to encounter, briefly, one or two or five or six other parties, passing them or being passed. In that mere knowledge there is a fracture of solitude, a using up of wildness.

You could see it, on that raft trip, in the quiet, almost embarrassed greetings that were given in return for ours, whenever two or three canoes passed us in a canyon of the Bend or in one of its long, winding, birdloud desert stretches. Sometimes, more rarely, you would see it in the set jaw and averted gaze of some possessive African duck type who passed in hostile silence. I had come with a good-sized party of people on that trip and did not expect solitude, but if I had come with such expectation I think I'd have been hostile too.

There is irony. On that long-ago cheerful journey we made down the Conchos not knowing what to expect, we undoubtedly saw more human beings in an average day than you can count on seeing now along the Rio Grande, but because they so honestly and unthinkingly belonged where they were, they left the wildness intact for us and we possessed the aloneness that, without defining it, we had been looking for when we came. And in contrast, on the magnificent, admirably preserved river of the Bend, where you see only a few people who want to belong but don't really, aloneness is hard to have.

Maybe we could all wear Mexican straw hats.

OTIS AULTMAN

JOHN REED

from *Insurgent Mexico* (1914)

MERCADO'S FEDERAL ARMY, after its dramatic and terrible retreat four hundred miles across the desert when Chihuahua was abandoned, lay three months at Ojinaga on the Rio Grande.

At Presidio, on the American side of the river, one could climb to the flat mud roof of the Post Office and look across the mile or so of low scrub growing in the sand to the shallow, yellow stream; and beyond to the low mesa, where the town was, sticking sharply up out of a scorched desert, ringed round with bare, savage mountains.

One could see the square, gray adobe houses of Ojinaga, with here and there the Oriental cupola of an old Spanish church. It was a desolate land, without trees. You expected minarets. By day, Federal soldiers in shabby white uniforms swarmed about the place desultorily digging trenches, for Villa and his victorious Constitutionalists were rumored to be on the way. You got sudden glints, where the sun flashed on field guns; strange, thick clouds of smoke rose straight in the still air.

Toward evening, when the sun went down with the flare of a blast furnace, patrols of cavalry rode sharply across the skyline to the night outposts. And after dark, mysterious fires burned in the town.

There were thirty-five hundred men in Ojinaga. This was all that remained of Mercado's army of ten thousand and the five thousand which Pascual Orozco had marched north from Mexico City to reinforce him. Of this thirty-five hundred, forty-five were majors, twenty-one colonels, and eleven generals.

I wanted to interview General Mercado; but one of the newspapers had printed something displeasing to General Salazar, and he had forbidden the reporters the town. I sent a polite request to General Mercado. The note was intercepted by General Orozco, who sent back the following reply:

> *Esteemed and Honored Sir: If you set foot inside of Ojinaga, I will stand you sideways against a wall, and with my own hand take great pleasure in shooting furrows in your back.*

But after all I waded the river one day and went up into the town. Luckily, I did not meet General Orozco. No one seemed to object to my entrance. All the sentries I saw were taking a siesta on the shady side of adobe walls. But almost immediately I encountered a courteous officer named Hernandez, to whom I explained that I wished to see General Mercado.

Without inquiring as to my identity, he scowled, folded his arms, and burst out:

"I am General Orozco's chief of staff, and I will not take you to see General Mercado!"

I said nothing. In a few minutes he explained:

"General Orozco hates General Mercado. He does not deign to go to General Mercado's cuartel, and General Mercado does not *dare* to come to General Orozco's cuartel! He is a coward. He ran away from Tierra Blanca, and then he ran away from Chihuahua!"

"What other Generals don't you like?" I asked.

He caught himself and slanted an angry look at me, and then grinned:

"Quien sabe . . . ?"

I saw General Mercado, a fat, pathetic, worried, undecided little man, who blubbered and blustered a long tale about how the United States army had come across the river and helped Villa to win the battle of Tierra Blanca.

The white, dusty streets of the town, piled high with filth and fodder, the ancient windowless church with its three enormous Spanish bells hanging on a rack outside and a cloud of blue incense crawling out of the black doorway, where the women camp followers of the army prayed for victory day and night, lay in hot, breathless sun. Five times had Ojinaga been lost and taken. Hardly a house had a roof, and all the walls gaped with cannon shot. In these bare, gutted rooms lived the soldiers, their women, their horses, their chickens and pigs, raided from the surrounding country. Guns were stacked in the corners, saddles piled in the dust. The soldiers were in rags; scarcely one possessed a complete uniform. They squatted around little fires in their doorways, boiling cornhusks and dried meat. They were almost starving.

Along the main street passed an unbroken procession of sick, exhausted, starving people, driven from the interior by fear of the approaching rebels, a journey of eight days over the most terrible desert in the world. They were stopped by a hundred soldiers along the street, and robbed of every possession that took the Federals' fancy. Then they passed on to the river, and on the American side they had to run the gantlet of the United States customs and immigration officials and the Army Border Patrol, who searched them for arms.

Hundreds of refugees poured across the river, some on horseback driving cattle before them, some in wagons, and others on foot. The inspectors were not very gentle.

"Come down off that wagon!" one would shout to a Mexican woman with a bundle in her arm.

"But, señor, for what reason? . . ." she would begin.

"Come down there or I'll pull you down!" he would yell.

They made an unnecessarily careful and brutal search of the men and of the women, too.

As I stood there, a woman waded across the ford, her skirts lifted unconcernedly to her thighs. She wore a voluminous shawl, which was humped up in front as if she were carrying something in it.

"Hi, there!" shouted a customs man. "What have you got under your shawl?"

She slowly opened the front of her dress, and answered placidly:

"I don't know, señor. It may be a girl, or it may be a boy."

These were metropolitan days for Presidio, a straggling and indescribably desolate village of about fifteen adobe houses, scattered without much plan in the deep sand and cottonwood scrub along the river bottom. Old Kleinmann, the German storekeeper, made a fortune a day outfitting refugees and supplying the Federal army across the river with provisions. He had three beautiful adolescent daughters whom he kept locked up in the attic of the store, because a flock of amorous Mexicans and ardent cowpunchers prowled around like dogs, drawn from many miles away by the fame of these damsels. Half the time he spent working furiously in the store, stripped to the waist; and the remainder, rushing around with a large gun strapped to his waist, warning off the suitors.

At all times of the day and night, throngs of unarmed Federal soldiers from across the river swarmed in the store and the pool hall. Among them circulated dark, ominous persons with an important air, secret agents of the rebels and the Federals. Around in the brush camped hundreds of destitute refugees, and you could not walk around

OTIS AULTMAN

a corner at night without stumbling over a plot or a counterplot. There were Texas Rangers, and United States troopers, and agents of American corporations trying to get secret instructions to their employees in the interior.

One MacKenzie stamped about the Post Office in a high dudgeon. It appeared that he had important letters for the American Smelting and Refining Company mines in Santa Eulalia.

"Old Mercado insists on opening and reading all letters that pass through his lines," he shouted indignantly.

"But," I said, "he will let them pass, won't he?"

"Certainly," he answered. "But do you think the American Smelting and Refining Company will submit to having its letters opened and read by a damned greaser? It's an outrage when an American corporation can't send a private letter to its employees! If this don't bring Intervention," he finished, darkly, "I don't know what will!"

There were all sorts of drummers for arms and ammunition companies, smugglers and *contrabandistas*; also a small, bantam man, the salesman for a portrait company, which made crayon enlargements from photographs at $5 apiece. He was scurrying around among the Mexicans, getting thousands of orders for pictures which were to be paid for upon delivery, and which, of course, could never be delivered. It was his first experience among Mexicans, and he was highly gratified by the hundreds of orders he had received. You see, a Mexican would just as soon order a portrait, or a piano, or an automobile as not, so long as he does not have to pay for it. It gives him a sense of wealth.

The little agent for crayon enlargements made one comment on the Mexican revolution. He said that General Huerta must be a fine man, because he understood he was distantly connected, on his mother's side, with the distinguished Carey family of Virginia!

The American bank of the river was patrolled twice a day by details of cavalry, conscientiously paralleled on the Mexican side by companies of horsemen. Both parties watched each other narrowly across the Border. Every once in a while a Mexican, unable to restrain his nervousness, took a pot shot at the Americans, and a small battle ensued as both parties scattered into the brush. A little way above Presidio were stationed two troops of the Negro Ninth Cavalry. One colored trooper, watering his horse on the bank of the river, was accosted by an English-speaking Mexican squatting on the opposite shore:

"Hey, coon!" he shouted, derisively, "when are you damned gringos going to cross that line?"

"Chile!" responded the Negro. "We ain't agoin' to cross that line at all. We're just goin' to pick up that line an' carry it right down to the Big Ditch!"

Sometimes a rich refugee, with a good deal of gold sewed in his saddle blankets, would get across the river without the Federals discovering it. There were six big, high-power automobiles in Presidio waiting for just such a victim. They would soak him one

OTIS AULTMAN

hundred dollars gold to make a trip to the railroad; and on the way, somewhere in the desolate wastes south of Marfa, he was almost sure to be held up by masked men and everything taken away from him. Upon these occasions the High Sheriff of Presidio County would bluster into town on a small pinto horse—a figure true to the best tradition of "The Girl of the Golden West." He had read all Owen Wister's novels, and knew what a Western sheriff ought to look like: two revolvers on the hip, one slung under his arm, a large knife in his left boot, and an enormous shotgun over his saddle. His conversation was larded with the most fearful oaths, and he never caught any criminal. He spent all of his time enforcing the Presidio County law against carrying firearms and playing poker; and at night, after the day's work was done, you could always find him sitting in at a quiet game in the back of Kleinmann's store.

War and rumors of war kept Presidio at a fever heat. We all knew that sooner or later the Constitutionalist army would come overland from Chihuahua and attack Ojinaga. In fact, the major in command of the Border Patrol had already been approached by the Federal generals in a body to make arrangements for the retreat of the Federal army from Ojinaga under such circumstances. They said that when the rebels attacked they would want to resist for a respectable length of time—say two hours—and that then they would like permission to come across the river.

We knew that some twenty-five miles southward, at La Mula Pass, five hundred rebel volunteers guarded the only road from Ojinaga through the mountains. One day a courier sneaked through the Federal lines and across the river with important news. He said that the military band of the Federal army had been marching around the country practicing their music, and had been captured by the Constitutionalists, who stood them up in the market place with rifles pointed at their heads, and made them play twelve hours at a stretch. "Thus," continued the message, "the hardships of life in the desert have been somewhat alleviated." We could never discover just how it was that the band happened to be practicing all alone twenty-two miles from Ojinaga in the desert.

~

FOR A MONTH LONGER the Federals remained at Ojinaga, and Presidio throve. Then Villa, at the head of his army, appeared over a rise of the desert. The Federals resisted a respectable length of time—just two hours, or, to be exact, until Villa himself at the head of a battery galloped right up to the muzzles of the guns—and then poured across the river in wild rout, were herded in a vast corral by the American soldiers, and afterward imprisoned in a barbed-wire stockade at Fort Bliss, Texas.

But by that time I was already far down in Mexico, riding across the desert with a hundred ragged Constitutionalist troopers on my way to the front.

DON HENRY FORD, JR.

from *Contrabando* (2004)

DURING THE LATE SUMMER MONTHS of one year in the early eighties I found myself broke. (Summer tends to be a bad time for those who make their living smuggling Mexican marijuana.) I had not been able to find anything for some time other than poor quality leftover shit no one would pay for. I calculated I might be able to go directly to the growers I knew high in the Sierra Madres between Durango and Sinaloa and be the first to arrive with a fresh product. I was so broke that I had to borrow several hundred dollars from a potential buyer in exchange for a promise to give him a special price on a couple of pounds upon my return.

I took $140 and bought a one-way plane ticket to Mazatlán, and then rented a ten-dollar motel room after managing to sneak through customs at the airport, because I had no luggage. (I often obtained visas with little more than a $20 bill and an affidavit prepared in front of a notary swearing that I was an American citizen.)

The following day, I walked to the outdoor marketplace and bought a large canvas backpack and a poncho for the mountains, after turning my dollars into pesos. I then went to the bus station and bought a ticket to Durango, Durango.

At that time there were several classes of buses operating in Mexico. The bus I chose was one of the cheapies. All seats were occupied and people stood in the aisles. Regardless of how full the bus might be, the bus driver stopped for anyone and everyone wanting a ride, cramming them in for a little extra cash that went right into his pocket. Vendors carried their wares, including live chickens and baby pigs, and almost anything imaginable.

When we got to my friend's place high in the mountains, I weaved through people to the front of the bus and asked him to stop, and got off while my fellow passengers stared in amazement. There were very few reasons why a young white gringo would want off in this area.

After the bus pulled away, I walked up a steep, slippery, wet trail through lush green foliage to a collection of homes shared by the town's inhabitants and asked a woman for my friend.

Rarely were there any men visible in this village, but I knew they were there, watching. Always watching.

Mazatlán had been hot and humid; up here, it was cold. From past experience, I knew that would be the case, hence the wool poncho. Smells of wood smoke permeated the air.

Daniel came walking up dressed in the clothes of a peasant, though not the traditional variety one would expect of an older man. He wore pastel green jeans with an embroidered leather belt and a battered hat. Huaraches protected rough, calloused feet from the ground. If one looked a little closer, the lump of a 9mm semi-automatic handgun could be seen in his waistband. In fact, every male member of this community from about twelve on up was armed in similar fashion.

Knowing it was illegal for men to carry arms in Mexico, I once asked Daniel what they did when cops showed up.

"We shoot them," he replied.

"What if the soldiers come?" I asked.

"That depends on how many come. If a few come, we kill them. If too many come, we run and hide."

"What if they catch you?"

"Then most likely, they will kill us."

"Can you not pay them off?"

"No, not us. It is said that others can and do. We are poor. We cannot do this."

At this particular *ejido*, the men never slept in their homes, opting for the safety of the mountains, with no cover other than a sleeping bag and a sheet of plastic to protect them from the elements. It seemed to rain damn near everyday up in those mountains, and with the elevation, it got cold. During the day, they would go to their homes, but not without setting up surveillance on the road passing by their town. There was no way short of a helicopter, perhaps, to approach this town without being observed far in advance of your arrival. None of these men would accept dollars for marijuana because when they tried to spend them, dollars would create suspicion.

On this particular occasion, I had only enough money to buy around four or five pounds of marijuana at about the equivalent of fifty dollars a pound, if I were to keep enough to get home on. I explained this to Daniel.

They had just begun to harvest early buds, but he had enough decent *sinsemilla* bud to fill my backpack and that he did, with around ten or twelve pounds.

He then asked, "Can you sell goma?"

"What?" I asked.

"Goma . . . Opio." He showed me some dark, gummy crap wrapped in a piece of plastic.

"No," I replied, and then a stupid thought came to mind. I disliked heroin and wanted nothing to do with buying, selling, or using it. I did have acquaintances who used the stuff. I consistently tried to get them to quit. The thought occurred to me they might be able to smoke opium to ease their cravings while breaking their addiction to heroin, so I bought the small piece he showed me.

I paid him for the marijuana and agreed to come back with the remainder of the money owed in addition to more I would be able to make off of what I had, to be applied to a larger load once I proved there was good product available. That evening we walked several miles through mountain trails to another spot above the highway and waited for a bus to come along. When one did, I ran down the side of the hill and flagged it down.

The bus did stop; stares of all the bus's passengers greeted me as I boarded with a backpack full of marijuana. I paid to go to Durango, and off we went. The driver of the bus smiled knowingly. I sweated through the tiny town of La Ciudad, where I knew there were often soldiers checking traffic, but on this day, there were none. We arrived at a bus station in Durango, crawling with cops. I got out like I owned the place, walked right past the cops, up to the ticket counter, and bought a ticket to Camargo, Chihuahua.

Once again, I boarded a bus, but this one was a *Chihuahuense* bus with two daredevil drivers and a souped-up engine. The drive to Parral and then over to Camargo was a white-knuckle ride all the way. I felt lucky not to be represented by one of those white crosses alongside the road by the time we arrived.

The bus continued on to Chihuahua, but I knew if I went that way I would have to go through a checkpoint between Chihuahua City and Ojinaga, which was something I was unwilling to try. At that time, the road from Camargo to Ojinaga was not completed, but was paved for about ten miles on either end; the rest was dirt and rocks. Very rarely was the *aduana* checkpoint manned.

I took off walking with my backpack toward Ojinaga. After about five miles, I got a ride to the place where the pavement ended with some road construction workers in the back of their dump truck. I was let out and began to walk again through the dry desert terrain. This time I walked ten or so miles before a pickup load of men stopped to give me a ride. I got into the bed of the truck and off we went, bumping merrily over the wash-boarded dirt road.

A few miles later we came across a man with a huge sack of Tupperware-like bowls and dishes, bundled in a huge tarp. The driver of the pickup stopped. The man, an elderly type, muscled the huge bundle of his wares into the bed of the truck and joined me for the ride.

The man was heavy-set and had on the clothes of a peasant but seemed to be content with his life as a traveling salesman. I could tell he was curious about what a gringo might be doing in this particular part of the world. We talked for some time. For some reason, I decided I should tell him what I was up to before we arrived at the tiny village where the *aduana* was located.

"You have what?" he asked incredulously, when I told him about my cargo.

"Marijuana," I replied.

With a look bordering panic, he replied, "You should not do that here! It is very dangerous. Have you not heard of El vibora?"

"No."

"El vibora controls that around here. If you want to buy, you must go see him. He will kill you for what you do! You must talk to El vibora to do that here."

I had never heard of Manuel Carrasco, but this guy sure as hell had. He proceeded to tell me about him. Years later, I would read about Carrasco and learn he was no longer the main man around Ojinaga. Apparently this vendor failed to receive that news. Before we got to the village, he knocked on the back window of the pickup truck, got them to stop, unloaded his wares in the middle of the desert and continued walking with his heavy load, shaking his head at me as we drove off toward the checkpoint.

I myself was tired of walking and decided to take my chances, hoping there would be no one manning the checkpoint. I watched with anticipation and apprehension as we approached and then breathed a sigh of relief when no one was there. My ride carried me all the way to Ojinaga. I checked into a motel and stashed my backpack in a room. I then went walking through the streets until I spied a group of conspicuous-looking young men. I approached them.

"Do any of you know how to get across the river on foot?" I asked.

"Where do you want to go?" one small-statured young man asked, with one eye looking at me and the other looking off to the side.

"Marfa," I replied. "I will pay someone to take me."

"Why don't you walk across the bridge?"

At this point, I took a big chance. I was prone to do such things.

"Because I have marijuana."

"How much will you pay me?" he asked.

We agreed on a price and I told him he had to come with me right then and there or not at all. Past experiences had taught me not to let him out of my sight after revealing what I had in my possession.

We went straight back to my room, got the backpack and rented a taxi to take us to some location about 15 miles or so west of town. There, I bought a kilo of Gamesa crackers, similar to shortbread cookies, and then, off we went, like so many wetbacks on any given night. We walked under cover of darkness and then, for no apparent reason we stopped, waiting quietly.

"Why are we waiting?" I asked.

"They are over there . . . La migra!"

Sure enough, after about fifteen minutes, lights flashed on, searching for us. Rather than go north, we walked downstream and waited again. We reached an area where he thought it would be safe to cross. To my surprise, there was no river to cross. Apparently the Rio Conchos—from the Mexican side, further downstream—supplied most of the water I was accustomed to seeing; all water upstream from that location had been removed for irrigation purposes. What was left was neither *grande* nor *bravo*. There was, however, a ditch full of mud, nearly waist deep. He removed his pants and shoes and waded through. Foolishly, I did not remove mine. On the other side of the ditch we encountered a large strip of plowed ground the border patrol maintains to tell where people have come across. We walked backwards across this area.

We played cat and mouse with the border patrol the rest of the night, walking for what I estimate was thirty miles. I kept telling my companion we were going the wrong direction. We filled used plastic soda bottles with muddy water after drinking out of puddles found in arroyos. I was thankful I could not see the water. I had to drink something. I can remember almost falling asleep while still walking, which was a first for me. At daybreak, we stopped.

We talked for some time while resting. He told me he would go no farther, and I would be on my own from that point forward. I gave him the last of the Mexican pesos I had left. During our conversation, he described several arrests he had endured in Mexico and the torture he had received. To prove what he said, he showed me scars on the calves of both legs where bare electrical wires had been wrapped while his feet rested in a bucket of water. The extension cord had been plugged into a wall socket. He also claimed that his eye strayed because he had been repeatedly shocked in the face with a cattle prod, causing him to lose control of the travel of that eye. The damage was permanent.

Before leaving, he counseled me, telling me that what I was doing was foolish. He then removed a loaded .45 from his waistband and said, "If I were a bad man, I could take all your money and the marijuana too."

"You already have all of my money!" I replied, smiling.

There was nothing left for him to steal, other than a backpack full of marijuana in hostile territory; otherwise, I might possibly have been robbed and/or killed.

"You are crazy!" He turned to head back to Mexico. "Vaya con Dios!" he said over his shoulder. Sometimes there is a bond between crazy people.

I was so exhausted and sleepy I could hardly keep my eyes open. I lay down and went to sleep on hard packed ground littered with rocks. When the sun came out, the heat soon followed. I woke up and took a look around by the light of day.

To my dismay, I was about two miles from Presidio, which meant that including the walking I had done the day before between Camargo and Ojinaga, I had covered about 45 miles on foot over the previous 24 hours and was only two miles into U.S. territory. My clothes were caked in mud and my feet wet and blistered. I still had sixty miles to go to reach Marfa.

I got up and began trudging through the desert. I had planned to walk all the way to Marfa. I made it about fifteen miles and could go no farther. I was bone tired. The blisters began to bleed and each step hurt terribly. Unless perhaps you run marathons or climb mountains, it will be hard to understand the level of exhaustion a body can reach. The point can come when it just quits. I was near that point.

In desperation, I walked out to the highway and began flagging cars. When a border patrol vehicle came by, I flagged him too, figuring that was one sure way to make sure he didn't stop. He drove on by. Finally, a well-dressed Mexican national working for the Mexican consulate picked me up. I must have been a hell of a sight. I placed my backpack in the trunk of his sedan and off we went. He dropped me off in Marfa.

I started walking toward Fort Davis. Soon, I got a ride with another Mexican national in a pickup truck. I guess I looked too dirty for anyone from our country to stop. I tossed the backpack into the bed of his pickup and we headed toward my home. He delivered me at the doorstep of my house. I was able to sell the marijuana at a premium price and return for more, but I will never forget the price I paid for that load—a price that cannot be counted in dollars. It took several days for me to recover to the point where I could once again walk normally. I gave the opium to my *tecato* friends after smoking a little to see what it was like.

"You can smoke this to ease your cravings," I told them. In less than a day, they had figured out some way to cook the shit up and shoot it into their veins. So much for good intentions.

ROBERT DRAPER

"Soldiers of Misfortune" (1997)

ON MOST AFTERNOONS at the edge of El Polvo, the low-water crossing that connects Redford, Texas, with Mexico, a visitor who survives the mind-wilting border heat may hunker beside the Rio Grande and be rewarded with a tableau as pastoral as any in Texas. The vision is preceded by an ethereal tinkling, the barest fingerprint of a sound. Then, spilling down from the northern plain, the goats come into view. There are perhaps forty of them, accompanied by a dog of obscure pedigree. Two of the goats wear bells around their necks. Quietly gnashing at the weeds, they make their unhurried way to the water.

Behind the animals a man and a boy materialize on horseback. Ezequiel Hernandez, Sr., is a solidly built, middle-aged native of Palomas, a pueblo almost visible from here. He wears a cap and a solemn but profoundly weary expression. In silence he surveys the mangy splendor of his world. His ten-year-old son, Noel, sits atop his pony with the slack posture that suggests an easy familiarity with goat herding. In this communion even the boy appears ancient. Meanwhile, the river glints like a shivering sheet of tinfoil. Across the water a lone man stands beside a dusty pickup staring vaguely at America, waiting.

Simplicity shaded with ambiguity. That is El Polvo (literally, the Dust) and the border as a whole. Its beauty is not the innocent kind. Even the boy knows that. His older brother, 18-year-old Ezequiel Junior, who owned this very flock of goats, was shot to death here on May 20 by U.S. Marines. Likely the inscrutable figure on the other side of the river knows about the killing, and in any case, he is no innocent, as the visitor will later see for himself. But there are crimes and there are outrages. Hernandez's death at the hands of a 22-year-old California-reared Marine named Clemente Banuelos was at least the latter, no matter what a jury decides about the former. Newspaper readers all over America now know what tiny Redford (population: 107) always knew—that the soft-spoken, hard-working high school sophomore was as law-abiding and unthreatening as anyone drawing breath could possibly be.

Quite properly, the Texas Rangers are preoccupied with what took place the day Hernandez—carrying his grandfather's old .22 rifle to fend off a pack of wild dogs that had been ravaging his herd—allegedly fired on four low-to-the-ground shaggy figures that turned out to be heavily armed and camouflaged Marines. The investigators have already voiced their skepticism as they square the soldiers' statements against the autopsy report, the shooting distance, the position of Hernandez's body, the time discrepancies, and the evidence gathered at the scene of the incident. District Attorney Albert Valadez has intimated his desire to try Corporal Banuelos for murder, and Hernandez's parents have hired an attorney to pursue a wrongful death lawsuit against the U.S. military. While his family awaits justice, the rest of the world awaits the truth.

Senseless though the tragedy was, the greater outrage is this: Ezequiel Hernandez's killing was eminently predictable. We could expect no less, really, from the quiet but growing movement to militarize an area populated by civilians. Just what was the Marines' mission at El Polvo? Was it, as we have been led to believe, an honorable episode in America's much-ballyhooed War on Drugs? The evidence plainly suggests otherwise. From inception, the Marines' mission in Redford was trivial, politically and bureaucratically freighted, and doomed to fail—a blundering bullet, in effect, with Ezequiel Hernandez's name on it.

~

FROM WHERE I SAT the day I observed the Hernandezes and their goats, El Polvo didn't look like a battlefield. Later, however, as I walked through the scrubby trails paralleling the river, I found abundant evidence of the Marines' presence there a month before: more than a dozen empty packages of military rations, plastic military utensils, camouflaging burlap, and the duct tape used to secure it to the soldiers' uniforms.

Then, after discovering a piece of wire poking out of the dirt road at the river's edge, I dug. What I uncovered, about a foot below the surface, was a heavy plastic box, similar to a car battery, with ten-foot wires dangling from each side. "U.S. Government" read the inscription on the box, which turned out to be a sensor used to monitor movements at trafficking areas. A Redford resident I talked to had seen a U.S. Border Patrol vehicle parked at this spot late one night, about a week before Hernandez was shot. I reported this to a senior Border Patrol official. He denied the sensor was theirs and suggested that I ask the military agency that had coordinated the mission at El Polvo. I did, but a spokesperson said the sensor wasn't the military's either.

Abandoned there in the dirt, the devious instrument seemed a forlorn and impotent creature—a fitting symbol for the wayward mission it was intended to serve, and maybe for the War on Drugs as a whole. What was a U.S. government sensor doing out here in the middle of nowhere? El Polvo, just south of Redford, is one of dozens of nearby informal crossings, a relatively shallow stretch of the Rio Grande that can be easily waded across by small-time dealers. The real drug action goes on in ports of entry like Presidio-Ojinaga, sixteen miles away, where notorious smugglers like Pablo Acosta Villareal and Amado Carrillo Fuentes have made millions sneaking drugs into the U.S. The fact is that the War on Drugs, if it is to be won by interdiction, will be won at the ports of entry and not by collaring flunkies who ford the Rio Grande with bundles of pot held over their heads. But like all wars, this one must be fought on all fronts. So while U.S. Customs makes the big busts at the ports, the woefully undermanned Border Patrol must monitor the vast riverbanks where the odd nickel-and-dimer might pop up.

This is where the story of Ezequiel Hernandez's tragic demise begins: with the best of intentions. In the early summer of 1996 Border Patrol assistant chief patrol agent David Castañeda met with two informants who alerted him to a drug-backpacking operation in force at El Polvo. The news discouraged Castañeda. "In the past couple of years," he told me, "we had hurt the organizations in Ojinaga by turning the people we'd caught over to the state, meaning they'd have to spend twelve to eighteen months in jail before even coming to trial. Word got around Ojinaga to the point where the operators had to go all the way down to Durango to recruit new backpackers. But the confidential sources told me they were recruiting in Ojinaga again."

Specifically, they would later learn, a Cuban-born *traficante* named El Cubano was signing up so-called mule trains consisting of teams of five that would haul 175 to 200 pounds of pot in backpacks across El Polvo. Each backpacker would be paid about $1,500 and get counterfeit identification papers along with a free ride into the American interior, where they could then seek honest work. El Cubano's operation was small but steady, and it took place at late-night hours, when the Border Patrol's skeleton crew was ill-equipped to react. Castañeda knew his agency needed outside help, but he also saw the operation for what it was—hardly a mission requiring immediately deployable troops. "When we need urgent assistance," he told me, "we call on the Texas National Guard." In this case the call went out to Joint Task Force 6.

~

LIKE A GRIMACING CHESHIRE CAT, the military's presence along the border is both more and less than it appears. For example, Joint Task Force 6 (JTF-6), the agency that coordinates anti-drug activities for the U.S. Department of Defense, subsists on a minuscule operating budget of $25 million. As its spokesperson, Maureen Bossch, insisted to me, "There has not been a recent increase in the militarization of the border. We're such a small part of the overall fight against drugs." Yet from its command post in El Paso, JTF-6 deploys a U.S. military force that is allocated $808 million for use in the War on Drugs—astonishingly, more than Customs, the Border Patrol, the FBI, or even the Drug Enforcement Administration.

More to the point, militarization of the border occurs not simply by funding soldiers to stand shoulder-to-shoulder with guns pointed at Mexico. Instead, a civilian zone becomes militarized when the rules of war are imposed upon it. That is precisely what transpired in May of this year, the moment four JTF-6 Marines set foot in El Polvo.

Created in 1989 by then-Secretary of Defense Dick Cheney, JTF-6 also owes its existence to then-Joint Chiefs of Staff chairman Colin Powell, who envisioned a key role for the military in the Bush administration's National Drug Control Strategy. When one considers the political inclinations of both Powell and Cheney, one can imagine the public-relations value they saw in this maneuver. Others in the military were less sanguine. As one Defense Department spokesperson told me, "We were ordered to get into the counter-drug policy, and believe me, we were dragged in kicking and screaming. There are a lot of hard, complicated issues to be faced when you're talking about military personnel on U.S. soil. But there was strong pressure for the military to be more involved in the drug fight. For a lot of lawmakers, this is their big political shtick."

Beneath the rhetorical bravado, however, one finds a war that is being carried out with a near-total absence of urgency. In the dull, workaday setting of vast Biggs Army Air Field, part of Fort Bliss near El Paso, some 169 soldiers and support personnel toil at JTF-6, including its commander, Brigadier General James Lovelace, who, like his predecessors, will serve eighteen months before moving on to the next post. This lack of continuity exasperates other senior colleagues in the federal drug war—including one senior official at another agency who says of JTF-6: "It's basically a way station where a one-star general gets a second star, and then he moves on."

The wheezing bureaucracy that directs the military's drug warriors hardly provokes an image of a lean, mean fighting machine. It takes months for JTF-6 translators to provide a wiretap transcript and usually a year to deploy an operational military unit. Its so-called rapid support unit renders assistance in about a month, according to spokesperson Bossch. In memos distributed to local, state, and federal drug-fighting agencies, JTF-6 regularly promotes what a senior official at another agency terms "services *they* want you to use, as opposed to what we need." Canine training, first-aid instruction, fence building, map reading—all useful, but are they unique or simply a way for one agency to spend another's money?

JTF-6's biggest federal client is the Border Patrol, an agency whose primary function is not narcotics interdiction, but people interdiction. When I asked a senior Border Patrol official at the Marfa sector about what use he had made of the military through JTF-6, he enthused, "They improved a shooting range out at the Marfa airport and saved us seventy percent of the cost. They also built a radio workshop for us much cheaper than we could've done it."

Compared with such dubious pursuits, the interdiction mission against El Cubano's backpacking operation must have resembled the invasion of Normandy in the eyes of the officials who reviewed it for merit. In truth, though, when U.S. Border Patrol assistant Marfa sector chief Rudy Rodriguez penned the proposal last June or July, he knew that the request for several LP/OPs (listening posts-observation posts) to be stationed in and around El Polvo wasn't actually going to snare El Cubano. "The backpacking situation had something to do with the request," Rodriguez told me recently, "but it wasn't just that. I knew there wasn't a pattern I could point them to by the time they got there. Mainly, we wanted to use them here as a force multiplier because of our lack of personnel."

Though Bossch of JTF-6 would later explicitly tell me, "We're not a force multiplier—they're not using us for that purpose," it seems clear that despite all the sophisticated gadgetry offered by the military, Rodriguez called upon JTF-6 for one basic reason. The Border Patrol Marfa sector—having been reminded once again that a small-time smuggling scheme could crop up anywhere within its 115,000-square-mile jurisdiction and operate with impunity—needed more bodies and didn't care where it got them.

Perhaps an objective review board would have seen through Rodriguez's request and discarded it. But there is nothing remotely objective about Operation Alliance, the bizarre outfit at Biggs Field that evaluates all agency requests for military assistance. Funded by the very federal agencies (such as the Border Patrol and Customs) that file the lion's share of the requests, Operation Alliance's nineteen members happen to work for those agencies as well. Not surprisingly, then, the organization—which, apart from receiving policy guidelines from Washington, answers to no agency—

dutifully passes on to JTF-6 85 percent to 90 percent of the requests (or about 1,500 annually), according to Operation Alliance's senior tactical coordinator, Brian Pledger.

Predictably, Operation Alliance rubberstamped the Marfa sector's request. The proposed mission, like all others, was then forwarded to one of JTF-6's four lawyers. What followed was a painstaking, time-consuming review to determine whether the project in any way violated the Reconstruction-era Posse Comitatus statute, which was enacted to ensure that the military does not get into the business of domestic law enforcement. (Though watered down somewhat in the eighties, the statute still limits domestic policing on the part of the DOD in ways that do not apply to the National Guard, the Border Patrol, Customs, the FBI, and the DEA.) In signing off on the El Polvo mission, the JTF-6 lawyers would, in effect, give the lie to the fiery oratory of politicians who promised their constituents, amid the popping of flashbulbs, to wage this war the old-fashioned way.

Shortly after one of the attorneys okayed Rodriguez's proposal, a JTF-6 message went out to every Army and Marine base in America, soliciting volunteers for an operational mission along the Texas-Mexico border. The message billed the El Polvo mission as a real-world encounter with drug smugglers, a challenge more bracing than the usual numbing base drill. All the same, it was a military exercise. The unit that signed up for the operation would do so not to win the War on Drugs but to satisfy one portion of the unit's "mission essential task list"—the checklist of duties any outfit must fulfill before becoming eligible for deployment in an actual battle. According to Bossch, the unit that was selected was simply the first that volunteered. That happened to be the 5th Battalion, 11th Marine Regiment, an artillery unit stationed at Camp Pendleton in San Diego County, California.

In October, fully four months after Castañeda had received word about the backpacking operation, the Border Patrol met with JTF-6 and Camp Pendleton officials to plan their mission. In that span of time the backpackers had doubtless altered their route, as smugglers do. Nonetheless, Castañeda, Rodriguez, and the military advisers elected to station an LP/OP unit near El Polvo, with a sensor to be buried at the crossing to signal comings and goings. Meanwhile, the 5th Battalion was transported to Biggs Field, where the troops engaged in situational military exercises, strategy sessions, and Posse Comitatus statute seminars for a few weeks. Following this, the unit returned to Camp Pendleton and intensified its mission planning, which included setting up a prototype operational center. All in all, the Marines engaged in a phenomenal flurry of activity, considering that the initial justification for the mission had long since evaporated.

Included in their standard military training was something known as the Joint Chiefs of Staff Standing Rules of Engagement. In essence, the rules of engagement dictate that when a soldier perceives an imminent threat to the lives of his fellow soldiers, he responds not as a police officer would—with a warning or with intent to disarm or wound—but instead as a warrior would on a battlefield. As Marine colonel

Thomas Kelly explained in a press conference two days after the death of Ezequiel Hernandez, "If you reach the point where you fire for fear of your lives, then you usually fire to kill."

Rudy Rodriguez of the Border Patrol knew, as he put it, "In times of stress, you revert to your training." According to Rodriguez, "I mentioned to the planners when they were making their threat assessment, 'You'll see guns everywhere all along the border.' I told them, 'In daytime, a guy with a gun is not a threat.'"

Apparently, the planners forgot to pass this information on to U.S. Marine corporal Clemente Banuelos.

~

BY LAW, the military is required to gain permission from a landowner to conduct an exercise on private property. Unlike the other border states, Texas is composed of very little public land, and the difficulties involved in securing landowner permission therefore help explain why less than 10 percent of JTF-6's approximately 3,300 missions have taken place in our state, according to Bossch.

The mission at El Polvo presented the worst of all possible scenarios. The military indeed received permission to encamp on acreage just downriver from the crossing. Unfortunately, the landowner resided in Kermit, 221 miles north of Redford, and seldom visited his border property. The other townsfolk had no way of knowing that the Marines would be descending on El Polvo. For that matter, the Presidio County Sheriff's Department didn't know either. And because there was no one to tell Redford about the Marines, no one, conversely, told the Marines about Redford. Colonel Kelly of the Camp Pendleton unit would later tell the press, "We key off of law enforcement. They have a good feel for the community. They live it, they breathe it, and they're part of it. So we depend upon law enforcement's judgment as to what there is to find." This kind of communication did not occur. Kelly also said that military intelligence gatherers actually visited El Polvo three to four days before the unit was deployed there. And, of course, either JTF-6 or the Border Patrol visited the crossing and buried a sensor. Yet throughout all this preparation, the military never gathered the one bit of information that everyone in Redford knew, the one kernel of intelligence that would have saved both the mission from being aborted and, incidentally, a life—nearly every afternoon from about five to six, a young man named Ezequiel Hernandez, Jr., brought his flock of goats to the riverbank.

On May 12 an advance team of Camp Pendleton officials arrived in Marfa and set up shop in a mobile home on a lot behind the sector headquarters of the Border Patrol. Two days later a C-130 airplane conveyed the remainder of the 5th Battalion to Marfa. Of the 120 or so soldiers, about 10 would remain at the command center on the Border Patrol lot—where, among other things, they would receive signals of movement from the sensor buried near El Polvo. Sixteen of the remaining Marines would be deployed at four designated LP/OP sites, 4 soldiers per location, rotating every few days to keep the troops fresh. The following day, May 15, 16 Marines were sent to their posts, officially, if secretly, inaugurating the military's fourteen-day mission.

Unit 513, stationed near El Polvo, consisted of four noncommissioned Marine corporals: Ronald Wieler, Jr., Ray Tomes, Jr., James Matthew Blood, and the team leader, San Francisco native Clemente Banuelos. For the next five days, the four young men (all of them between the ages of 19 and 22) lived day and night in the mesquite brush of a country where temperatures routinely soar into the triple digits. Each wore a ghillie suit, camouflage that covered him from head to toe in stringy brown and green burlap strips, their M-16 rifles similarly obscured, with their faces darkened, so that the Marines looked like nothing so much as large blobs of foliage— or, as some would later suggest, Bigfoot. While living on military rations and sweltering in their bulky garb, they looked through their binoculars, listened to the sensor reports on their radios, and in general came to know the world of the border through the eyes and ears of trained warriors.

"Every night they saw vehicles crossing," Rodriguez told me. Of course, this wouldn't surprise Redford residents, most of whom had family on the other side and routinely crossed over themselves. Furthermore, El Polvo has long been a corridor for *contrabandistas*—though the goods in question tend to be clothes, electronic wares, or frozen chickens being ferried into Mexico. So what, exactly, was there for the Marines to see? According to Rodriguez, on the third or fourth night, Unit 513 observed the crossing of ten illegal aliens, who were subsequently apprehended by the Border Patrol. But they weren't carrying drugs, and they bore no connection to El Cubano's smuggling scheme. According to David Castañeda, the Marines never once observed any backpackers; and though El Cubano was arrested a month later, credit for his apprehension would go to the Mexican police rather than anyone on the American side of the river.

In short, Unit 513 saw and did nothing during its five-day observation period at El Polvo to fulfill anyone's notion of an anti-drug mission. But on the afternoon of Tuesday, May 20, while encamped at their "hide site" near the banks of the Rio Grande, the four Marines did see someone. It was a Mexican man on horseback, across the river, gazing at America and waiting.

~

THERE IS NO WAY TO KNOW for certain whether the horseman was the same man beside a parked truck I saw 22 days later, when I visited El Polvo and watched the father and brother of Ezequiel Junior take the goats to the water. There is also probably no way to know for sure what he was up to. We do know that he unwittingly triggered the calamitous accident that was waiting all along to happen. The sighting of this man prompted the four Marines to move to higher ground—within view of Hernandez, who stood watch over his flock with a rickety .22 in hand, prepared to fire on the pack of wild dogs from town that had recently mutilated one of his goats.

The world of fact grows murky here. Did the teenager see the Marines? And if so, could he tell who or what they were? (Said Colonel Kelly at the press conference: "It is the team's impression that there is no mistake that they were identified as humans.") Or, considering their bushy camouflage and the standard duck-walking movements of stalking Marines, did he believe them to be dogs? Border Patrol officials confirm that a Marine radioed word that they had been fired upon—twice, according to two Marines in their statements. The Marines say that they then shadowed Hernandez (for how long is unclear) and that he not only did not retreat but eventually raised his .22 to fire at one of them. The Rangers have already expressed doubt over this scenario, considering that Banuelos shot the right-handed Hernandez in the right side, which would not have been exposed to the team leader if Hernandez had been aiming in the other Marine's direction. Instead, judging from the entry point of the single lethal bullet, one might conclude that Hernandez was turning to go back home with his goats.

Regardless, Banuelos fired his M-16 once. According to the Marines, Hernandez staggered, then fell backward into a three-foot fire pit. That, at least, is where the Border Patrol found him 22 minutes later. The Marines made no attempt to revive Hernandez, though, as the autopsy would later establish, he bled to death; in other words, he did not die instantly. Did the Marines let him die because they were not required to save his life? Or was it in their best interests, judging by what happened at El Polvo, that Ezequiel Hernandez be prevented from describing his version of the events?

We know this: The Marines at no time told him, as a lawman might, who they were and what their business was. Citing the windy conditions of that afternoon (though that, too, is a matter of dispute) that would have made verbal communications difficult, Colonel Kelly told the press, "In order to get the attention of the individual, they would've had to expose themselves. And there was no requirement under the rules of engagement about having to do that."

We also know this: Though at the time of his death Ezequiel Hernandez actually had a U.S. Marines recruiting poster tacked to the wall of his bedroom, he did not know that the Joint Chiefs of Staff Standing Rules of Engagement applied to the world that was his back yard.

~

HERE IS THE REST OF ALL I KNOW. Twenty-two days after Ezequiel Junior was shot to death, I sat on a rock beside El Polvo and said, "Buenos tardes" to his father as he

passed me on horseback. "Buenos tardes," replied Ezequiel Senior, as did Noel, and then they followed their goats uphill toward home. But the man across the river on the Mexican side continued to stand beside his truck for almost an hour. He looked at me, and I looked at him. Neither of us seemed to be in any imminent danger.

Then, at about six-thirty, I heard the sound of an engine coming from the north. Looking up, I saw a large vehicle slash and jiggle its way through the brush-clogged dirt road. It was a large flatbed truck, piled at least six feet high with contraband—which, I could plainly see, consisted of nothing more than some seventy automobile tires precariously tied to the bed. Slowly, inexorably, the truck advanced upon El Polvo. It plowed noisily through the river, spraying water everywhere. A minute later it was across. Only then did the lone man beside the truck move. He waved to the driver of the contraband, hopped into his own vehicle, and drove off after him.

While watching the tire *contrabandistas* vanish into the Mexican interior that after-noon, it occurred to me that somewhere in somebody's headquarters, a sensor signal had been transmitted. Maybe somebody would hear the signal. Even if he did, the battle would be joined too late.

ARISTEO BRITO

from *The Devil in Texas* (1976)

"Well, what happened is that my parents emigrated when I was six years old. My papa found work on young Ben's ranch, which had previously belonged to his father, and he considered himself happy, although I had to help him out after school. Life went on like that until 1931, just like you said. The government got the idea that we were a nuisance, although they said they were throwing us out because they felt sorry for us. What they didn't want to understand was that it was worse over there. One day they showed up at home and examined our papers. My papa had emigrated with his papers all in order, but they told him that I was illegal and that I would have to go back to the country where I was born, Mexico. And if I didn't, the whole family would have to return. My mama begged and cried, and my father complained, but it was of no use. And I liked school so much. Well, in any event, I went to live with my grandparents, but I couldn't stand it. After six weeks, and despite my grandmother's warning, I got up real early to cross the river. (Grandma, I'm going over to the other side. No, child, don't cross the river. The field on both sides is dry. Don't cross. Can't you see the spiders are weaving a web to catch you under the water? Can't you see the green chiggers will get into your bones?) It was still dark, but trembling with fear and all alone, I dived in . . . . (Heavy shadows, like dying fish . . . splashing in the water . . . tracks that sink away.) My grandma didn't want to let me come, and as I walked along the road I seemed to hear her telling me to turn back . . . (Green shadows, your pupils the color of the sea . . . the weeping willow is crying bitter tears for you . . . turn baaaaack!) But I crossed over anyway, like an echo in the mountains. It seemed like everything was against me, because I no sooner was on the other side when it started to get darker and to lightning . . . (My eyes clouded over with gray clouds and a black sky . . . the earth trembled under my feet, the sky broke into pieces, luminous machete blows.) Then I really got scared, because if it rained I wasn't going to be able to go on, and I think it was fright that made me keep going, even though I knew that I couldn't protect myself if the rain caught me in the middle and I lost my way. And that's what happened. The rain caught me when I was only halfway across the field . . . (pelting my face, whiplashes on my back. Run! Take cover! Turn baaaack!) and the worst part is that it soon turned to hail and I began to be covered with bruises. (Tears, rain, icy ammunition. Have mercy!) My cap was useless, and like a madman I started to run while I cried. I don't even remember how I found the tree (under the sad weeping willow I shivered while the drops falling on the leaves of the plants applauded). I made my body into a ball and cried for a long time until I fell asleep. In the morning I started to walk again, but my heart was heavy, as if the whole world were making fun of me. And when I got there, I cried in my mother's arms like a child. (And you, Mama, you gave shape to time, fathoming the transparency of the sea. You liked to gather the waters of the lagoons and rivers in your round pupils. And although the rivers no longer flowed as before, you mended with the rocking of your chair. Don't you remember how I tickled your ribs, and that's how you filled the arroyos of your skin? A laughter of multiform water overflowing your linen petticoats. Life without measure. Teeming seas. A transparent sky that cuddles in your lap.)"

"I can see all that. But, then, how did they shoot you if it didn't happen then?"

"Ah, that was later when I started working, since I was no longer going to school. I was all alone in the fields cleaning up when the patrol appeared. The same ones. I believe that if it had not been for this hate, they wouldn't have recognized me. The fact is that they immediately came over to me. I just asked them to at least let me get my clothes and say goodbye. Well, they said fine, and tossed me into the car. They took me to my home, and they waited for me in the car till I took care of my business, and even though my parents raised a ruckus, it was no good. When I came out, I noticed that one of the patrolmen was drinking some water from one of the faucets a little ways off. The other seemed to be sitting in the car dozing. I don't know what came over me, but I got the idea to run, knowing that I couldn't get away. The one drinking water saw me and fired his gun to scare me. But then he started to run, and when he saw he wasn't going to catch me, he steadied himself so as not to miss. And like a fool I turned around to face him, and suddenly I felt the cold next to my heart. But I didn't feel any pain, just a huge surprise. I remember that I acted scared because when the two came to put the handcuffs on me, I held my joined hands out to them. Then, handcuffed, I picked my hat up and put it over my heart. They helped me get up and I walked with them to the car, but my legs said no. I think that my hat tried to cover the hole my life was flowing out of. But how can a hat hold on to your life? All of us who are going to die are funny, don't you think so?"

"That's for sure. But what are you doing here? You're not from Presidio."

"I'm from the world, sir. Like death. What does it matter if you're from here or from there? Ignorance is enormous, and it's all the same. Poverty, too. The reality is the hole I have here, sir."

"I am reality, gentlemen."

"And who are you?"

"I am Jesús of the river, I am of the water."

"You're nuts, you're of the earth like all of us."

"Of neither ashes nor of clay. I lived in the water, and I died in the water. I am all water."

"And why are you in the fort if you're made of water?"

"Because the fort is made of glass. It's an aquarium."

"Sure, right, nutball. An aquarium with doors of crumbling adobe. You're ridiculous."

"No, the doors are made of voices."

"Ours?"

"No, the devil's."

"That's not true, they're ours. They're cries, the whistling of men who want to cross the river. They are speaking to you, Jesús."

"No, they're the sirens of the sea. They love me, which is why they call to me."

"Yes, they want you. Dead."

"No, they want me to tell them fairy tales."

"Just your old stories, Jesús. What are they going to want your idiocies for?"

"Because my stories are the truth. I am also a siren."

"How so, Jesús?"

"Because my body is in Presidio, but my soul is in the river."

PART 4

Bend

OVER MOUNTAINS OF AUBURN VOLCANIC ROCK and down the river gorge from La Junta is a handsome shallow and vestige of the Comanche Trail. The Comanches' favorite raiding route to Mexico crossed the river here. They called the river *ocuebi*. Now the spot is shadowed by the controversial resort of Lajitas. An Austin telecom nouveau riche named Steve Smith had poured hundreds of millions of dollars into his dream of creating a golf resort a few miles from Big Bend National Park. Many local residents were opposed to Smith's development, and few seemed to believe the claim that his outfit had discovered a limitless aquifer that would relieve the development's stress on the Rio Grande. Cell phones didn't work out here. Computers were troubled. A woman who moved to Lajitas with one of the construction companies told me with a laugh that the whole operation lost its power for a couple of days when a bear in the mountains decided to gnaw on some wire. Still, Smith and the Lajitas development were responsible for a thick wad of paychecks, which were hard to come by in Big Bend. Some of the happiest beneficiaries were residents of Paso Lajitas, across the river and near a nineteenth hole where duffers, who never appeared to be numerous, were invited to whack a ball they couldn't retrieve in the cause of international golf.

Smith's company and most of the contractors who swarmed into Lajitas took pains to ensure their employees in Paso Lajitas were properly documented by the INS, but most workers came across in a rowboat. One Friday in May 2002, people were lined up buying provisions and cashing their checks at the Lajitas Trading Post, which had existed many years before the development and had gained fame for its beer-drinking goat, the "mayor" of Lajitas. Suddenly dust swirled from a low-flying helicopter, and people with dogs, guns, and black coveralls were running around in "Operation Green River Tours." Border Patrol agents arrested 21 people for illegally entering the United States, among them the 18-year-old youth who ferried people back and forth in a jonboat. His boat was confiscated, and he sat in jail in El Paso for a month before he was deported to Mexico.

Two weeks later the Border Patrol raided Lajitas again, arresting seven more. "They were breaking the law," Smith said mildly, as we chatted in his restaurant one morning. "There's not much you can say." But to reach the Ojinaga-Presidio bridge, legal workers from Paso Lajitas faced a four-hour trek over a bad dirt road, a line of people approaching U.S. officials at the bridge, then more than another hour's drive back through the gorge on the Texas side. The families of some workers had left the village and moved to Ojinaga, and Lajitas employers were offering a four-day workweek and dormitory arrangements to the artisans and laborers. Simon Garza did not grow up in the Big Bend country, but he was the longtime chief of the Border Patrol's sector at Marfa. He told a reporter from the *Texas Observer* that up to 170 people a day had been illegally crossing at Lajitas: "I can't tolerate that level of activity on a portion of my river."

His river? Nearby Terlingua is a defunct mercury- and silver-mining town that has been reclaimed by desert lovers, hermits, and eccentrics; its response to the raids was furious. Mimi Webb Miller, the longtime friend of Pablo Acosta, claimed that her daughter, a U.S. citizen, was hauled off by agents who left her infant in care of a 90-year-old woman with a walker. Another Terlingua woman said that teenagers were buzzed and followed by a helicopter as they were walking to a spring prom. Toward the end of summer in 2002, area residents blew off steam in a packed Terlingua community center. The Border Patrol and the INS did not send representatives, but U.S. Customs and the Park Service did. Frank Deckert, the superintendent of Big Bend National Park, who was nearing retirement, made no secret of his exception to the crackdown. For decades park visitors had been taking rowboats across the Rio Grande and having a beer in the villages of Boquillas and San Vicente. Now if they did that they were threatened with arrest, accused of violating Homeland Security. The policy frightened tourists, alienated residents of the villages, and obstructed the work of Los Diablos--firefighters from the Big Bend villages who had been cleared by Customs to help fight range and forest fires all over the U.S. In a briefing statement on the policy, Deckert warned: "A noticeable drop in park visitation could occur, since the lure of visiting quaint Mexican villages is important to many visitors. The lifeblood of park neighbors in the villages will be drained without the support of U.S. tourist and humanitarian organizations. As a result, they will be more likely to resort to far more serious illegal activities in order to survive."

Deckert was diplomatic, hopeful that a compromise suited to local circumstance and reality could be reached. His chief river ranger, Marcos Paredes, was more outspoken. "I'm baffled by it," he said of the crackdown. "That border has never been a hard fast line. People do come across, and they're not going to stop. Contraband has always been a part of life on the border—whether it's cocaine or chickens or blue fountain pens. But people in San Vicente never even wanted a tourist economy. They're just trying to hang on to a traditional way of life. To say people in these villages pose a security threat is just absurd."

~

MAYBE THE WHIRLWINDS ARE GHOSTS. Maybe the devil does swing across the Rio Grande. The Chisos Mountains that crown the national park got their name, according to legend, from an Indian word for ghosts. So many things attempted out here appear to wind up strangely cursed. Mescalero Apaches occupied semipermanent camps called *rancherías* in the Chisos Mountains; the cavalry did not pry loose their grip on Big Bend until the 1880s. The cattle growers arrived as soon as it was safe. A salesman from Mississippi named J. O. Langford headed west in 1909 with hopes of curing his malaria, and described his exhilaration on first seeing the prairie of Big Bend: "Clear up to the rocks of the highest ridges it grew, almost hiding the glistening rimrocks, and down on the slopes and down in the valleys, only the tallest of desert plants stood above it. Looking at it then, it seemed to me there was enough grass growing in the Big Bend country to fatten every horse and cow in the United States."

Unfortunately, the ranchers went about stocking the range like they believed that. The worst overgrazing occurred as governmental agencies converted Big Bend from private ranchland to a public nature preserve. The state of Texas acquired most of the Big Bend parkland by 1942, but during the two years required to complete transfer of the acreage to the National Park Service, ranchers eagerly took advantage of the wholesale grazing. Some foothills and clearings of the Chisos are still filled with dense and tawny prairie, but the fabulous riches of grass described by Langford are as used up and finished as the mountain veins of mercury and silver.

Still, Big Bend has not lost that feel of being on the edge—it is Texas's far outpost. The clearness of the skies has been smudged by coal-burning power plants along the border in Mexican towns downstream, but the hike to the Chisos's South Rim delivers a majestic vista of the Rio Grande plain and the cordilleras beyond. Though the long drought has punished the whitewater outfitters and guides, when a rain at last comes and the river is up and running, a canoe or raft is the best way to experience Big Bend. One of the canyons' many devotees was U.S. Supreme Court justice William O. Douglas. In 1967 Douglas published a notable book about vanishing wilderness, *Farewell to Texas*. With astonishment, the jurist described seeing chinks and iron stakes in remote canyon walls—the U.S. Army Corps of Engineers had seriously proposed damming the river and filling the Big Bend canyons with a vast new lake.

Another tourist who said he enjoyed floating the Rio Grande was Henry F. DuPont. In Heath Canyon, a few miles downriver from the national park, the DuPont Corporation had bought from Dow a fluorspar mining and refining operation in a Mexican village called La Linda. Declining prices and Chinese dominance of the fluorspar market prompted DuPont to close its operation in 1986, turning the company town into a ghost town. A two-lane Texas highway and bridge across the Rio Grande had connected La Linda with railway access in the nearby small town of Marathon. DuPont sold the bridge and a parcel of land to the National Parks Conservation Association. For a few years it was used by occasional tourists and binational Latino families, but U.S. Customs closed the bridge in 1997, building a concrete and steel barricade across it. The official reason for the bridge's closure was an alleged shootout on the span between Mexican officials and drug dealers; Customs also acknowledged that it was difficult to find agents eager to work a bridge with hardly any traffic in the middle of nowhere. After the bridge closed the only occupants of the community were the last manager of DuPont's operation, a shy engineering geologist named Andy Kurie, who lived on the Texas side; and a small contingent of Mexican soldiers, who waded the river or climbed across the barricade and bought lunch at a café Andy sometimes kept open, along with a little-used motel.

JAMES EVANS

Andy's wife spent most of her time at their other home in Marathon. The place in La Linda was always more or less for sale, but in solitary contentment Andy stayed on in a house filled with books, geological maps, and souvenirs and memories of his Mexican adventures. He walked out periodically to be among his dogs and check and record his climatological data. Ask him how hot it was, as I did one day, and he would hold up his palm. Written large with a ballpoint was the latest thermometer reading, 106.

The celebrated Chisos Mountains of Big Bend National Park are a small northern promontory of a mountain range called the Maderas del Carmen. Maps of Mexico have long shown a large green area south of the Rio Grande that was billed as a future "companion park" of Big Bend. Mexico was not going to open a national park of the U.S. variety, but it had restricted use and granted resource protection to private landowners in an area called Museo del Carmen. About the size of Big Bend National Park, Big Bend Ranch State Park, and the Black Gap Wildlife Preserve in Texas, the refuge contains forests of Douglas fir and some canyons that are 3,000 feet deep. The mountains on the eastern slope of the Sierra Madres catch the winds off the Gulf of Mexico, so the vegetation is lush. Here one could see black bears, golden eagles, mountain lions, flocks of parrots. A U.S. botanist who roamed the wilderness encountered three species of orchids he'd never seen before.

The National Parks Conservation Association accepted ownership of the American side of the La Linda bridge with hopes and expectations that the Sierra del Carmens would one day beckon American ecotourists. Though the desert terrain in Mexico looks surreal and forbidding, a system of graded but improvable roads into the interior and highlands was built during the mining era. An adventure-sports enthusiast named Alberto Garza was a scion of a Monterrey family that pioneered Mexican steel, glass, and beer industries. His part of the business empire was managing the solid waste of clients such as the city of Tijuana and Pemex, the national oil company, but his passion was a nonprofit preserve in the Museo devoted to ecotourism. In the mountains he had built a base camp with tent dormitories, a dining hall, a bar with good wine and tequila. Garza was a leader of a big-name alliance of political and private-sector supporters on both sides of the border. He hoped to see the preserve frequented by upscale Mexican, French, and German tourists who loved rappelling and hang gliding, as he did, but Garza knew that to really get it off the ground, he had to lure Americans. To that end, he had been running six-hour shuttles into the Museo from tiny Boquillas, but his best hope was for the reopening of the bridge at La Linda. Garza had employees and investors working on plans to build hotels and restaurants in the deserted mining town. Andy Kurie dreamed of how that might transform his beloved ghost town.

Then came September 11 and the Department of Homeland Security. Interpretations of memos written in Washington abruptly put their dreams on hold.

And that lay somewhat apart from the bizarre status of the La Linda Bridge. One day in 2002 the Washington-based parks association received a letter from the U.S. Coast Guard.

A classic of one-page federal prose, the letter proclaimed that the Rio Grande, being an international boundary, was legally a navigable stream under its jurisdiction. The La Linda Bridge, through its closure, had become a hazard to navigation. Under the law it had to be torn down. And the owner of the bridge had to pay for it.

Embarrassed by the publicity and the cartoons of Coast Guard cutters on the waist-deep Rio Grande, the service granted a three-year moratorium on the order while an alliance of people in West Texas and northern Mexico tried to work with government officials and conservationists to find a suitable owner for the bridge; finally, the Mexican conservationist Alberto Garza and the nonprofit Rio Grande Institute of Texas proposed to buy and operate the bridge as an official port of entry. Some residents of the Trans-Pecos warned that the bridge and the promised highway improvements in Mexico would turn loose the sixteen-wheelers of the North American Free Trade Agreement on Big Bend. The traffic in commercial trucks between the two countries exceeds four million annually, and a big new highway is being built to connect Mexico's cities on the Pacific with Texas. Among other ills, some locals predicted, the traffic would squash a wealth of rare snakes for which the road to La Linda is known. But the mission to save the bridge seemed to be making progress when, without informing anyone in advance, the Parks Association abruptly sold the Rio Grande property for $3,000 to a woman named Deborah Calvert, who lived in Terlingua. She told an environmental lawyer who volunteered to represent her in negotiations with Garza and the Rio Grande Institute that the last thing she ever meant to buy was a Rio Grande *bridge*. Her idea of a good time was the annual chili cook-off in Terlingua. She had just wanted to own a little place with a nice view.

An exasperated Marco Paredes, the chief ranger at Big Bend National Park, favored reopening the bridge. "It's nearly three hundred miles from Presidio to Del Rio. Not to have a point of entry anywhere along that stretch of river is unconscionable. It would be crazy to tear that bridge down."

Paredes had been a whitewater guide for Far-Flung Adventures for many years, and he used to outfit horse treks in the Sierra del Carmens. His job as a river ranger extended beyond the park to the Lower Canyons, which are protected under the National Wild and Scenic Rivers System. Paredes told me that before his job became more administrative, he spent more than 150 days a year navigating the Rio Grande, and he brightened when we talked about recent monsoon rains that had put rafts, canoes, and kayaks back afloat in Big Bend. "I'm going to the Lower Canyons in a few days," he said. "Where else in Texas can you go out for a week and not see another soul? It's good for your head to get off where even radios don't work."

FRANK ARMSTRONG

ROBERT T. HILL

from "Running the Cañons of the Rio Grande" (1901)

AT NOON, OCTOBER 5, 1899, we pushed out into the river at Presidio, and started on our long journey into the unknown. I do not claim to be the only man who has traveled the tortuous and dangerous channel of the frontier stream; for one man, and one only, James MacMahon, has made at least three trips down the river. Mine, however, was the first exploring expedition to pass the entire length of the cañons, and, with the exception of MacMahon's, was the only attempt that succeeded. Others, like Gano and Neville, have passed the fearful twelve miles of the Grand Cañon de Santa Helena. The only government expedition, the International Boundary Survey, pronounced the cañons impassable, and gave up the attempt to survey them, except the lower hundred miles of the course, which Lieutenant Micheler passed through.

MacMahon was interested neither in science, exploration, nor travel. He ventured the stream without knowledge of its dangers, and merely because, as a lifelong hunter and trapper, he knew that the beaver probably lived along its unmolested banks.

These animals alone interested him, and a map made by him, if he could make such a thing, would note only beaver banks and danger-spots, for these were all that he saw. Unguided and alone, he loaded his boat with traps, placed it in the stream, and slowly drifted down to Del Rio, braving a thousand dangers and making the first successful passage. This man, whose name has perhaps never before appeared in print, had spent his long life in such exploits, and is one of the few old-time trappers still to be found in the West.

The finding of MacMahon was the first of the dozen fortuitous circumstances which made my trip possible, and there was not a day that his knowledge of the dangers of the stream did not save us from loss and destruction. Always kind and unobtrusive, he was as cautious as a cat, being at times apparently over-careful. He was ever on the lookout for a safe channel in the treacherous current, beaver slides on the banks, and border Mexicans in the bushes.

Hardly had we begun to enjoy the pleasant sensation of drifting down the stream when a roaring noise was heard ahead. This came from seething and dangerous torrents of water foaming over huge rounded boulders of volcanic rock which everywhere form the bottom of the river. Reaching these rapids, we had to get out of the boats and wade beside them, pushing them off or over the stones, or holding them back by the stern-lines. This process had to be repeated many times a day for the entire distance, and, as a consequence, all hands were constantly wet. The swift current and uncertain footing of the hidden rocks make these rapids very dangerous. A loss of balance or a fall meant almost certain death. It was our very good fortune not to upset a boat or lose a man. Ware was especially cautious at such places, for only a year before, while on a hunting and fishing expedition on the Lower Rio Grande, his companion had been drowned in a place of this character.

The first twenty miles lay through a low, broken desert country. The river-banks were of muddy silt, with here and there a lone cottonwood or willow. Ahead of us loomed the Bofecillos Mountains of Texas and the San Carlos Sierra of Mexico, closing in upon the river.

This region is infested by thieves and murderers, and MacMahon was watchful. Our loaded rifles lay beside our oars, and every bush and stone was closely scanned for men in ambush. The special objects of terror were a famous Mexican, Alvarado, and his associates. Alvarado possessed a mustache one side of which was white and the other black. From this he was called "Old White Lip." To his hand had been charged the murder of several men who had attempted the river route, and it was he who, MacMahon avowed, the year before had riddled his sleeping camp with rifle-balls. At night we secreted our camps in thickets of carrizo, a kind of cane which grew on the low sandbanks, and each man slept with a loaded Winchester beneath his pillow.

The second morning we reached the appropriately named village of Polvo ("dust"), the last settlement for one hundred and fifty miles. It consists of half a dozen dreary adobe houses on a mud-bank, the remains of the old United States military post of Fort Leaton. Here the hospitable storekeeper, an agreeable white man who for some unknown reason had chosen this dreary place of exile, entertained us by showing us the splotches of blood upon the floor and wall behind his counter, where his predecessor had been robbed and murdered the year before, supposedly by Alvarado and his friends. Before I saw this gruesome sight I had not entertained sufficient respect for MacMahon's precautions. Thereafter I was more careful to keep my firearms handy. While at this store, remarks were made by some of my men which led me to suspect that they were secretly planning to retaliate upon Alvarado. Here was a possible motive for undertaking a journey the dangers of which they depicted in vigorous terms. In vain I protested that this expedition was for scientific purposes, and not for vengeance. They only replied that they would shoot Alvarado on sight, "like any other varmint."

A few miles below Polvo the huge chocolate-colored cliffs and domes of the Bofecillos Mountains began to overhang the river, and before night we entered the first of the series of cañons of the Rio Grande, in which we were to be entombed for the succeeding weeks. This bears the cheerful name of Murderer's Cañon, for here, a year or two before, the body of a supposed victim of Alvarado was found lodged on a sandbar. This and the Fresno Cañon, a few miles below, are vertical cuts about six hundred feet deep through massive walls of red volcanic rock. All the other cañons are of massive limestone. The rocks are serrated into vertical columns of jointed structure, and when touched by the sunlight become a golden yellow. The skyline is a ragged crest, with many little side cañons nicking the profile. When evening came we were glad to camp on a narrow bank of sandy silt between the river and its walls. Lying upon our backs and relieved of the concentration of our wits upon the cares of navigation, we were able to study and appreciate the beauties of this wild gorge.

The river itself, here as everywhere, is a muddy yellow stream. In places, patches of fine white silt form bordering sand-bars; about twenty-five feet above these there is a second bench, covered by a growth of dark-green mesquite. The whole is enclosed by vertically steep, jointed rock walls. The thread of water and the green ribbon of the mesquite bench are refreshing sights, for immediately above the latter, on both sides, the desert vegetation always sets in.

Toward sunset I scaled a break in the cañon to reach the upland and obtain a lookout. Above the narrow alluvial bench forming the green ribbon of river verdure I suddenly came upon the stony, soil-less hills forming the matrix out of which the valley is cut, glaring in the brilliant sunshine and covered with the mocking desert flora. The sight of this aridity almost within reach of the torrent of life-giving waters below, the blessing of which it was never to receive, was shocking and repulsive. It also recalled a danger which ever after haunted us. Should we lose our boats and escape the cañons, what chance for life should we have in crossing these merciless, waterless wastes of thorn for a hundred miles or more to food and succor?

Below the mouth of Murderer's Cañon the rapids were unusually bad and dangerous, and it required all hands but one, who stood guard with cocked rifle, to wade beside the boats and preserve them from destruction. As this cañon suddenly ends, its vertical walls continue north and south, as the front of the mountain which it has crossed. We then entered a valley which presents a beautiful panorama of desert form and color. The hills are of all sizes and shapes. Those on the outer border are dazzlingly white, chalky rocks, surmounted here and there by black caps of volcanic rock. The slopes are vermilion foothills of red clay. Still lower are the river terraces of the desert, yellow clay and gravel, the whole threaded by the narrow fringe of fresh green along the river.

In this wild country lived the notorious Alvarado. Only a most fortunate mistake prevented my men from carrying out their threat to exterminate this bandit. Alvarado had a surname as well as a Christian name, and when they were told that the next ranch down the river was Ordonez's, they did not understand that this was another name for Alvarado until after we had passed him with an infant in his arms, serenely watching us float down the stream. I breathed easier on finding this out, but the men swore audibly and long at their misfortune in not recognizing the supposed monster.

Still lower down the river this region becomes more weird. Immediately adjacent to the stream there are great bluffs of a dirty yellow volcanic tuff, which weather into many fantastic, curvilinear forms. One of these, two hundred feet high, stands out conspicuously from its surroundings, an almost perfect reproduction of the Egyptian Sphinx. This, with the sterility of the surroundings and the dirty mud colors, constantly recalled the character of the Nile.

We were relieved to see before us the entrance of another vertical "shut-out," or cañon, into which we passed at about four o'clock in the afternoon, and found a suitable camping ground, hemmed in on each side by vertical walls and out of rifle-range from above. This cañon was only a mile or two long, and was very similar to Murderer's Cañon in its scenic and geologic features.

The next day the river followed a sinuous course through a most picturesque district which we named the Black Rock Cañon. This widely sloping, terraced cañon cut one thousand feet below the summit of a level plateau. The edges of this plateau were lozenged by erosion into symmetrical buttes with great flat caps and scarp lines above terraced slopes, the graceful curves of which wound back and forth from the river's edge. The tabled tops and lower slopes of these buttes were thick strata of dazzling white chalk, while between them was an immense bed of black lava, which always occupied the same relative position between the white bands, as if kind nature had painted a stripe of black about the hills to break the monotony of the desert glare. All day we wound through these hills, now beneath vast bluffs at the water's edge, and then again in more open spaces, each revealing a new and more beautiful vista.

Toward evening a graceful sweep of the river brought us into a more open basin opposite the mouth of the San Carlos Creek. This stream, which can barely be said to flow, comes in from the Mexican side, and is the only flowing tributary of the Rio Grande that we passed between the Conchos and the Pecos. Near its headwaters in the wild and rugged San Carlos Mountains is a little settlement of Indians, the remnant of a once famous, desperate tribe from which the creek and the mountains take their names. Opposite is a wide, sloping plain of limestone, from the center of which rises a wonderful symmetrical butte a thousand feet high, the summit of which is a head presenting the profile of an old man, which we named the Sentinel, from the watch which it kept over the entrance of the Grand Cañon.

We traveled fully one hundred miles to this point by river, but as the crow flies it is only about fifty miles below Presidio. We camped on the Texas side, beneath a limestone bluff. A mile below us down the river was a vast mountain wall, the vertical escarpment of which ran directly north and south across the path of the river, and through which the latter cuts its way. The river disappears in a narrow vertical slit in the face of the escarpment. This mountain is the Sierra Santa Helena, and the rift in its face is the entrance to the so-called Grand Cañon of the Rio Grande. Why this particular cañon is called Grand is not known, for many of the cañons below were not only as deep, but far longer and in every way equally deserving of the name. But Texas is poor in topographic names; most of the features are without names at all. This was the case even with the great mountain through which this cañon passed. Later the Mexicans told us that the feature was called the Sierra de Santa Helena, and this particular cañon will be spoken of as the Grand Cañon de Santa Helena.

The Sierra de Santa Helena is an elongated, quadrangular mountain block half a mile high, twelve miles wide, and fifty miles long, and lies directly across the path of the river. Its summit is a plane surface slightly tilted to the west. The edges are precipitous scarps. Imagine this block cut through vertically with the finest saw, and the rift of the saw will represent the cañon of the river.

Before entering the cañon, let us look at it as did Dr. G. G. Parry of the Mexican Boundary Survey, who, deeming it impassable, climbed the heights and saw it from above. The general surface of the plateau presents no indication of a river-course, and you are not aware of its presence till you stand suddenly on its abrupt brink. Even here the running water is not always visible, unless advantage be taken of the projecting points that form angles along the general course of the river. From this dizzy height the stream below looks like a mere thread, passing in whirling eddies or foaming over broken rapids; and a stone hurled from above into this chasm passes completely out of sight behind the overhanging ledges. From the point formed by its last projecting ledges the view is grand beyond all conception. You can here trace backward the line of the immense chasm which marks the course of the river till it emerges from its stupendous outlet.

The next morning, after the customary involuntary wetting at the rapids by which we made our nightly camps, we rowed straight for the narrow slit in the mountain. The river makes a sudden bend as it enters the cañon, and almost in the twinkling of an eye we passed out of the desert glare into the dark and silent depths of its gigantic walls, which rise vertically from the water's edge to a narrow ribbon of sky above. Confined in a narrow channel less than twenty-five feet wide, without bench or bank upon which to land, our boats glided along without need of oars, as we sat in admiration of the superb precipices which hemmed us in on each side. The solemnity of the scene was increased by the deathlike stillness which prevailed and by the thought of those who had tried the journey and either lost their lives or narrowly escaped destruction. The walls rose straight toward the sky, unbroken by bench or terrace, and marked only by an occasional line of stratification in the cream-colored marbles and limestones which composed them. The waters flowed noiselessly and swiftly through this cañon, with hardly a ripple or gurgle except at one place. Their flow is so silent as to be appalling. With the ends of our oars we could almost touch either wall. The solemnity and beauty of the spectacle were overwhelming.

We had gone only a few miles when a halt was suddenly forced upon us. Directly ahead was a place where one side of the great cliffs had caved away, and debris spread across the narrow passage of the river. This obstacle was composed of great blocks of stone and talus rising two hundred feet high, which, while obstructing the channel, did not dam the waters, but gave them way through the interstices of the rocks. The boulders were mostly quadrangular masses of limestone fifty feet or more in height, dumped in a heterogeneous pile, like a load of bricks from a tip-cart, directly across the stream. At this place, which we appropriately named "Camp Misery," trouble began. Although the obstruction was hardly a quarter of a mile in length, it took us three days to get our boats across it.

A landing was made upon the rocks, and scouts were sent out to explore a route across them. In the course of three or four hours we found that it would be necessary to pack the contents of the three boats over these stones, first uphill to an altitude of one hundred eighty feet, and then down again to the stream below the obstruction. Crevices were found between the boulders where a foothold could be obtained, and the articles were passed hand over hand to a height of one hundred feet. Our faithful Mexican, with ax in hand, then cut away the thorns and daggers and made a path along the base of the cliff for the remainder of the way. It was not until the following night that the last piece of baggage was transferred.

The handling of the equipment was an easy task in comparison with a greater difficulty that lay before us. The three boats, each weighing three hundred pounds, were yet to be lifted over the vast cubes of limestone along the immediate course of the river, around and between which the water dashed with the force of a mill-race, and where a slip of the foot on the smooth rocks meant certain death.

Foothold had to be sought on these great stones, and often precious hours were lost in seeking a means to ascend them. This was sometimes accomplished by throwing lariats, the dangling ends of which were scaled hand over hand. Once upon the summit of the rocks, the boats were pulled and pushed up by the exertion of all the crew. Three days were consumed in this task before we passed our final night at Camp Misery, ready to resume our journey the following morning. At the place where we ate and slept there was not a foot of flat earth to lie upon, and we sought such perches as we could obtain upon the sharp-cut edges of the fallen limestone blocks, above danger of flood. For myself, by a liberal use of the geologic hammer, I widened out a crevice in the stone, in which, by lying crooked, I managed to pass the nights.

During our three days' stay at Camp Misery we had abundant opportunity to observe the majestic features of the great gorge in which we were entombed. The scene within this cañon is of unusual beauty. The austerity of the cliffs is softened by colors which camera or pen cannot reproduce. These rich tints are like the yellow marbles of Portugal and Algiers, warmed by reddening tones which become golden in the sunlight. The cliffs are often rigid and geometrically vertical, but usually the severity is modulated by gently swelling curves which develop at the edges of the horizontal strata or vertical joint-seams. In many instances the profiles are overhanging or toppling. This was forcibly illustrated on one occasion, when, having selected a spot on which to make my bed, my attention was directed by the men to an immense boulder so delicately poised upon the very edge of the cliff immediately above me that the vibration of a rifle-shot would apparently have dislocated it and sent it thundering down.

Here and there the surging waters at the angle of a bend, beating straight against the limestone, have bored great caves beneath the bluffs at the water's edge. In places gigantic columns five hundred feet high have been undermined and dropped down a few feet without tumbling, so that they now lean in uncertain stability against the main wall.

From above, the skyline was of never-ceasing interest, whether bathed in sunshine while shadows filled the vast crevices below, or flooded with the glorious moonlight which is one of the characteristics of the desert. Frequently there were vast caverns a hundred feet or more below the crest-line, into which we could look from below and see their other ends opening out upon the plain above. Castellated and turreted forms in natural mimicry of the feudal structures of the Rhine were frequent. One of these, opposite our camp, was so natural that upon awakening one moonlit night and seeing it above me it took several moments for me to dispel the idea that it was a genuine castle, with towers, bastions, portcullis, and port-holes.

A striking feature of this cañon was the absence of animal life. There was little sign of bird, rabbit, wolf, squirrel, or other animal, so common upon the uplands above. The only indigenous creature we saw was a small species of bat, new and unknown to me, which fluttered about at night. A single covey of blue quail, which in some manner had made their way into these depths, were so frightened by our intrusion that it was pitiful to see their vain attempts to fly out to the cliffs above. Time and again the mother bird called her flock together and led an attempted flight to the summit. The quail is not noted as a soarer, the trajectory of its flight being almost as flat as that of a rifle-ball. They rose two hundred or three hundred feet, with a desperate whirring of their wings, and then fell back almost exhausted into the rocky debris of the cañon.

While buried in this cañon at Camp Misery, we were constantly impressed by the impossibility of escaping from it in case we should lose our boats or be overwhelmed by sudden floods. Leisure moments were devoted to looking for some possible manner by which the vertical walls could be scaled. For its entire length there is no place where this cliff can be scaled by man. In order to reach its summit, after finishing my river-trip, I made a special overland journey from Marathon, and succeeded in surmounting the vegetation, some which are black-capped volcanic hills; others are of dazzling yellow sandstone; still others show stripes of stratified vermilion and chocolate colors.

Day after day we drifted through this weird desert, hemmed in by low bluffs of dirty yellow soil, and seeing few signs of human habitation. One day we ran across three or four Mexicans leisurely driving a herd of stolen cattle across the river into Mexico. This is the chief occupation of the few people who choose this wild region for a habitation. A little later we were greeted at our camp on the Mexican side by a white man accompanied by seven or eight Mexicans, all fully armed. Ware recognized him as a notorious ex-convict known in Texas as "Greasy Bill." Later, upon my return to Marathon, I learned from the rangers that he was the outlaw most wanted in Texas, and that only the year before he had murdered an old man named Reed, who kept a store on the Texas side.

We were now nearing the apex of the Great Bend. The river had never been correctly meandered, and we naturally looked for the point where the stream which we had followed so many miles in a southwesterly direction should turn toward the north. Five times we came to the southern apex of bends in the stream, each time thinking we had made the turn, before we finally reached the most southern point in our journey. Our general course then changed from a southwest to a northwest, which we were to follow for many days.

Just after making the turn we entered the first of the two cañons known as the Little and the Big San Vincente cañons respectively. These cut through a long, low sierra within the general area of the Terlingo valley. Directly through and across the front of the sierra a vertical black line could be seen marking the vast chasm through which the stream makes its way. As we neared the entrance, the river presented the appearance of apparently plunging into a seething hole without visible outlet. This cañon, like the Grand Cañon de Santa Helena, is cut through limestone, but the strata are tilted and bent into many picturesque effects. The bends of the stream in its depths are more numerous, and the walls are broken by the entrance of many lateral cañons presenting pinnacled and terraced cream-colored sides. In this cañon we saw a Rocky Mountain sheep far above us upon an inaccessible ledge. Serafino took one shot at him, and he tumbled back in a majestic leap.

The passage of the San Vincente cañons took only a few hours, and at noon we found ourselves in the eastern or Tornillo extension of the Terlingo Desert, near the ruins of the old Mexican Presidio de San Vincente. These ruins were seen in 1852 by the Mexican Boundary Survey, and were apparently as ancient and deserted then as today. They consist of extensive roofless walls of old adobe buildings standing in an uninhabited region, upon a low mesa a mile or two from the river. The people of the Big Bend region have a tradition that in the days of the Spanish regime they were the site of a prison where convicts were kept and worked in certain mythical mines in the Chisos Mountains. They are the ruins of an old Spanish frontier military post.

The following morning we passed another short cañon, through a mountain region similar to that of San Vincente, which was picturesque in every detail. Beyond this we arrived at the village of Boquillas, where we encountered the first and only American civilization upon our expedition.

At this point, and for about fifty miles down its course, the river is reinforced by a remarkable series of hot springs bursting out of vertical fissures. The first noted of these was in the middle of the stream, and its presence was made apparent by the beautiful, limpid water welling up in the midst of the muddy current. Roughly estimated, the volume of the stream is doubled by springs of this character as it passes through these mountain gorges.

Boquillas is a widely divided settlement that owes its existence to a near-by silver-mine in the adjacent mountains of Mexico. Upon the American side there are a store, a custom-house, and a post-office. These are connected with the Mexican side of the river by a great wire-cable carrier a quarter of a mile long, terminating in Mexico at a smelter where enterprising Americans are reducing the ore found in a vast pocket twelve miles away in the Sierra del Carmen.

Two miles below the smelting-works is a densely crowded village of two thousand Mexican inhabitants. This, like other Mexican towns along the Rio Grande, presents none of the neatness or artistic suggestion of the villages of other parts of Mexico. There is no sign of stucco, whitewash, or of ornamentation of other kind. Streets and walls and interiors are all a continuation of the dirty adobe soil of which the houses are built, made no less repulsive by the filthy pigs, burros, chickens and other inhabitants which seem to possess no separate apartments. It is rumored that the ore is becoming exhausted, and that within a few months the industry will cease. Then the inhabitants of the three Boquillas will disperse like the flakes of white cloud that sometimes dot the sky, and the solitude of the desert will again reign the entire length of the Big Bend.

East of the Boquillas group of settlements the wonderful western escarpment of the Sierra del Carmen rises straight above our path. Although the crest, which makes a gentle arch, is less regular than that of the opposing escarpment of the plateau of Santa Helena, it is higher and of grander relief. Surmounting the center of the arch of the plateau is a single steeple-like peak, which may be termed the Boquillas Finger. This landmark, like the Chisos summits, was often in sight from points one hundred miles away.

Across the center of the Sierra del Carmen, which rises seventy-five hundred feet above the sea, the river cuts another vertical chasm, which is even more worthy of the name of the Grand Cañon than that of the Sierra de Santa Helena. The Mexican Boundary surveyors, upon encountering it, were obliged to make a detour of fifty miles around the mountain to approach the river again, where they finally gave up the attempt of further exploration, and reached the lower Texas country by a long journey through Mexico. The cañon profile presents a summit nearly five thousand feet above the river. The river itself, in approaching this mountain, first turns from side to side in short stretches, as if trying to avoid the mighty barrier above it, and then, as if realizing that it is constantly becoming involved in the maze of foothills, suddenly starts across the sierra.

In crossing this mountain the river pursues a tortuous course made of many small rectangular bends, around each of which a new and more surprising panorama is presented. The walls of the cañon are of the same rich cream-colored limestone rocks as those which make the cañons of Santa Helena and San Vincente. Owing to the dislocation of the strata, the rocks are more varied in form, and are broken into beautiful pointed salients and vertical columns. Wonderful indeed are the remarkable forms of rock sculpture. Among these was a vast cylindrical tower like the imaginary pictures of Babel, standing outward of the cliff-line and rising, through perspective, far above. Upon the opposite side was another great Rhine castle. Frequently, lonely columns of rock five hundred feet or more in height stood out from the front of the cliff in an apparent state of unequal equilibrium. Caverns of gigantic proportions also indented the cliff at many places. Again, the great yellow walls were cut from base to summit by wonderful fissures filled with white calcite or vermilion-colored iron ore. Huge piles of talus here and there encumbered the bases of the cliffs.

The moon was full while we were in this cañon, and the effects of its illuminations were indescribably beautiful. Long before its face could be seen, its light would tip the pinnacles and upper strata of the cliffs, still further gilding the natural yellows of the rocks. Slowly this brilliant light sank into the magma of darkness which filled the cañon, gently settling from stratum to stratum as the black shadows fled before it, until finally it reached the silent but rapid waters of the river, which became a belt of silver. Language cannot describe the beauty of such nights, and I could never sleep until the glorious light had ferreted out the shadows from every crevice and driven darkness from the cañon.

WOODY GUTHRIE

from *Seeds of Man* (1976)

MANUEL KICKED HIS SHOES OFF and pushed them under the army cot with a natural smile that came from the ringing of the boys' voices in his ears. He lowered his voice to a loud whisper to tell me, "I t'ink you name Woodachook? Sam't'ing lak?"

"'At's my monicker," I told him. "I aim t' take a look around t' see if I can locate a can er so of them there Vye-enna sausages that y' like sa good. I go see."

"No," Manuel whispered out. "Rio say he moosta see you. Now. Queecka. Atta the sundown. Savvy?"

"Where at?"

"De Rio Grande."

"Th' Ryoe Grandey? God sakes! Sun's already sunk down. I don't know how t' find no Ryoe Grandey. Which part?"

"Sheepa trail back de house. Rio meet opp weetha you where the trail cross ov'r

FRANK ARMSTRONG

goats road onna reever bank. Rio there now. You ron queeck. You back queeck. I save planty dry beef, planty sassaja for Rio, for you, also. Now ron."

I ran back to the truck, puffing, out of wind, saying, "I gotta run meet Rio, boys, over here'n some other house 'crost th' town. Go ahead, open up some dried beef, pork'n's, and some cream for th' coffee. Oh, Eddie, dig out a few of them cans of doggy sausages. Save some back for me 'n' Rio. Bye-bye."

I made both legs fly. I hit that sheep trail and every root and weed along it, and from the high side of a slope I got my skin whipped raw with some kind of a long, hard-tail cat-whisker grass. But I kept on, like Manuel told me; I outrun the sun going down.

Up, down, along, and around several ditches, low hills, through goat grasses, sheep bushes, seeds that stuck in my hair and shirt collar.

I hit a roily, rocky, uphill path that twisted over itself three or four times, till it carried me up above the little feathery treetops and I stopped to grab my breath at the spot where the path started down again. I saw a long, wide, shallow, ribbony stretch of water moving at a lazy gait down its mountains, down its valleys. I figured the downhill run wouldn't take my wind so bad, so I trotted down the path in a long, muley lope, flatfoot Indian style.

I ran in under the leaves of a few trees which had the blown cottony seeds I knew belonged to the cottonwood. I stopped once more to look under and partly behind several of the oversize, papery-soft cottonwoods that grew at the edge of a bluff a hundred feet or so over a pool of the Rio's bluest waters. I caught sight of several women, girls, babies, in the pool splashing and swimming back and forth. Their voices had a sharp echo and a clear sound as they laughed, pushed, splashed, and ducked one another down under the water. I could not see any clothes on any of them. I pulled my shirt wider open and hid behind the tree trunks to see the sights. I guess my eyes got so full of pretty swimmers that my memory went dog blank on me. I forgot the old truck. Forgot all about Papa, Jeff, Eddie, and that there ever did live by these waters and rocks a man as old as the weather itself, by that very same name, yes, Rio. Gold and silver mines slipped my senses. Pampa, wheat plains, oil fields, sheriffs' badges, guns, jails, money, sheep yonder, cattle rooting grass out from under flat hilltop rocks. Sun gone. Light still here. Just me. Me here. Just me here. Boy, what I wouldn't give, just to be able to get that little meaty maiden down there with that long handful of black curls waving down acrost her sunburnt shoulders. How come I had to meet up with you while I'm up here, hid out in back of this old cottonwood?

That long, stringy-bean one down there, with that pair of hard-set knockers, hair all piggytailed up around over her head there, long, loose, easy-swung, limbery legs, I might have more fun playing around with her, but I'd have to climb a packing crate to ever kiss her.

Great God Almighty Lord Jesus in the High Rock! Why did you ever hate this one of your sons enough to send me off down here away from Helly Cat Cliffman, and lose me here along these old bumpy rocks; and Lord, what made you stick all these old cactus grass blades, these old devilish thorny stickers, these old bullheads, these old skin itchers, these old brushy limbs, these old cottonwoods, in between this juicy pretty little piece of pussy meat yonder with her legs all spread out so wide apart on that mossy flatrock? Put me where that flatrock is, Lord, turn me into that moldy green moss. Set me closer, Dear Lord, closer, and then closer, closer, closer, till I'm close as I can ever get, and then take me, Lord, and smear me just one little froggy hair closer.

Trees and skies and sundown waters. And that little way her breasts move while she ducks her head and mouth down, and she laughs that way that echoes up and down my roots and tree leaves. Now she leans back on her hands and drags her foot up like a rock seat, bends her knee and crosses both legs and her curls rub on the rock moss.

Sundown swimmer. Water's daughter. Shady sand pool hid from men's eyes. I'm the only son to suffer here, to stand and kiss your tree bark and to dream this warm tree is you, but my tree can't spread its legs out and can't laugh that way you're laughing.

This feeling. It comes every time I get close to some girl I like real good. Warm-like, I guess, and blind, and dizzy, sort of blood kin to these tree vines, sorta tuned up to the berry patch, and shot full of this girl laughing.

"Thees ees where our two trails cross." I heard a voice somewhere at my back. I spun around on my heels and looked about. "Here. Over here. Do you see anyt'ing down there whicha you like?" The words drifted on the breeze, but I could not, to save me, find the spot they were coming from.

I recalled several stories about men that got killed for peep-tomming at Indian girls taking their daily baths. My neck got so tight it was hard for me to say a word. I did say, "Hmmm. Come on out."

"Gass who eet ees anda I weel walk out."

"Ole Man Rio," I laughed out.

"You right. I lose. I come." Rio's blanket hid him so well in the weaving clump of grass that my eyes could hardly see where he came out from. "I you slave. Say whata you wish, and Rio will get him and give him to your hands."

"'Tain't no him." I shook my head.

"No?" He walked over and patted my back. "Whatta could eet be, then, eef she ees not a him."

"She's a her."

"Oh. How far do I, Rio, have to walk to catch her for you, eh?"

"Not fer. She's real, real close." I pointed my finger around the cottonwood bark towards the river pool. "Right down yonder, see; take a free look."

"Mmmm." Rio looked down the slope. "I see de poola. I no see de she. You craze."

"I'm crazy? You're loco poconut." I motioned down at the rock pool. "Me craze? You craze. Look real close."

"You point. You show."

I pointed over his back as he squatted low and bent over to cover his eyes and to look. "I be dam-bern," I told Rio.

All of the women, girls, and babies were gone. The pool did not have even a wind ripple on it. It looked as quiet and still as Tuesday in the dead house. Gone. Took her toes and took her legs, and took her laugh, and gone. Curls went with her, I suppose. Wish I knew which way she went. That silly echo of her laughing still bounced around in my ears. That nice warm feeling, she took most of that with her when she left.

"Craze." I pointed to my temple.

"Eet eesa very bad."

MOLLY IVINS

"Mayor of Lajitas Not the Goat He Used to Be" (2002)

MARATHON—In the annals of West Texas law enforcement, few episodes rival the recent (well, relatively recent) unfortunate occurrence involving the major of Lajitas. As visitors to that border metropolis in the Big Bend are aware, the mayor of Lajitas is an alcoholic goat named Clay Henry.

The incumbent Mayor Henry is the third of his line, making this, we believe, the only democratically elected dynasty in the country. If you give the mayor a longneck bottle of beer, he'll swig it—just like most of his constituents. The Sober Party ran a canine against him in the last election, but it didn't have a dog's chance.

First thing one morning just a few months ago, Steve Houston, the county attorney, gets a call from Richard Hill, constable in Lajitas, announcing they're dealing with a serious situation: Someone castrated the mayor. A vet is en route at high speed from Alpine, but it's unclear whether the goat will live or not. Local feelings were running high against the perps. Some felt there was danger of a possible lynch mob. Constable Hill got right on it.

As it happened, there was a Mexican maid cleaning one of those houses in Lajitas owned by some rich guy who lives in Houston, and while cleaning the fridge, she finds a bag containing what could be the key pieces of evidence. Thinking nothing of it, she puts the evidence in the garbage, which goes to the Dumpster. But after hearing of the dastardly attack on the mayor, she reports the suspicious occurrence to the constable, who then heroically goes through the garbage in the Dumpster until he finds the evidence.

(We now pause for a point of border law enforcement that needs to be made more forcefully to the nincompoops at the Department of Justice in Washington. There is some pressure from up there for the local laws to get involved in immigration enforcement. The reason this is a terrible idea is because if calling 911 is the same as calling La Migra, illegal workers won't call to report crimes, leaving them even more vulnerable to human predators than they already are. The case of this upstanding non-citizen who found the mayor's privates is but one example of what wouldn't happen if the fools in Washington had their way. And now, back to the story.)

Further excellent law-enforcement work tracks down first the owner of the house and then the alleged perps, to whom he had loaned it for the weekend. The main alleged perp is from a nearby town with a bad reputation (not Terlingua), and this is where a certain class element enters the story.

The alleged perp and his friends had done some work for the absentee homeowner, who made his house available to them as a reward. On Sunday morning, they're drinking near the trading post and one of those rich guys who keep buying up Lajitas was showing around a lady (who might have been a movie star from Hollywood, according to some unreliable source)—and he wants to show her Clay Henry's talent with the bottle.

But it's Sunday a.m. with no beer for sale, so this rich guy asks the perps if he can get a beer from their stash, and they oblige. Then he takes their perfectly good greenbottle beer and gives it to the goat, which the alleged perp feels is an insult. Why he decided to take his revenge on the goat is unclear, except they were all pretty drunked up, according to several sources.

The perp is charged with torturing an animal and possession of a deadly weapon. County Attorney Houston and District Attorney Frank Brown tried to figure out a way to charge the guy with injury to a public official, which the Texas Legislature, naturally, has made into a crime that carries heavy time, but they couldn't get Clay Henry to fit the legal definition of "person."

Meantime, Clay Henry has recovered and is drinking again, heavily. Dan Carroll of Lajitas Resort told the *Alpine Avalanche*, "Clay Henry's health is fine now, although he obviously won't make a complete recovery."

JOHN SPONG

"Sand Trap" (2002)

THE DESERT SPORTS LOGO on the river guides' truck was scarcely visible through the gathering dust as we crawled to the ghost town at Terlingua after a day trip to Mariscal Canyon. It's a long drive even by Big Bend standards: two hours creeping over bone-dry washes, past ruins of sunbaked adobes that never had a chance, through a sea of scattered cactus, creosote bushes, and endless, merciless Texas. And that's just to get to the paved road that is itself another hour from Terlingua.

It's a measure of the people who choose to live out here—and it is always a conscious choice—that not once on such a drive will you hear anyone ask, "Are we there yet?"

The three Desert Sports guides in the truck that January afternoon shared that mind-set. The de facto honcho was Jim Carrico, the former superintendent of Big Bend National Park generally regarded as having made the destination great. Jack

Kinslow was along too, an Austin retailer who had decided to retire early and refuel in the ghost town instead of having a midlife crisis. Driving the truck was a small, wiry woman with a been-there, made-do-with-that manner who was identified only as Taz.

These folks don't mind a three-hour drive because frequently enough it's a trip like this one, from Mariscal's sheer 1,500-foot limestone walls to the porch outside the storefronts of the ghost town, where each afternoon the community's more refined element gathers to drink a cold beer and watch the sunset soak the western face of the Chisos. For locals, a long drive is like the months with no rain or the summer days when the thermometer hits 100 well before the clock strikes noon. It's simply what a West Texas sunset costs.

But while peace of mind might shoo away such pedestrian concerns as the time of day, that security is suddenly looking tenuous. Part of the desert rat's repose is knowing that people who don't love the desert don't come out here, but the real world is creeping closer than was ever thought possible. So the discussion in the truck turned, as does every conversation in West Texas these days, to Steve Smith and his plan to create the Southwest's most exclusive golf resort twelve miles west, in Lajitas.

Smith might be one of the few people ever to visit Big Bend and think it did not look enough like the Lakeway resort outside Austin. He was a savior when he bought this ramshackle resort two years ago, keeping the third leg of the Study Butte-Terlingua-Lajitas puebloplex (population: 300) from falling into the hands of a California hotelier. But then his construction site grew to look like war-torn Afghanistan, with great plumes of dust rising over the desolate hills.

Rumors reached Final Conflict proportions: He was building a new runway for Southwest Airlines, a casino across the river, and horror of horrors, cell phone towers. When the unofficial mayor of Lajitas, a beer-drinking goat named Clay Henry, became the unlucky recipient of a back-alley castration last November, the scuttlebutt was that an irate local had nailed the bloody cojones to the clubhouse door at the golf course as a message to Smith. An alternative explanation had Smith emasculating the goat to send out a message of his own. Neither of these stories was true, but Smith was moving too fast to dispel them. Since the Desert Sports folks knew I'd spent the previous day with Smith, they wanted to hear the truth. It was just as amazing.

Smith and company are spending like the Clampetts: $40 million to date, $40 million more this year, all in cash dollars. They are building two eighteen-hole golf courses, a 25,000-square-foot clubhouse, and a 32,000-square-foot spa. An outdoor amphitheater that can seat three thousand people is already finished, and a world-class restaurant that will spotlight desert game is almost done. Smith plans seven hundred homes, the high end on two-acre lots that will sell for $1 million apiece.

"Who's going to spend all that money to build in the desert?" asked Carrico.

"I asked Smith's adman that," I replied. "He's Tim McClure, the M in GSD&M. He says, 'All it's going to take is one person with major league Hollywood credentials or major league sports credentials, and it'll all be over. If Tom Cruise or Tiger Woods goes out there and plays golf, he'll fall in love with the place, and it'll all be over.'"

Taz shook her head as the truck pitched forward. Carrico kept firing away like he was working on a bucket of range balls, something he admittedly had never felt the urge to do. "Did he say whether people with major league credentials would mind living across the highway from an RV park?"

"He says there is no more RV park. The first thing he told Smith was, 'Steve, you don't have an RV park. You have Maverick Ranch.'"

"Maverick Ranch?"

"Yeah. He says the people who will buy slips in that park aren't like the rest of us. They're 'mavericks,' spending their twilight years crisscrossing the country in half-a-million-dollar motor homes, just playing golf and living."

"And the slips are supposed to cost $100,000 apiece?"

"To start. They'll end up as high as $175,000."

And that's just the beginning. Maverick Ranch will have a pond stocked for fishing. There's talk of a small recording studio and plans to honor the mayor—who recovered from his unelective surgery, by the way—by selling Clay Henry Bock beer. The restaurant will sell a line of sauces and dressings, and the spa will market its own beauty and skin-care products made from native plants.

That was all Taz could take. Keeping one hand on the wheel and one foot on the gas, she turned all the way around to face me. It was of no concern that she wasn't watching the road; there's not much to run into in the desert. But there was a crazed look in her eyes.

"What the hell are you talking about?" she asked. "Lajitas mud packs made with real Rio Grande mud? Are they absolutely nuts?"

"Careful, Taz," I said. "McClure's in love with this project. He said, 'If I had the money, I'd go out there and buy *Terling-you-a*.'"

She looked like she was going to come over the seat and get me. "He called it '*Terling-you-a*'?"

"Some people say this is just going to be a second ghost town," Smith had said the previous afternoon on the patio of his home. "They say, 'Smith's going to build this party, and nobody's going to come.' What will happen if they're right? I kind of tongue-in-cheek tell them, 'Well, at least me and my friends will have a really nice golf course to play.'"

He was overlooking the resort, watching his dream come together, the grass trying to green on the course, the bulldozers and the backhoes making room for the spa and clubhouse. Here stood Smith as plaid-and-khaki land baron, short and stout, with a patron's gray mustache and a dream to turn the desert into a billionaire's playground. But as he lazily pulled a mouthful of vodka from a tall glass of Grey Goose and ice, he gazed out over his empire with a distinct, look-where-I've-landed wonderment.

The Legend of Steve Smith has him selling strings of dried chile peppers by the highway outside Austin in the mid-eighties. During the months when profits didn't keep pace with bills, his wife, Sarah, would sneak their two kids into public swimming pools at night to bathe them. By the mid-nineties he'd amassed a fortune of nearly $1 billion, all by dint of a winning personality and a multilevel marketing plan. The company he helped build, Excel Communications, sold long-distance service, but the moneymaker was Smith's Amway-style sales model, a pyramid and a product.

It was one of the fastest companies ever to reach $1 billion in annual sales, and at its peak, the top sales rep made more than $1.5 million a month. Smith got a cut of every transaction.

He purchased Lajitas on a whim in February 2000. He had seen an ad for the auction of the resort—a nine-hole golf course, hotel, Old West boardwalk, and RV park on 22,000 acres—in *Millionaire* magazine and decided on the morning of the sale to make an appearance. Forty-five minutes before the auction opened in the Lajitas saloon, he arrived by helicopter and took a seat in a tall wing chair at the front of the room that prevented the spectators from seeing his face.

He outbid a San Francisco hotel magnate for a sale price of $4.25 million and, to the further relief of the locals, promised that very little would change.

Sometime thereafter he developed his vision. "When I bought this place, I had absolutely no idea what I was going to do," he said. "I thought I'd dress the existing nine-hole course up a bit, so I got a golf course designer out here. By the time he was through working me over, we had a whole new championship course with wall-to-wall Bermuda and then a whole other course to go with it."

Later that summer, he decided he needed another attraction. "I thought that if we built a little spa here, it could be a family affair," he said. "There'd be a spa for the ladies and a pool for the kids, while the guys all played golf."

Again, consultants re-imagined his modest spa and clubhouse as the palaces now under construction. Then the scale had to explode. "There's no place in the U.S. that's as hard to get to as Lajitas," he said. "We were driven to attract people who had the means to come to a very private place, meaning they had to own or have access to their own aircraft."

Meaning also $1 million lots, $175,000 RV slips, $250-a-night hotel rooms, an equestrian center, a hunting lodge, and whatever Smith thinks of next. The big lure

JAMES EVANS

for those who could afford it would be that no one else could. The ball was rolling on what Smith now called the Ultimate Hideout.

~

IT DIDN'T TAKE LONG for a homemade koozie reading "The Ultimate High Doubt" to appear, but that was no surprise. Terlinguans had derided "Lahideous" for years, two communities distinguishable not so much as the haves and the have-nots but as the resourced and the resourceful. Thirty years ago it was common to see desert rat foursomes walking improvised links just off Texas Highway 118 near Study Butte, each duffer with a couple of clubs and a sheet of AstroTurf. Drop the Turf, place the ball, give it a ride, track it down, repeat. Desert golf.

Country club golf, complete with real country club grass, came to the region in

1978, not long after Houston real estate mogul and kingmaker Walter Mischer purchased a vast stretch of land around the little U.S. cavalry outpost known as Lajitas. Back then, the area contained little more than barrack ruins, an old church, and a trading post. Mischer dreamed of Palm Springs, Texas, but he never figured out how to sell golfers on a course where it was too hot to play five months out of the year. By the nineties he had turned management over to his kids and grandkids. The desert had all but reclaimed Lajitas by the time Smith rode into town.

Terlingua's cynics watched him with a wary eye, keeping score on the porch while the desert punished his early missteps. More than one hundred trees transplanted last April didn't make it through summer. Bermuda sprigs planted in October and again in February—read: the golf course—browned twice with winter freezes. They complained that Smith would close the traditional, unofficial border crossing from his land over to Paso Lajitas, preventing some fifteen kids living in Paso from legally attending school in Study Butte. (Smith said he would close the crossing only to vehicular traffic; the $2 boat ride that tourists took across and the "school boat" that ferried the kids each day would continue. But that was before the advent of Homeland Security.)

What seldom got mentioned were things Smith did right, like the way he relocated his new runway because flight patterns could have threatened the peregrine falcon habitat in Santa Elena Canyon. Little was made too of all the people he was employing from both sides of the border, the baseball field for kids he was building near Study Butte, and the $34,000 check he wrote to the Terlingua school-library fund. Of course, many of his moves were to protect his investment, like securing a medical clinic and an EMS service he would need to get rich folks to visit him, but he promised to keep them affordable to the community.

Nothing, though, could have split open the cultural divide like the issue of water. Since last Thanksgiving Smith has sprayed 750,000 gallons of it a day on his golf course. For people who rely on water-catchment systems on their roof, that may sound obnoxious, but for people with wells connected to the same water supply, it's downright scary.

Smith is not worried. "We had a lot of hydrogeological work done, and it in effect says that we're sitting over our own aquifer," he said. His reports project that annual rainfall will return 6,400 acre-feet of water to the aquifer Smith shares with Terlingua and northern Mexico. Smith's most liberal estimates for a full seven-hundred-home development require around 3,400 acre-feet.

Brewster County officials, however, are not convinced. They say that rainfall during the current ten-year drought has been half of what Smith projects. Furthermore, they think only one percent of that—not Smith's ten percent—will recharge the aquifer, producing just 320 acre-feet a year. Both the county and the national park are looking for money to conduct full studies of their own.

In the meantime, there are checks on what Smith can do. County judge Val Beard says Smith will need to show proof of a thirty-year water supply before the county commissioners' court will say grace over his first subdivision plats, and her husband, Tom, will want similar assurances as the head of the county's new water conservation district. Under rules adopted in March, the district will determine if Lajitas' usage leaves enough water to sustain the rest of the area. To Smith's credit, his right-hand man, Richard Hubble, put meters on the Lajitas wells to gauge depletion long before the district required them, and Smith offered to pay for the same on the Terlingua municipal well to ensure that Lajitas isn't draining Terlingua's supply.

But the critics keep coming. Tony Fallin, a lifelong visitor to the area, is the hydrogeologist Smith gives primary credit for finding his water, but Fallin has jumped ship. After quitting Smith a year ago, he took up residence near the ghost town in a cinderblock structure with "Passing Wind" written on a sign over the gate, from where he mailed out two- and three-thousand-word handwritten diatribes to Hubble, government officials, and the press at least once a week. The letters typically began with declarations like "The pigs are coming home to roost!" Although he stands by his estimate that the aquifer is the size of "a small Lake Erie," he has halved his recharge projections to reflect the current drought. More to the point, he can't abide Lajitas' taking such a disproportionate share of the water—least of all for something with as little place in the desert as an oasis golf course.

One of Smith's measures that has actually been applauded in the community is the creation of a 64-acre bird sanctuary on and around an island in the river. To fashion it he cleared thousands of the dreaded salt cedar trees, the non-native scourge of the park that sucks nearly three hundred gallons of river water a day per tree. Smith estimates that the salt cedar removal has returned a million gallons of water to the river daily, and the mature cottonwoods he planted in their place have already attracted a whole bunch of birds, quietly pleasing area birders.

But what the desert taketh away, it can give back in a hurry. Locals say violent flash floods rage down the Rio Grande every ten years or so, and without the salt cedar to hold down the island or sufficient time for the cottonwoods to root, one such storm could carry the bird sanctuary and a large section of golf course all the way to Boquillas Canyon. If that happens, park officials worry not only that the course's structures and trees will collect in tight spots on the river but also that fertilizer and exotic plants will affect the ecological balance in the park. The cottonwoods will root in two to five years. The next ten-year flood was due last year. Smith has no answer for that scenario but to pick up the mess and rebuild.

SMITH GAVE NO REAL TIMETABLE for moving people in, which may indicate he's becoming aware of the desert's limitations. A golf event to be televised nationally in
June has been pushed back, hopefully no further than to the fall. The grass should be
in by then. He has taken "reservations" on just one slip in Maverick Ranch and four
of the smaller lots across the highway from where he'd put Tiger and Tom, but sales
can't be finalized until the plats for those areas are approved by the county. The
Maverick Ranch plat was approved in late March, but Smith won't even apply for the
subdivision plats until this summer.

Smith does talk about an overall eight-to-ten-year process, after which he hopes
to step down and play golf while the community runs itself. And if his billionaires
decide 100 degrees is not a bearable, dry heat? "We're not really anticipating what'll
happen if this doesn't work," he said. "We're focusing on what we have planned.
That's the only way I know how to do things."

"It's weird that such nice people have created such dissonance," said a neighbor of
Smith's, Collie Ryan. She has been a squatter in Lajitas for twenty years, living without electricity or water in a gutted school bus near what is now Smith's spa site. She
supports herself by selling hubcaps that she paints with intricate Native American
designs and works on a patio she created with rocks she carried to her little oasis. It's
a quirky, beautiful spot, typical of the whole of Big Bend: You either feel immediately
at home or you miss your air conditioning.

Smith told her last year that she could stay on his property as long as she wanted,
so she has positioned herself as a go-between for the developer and the desert. "Right
now," Ryan said, "it's two camps: the quote 'nature lovers' and the quote 'nature
haters,' us 'poor folks' and them 'rich boogers.' The water process with the county
should awaken the 'we.' It'll increase Smith's understanding of our resources, limit his
ability to act, and force him to communicate. Maybe then some of us who love
nature so much can teach them to appreciate it too, which will be good. The richer
you are, the more you need this place."

Ryan views it all with some ambivalence. On the one hand, she says she can hear
the salt cedar cry when they are ripped from the earth. On the other, she looks
forward to selling a couple extra $125 hubcaps a month to Smith's high-rolling friends
once the construction is done.

PART 5

I GREW UP AT A DISTANCE and remove from the Rio Grande. The big river that ran through the country of my youth was the Red, and the strange other place beyond it was just Oklahoma. Prowling the red light districts of Mexican border towns was supposed to be a rite of passage for boys from Texas. For youths in my hometown, the closest Mexican bordello was 400 miles through the grassland and mesquites, almost a straight shot south. Across the river from Del Rio, Ciudad Acuña was then known, before an apparent gain in population, as Villa Acuña—officially a village, not a city. Or to yahoos like myself, it was simply "Coon-yah." The cars would go zooming through the chaparral over a rise and then at the bottom of a dun valley the drunk and hooting boys would see the border towns and the river's narrow but lovely string of trees, laid out like young limbs for the taking. Beyond the river, damn, was Old Mexico. God help those whores.

As a boy I never made it to a Boys' Town across the Rio Grande. It wasn't a matter of scruples; my friends and I never had a car in those days that would reliably make a round trip of 800 miles. My first brush with people from Mexico came when I was past thirty. I was living in the Hill Country west of Austin on the Paisano Ranch of J. Frank Dobie, which has been made into a fine retreat for aspiring writers. It was the first time I had experienced rural living since my grandparents retired to town from a cotton farm. I worked in the mornings then ran a couple of miles to the mailbox with my collie, and on warm days walked back and cooled off with a plunge in a clear-running creek. I had my first hair-raising encounter with a coiled and glaring rattlesnake, planted my first garden, and read a couple of Dobie's books. Then I read John Graves's *Hard Scrabble*, his reflections on his own special place and somewhat working cattle ranch. I particularly enjoyed a chapter of droll "fictions" about undocumented workers that he called "Helpers." Graves wrote: "In pairs and threes and fours most usually they come, following various underground-railway routes they know or have been told of, or cast up in our hills by some concatenation of accidents. South Texas close to Mexico has far more than does our neighborhood, but the wages they get there are lower too and there is always among them a sort of hydraulic pressure northward, Chicago being for some reason a legendary El Dorado, seldom reached . . . " He wrote that usually there was an older man who had gone north before, often another man hanging back while he talked, and then a boy. The expression Graves used was *mojados*, wet ones. It occurred to me while reading his book that to my knowledge I had never met an honest-to-god wetback.

A cool front had blown through with a rain, and then the skies cleared. I was starting the bright morning's work in Dobie's front room when a ruckus erupted in the kitchen. My dog was sure after something; I hoped it wasn't a snake. I came through the house tentatively, and found standing outside the back door three dark-skinned men, glances intent upon the collie. It was as if they had walked right out of Graves's book! I got the dog calmed down and ushered them inside, jabbering—set about frying them bacon and eggs. They must have thought I was daft. It was a crisp morning, and they all had colds. The older two were mestizos, and the boy had the stony features of an Indian. He wore jeans and a tattered shirt and jacket and, of all things, a Davy Crockett coonskin cap. Only it was dyed bright indigo. He had turned it around smartly, so that the raccoon's tail hung past his ear and jaw.

The oldest one did all the talking. He remarked that a pretty river ran near my house, and I agreed. I asked him where they came from. "Guanajuato," he replied.

"How did you get here?" I asked in my faltering Spanish. He swallowed eggs and toast and on the table made the sign of walking with his index and middle fingers.

"You *walked* from Guanajuato?" I said. It was close to 800 miles.

"Yes."

"Where did you cross?"

"Piedras Negras," he replied—the border town meaning Black Rocks, whose Texas sister is Eagle Pass. "We came to San Antonio, but there was no work. Someone said we should go to Johnson City. Do you know the way to Johnson City?"

I nodded and pointed west toward the hometown of Lyndon Johnson. "How far?" he asked.

I calculated in kilometers and said, "Sesenta," sixty.

"Aieee," they said in pained unison, except for the boy. The collie had sat down at his feet, and they were staring at each other.

The oldest *mojado* asked if I had any work for them, and I told him I was sorry, but I didn't. I didn't know what to do with them. Finally I dumped the skillet and their plates in the sink and grabbed a jacket. I could at least find people who could carry on a conversation with them. I drove them to the barrio on Austin's east side. As the immigration laws were then written, I later learned, I was committing a serious crime just by giving them a ride. When I let them out on Chicon Street I said, "Buena suerte," good luck, and extended a five-dollar bill to the oldest one. He gave me a look like I was insane and snatched it.

I couldn't think of any way to express my thoughts in Spanish, so I pointed at the Indian kid and blurted in English. "The boy," I said. "Tell him to get rid of that hat. They're not worn here. He's going to get you caught."

~

ANOTHER DAY, seventeen years later, I was struck again by how I had grown up knowing so little about the peoples and cultures on and beyond the Rio Grande. I sat in the parking lot of a shopping center in Eagle Pass. Eric Fredlund, an anthropologist who had befriended the Kickapoo Indians, was taking me to Nacimiento, the Mexican reservation and adopted holy land of the small border tribe. Fredlund had gone inside a store to buy some sunglasses and cigarettes, leaving me in a Chevy Blazer with Joe Hernandez, our driver, guide, and translator. Joe, whose Kickapoo name is Ta-Pe-A-ah, was 23 then, five feet ten with thick broad shoulders, a laborer's build. He wore boots, jeans, a cap, and sunshades that masked a large shy face. There is a Lake Kickapoo in the part of Texas where I grew up, and, just to break the silence, I asked Joe if he knew the place. He looked back over the seat and replied quietly, "No. We're kind of allergic to lakes."

I blinked and asked him what he meant. "When I was a kid," he said, "I used to drive up to Del Rio a lot, to that big lake there, Amistad. But my dad told me he didn't want me going up there. That lake, it makes big rains."

I mused on the cryptic remark as we crossed the Rio Grande and drove south from Piedras Negras into the Coahuilan chaparral. Allergic to lakes?

The Kickapoo came from the Great Lakes; they speak Algonquian and still tell stories of French explorers who found them around Lake Michigan in the early 1600s. Their migration to the borderlands of Texas and Mexico—which made them citizens of two nations— is one of the most remarkable odysseys in North American history, and they undertook it to sustain a religion and way of life that abounds with supernatural beings and events.

Yet Texans know the Kickapoo—if they know them at all—as a poverty-stricken people who for decades lived as squatters under the Rio Grande bridge at Eagle Pass. (Since 1987 they have occupied a bleak 123-acre reservation on the outskirts of town, nestled against a bend of the river.) They are footnotes in a Texas frontier lore dominated by Comanches, Apaches, and Cherokees; it is a common belief today that Texas has just two tribes, the Alabama-Coushatta of the Big Thicket and the Tigua in El Paso. Yet the Kickapoo have played a lively role in Texas history, and their culture is arguably more intact than that of the better-known tribes. In anthropological circles, the Kickapoo have a reputation as the most unassimilated tribe in the contiguous United States. Along the border one sees them driving pickups, wearing shades, listening to country or rap music, but even in those moments they perceive a spiritual world to which most of us are blind.

I had been reading a monograph Fredlund was drafting about his work with the Kickapoo. "One informant told me of an incident," he wrote, "that occurred when he was traveling in the Midwest in a pickup truck with an elderly male relative. In the distance they saw a tornado heading in their direction at a high rate of speed. The man instructed him to stop the truck and get out quickly. The old man then said a prayer to the 'grandfather' who *was* the tornado. The funnel cloud rose off the ground and passed over their heads, returning to earth a half mile beyond where they stood, and resumed its path of destruction. The older man explained that there is no reason for a Kickapoo man to fear a tornado provided one is in harmony with the nature and spirits of the grandfathers and knows how to get the latter's attention."

The troubles of contemporary Kickapoo are legion, but in the view of tribal elders and administrators, two in particular imperil their existence as a distinct culture. Deer hunting is a sacrament among the Kickapoo; in their religion a father cannot baptize and bestow a tribal name on an infant unless he can contribute to the rite four slain deer. The animals are scarce at Nacimiento, their Mexican preserve, and rare as polar bears on their U.S. reservation, downriver from Eagle Pass. Mexican law tries to accommodate their need, though game regulations and posting of private property there have recently grown more restrictive, and in Texas the dual constraints are unrelenting. Few Kickapoo earn more than $7,000 a year, and even if they could afford a private hunting lease, babies are born year-round, not just in the state's autumn hunting season. They would get caught poaching and fined $500, to them an impossible sum, so they worked it off on county road gangs. What else were they going to do? Let their children go nameless?

The second crisis, addiction, threatened to do what 350 years of hardship could not: extinguish the traditional Kickapoo way of life from the earth. Like many Native Americans, the Kickapoo seem incapable of moderate social drinking; their elected council forbids consumption of alcohol on both reservations, though of course that doesn't solve the problem. But the intoxicant that terrified the elders was common spray paint. About 450 people were legal members of the Texas Kickapoo tribe. At least 80, most of them adults, were addicted to paint fumes. Fredlund worked for the state, but part of his assignment was to write a grant proposal on the Kickapoo's behalf to the federal Center for Substance Abuse Treatment. His proposal had won a five-year, $2.6 million grant that made Eric a celebrated figure among the Kickapoo.

As we drove by power plants and coal mines and the Sierra Madres came into view, Joe Hernandez readily shared his experience with the anthropologist. He told us of his own addiction when he was twelve and thirteen. Nothing mattered to him but the visions brought on by the paint. He once saw his father looming tall as a giant. He likened other hallucinations to the flickering, jerky effect of dancers under a strobe light, and there were sounds as well—he could hear his blood racing, his heart was a drum. "Every day, every day," he said with a sigh. "You don't want to do nothing else. I wouldn't eat, and I kept getting caught by my parents. Even now when I smell paint, I still want to do it. But I had to quit. I didn't want to lose my dad."

On the rough gravel road that leads to Nacimiento, solvent abuse seemed even more of an aberration, something absurd and far away. The air was very clear, and above the light green mesquite and huisache foliage, the Sierra Madres rose in subtly varied shades of cobalt blue. They spread in an arc around us, but the succeeding wedges looked almost equidistant, packed into a vertical plane. I had never seen mountains quite like them. Joe spoke happily of going off on horseback on hunts of several weeks' duration and bringing back bear, turkey, and the deer that granted him the favor of naming his two small children. I remarked on a striking arrangement of peaks toward the west. Joe glanced at them and mystified me again. "We can't go over there," he said. "There's lots of big cats." Later I read in an anthropology book about the Kickapoo that large wild cats carry a strong taboo. Joe's explanation was less esoteric. "They make bad winds."

~

AT NACIMIENTO a Kickapoo spiritual leader who was in his eighties related in droll fashion the encounter that changed Kickapoo life forever: "The first white people we met were French. We traded them deer hides and they said, 'Ah, these are very good hides.' Then they asked us for a small place to sleep."

For the next 200 years the Kickapoo were constantly at war. They fought the French and simultaneously fought their tribal enemies, the Iroquois, who came at them from the east, and the Sioux, who attacked from the west. The made peace with the French and helped them fight the English. After the American Revolution, they fought the settlers and soldiers of the United States. As a warring people they once besieged Detroit, were ferocious allies of the Ottawa chief Pontiac, and were among the losers of the Battle of Tippecanoe. Exhausted, they signed a peace treaty in 1819 and consented to forced removal from their northern homeland to a reservation in southeast Missouri. But they didn't like that place, and for most of the nineteenth century they resisted the swallowing giant called America by fleeing it southward. They left bands of themselves in Kansas and Oklahoma, but they were gypsies of the plains. They were unlike the tribes they moved among. They greatly preferred deer to buffalo as prey, and though they valued horses as an improvement over walking, they never made horsemanship into a martial and material culture. Nor did they fear the fierce horse and buffalo peoples. Around Nacogdoches, Spain (and later Mexico) set up the Kickapoo as a military buffer against "wild tribes." When Texas gained independence, it pressured all Indians to leave the republic and then the state. South of the Rio Grande, the Kickapoo again enlisted as protectors from the raids of Comanches and Apaches, and in gratitude Mexico gave them 17,000 acres at the foot of the Sierra Madres in 1852.

The antipathy between the Kickapoo and Texans continued to be mutual and brutal. In 1865 a troop of Texas Rangers and Confederate soldiers attacked a Mexico-bound party of Kickapoo at Dove Creek, near San Angelo, and got themselves roundly thrashed. Still, fifteen Kickapoo deaths in that battle triggered a war of vengeance against Texans that lasted until 1873. U.S. general Phil Sheridan temporarily pulled Colonel Ranald Mackenzie and his cavalry troops away from their pursuit of the Comanches and Kiowas in North Texas. Without consulting Mexico on the matter, Sheridan sent the troops across the Rio Grande against the Kickapoo with the reputed orders: "Let it be a campaign of annihilation, obliteration, and complete destruction." After that bloodshed, more Kickapoo were coerced into Oklahoma residence; they agreed to go as long as the route bypassed Texas.

The next generation of Kickapoo living in Mexico suffered at the hands of Pancho Villa and other Mexican revolutionaries. Still, at long last they were where they wanted to be. Kickapoo might have never again intruded much on Texas if not for a calamitous drought that began in 1944 and lasted seven years. At Nacimiento they had no water except for barely trickling springs. Their wheat crops failed, their cattle starved, and the mountains nearby were largely hunted out. Though Mexico had been generous with loyalty and land, it offered neither jobs nor government assistance. So the Kickapoo became migrant farmworkers—and the lowly and despised of Eagle Pass.

In a way they lived as they always had. They clung to their language, returned to Nacimiento for the spring holy season, celebrated ultrasecretive rites of spring renewal, then divided into kinship groups for the year's economic production. But instead of hunting, now the young and able-bodied weeded sugar beet fields in Montana and Wyoming and picked cherries in Utah, and harvested apples and onions in Colorado. Later they found the approach could be applied to work caused by spring storms; they are able roofers. Until they moved to their reservation in 1987, the staging ground for the annual treks was the long floodplain under the Rio Grande bridge at Eagle Pass, where they built wickiups, but not with the cattail reeds and finely detailed craft of their ceremonial houses at Nacimiento. As if to acknowledge their transience and diminished state, they cobbled the domed structures together with plywood and tarp. They had no water, sewage, or privacy. People hurled down insults and trash.

W. D. SMITHERS

ABOUT TEN MILES OFF THE PAVED ROAD that winds from the foot of the Sierra Madres to Big Bend, Joe Hernandez steered his Blazer through a tiny wan village. The Kickapoo preserve lay across a tree-lined Rio Grande tributary called the Sabinas, which could only be crossed at a rocky ford. Nacimiento, which in Spanish means birthplace, was several hundred yards beyond the crossing. There were some houses of gray cinderblock in the Kickapoo enclave, but the dominant architecture was the traditional loaf-shaped wickiups made of the cattail reeds. People were strolling, chatting in groups, sitting on straw cots under the shade of their summer porches—a scene of leisure. As the day wore on, I could understand how the Kickapoo hold such land holy. Under oak-forested mountains cut with dramatic rock cliffs, the village sat beside the clear-running stream we had forded. Its fountainhead emerged from a jumble of smooth white rocks amid thick and towering trees. As Joe and I strolled through the bottom, a tanager swooped past us. I asked him if they had a name for their sacred stream. "No," he said. "We just call it River."

Like many in the tribe, Joe has had no formal schooling, yet he has learned to read and write a little, and is fluent in three languages (he is least confident in English). "I was always with my dad, learning the tradition," he told me. "But then I found out about money. I know now I was supposed to be going to school."

Nacimiento had no water pipes or sewage systems, though Mexican officials were encouraging the tribe to start selling water meters. A clock and small refrigerator in the Hernandez family's flat-roofed concrete house testified to the arrival of electricity that year. Joe said that his dad was a boy when the lines and poles were first promised. "I respect them for doing it," he said nonetheless. The walls were decorated with family photos and a wanted poster of a woman accused of defrauding the Kickapoo. Joe showed us his family's most prized material possession, an 1894 model lever-action .30-30 Winchester rifle. Outside, we examined their wickiup, and in a small fenced pasture walked among gaunt horses and a mule. Joe affectionately rubbed the neck of a palomino gelding named Flaco, which means Skinny. He asked if I wanted to ride his hunting horse. I told him it would be a pleasure.

But we never got the tack out because Joe's dad drove up in an old red Ford pickup. Eric had been trying to acquaint me with the mysteries of tribal kinship and had told me to watch for the change in Joe's manner when he was around his father. He grew quiet and seemed wary of looking at his dad closely and directly, even as they talked. Jose Hernandez had an immense head and a thick shock of gray hair. He spoke only Kickapoo and Spanish.

Jose was a member of the Traditional Council of elected leaders, and as we talked in Spanish with our forearms resting on the rails of his pickup, he picked up a can of processed meat in the truck bed and revolved it in his hands. After a while he chuckled, handed it to me, and gestured at the label. Canned in Denmark, it was routed toward the Kickapoo by a hunger relief agency of the United Nations. Jose said he worried most about the hunting. "We have no books," he said. "Our customs are all in our heads." All the negotiations and entreaties he described were directed at Mexican officials; I asked him if the tribe had tried to communicate with anyone public or private in Texas, where overpopulations of whitetail deer are a widespread problem. He looked skeptical and said he wouldn't know how to begin. As we left, I told Jose that I hoped I saw him again. "Ojalá!" he replied: May God grant.

~

IT SEEMED THAT MY FIRST EXPOSURE to the Kickapoo and their home in the Sierra Madres would end on that tranquil note—but it was not to be. The next morning, Eric and I emerged from our motel rooms in Múzquiz, a pleasant town on the main highway not far from Nacimiento, and found Joe waiting in the car. With him now was a strapping young man named Fernando, his friend since childhood. Fernando prefaced his replies to almost all our remarks with a soft, musically phrased, "Well, I don' know." Fernando was drinking beer and soon passed out in the front seat. We left him there and went into a roadside cantina, where we bought soft drinks. Inside, some Mexican men in ranching attire greeted Joe warmly, inquired about his father, and invited us to join them at their table. One of the men was a former mayor of Múzquiz. When Joe brought up the problem with deer hunting, the man replied carefully, with a politician's aplomb. "This is a matter of law, just like in the United States." As we stood to leave, the man suggested gently to Joe that he might want to check on some Kickapoo who were up the road a way.

About a dozen men were passing the time and bottles of sugarcane liquor in a shaded bar ditch; they had a nice view of the Sierra Madres. As Fernando dozed on and Joe grinned at their jests—they took pleasure in reminding him of a Comanche in his bloodline—Eric and I took seats on the ground among them and discreetly tried to decline the quart bottle making the rounds. But it wasn't easy: refusing to drink with them was deemed a pejorative act. Finally I relented and took a swallow. The stuff was sweet and terrifically strong. The man next to me was not appeased. He had a dark pitted face, and his eyes kept coming back to mine. "My name is Dave," he said, with apparent reference to some past slight. "Don't call me Chief."

"Pleased to meet you, Dave."

"Dave," he emphasized. "Don't ever call me Chief."

Most of the men lived among the Oklahoma Kickapoo. They hold Nacimiento sacred, too, and often move back and forth between McCloud and Eagle Pass. "These are my uncles," Joe explained, turning up the bottle for the first time.

It came back to me that for the convenience of outsiders, Kickapoo lump a great number of male relatives into the term "uncle." If an uncle asks you for a gift, you can't refuse him. I recalled this with a sinking sensation when they asked Joe to drive into Múzquiz and fetch them several more bottles of cane liquor. Fernando's head fell back as Joe lurched away in the Blazer. His *uncles* made him do it.

A little old man whom they called Coni eased forward and went to sleep with his head on the shin of a younger fellow. As if in a slow-motion topple of dominos, that man turned and slumped until his cheek was lying in the dirt. A string of drool leaked from his mouth and in time formed a small cone of mud. As my gaze fastened on this, another man sought to reassure us, or perhaps himself. "I just do this ever' once in a while," he said. "For the good times."

One whose name was Fidel wasn't buying that. Fidel fixed on me a stare of immense sadness and said: "I been doing this since 1975. I lost my house, I lost my wife. I lost everything. I gotta get straight."

As the bottle continued round, Eric leaned over and murmured a witticism of treatment-speak: "This is a novel kind of needs assessment."

I expect my smile was a little tight. We were deep in a foreign country, and we were starting off the day in a ditch full of drunk Indians!

Joe rolled up then, flung the door open, and strode toward us with two paper sacks filled with quart bottles. Joe turned the first one up and held it skyward for a long time. "I love these peoples," he said, and almost fell.

Eric finally convinced Joe that we had to go, and coaxed the keys away from him. He navigated Múzquiz, but on the way down we hadn't paid much attention to landmarks. There were no highway signs in the towns, and soon we were lost. I asked some kids on the road if they knew the way to Texas; they shrieked with laughter.

We parked in front of a store, trying to regain our composure. Fernando woke up with a jerk, shook his head, slapped his face, and took command of the situation. "I don' wan' you to think we drink like this all the time," he said in his soft singsong accent, and set out for home at ninety miles an hour. Joe was aware enough to feel badly about what had happened. In apology he offered Eric the gift of his dog, and dug in his wallet until he found its vaccination papers. Fernando firmly gripped the wheel and hardly spoke or glanced as trucks on the narrow highway soughed past. Eric looked at me with a wild grin. "They can really drive, can't they!"

STEPHEN HARRIGAN

"Highway One," from *Comanche Midnight* (1995)

THE LINES ON THE MAP reminded me of an erratic riverbed, constantly meandering and shifting, a series of braided channels that ultimately led to the same destination. Each variant of the braid had its own name: the Upper Presidio Road, the Lower Presidio Road, the Camino Pita, the Camino de los Tejas, the Camino Arriba. The reason for this web of routes is easy to understand. In its early existence the road was a faint track, hardly more than a suggestion. Almost every expedition that used it found a way to improve upon it. Over time the travelers discovered more-efficient river crossings or routes that would help them skirt natural obstacles such as El Atascosa, the boggy alluvial plain south of San Antonio, or the dense forest—El Monte—near present-day Bastrop, under whose gloomy canopy the Spanish soldiers tended to grow anxious and disoriented. It is believed that when the Apaches, pressured by the Comanches to the north, began to raid below the Hill Country, the road looped south into the less hospitable brushland to avoid them.

BUT ALL THE ROUTES began in the same place, at a frontier outpost known as San Juan Bautista that sat in a pecan glade on the south bank of the Rio Grande. At the time the Camino Real was created, San Juan Bautista was nothing more than a remote settlement built around a mission and the presidio that guarded it. Over time, however, it became a major staging area for the royal expeditions that filtered up to the unknown lands of Texas.

The town that grew up around San Juan Bautista is called Guerrero and is enthrallingly old. I drove there one day in late spring, crossing the border at Eagle Pass, driving through Piedras Negras, and heading about thirty miles east into the Mexican state of Coahuila. In mid-afternoon, the streets and square of Guerrero were empty, and the town had the echoing stillness of a stopped clock. There were no sounds except those that might have been heard here three hundred years ago—the creaky calls of Chihuahuan ravens, the crowing of roosters, the noise of the wind rushing through the pecan leaves overhead. The parade ground of the old presidio had become the town square, and many of the ancient buildings from Spanish colonial times—the presidio captain's house, the paymaster's house—were not only still standing but still in use. Some of the houses now had modern stucco fronts, but along their sides I could see the bare walls of stacked stone, the mortar long since eroded away.

Other structures were vacant and half fallen-in. I chose one and walked inside. Most of the roof had collapsed, and the floor was a weedy mass of rubble and broken bottles. The house had been unused for so long that a large tree had grown inside of it, though in an adjoining room the old roof beams were still in place, supporting a few remaining scraps of brittle sod overgrown with prickly pear.

Emerging through a low doorway, I stood for a moment in the sun and gazed across the square, at the former *plaza de armas* of the presidio. The occupants of this house might have stood in this same spot, watching the various *entradas* assemble and march off in high spirits toward the Rio Grande, the first of the many rivers they would cross in their journey through what is now the state of Texas.

Those early expeditions crossed the Rio Grande at a place several miles distant, called Paso Francia—"Frenchman's Crossing." It was called that for a reason. Near the end of the seventeenth century, Spain's claim that it possessed the land beyond the Rio Grande was not much more than rhetoric. In fact, the march of Spanish civilization had just about stalled out in the deserts of northern Mexico. Texas was a looming wilderness at the farthest margin of Spain's farthest frontier. There was no compelling reason to venture into it, and hence no need for a royal road.

But the Spaniards were roused to action when they heard rumors that the French had invaded Texas from the Gulf of Mexico and had planted a colony somewhere on the coast. These rumors were given alarming credence in 1668, when Alonso De León, the governor of Coahuila, happened upon a Frenchman living in an Indian village about sixty miles north of the Rio Grande, west of present-day Uvalde. The man was about fifty years old and crazy, but he had managed to entice the Indians into treating him like a potentate. De León found him sitting on a cushion made of buffalo hide while members of his court cooled him with feather fans. He was surrounded by a bodyguard of forty warriors.

When he saw his visitors, he jumped up from the cushion, pumped their hands in greeting, kissed the priest's scapular, and happily announced in his fractured Spanish, "Yo *frances*! (I French!)"

"I am going about assembling many Indian nations," he told De León, "to make them my friends; those who do not wish to join me, I attack and destroy with the aid of my Indian followers."

Exactly who he was, what he was up to, and where he had come from nobody ever really knew—least of all the befuddled Frenchman himself. But something he told De León helped change the course of history. He said that a French settlement—with a fort and a township—had been established on the banks of a "large river to the east" and had been there for fifteen years.

There was indeed a French fort. De León spent the next year looking for it and in the process opened up the route of the Camino Real. But instead of a formidable French presence, he found only a ruined and looted stockade, the ground strewn with pig carcasses, rotting books in leather bindings, and a woman's skeleton still wearing the tattered scraps of a dress. That was all that was left of Fort St. Louis, the colony that the French explorer Sieur de la Salle had attempted to establish on Matagorda Bay. La Salle himself had been killed by his own men, and the rest of the desperate colonists had been overrun by Karankawas.

The French threat seemed to have taken care of itself, but because of it the Spanish road into Texas had been opened, and De León's next discovery helped guarantee that it would remain so. Traveling north and east, pursuing rumors of French survivors, he entered the country of the Hasinai, a confederation of tribes whose name in all its variations—Tayshas, Taychas, Tehas, Teias, Texia, Teisa, Teyans, Tejas—meant "friend." De León found the "kingdom of the Texas," and it indeed seemed to be a land of friendship and welcome. These Caddoan people were settled and affluent—skilled farmers who kept their surplus maize and beans in watertight cribs inside their huge conical houses. To the Spaniards' astonishment, they had even been visited by the Woman in Blue.

The Woman in Blue was a weird spiritual phenomenon of seventeenth-century

Spain. In physical reality, she was a Castilian abbess named Mother María de Jesús de Agreda. María de Agreda never left her convent in Spain—but she became famous for her claims that she was able to transport herself to faraway Texas. There she appeared before the Indians as a beautiful woman in a blue cloak, bewitching them into Christian belief.

So far, the Woman in Blue had shown herself only to the Indians living along the Rio Grande, but now here was evidence that her spirit was roving deep into the unknown lands to the east. It is reported that the Hasinai chief whom De León encountered even had a portable altar, complete with figures of Christ and the saints, in front of which a light was kept burning in perpetual veneration. The chief told Father Damian Massanet, the priest accompanying De León, that he would welcome further spiritual instruction.

So all at once New Spain had compelling business in distant Texas. It would establish presidios to guard its borders against the French and missions to turn the Indians into servants of God and Spain. To do all this, it would need a road.

~

THE ROAD CAME INTO BEING slowly, league by league, river crossing by river crossing. It was never actually "built" but simply improved upon, its route modified by almost every expedition that used it. To call it a road at all is misleading. The Camino Real was not nearly as imposing, for instance, as the broad curbed highways the Anasazi Indians had built hundreds of years before, far to the west in the New Mexican desert. The Spanish road was a track, rarely wider than a single oxcart, and often so indecipherable that the professional explorers who followed it routinely got lost.

When I left Guerrero, traveling northeast toward San Antonio, I was following the general trend of the Camino Real, but there was hardly any physical evidence to mark the actual route of the old road. I crossed the Nueces, the Hondo, the Medina, glancing down at the rivers from the highway bridges as I sped across, thinking of the Spanish horses churning madly in the water, and the soldiers and Indians ferrying sheep across one at a time.

The crossings were routinely hazardous. On Domingo Ramón's 1716 expedition, eighty-two horses were drowned trying to reach the far bank of the Medina. Ramón, sensing the devil's hand in this calamity, ordered a mass the next day "to crush him." Don Domingo de Terán, starting out on the first expedition to establish the missions in East Texas, lost forty-nine saddle horses to the Rio Grande. "However, the great power of Our Lady of Guadalupe, the North Star and protector of this undertaking, carried our weak efforts in this task to a successful ending."

Day by day these *entradas* had staggered down the rude path of the Camino Real—the soldiers outfitted in buckskin or quilted cotton, plodding along under the weight of their harquebuses and leather shields; the friars and lay brothers in their brown robes, a few of them heroically barefoot, the rest with their gnarled and swollen feet encased in sandals; the mission Indians driving herds of goats and sheep; the oxcarts packed with trading goods and religious implements, including holy-water fonts and ovens for baking communion wafers; and the banners overhead, bearing the images of Our Lady of Pilar or Our Lady of Guadalupe or Saint James the Moor-Killer.

When I reached San Antonio, I traveled along Mission Road, more or less following the course of the old road as it passed icehouses and auto-repair shops and Pig Stands, almost incidentally passing the missions of San Juan Capistrano, San Francisco de la Espada, San José and Nuestra Señora de la Purísima Concepción. These missions were begun by the Spaniards early in the eighteenth century, after those in East Texas had been abandoned and the padres were ordered to retrench along the San Antonio River, where the local Indians proved to be ultimately more agreeable than the Hasinai.

Domingo Ramón's expedition of 1716 had been the first to describe San Antonio Springs, the glorious headwaters of the San Antonio River. It was near there, two years later, that the village of San Antonio de Bexar was founded. The first mission to be built in the town—San Antonio de Valero—was moved twice, allowed to fall into ruin, and finally secularized in 1793. For a time it served as the headquarters for a Spanish cavalry from a town in Mexico named Alamo de las Parras.

I parked my car in a lot by the San Antonio River and walked through the lobby of the Hyatt Hotel to Alamo Plaza. Standing in front of the chapel, I reckoned that the Camino Real would have passed a few hundred yards to the east, and I tried to imagine Santa Anna's forces wheeling into position for the siege. Striking out in 1836 from Mexico to suppress the rebellion in Texas, Santa Anna had driven his army up the road in a cold-blooded forced march that left many of them buried along the way, his bewildered conscripts from the tropical jungles of the Yucatan dropping from exposure in a freak blizzard.

And this is where the Camino Real had led him. The Battle of the Alamo was no accident. By 1836 Anglo-American immigrants had for several decades been on a collision course with the Spanish and Mexican governments that held Texas, and now the two cultures hurtled toward each other from opposite ends of the Camino Real like locomotives on a single track. The wreck had to occur someplace, and that someplace—sitting smack in the middle of the road—was the Alamo.

DICK J. REAVIS

"Gateway to Texas" (2003)

NORTHEAST OF VILLA UNION, nearly on the banks of the Rio Grande, the village of Guerrero (population 2,000) maintains the role that it assumed three centuries ago, when, as Presidio del Rio Grande, it was the gateway to Texas.

Most of the expeditions that colonized Texas left from Presidio del Rio Grande, and most colonial cattle drives went through there, using two hard-bottom, shallow-water river crossings.

In colonial days, three missions made their homes at Presidio del Rio. One was called San Francisco de Valero. That mission became San Antonio de Valero—the Alamo—when its presiding priest, Father Antonio de Buenaventura Olivares, moved to San Antonio in 1718.

A second, San Bernardo, is still standing, thanks in part to work conducted by an archaeological team from the University of Texas at San Antonio.

Ruts, or swales, from the Camino still run through Guerrero, and in recent years, locals have come to know them for what they are.

"I was born ten meters from the Camino Real, but until four or five years ago, I didn't know what it was, because my parents called it the Old Road," says the shepherd and school bus driver Enrique Cervera Rodriguez, age 65.

Cervera began his studies in the mid-1990s, after attending a conference held along San Antonio's Riverwalk. There he met Eagle Pass historian and Quemado native John Stockley, a retired civil servant, now 69. Stockley took an interest in Guerrero's past, he says, "after I got ahold of archaeologists to learn something about the people who made the arrowheads I'd been picking up since I was a boy."

Today, Stockley and Cervera often compare notes, sometimes at Guerrero's city hall, where Cervera's wife, Blanca Estela López Zapata, is an elected official, the town's *sindico*, or custodian of municipal assets.

There were no distaff officials in Presidio del Rio Grande, and very few in Mexico, until after the Mexican Revolution of 1910–1920. But afterwards, scores of women like López found a place for themselves, and a way out of rural isolation, through political participation.

López, who has also twice been elected to Guerrero's city council, says that her activism in the now-faded National Peasant Confederation opened doors to her. "I was just a campesinita from a corner of the land," she says, noting that she attended only junior high. "But I wanted to do something more, to see the world that lay beyond the mountains."

Because Guerrero has a limited economy—most of its people work in industrial plants at Piedras Negras, 25 miles away—she and her husband have encouraged their four children to attend college. Two of them are now enrolled.

"I tell my children to study—because, even if I went to school in the country, look at what I could do," she says with satisfaction. "If they get a modern education, there's no limit to what they can achieve."

Both she and her husband take pride in the belief that none of their children will cross the Rio Grande, headed north, as many of Guerrero's inhabitants have done.

"This town has always been a kind of incubator," laments mayor Jesús Saucedo, 58. "Always, as soon as they turned eighteen, people headed toward the river. Wherever you go in the United States—Dallas, Chicago, San Jose, Eagle Pass, San Antonio—there are people from Guerrero."

Life has changed in Mexico and Texas over the past 300 years, but some things about the Camino Real region, it seems, remain always the same. Stockley and Cervera insist that the Camino Real helps migrants cross the border today, as it always has. Illegal aliens, they say, use Presidio del Rio Grande's low-water fords, Paso de Francia and Paso Pacuache—the same crossings used by Father Olivares and General Santa Anna.

Flying on a tether between the two historic fords, on the American side of the Rio Grande, is a large, white blimp, loaded with aerial surveillance devices. The blimp's purpose, drug enforcement officials say, is to track aircraft that might be smuggling drugs, not to assist illegal aliens. But Stockley observes: "They have a pretty easy time finding the pasos, because they can follow the balloon."

LARRY MCMURTRY

from *Lonesome Dove* (1985)

AUGUSTUS SOON FOUND THE HORSE HERD in a valley south of the old line camp. Call had predicted its location precisely, but had overestimated its size. A couple of horses whinnied at the sight of riders but didn't seem particularly disturbed.

"Probably all Texas horses anyway," Augustus said. "Probably had enough of Mexico."

"I've had enough of it and I just got here," Jake said, lighting his smoke. "I never liked it down here with these chili-bellies."

"Why, Jake, you should stay and make your home here," Augustus said. "That sheriff can't follow you here. Besides, think of the women."

"I got a woman," Jake said. "That one back in Lonesome Dove will do me for a while."

"She'll do you, all right," Augustus said. "That girl's got more spunk than you have."

"What would you know about it, Gus?" Jake asked. "I don't suppose you've spent time with her, a man your age."

"The older the violin, the sweeter the music," Augustus said. "You never knowed much about women."

Jake didn't answer. He had forgotten how much Gus liked argument.

"I guess you think all women want you to marry them and build 'em a house and raise five or six brats," Augustus said. "But it's my view that very few women are fools, and only a fool would pick you for a chore like that, Jake. You'll do fine for a barn dance or a cakewalk, or maybe a picnic, but house building and brat raising ain't exactly your line."

Jake kept quiet. He knew that silence was the best defense once Augustus got wound up. It might take him a while to talk himself out, if left alone, but any response would just encourage him.

"This ain't no hundred horses," he said, after a bit. "Maybe we got the wrong herd."

"Nope, it's right," Augustus said. "Pedro just learned not to keep all his remuda in one place. It's almost forty horses here. It won't satisfy Woodrow, but then practically nothing does."

He had no sooner spoken than he heard three horses coming from the north.

"If that ain't them, we're under attack," Jake said.

"It's them," Augustus said. "A scout like you, who's traveled in Montana, ought to recognize his own men."

"Gus, you'd exasperate a preacher," Jake said. "I don't know what your dern horses sound like."

It was an old trick of theirs, trying to make him feel incompetent—as if a man was incompetent because he couldn't see in the dark, or identify a local horse by the sound of its trot.

"'Y god, you're techy, Jake," Augustus said, just as Call rode up.

"Is this all there is or did you trot in and run the rest off?" he asked.

"Do them horses look nervous?" Augustus asked.

"Dern," Call said. "Last time we was through here there was two or three hundred horses."

"Maybe Pedro's going broke," Augustus said. "Mexicans can go broke, same as Texans. What'd you do with the *vaqueros*?"

"We didn't find none. We just found two Irishmen."

"Irishmen?" Augustus asked.

"They just lost," Deets said.

"Hell, I can believe they're lost," Jake said.

"On their way to Galveston," Newt said, thinking it might help clarify the situation.

Augustus laughed. "I guess it ain't hard to miss Galveston if you start from Ireland," he said. "However, it takes skill to miss the dern United States entirely and hit Pedro Flores' ranch. I'd like to meet men who can do that."

"You'll get your chance," Call said. "They don't have mounts, unless you count a mule and a donkey. I guess we better help them out of their fix."

"I'm surprised they ain't naked, too," Augustus said. "I'd had thought some bandit would have stolen their clothes by now."

"Have you counted these horses, or have you been sitting here jawing?" Call said brusquely. The night was turning out to be more complicated and less profitable than he had hoped.

"I assigned that chore to Dish Boggett," Augustus said. "It's around forty."

"Not enough," Call said. "You take two and go back and get the Irishmen."

He took his rope off his saddle and handed it to the boy.

"Go catch two horses," he said. "You better make hackamores."

Newt was so surprised by the assignment he almost dropped the rope. He had never roped a horse in the dark before—but he would have to try. He trotted off toward the horse herd, sure they would probably stampede at the sight of him. But he had a piece of luck. Six or eight horses trotted over to sniff at his mount and he easily caught one of them. As he was making a second loop and trying to lead the first horse over to Pea, Dish Boggett trotted over without being asked and casually roped another horse.

"What are we gonna do, brand 'em?" he asked.

Newt was irritated, for he would have liked to complete the assignment himself, but since it was Dish he said nothing.

"Lend 'em to some men we found," he said. "Irishmen."

"Oh," Dish said. "I hate to lend my rope to an Irishman. I might be out a good rope."

Newt solved that by putting his own rope on the second horse. He led them back to where the Captain was waiting. As he did, Mr. Gus began to laugh, causing Newt to worry that he had done something improperly after all—he couldn't imagine what.

Then he saw that they were looking at the horse brands—H I C on the left hips.

"It just goes to show that even sinners can accomplish Christian acts," Augustus said. "Here we set out to rob a man and now we're in a position to return valuable property to a man who's already been robbed. That's curious justice, ain't it?"

"It's a wasted night, is what it is," Call said.

"If it was me I'd make the man pay a reward for them horses," Jake said. "He'd never have seen them agin if it hadn't been for us."

Call was silent. Of course they could not charge a man for his own horses.

"That's all right, Call," Augustus said. "We'll make it up off the Irishmen. Maybe they got rich uncles—bank directors or railroad magnates or something. They'll be so happy to see those boys alive again that they'll likely make us partners."

Call ignored him, trying to think of some way to salvage the trip. Though he had always been a careful planner, life on the frontier had long ago convinced him of the fragility of plans. The truth was, most plans did fail, to one degree or another, for one reason or another. He had survived as a Ranger because he was quick to respond to what he had actually found, not because his planning was infallible.

In the present case he had found two destitute travelers and a herd of recently stolen horses. But it was still four hours till sunup and he was reluctant to abandon his original ambition, which was to return with a hundred Mexican horses. It was still possible, if he acted decisively.

"All right," he said, quickly sorting over in his head who should be assigned to do what. "These are mainly Wilbarger's horses. The reason they're so gentle is because they've been run to a frazzle, and they're used to Texans besides."

"I'd catch one and ride him home, if I could find one that paces," Jake said. "I'm about give out from bouncing on this old trotter you boys gave me."

"Jake's used to feather pillows and Arkansas whores," Augustus said. "It's a pity he has to associate with hard old cobs like us."

"You two can jabber tomorrow," Call said. "Pedro's horses have got to be somewhere. I'd like to make a run at them before I quit. That means we have to split three ways."

"Leave me split the shortest way home," Jake said, never too proud to complain. "I've bounced my ass over enough of Mexico."

"All right," Call said. "You and Deets and Dish take these horses home."

He would have liked to have Deets with him, but Deets was the only one he knew for certain could take the Wilbarger horses on a line for Lonesome Dove. Dish Boggett, though said to be a good hand, was an untested quality, whereas Jake was probably lost himself.

"Gus, that leaves you the Irishmen," he said. "If they can ride, you ought to catch up with these horses somewhere this side of the river. Just don't stop to play no poker with them."

Augustus considered the situation for a minute.

"So that's your strategy, is it?" he said. "You and Newt and Pea get to have all the fun and the rest of us are stuck with the chores."

"Why, I was trying to make it easy for you, Gus," Call said. "Seeing as you're the oldest and most decrepit."

"See you for breakfast, then," Augustus said, taking the lead ropes from Newt. "I just hope the Irishmen don't expect a buggy."

With that he galloped off. The rest of them trotted down to where Pea and Dish were sitting, waiting.

"Pea, you come with me," Call said. "And you—" looking at the boy. Though it would expose Newt to more danger, he decided he wanted the boy with him. At least he wouldn't pick up bad habits, as he undoubtedly would have if he'd been sent along with Gus.

"All you three have to do is get these horses to town by sunup," he added. "If we ain't back, give Wilbarger his."

"What are you planning to do, stay here and get married?" Jake asked.

"My plans ain't set," he said. "Don't you worry about us. Just keep them horses moving."

He looked at Deets when he said that. He could not formally make Deets the leader over two white men, but he wanted him to know that he had the responsibility of seeing that the horses got there. Deets said nothing, but when he trotted off to start the horses he took the point as if it was his natural place. Dish Boggett loped around to the other point, leaving Jake to bring up the rear.

Jake seemed largely uninterested in the proceedings, which was his way.

"Call, you're some friend," he said. "I ain't been home a whole day and you already got me stealing horses."

But he loped off after the herd and was soon out of sight. Pea Eye yawned as he watched him go.

"I swear," he said. "Jake's just like he used to be."

~

AN HOUR LATER they found the main horse herd in a narrow valley several miles to the north. Call estimated it to be over a hundred horses strong. The situation had its difficulty, the main one being that the horses were barely a mile from the Flores headquarters, and on the wrong side of it at that. It would be necessary to bring them back past the hacienda, or else take them north to the river, a considerably longer route. If Pedro Flores and his men chose to pursue, they would have a fine chance of catching them out in the open, in broad daylight, several miles from help. It would be himself and Pea and the boy against a small army of *vaqueros*.

On the other hand, he didn't relish leaving the horses, now that he had found them. He was tempted just to move them right past the hacienda and hope everyone there had gone to bed drunk.

"Well, we're here," he said. "Let's take 'em."

"It's a bunch," Pea said. "We won't have to come back for a while."

"We won't never come back," Call said. "We'll sell some and take the rest with us to Montana."

Life was finally starting, Newt thought. Here he was below the border, about to run off a huge horse herd, and in a few days or weeks he would be going up the trail to a place he had barely even heard of. Most of the cowpokes who went north from Lonesome Dove just went to Kansas and thought that was far—but Montana must be twice as far. He couldn't imagine what such a place would look like. Jake had said it had buffalo and mountains, two things he had never seen, and snow, the hardest thing of all to imagine. He had seen ridges and hills, and so had a notion about mountains, and he had seen pictures of buffalo in the papers that the stage drivers sometimes left Mr. Gus.

Snow, however, was an entirely mysterious thing. Once or twice in his lifetime there had been freezes in Lonesome Dove—he had seen thin ice on the water bucket that sat on the porch. But ice wasn't snow, which was supposed to stack up on the ground so high that people had to wade through it. He had seen pictures of people sledding over it, but still couldn't imagine what it would actually feel like to be in snow.

"I guess we'll just go for home," Call said. "If we wake 'em up we wake 'em up."

He looked at the boy. "You take the left point," he said. "Pea will be on the right, and I'll be behind. If trouble comes, it'll come from behind, and I'll notice it first. If they get after us hot and heavy we can always drop off thirty or forty horses and hope that satisfies them."

They circled the herd and quietly started it moving to the northwest, waving a rope now and then to get the horses in motion but saying as little as possible. Newt could not help feeling a little odd about it all, since he had somehow had it in his mind that they were coming to Mexico to buy horses, not steal them. It was puzzling that such a muddy little river like the Rio Grande should make such a difference in terms of what was lawful and what not. On the Texas side, horse stealing was a hanging crime, and many of those hung for it were Mexican cowboys who came across the river to do pretty much what they themselves were doing. The Captain was known for his sternness where horse thieves were concerned, and yet, here they were, running off a whole herd. Evidently if you crossed the river to do it, it stopped being a crime and became a game.

Newt didn't really feel that what they were doing was wrong—if it had been wrong, the Captain wouldn't have done it. But the thought hit him that under Mexican law what they were doing might be a hanging offense. It put a different slant on the game. In imagining what it would be like to go to Mexico, he had always supposed the main danger would come in the form of bullets, but he was no longer so sure. On the ride down he hadn't been worried, because he had a whole company around him.

But once they started back, instead of having a whole company around him, he seemed to have no one. Pea was far across the valley, and the Captain was half a mile to the rear. If a bunch of hostile *vaqueros* sprang up, he might not even be able to find the other two men. Even if he wasn't captured immediately, he could easily get lost. Lonesome Dove might be hard to locate, particularly if he was being chased.

If caught, he knew he could expect no mercy. The only thing in his favor was that there didn't seem to be any trees around to hang him from. Mr. Gus had once told a story about a horse thief who had to be hung from the rafter of a barn because there were no trees, but so far as Newt could tell there were no barns in Mexico either. The only thing he knew clearly was that he was scared. He rode for several miles, feeling very apprehensive. The thought of hanging—a new thought—wouldn't leave his mind. It became so powerful at one point that he squeezed his throat with one hand, to get a little notion of how it felt not to breathe. It didn't feel so bad when it was just his hand, but he knew a rope would feel a lot worse.

But the miles passed and no *vaqueros* appeared. The horses strung out under the moonlight in a long line, trotting easily. They were well past the hacienda, and the night seemed so peaceful that Newt began to relax a little. After all, the Captain and Pea and the others had done such things many times. It was just a night's work, and one that would soon be over.

Newt wasn't tired, and as he became less scared he began to imagine how gratifying it would be to ride into Lonesome Dove with such a large herd of horses. Everyone who saw them ride in would realize that he was now a man—even Lorena might see it if she happened to look out her window at the right time. He and the Captain and Pea were doing an exceptional thing. Deets would be proud of him, and even Bolivar would take notice.

All went peaceful and steady, and the thin moon hung brightly in the west. It seemed to Newt that it must be one of the longest nights of the year. He kept looking to the east, hoping to see a little redness on the horizon, but the horizon was still black.

He was thinking about the morning, and how nice it would be to cross the river and bring the horses through the town, when the peaceful night suddenly went off like a bomb. They were on the long chaparral plain not far south of the river and were easing the horses around a particularly dense thicket of chaparral, prickly pear and low mesquite when it happened. Newt had dropped off the point a little distance, to allow the horses room to skirt the thicket, when he heard shots from behind him. Before he had time to look around, or even touch his own gun, the horse herd exploded into a dead run and began to spread out. He saw what looked like half the herd charging right at him from the rear; some of the horses nearest him veered and went crashing into the chaparral. Then he heard Pea's gun sound from the other side of the thicket, and at that point lost all capacity for sorting out what was happening. When the race started, most of the herd was behind him, and the horses ahead of him were at least going in the same direction he was. But in a few seconds, once the whole mass of animals was moving at a dead run over the uncertain terrain, he suddenly noticed a stream of animals coming directly toward him from the right. The new bunch had simply cut around the chaparral thicket from the north and collided with the first herd. Before Newt even had time to consider what was happening, he was engulfed in a mass of animals, a few of which went down when the two herds ran together. Then, over the confused neighing of what seemed like hundreds of horses he began to hear yells and curses—Mexican curses. To his shock he saw a rider engulfed in the mass like himself, and the rider was not the Captain or Pea Eye. He realized then that two horse herds had run together, theirs headed for Texas, the other coming from Texas, both trying to skirt the same thicket, though from opposite directions.

The realization was unhelpful, though, because the horses behind him had caught up with him and all were struggling for running room. For a second he thought of trying to force his way to the outside, but then he saw two riders already there, struggling to turn the herd. They were not succeeding, but they were not his riders, either, and it struck him that being in the middle of the herd offered a certain safety, at least.

It quickly became clear that their herd was much the larger, and was forcing the new herd to curve into its flow. Soon all the horses were running northwest, Newt still in the middle of the bunch. Once a big wild-eyed gelding nearly knocked Mouse down; then Newt heard shots to his left and ducked, thinking the shots were meant for him.

Just as he ducked Mouse leaped a sizable chaparral bush. With his eyes toward the gunfire Newt was unprepared for the leap, and lost a stirrup and one rein but held onto the saddle horn and kept his seat. From then on he concentrated on riding, though he still occasionally heard shots. He kept low over his horse, an unnecessary precaution, for the running herd threw up so much dust that he could not have seen ten feet in front of him even if it had been daylight. He was grateful for the dust—

it was choking him, but it was also keeping him from getting shot, a more important consideration.

After a few miles the horses were no longer bunched so tightly. It occurred to Newt that he ought to angle out of the herd and not just let himself be carried along like a cow chip on a river, but he didn't know what such a move might mean. Would he be required to shoot at the *vaqueros* if they were still there? He was almost afraid to take his pistol out of its holster for fear Mouse would jump another bush and he'd drop it.

While he was running along, trying not to fall off and hoping he and the horses wouldn't suddenly go over a cutbank or pile into a deep gully of some kind, he heard a sound that was deeply reassuring: the sound of the Captain's rifle, the big Henry. Newt heard it shoot twice. It had to be the Captain because he was the only man on the border who carried a Henry. Everyone else had already switched to the lighter Winchesters.

The shots meant the Captain was all right. They came from ahead, which was odd, since the Captain had been behind, but then the *vaqueros* had been ahead, too. Somehow the Captain had managed to get to the front of the run and deal with them.

Newt looked back over his shoulder and saw red in the east. It was just a line of red, like somebody had drawn it with a crayon, over the thick black line of the land, but it meant that the night was ending. He didn't know where they were, but they still had a lot of horses. The horses were well spread by then, and he eased out of the herd. Despite the red in the east, the land seemed darker than it had all night; he could see nothing and just exerted himself to keep up, hoping they were going in the right direction. It felt a little odd to be alive and unharmed after such a deep scare, and Newt kept looking east, wishing the light would hurry so he could see around him and know whether it was safe to relax. For all he knew, Mexicans with Winchesters could be a hundred yards behind him.

He wished the Captain would shoot again; he had never been in a situation in which he felt so uncertain about everything. Squint as he could, Newt could see nothing but dark land and white dust. Of course the sun would soon solve the problem, but what would he see when he could see? The Captain and Pea could be ten miles away, and he himself could be riding into Mexico with Pedro Flores' *vaqueros*.

Then, coming over a little rise in the ground, he saw something that gave him heart: a thin silver ribbon to the northwest that could only be the river. The fading moon hung just above it. Across it, Texas was in sight, no less dark than Mexico, but there. The deep relief Newt felt at the sight of it washed away most of his fear. He even recognized the curve of the river—it was the old Comanche crossing, only a mile above Lonesome Dove. Whoever he was with had brought him home.

To his dismay, the sight of such a safe, familiar place made him want to cry. It seemed to him that the night had lasted many days—days during which he had been worried every moment that he would do something wrong and make a mistake that meant he would never come back to Lonesome Dove, or else come back disgraced. Now it was over and he was almost back, and relief seemed to run through him like warm water, some of which leaked out his eyes. It made him glad it was still dark—what would the men think if they saw him? There was so much dust on his face that when he quickly wiped away the tears of relief his fingers rubbed off moist smears of dirt.

In a few minutes more, as the herd neared the river, the darkness loosened and began to gray. The red on the eastern horizon was no longer a line but spread upward like an opened fan. Soon Newt could see the horses moving through the first faint gray light—a lot of horses. Then, just as he thought he had brought the flood within himself under control, the darkness loosened its hold yet more and the first sunlight streamed across the plain, filtering through the cloud of dust to touch the coats of the tired horses, most of whom had slowed to a rapid trot. Ahead, waiting on the bank of the river, was Captain Call, the big Henry in the crook of his arm. The Hell Bitch was lathered with sweat, but her head was up and she slung it restlessly as she watched the herd approach—even pointing her keen ears at Mouse for a moment. Neither the Captain nor the gray mare looked in the least affected by the long night or the hard ride, yet Newt found himself so moved by the mere sight of them sitting there that he had to brush away yet another tear and smudge his dusty cheek even worse.

Down the river aways he could see Pea, sitting on the rangy bay they called Sardine. Of the hostile *vaqueros* they had met there was no sign. There were so many questions Newt wanted to ask about what they had done and where they had been that he hardly knew where to begin; yet, when he rode up to the Captain, keeping Mouse far enough away from the Hell Bitch that she wouldn't try to take a bite out of him, he didn't ask any questions. They would have poured out of him if it had been Mr. Gus or Deets or Pea, but since it was the Captain, the questions just stayed inside. All he said, at the end of the most exciting and important night of his life, was a simple good morning.

"It is a good one, ain't it?" Call said, as he watched the huge herd of horses—well over a hundred of them—pour over the low banks and spread out down the river to drink. Pea had ridden Sardine into the water stirrup deep to keep the herd from spreading too far south.

Call knew that it had been rare luck, running into the four Mexican horse thieves and getting most of the horses they had just brought over from Texas. The Mexicans had thought they had run into an army—who but an army would have so many horses?—and had not really stayed to make a fight, though he had had to scare off one *vaquero* who kept trying to turn the herd.

As for the boy, it was good that he had picked up a little experience and come through it all with nothing worse than a dirty face.

They sat together silently as the top half of the sun shot long ribbons of light across the brown river and the drinking horses, some of whom lay down in the shallows and rolled themselves in the cooling mud. When the herd began to move in twos and threes up the north bank, Call touched the mare and he and the boy moved out into the water. Call loosened his rein and let the mare drink. He was as pleased with her as he was with the catch. She was surefooted as a cat, and far from used up, though the boy's mount was so done in he would be worthless for a week. Pea's big bay was not much better. Call let the mare drink all she wanted before gathering his rein. Most of the horses had moved to the north bank, and the sun had finished lifting itself clear of the horizon.

"Let's ease on home," he said to the boy. "I hope Wilbarger's got his pockets full of money. We've got horses to sell."

LAURA GILPIN

ELMER KELTON

from *The Time It Never Rained* (1973)

THE WORKING CREW saddled fresh horses and rode into a new pasture to gather sheep for the next day's shearing. Those sheep would spend the night in a small fifty-acre enclosure known as a "trap." Its grass was purposely conserved for such overnight grazing or for a handful of hospital animals. Charlie remained in the pens, chalking out cull sheep to be sold, watching the putting-up of the wool.

When the riders returned at mid-afternoon to crowd their sheep through the trap gate, Manuel pulled away and rode toward the pens. Charlie sensed that the boy wanted to talk to him. He tilted a large metal can, poured ice water into the wide lid and handed it across the netwire fence. "Dry?"

"Awful dry," Manuel said, dismounting to take the water. He drank thirstily, pausing to slosh some around in his mouth and wash the dust down. He wiped his face on a half-rolled sleeve, leaving a streak where dust had turned to mud.

Charlie thought idly that he never used to see old-time cowboys roll their sleeves up. They believed in buttoning the sun out. But this was a new generation.

"Mister Charlie," Manuel said, "I rode up on three wetbacks hidin' out yonder in the brush."

"There's wetbacks passin' through here all the time."

"These sure do look hungry."

"Why don't they come on in? Ain't nobody goin' to hurt them."

"Too many people here. They're scared of the border patrol. Asked me if I thought you might have a few days' work for them. I told them you don't hardly ever hire a wetback."

Charlie nodded. "Once the border patrol catches you givin' them work, they'll rag you from then on. I got enough problems to put up with; I don't need the border patrol."

"That's what I told them." Manuel's eyes were concerned. "They're still awful hungry."

Charlie stared at the boy, irritated by his persistence. "You're the damnedest kid I ever saw to be pickin' up dogies all the time!"

Manuel ducked his head. Charlie was instantly remorseful for having spoken sharply. He considered a moment and said, "But hell, it shows there's a streak of kindness in you, *muchacho*, and kindness is one thing this world is short of. Think you could find them again?"

Manuel straightened. "They're right yonder." He pointed to a mesquite thicket.

"Tell them to come in and see me. I don't want nobody to leave this place hungry, Mexican or white." He put his hand on top of Manuel's old hat and affectionately pressed the crown down flat against the boy's head. "You doggoned dogie-hunter!"

Manuel smiled. "Thank you, Mister Charlie." He pulled the horse around and rode away faster than he had come.

Soon Charlie saw three men moving timidly toward the shearing pens from the cover of the brush. He watched, frowning, finally climbing over the fence to wait for them.

For generations the Mexican people on both sides of the Rio Grande had moved freely back and forth across the river to work and to live. International boundaries were fiction to them. They considered everything south of the Nueces River their own open and natural range. In recent times the United States government had tried to close the border. But old habits of a slow-changing people are not altered overnight by words on paper—words many could not even read.

These were from across the river; a man who knew Mexicans could tell that as far as he could see them. They carried the wetback's typical cloth satchels with colored stripes, and Charlie could see that the satchels were empty. If they had any food when they came across the river, it was long gone. Many came with no food at all, certain that as soon as they reached the north side of the Rio they would be in a bountiful land of milk and honey where no man was ever hungry, no pocket ever empty. These men's clothing had been patched until little was left for patches to cling to. Two wore leather *huaraches* which covered nothing more than the crusted soles of their brown feet. One wore an old pair of worn-out brogan shoes not as good, even, as the *huaraches*. A little in the lead came an old man with gray-salted hair and heavy gray mustache. The others were younger, one only fourteen or fifteen. A father and two sons, Charlie judged. Pity stirred him, and he knew why Manuel had been so touched. The old man was more than merely hungry. By his eyes, Charlie knew he was sick.

Thank God, he thought, *I was born north of the river.*

The old man removed his tattered straw hat, bowed stiffly as peons in Mexico had done for untold generations, and spoke in border Spanish: "Mi patrón, we are much indebted."

They were always courtly, no matter how bleak the circumstances. It was a trait of the humblest.

Charlie extended a pack of cigarettes to the old man. Mumbling his gracias, the *viejo* took a cigarette and passed the rest to the oldest son. The youngest came last, as was considered proper. He removed a cigarette and held the pack while Charlie lighted the old-timer's smoke, then the eldest son's. Charlie struck a fresh match for the boy, but the youngster shook his head and handed the pack to Charlie. He glanced at his father and put the cigarette in his shirt pocket. "I save it for later, patrón."

Keeping it for his father, Charlie knew. He started to put the pack back into his pocket, reconsidered and gave it to the old man. "Keep it," he said in gringo Spanish. "I have more."

The *viejo* thanked him again. He drew upon the cigarette with a deep and terrible hunger. He closed his eyes, losing himself in the luxury of the moment. He told his story then. To Charlie it was an old one he had heard a hundred times, always the same except for minor individual variations. They had come upon evil days in the country south of Ciudad Acuña the Mexican said sadly. For a long while now the good Dios had not chosen to send rain down on the state of Coahuila, and in truth, nowhere else along the border. The fields had fallen barren. Buckets dropped in the wells came up with mud, and finally only sand. The people's own little lands knew only poverty, and their patron—hit like the rest—had work now for no more than a few. The old man and his sons, as so many thousands like them, had come to "the other side" to find employment, to send money home to buy food and clothing for those of their family who must stay behind—the women, the little children.

"We do not beg, señor, or ask you to give us something we do not earn. We ask for a chance to work. We are hard workers, my sons and I."

Charlie rubbed the palms of his hands on his dirty khakis. There were so many of these people, so damn many of them, and always so hungry . . . He glanced into the old man's muddy eyes and looked away. For a moment he felt a twinge of guilt that these people were hungry and he was not, and then a brief resentment against them for arousing that guilt. Both passed quickly, the guilt and the resentment. "I am sorry, amigo. You know the laws of my country. You swam the river without papers, and it is prohibited that I hire you. Like you, I believe this law is unjust, but no matter, it is still the law. If the chotas catch you they will take you back across the river and make you walk home hungry. If they catch you *here*, they will also be angry with me."

"Señor, they can hurt us but little, for we are already hungry. And we do not intend to be caught."

"No one escapes the chotas forever. They have eyes that see in the dark. They will find you."

The old man's face began to fall. He repeated desperately, "We do not beg. We ask only to work."

Charlie shook his head. "I have no work for you. But you will not leave here hungry. Follow me."

He thought at first about taking them to Teofilo's camp. But except for the goat kids Charlie had furnished, the food there was Teofilo's. Garcia had bought and paid for it. Texas-born Mexicans—themselves often only one generation away from the river—often harbored resentment against the wetbacks. Despite their blood ties they considered them interlopers, a threat to their own jobs and security.

"We have food left at the big house. I will take you to la madama. She will feed you and give you food to carry along. Then you had better be on your way. If the chotas hear we are shearing today, they will probably come out to look us 'over. You will not wish to be here."

The old man said gratefully, "These are hard times that we must come to you this way. If ever the fates turn around, we shall do the same someday for you."

I hope to God not, Charlie thought.

He escorted them to the house and called Mary. He saw the pity in her eyes, and he tried to cover his own. Gruffly he said, "Some dogies Manuel found. Feed them." He glanced at the town road, looking for dust which might mean a border patrol car. The three Mexicans sat in the shade of the big live-oak trees and began to wolf down what was left of Mary's baked kid. Charlie was gratified when the young one took a big helping of the turnip greens. *I hope he eats them all.*

He thought about the apple pie from which Mary had given Tom a slice, then put the rest back up in the cabinet. Charlie had thought he would slip a slice of that tonight when she wasn't looking. He knew now it would probably go to the Mexicans along with everything else. She was generous to everyone but him.

He waited until Mary was in the house before he allowed his voice to soften. "When you are through, I would advise that you go on north. Perhaps you will find work farther away from the border."

"Buena suerte, patrón. May the dry time never fall upon you."

~

IN THE HURRY of the hot and dusty shearing pens, Charlie's mind soon drifted away from the three Mexicans. He heard nothing over the din of bleating sheep, the clattering protest of the cranky old shearing machine that seemed to have a malevolent will of its own. He stood at the tying table, critically examining a breaky fleece, the result of a sheep that had sickened sometime last winter, leaving a weak spot at that point of growth in the fiber. He was grumbling to himself, knowing he must sack this fleece apart from the good ones or risk its being found by a sharp-eyed wool buyer who then might dock his entire clip; they were always looking for an excuse to trim a man, he thought.

Charlie turned as an automobile's side window flashed a reflection across the tying table. He recognized the green government car, the round symbol on its door. Border patrol!

Damn chotas, always slipping up on you!

His first impulse was to look toward the house, but he managed not to. Maybe the three wetbacks had eaten and left. He got a grip on himself and moved through the shorn and unshorn sheep, shoving ewes and lambs aside with his knees. Two green-clad patrolmen climbed out of the car.

"Mister Flagg?"

Charlie nodded, and one patrolman extended his hand. The grip was firm and friendly. "Parker's my name. And this is Oliver Nance." Nance's face was cold and without cordiality, but Parker's easy drawl put Charlie partly at ease. Texas, he figured, or perhaps Oklahoma. He couldn't be all bad. The patrolman said, "We heard you were shearing, and we thought we'd like to watch a little. Oliver is new to this part of the country. He hasn't seen much shearing done."

Nance had no patience with pretense. "We came to see if you're working any wetbacks."

Charlie cast him a hard glance. The man was honest, anyway.

Parker frowned but said nothing.

Charlie said, "I don't work wetbacks."

Nance didn't ask a question; he made a statement. "Then you won't mind if we look around a little."

Too much honesty could get a man disliked. Tightly Charlie said, "Help yourself." He said more than that, under his breath. *Damnyankee! You could tell it as quick as he opened his mouth. Damnyankees always coming down here on us like locusts, thinking they're two notches better than Jesus Christ!* He had an old Texan aversion to Northerners. His heritage from a Confederate grandfather made it automatic that he class them all as damnyankees until they had proven to his satisfaction they were all right. That sometimes took a right smart of proving.

Nance studied Teofilo's shearing crew and started to climb over the fence into the pens. Parker said, "Those are all local Mexicans. You won't find any wetbacks in there."

"How do you know till you look?" Nance climbed over and shoved his way through the sheep, his eyes on the shearers.

Stupid as *well* as arrogant, Charlie thought irritably. This would be a slap in the face to Teofilo's men; to be mistaken for a wetback was considered no compliment. Maybe they would bounce Nance out of there on his butt. On reflection Charlie knew they wouldn't do that. They would simply turn on a cold contempt and mock him with their eyes. Generations of living in this country as a minority group had honed to a fine edge this ability of the Mexican people to put a *gringo* in his place without speaking a word or making any overt move that might invite stern reprisal. Charlie thought, *You've never been insulted, Yankee boy, till you've been insulted in silence by a Mexican who knows how to give you the treatment.*

Parker's jaw ridged. "I'll apologize for him, Mister Flagg. Occasionally they send us one of these new boys who already knows it all."

One of the shearers snickered, and the others followed suit. Even the tie-boys took it up.

People who lived long in the border country usually could tell at a glance whether a man was native-born or if he had recently arrived with muddy water dripping from his clothes. It showed in details hard to explain but easy to recognize—the clothing, the haircut, the general manner. To one who knew Spanish, a wetback was betrayed by his speech. Even a Yankee *chota* soon learned to know.

Motioning broadly with his big hands, Teofilo Garcia assured Nance that his shearers were all right. "Every man here is *puro* American, and votes Democrat."

Nance's face darkened in anger as the men quietly mocked him. He turned on his heel and pushed roughly back through the sheep.

With mild rebuke, Parker said, "I told you. If you get the locals mad at us, who's going to tip us off about the wets?"

Nance stiffly rejected any reproach. "I didn't like their attitude."

Charlie felt a glow of quiet triumph. He did not dislike border patrolmen, exactly; he realized they had a duty to perform. It was that duty which he disliked. In his view the wetback was no criminal; he was a hungry man desperately seeking work, and it took a lot of guts to set out across uncounted miles of unknown country in hopes of bettering oneself. Charlie identified because of his pioneer heritage. This gutsiness, he felt, was a character strength which was disappearing from American life. He was glad they still had it in Mexico.

He glanced in the direction of his house, and the breath went out of him. The three Mexicans were walking toward the pens, swinging those telltale cotton satchels. The satchels were full now, for Mary had been to the pantry.

Ay, Chihuahua! Didn't those innocents know what a *chota* looked like?

Parker saw them about the time Charlie did, and he glanced at Charlie in disappointment. Charlie was tempted to wave the three away, to shout for them to run. But that could get him sent to jail, or at least heavily fined. A ranchman could feed a wetback or even hire him to work without actually being liable to prosecution; no penalty had been provided. But the minute he advised him to run, he became an accessory to unlawful flight. So Charlie watched, numb, as the three Mexicans halted, realization striking them like a club.

"Alto!" Parker shouted. "Alto!"

The three took out for the brush as hard as they could run. The boy was far in the lead. The oldest son was hanging back, looking over his shoulder at the faltering old man.

Nance hurried to the green car, reached into the glove compartment and pulled out a pistol. Charlie's blood went cold. He wanted to shout, but no words came. He was sure Nance would fire at the fugitives. But Nance fired harmlessly into the air, causing a tied horse at the fence to lunge against the reins and snap them in two. The horse went trotting off in fear and confusion, stepping on one broken rein and jerking its head down. The old man stopped and raised his hands. The oldest son, seeing his father halt, turned and came back to stand dejectedly beside him. Only the boy kept running.

Parker waved for Nance to go after the young Mexican. Nance shouted something at the halted pair as he passed them on the run. He disappeared into the green tangle of mesquite. Parker walked out and brought the pair back. He allowed them to stop and pick up the satchels they had dropped when they started to run. The boy had held onto his. The old Mexican's eyes swam in tears of frustration. The younger man stood silent, defiant. Parker brought handcuffs out of the car. In Spanish he said, "I would not use these if you had not run."

The *viejo* said in a thin voice, "A man tries."

Charlie stood where he was until the pair were near him. Shaken, he said to the old man, "I am sorry. Why did you come back?"

"I would not go without thanking the patrón again. We had nothing to give you but our thanks."

And that, thought Charlie, came at a hell of a price.

While they waited for Nance, Charlie asked Parker, "What you goin' to do with them?"

"Jail a day or two. Then we'll ship them back across the river."

"They came here because they was hungry. They'll still be hungry when you send them back."

Parker flared. "Do you think you're telling me something new? What am I supposed to do about it? You know the law."

"I know the law is as blind as a one-eyed mule in a root cellar. Don't it ever bother you to take them back across?"

Parker studied the forlorn Mexican, and Charlie saw pity come into the patrolman's face. "I wake up nights . . . But hell, I don't pass the laws, I just carry them out. If it wasn't me, somebody else would do it. At least I try to treat them human. Some people wouldn't."

He glanced toward his partner. Nance trudged back, breathing heavily. His uniform was spotted with sweat, his face flushed with heat and anger. "Got away in the brush. Damn kid ran like a deer." He opened the rear door of the car and gave the old Mexican a shove. "Get in there!"

Sharply, Charlie said, "Take it easy. He's just a sick old man."

Nance whirled. "Don't you tell me what to do. You lied to us."

"I didn't lie. You asked if I was workin' any wets. These was passin' through and I fed them, that's all."

"If you ranchers would stop feeding them they'd quit coming. There are laws about that."

"And have a man starve to death in one of my pastures? There's a law about that too, a damn sight older than yours."

Parker tugged at Nance's sleeve. "Come on, Oliver."

Nance backed toward the car, eyes still hostile. "You ranchers think you're above the law, but you're not. I'll be watching you, Flagg."

Parker took Nance's arm. "Come on, I said. Let's go."

Nance slid into the driver's seat and slammed the door. Parker entered the other side where he could turn and watch the two wetbacks. The border patrol had not yet begun providing a grill between the back seat and the front in all of its vehicles. The pair seated behind the patrolmen could grab them and take over the car if the patrolmen's vigilance lapsed. But Charlie knew that was not the nature of the average man who came from across the river. Few criminals ventured deep into the ranch country, for travel was long and hard, and that kind gravitated more to the cities where pickings were varied and easy. These were humble men whose crime was that they refused to submit to hunger. Wetbacks might run or hide to elude capture, but once caught they were usually docile. In Mexico the ancient law of *ley fuga* was deeply ingrained, etched in blood. Even a common pickpocket might be killed for breaking away.

The pistol shots had brought an abrupt end to the shearing. Every shearer was standing against the fence, and the tie-boys had climbed up onto the sacking frame to watch. Some approved of the capture, some had been rooting for the wetbacks. Grumbling, Teofilo Garcia began trying to shoo the men back to work. The machine was using up gasoline. It took awhile; they had to discuss the incident in all its details first. When finally all were in their places and the wool was peeling again, Teofilo lumbered to the fence and leaned his considerable bulk against a cedar post, his shirttail hanging out, the knees of his old khaki trousers crusted with wool grease.

"Nothing here was your fault, Mister Charlie. Wetbacks like those, they get caught every day."

"They're so goddam hungry. . . "

Garcia shrugged. "Half the world is hungry. A man can't cry for all of them."

TOM MILLER

"Confessions of a Parrot Trooper,"
from *On the Border* (1982)

IN THE SIXTIES AND EARLY SEVENTIES, government agents used a composite profile to ferret out drug smugglers: white, male, shaggy hair, between eighteen and thirty-five, slightly nervous. But a typical parrot smuggler? No such thing. They are couples in Winnebagos. Grandmas in new Buicks. Teenagers in Volkswagens. Businessmen in Fords. Anyone in anything. The birds are hidden in cloth sacks and shopping bags, in hollow furniture and door panels, under the carburetor and around the engine. Even under women's skirts. A favorite ploy is to feed birds liquor-soaked bread to keep them tipsy and quiet for the crossing. Every parrot smuggler has a method.

Each year about two thousand parrots are intercepted at the border by customs agents, and the smugglers are warned not to try again. On rare occasions a bird-smuggling case will come before a federal judge. Except in the most extreme cases the defendant will get probation. The largest seizure in recent years occurred in 1978, when a California man was discovered with 562 birds in his station wagon. He received a sixty-day jail sentence and his birds got the death penalty.

~

THE CALIFORNIA MAN wasn't as wise as a fellow I met at a bar in Laredo frequented by local officials and other criminals. "I was at a birthday party for my brother a few years ago," he told me, "and a history professor from my college was feeling sad because one of his double yellow-head parrots had died. He was complaining that the laws were stupid—you could buy birds for fifteen or twenty dollars in Mexico, but by the time you find them in pet shops north of the border the price had multiplied twenty-fold or more. I was just amazed. I wanted to learn the whole parrot smuggling scam from beginning to end."

Today that student is the ringleader of a parrot-smuggling operation with branch offices throughout Texas, with possibilities of franchises all over the United States. He is working his way through college supplying all the birds he can to pet shops. "I didn't know what to look for on my first trip shopping for parrots, or how to tell if the birds were healthy or not. At the time I spoke only a little Spanish. With a friend who became my partner, I found a man in Ciudad Acuña who had parrots. We bought ten from him at twenty-five dollars a bird—although I found out later we could have bought them cheaper.

"I knew the area around Lake Amistad—my family used to go there on vacations when I was a kid. There is one place where the Rio Grande is about thirty-five yards across and fairly shallow. The current isn't very swift at that point and I knew I could swim the birds across there. We figured out what time the dam would close and when the customs men would leave.

"We put ten birds in one cage, and put the cage on a small, one-man rubber raft—the kind you play with in a backyard pool. The birds were pretty cramped and the weather was cold. We didn't know it was the wrong season for smuggling. Anyway, we put a cover on the cage and I shoved off. My partner drove around to the U.S. side to meet me at a rendezvous point.

"Crossing was no trouble. I was on the raft and the cage was between my legs. I paddled the backstroke over to the U.S. side. As soon as I beached I deflated the raft and started off along the three miles to my pick-up point. The first road I had to walk had thirty-foot-high fences lining it—I figured if someone comes down this road I'm a goner—so I started walking very fast. When I was almost in the clear I heard a noise like a jeep was coming. I thought, 'Oh shit, I must have tripped a sensor'—I'm very familiar with all the devices the Border Patrol uses and I got scared. I threw the cage in a ravine and ran to a grassy area and put my head down and thought, 'I'm not gonna move until somebody pulls me up.' I lay there five minutes and the noise kept getting louder. It turned out to be a train.

"Finally, I got to the highway with my cage. I was lying behind a bush waiting for my partner when a Border Patrol car slowly cruised down the same road I had just been on. Just after the Border Patrol left my partner arrived. I flagged him down, threw the birds into the back seat, hopped in the front, and we took off for San Antonio."

Three of the ten birds in the smuggler's first load died. The rest he took to a bird doctor. "He wanted to know what I was doing with a cageful of parrots. That seemed pretty suspicious to him since he didn't usually see thousands of dollars' worth of birds at once. I told him, 'A friend of mine has an aviary in Dallas, and he gave me the birds to sell in San Antonio. I've never seen my friend's aviary, and I don't want to sell any bad birds. That's why I want you to check them out.' He was a little wary, but he gave me some medicine to feed them. Since then I've read all sorts of books on how to feed the parrots, their health, and how to take care of them."

That first batch didn't sell very fast. "I had been after double yellow-heads, but as it turned out these were a different breed. Pet-store owners freaked out—they had never seen parrots like these in their lives. They said, 'Are these painted?' I said, 'You tell me. You run a pet shop, not me.' After a while I managed to sell all seven. One store owner looked at me like he was in a trance and said, 'Get me double yellow-heads—I'll buy all you can get.' By the way he said that, I knew I was on to something big.

"The man in Acuña never did have what I was after, but a contact I had farther downriver led me to a house full of birds in Nuevo Laredo. By this time I knew what I was looking for. The birds in Nuevo Laredo were the real McCoys—and they were young. Younger yellow-heads are worth more because they are easier to train. If you get an older one, he's going to be wilder than the rest.

"My customers always wanted to know whether they were buying male or female parrots. With a lot of birds the female is duller in color, but that's not always the case with parrots. The only way to find out is to feel the undercarriage of the bird: the diaphragm is shaped different in the two sexes. The only scientific way to sex parrots, though, is to have a vet insert a tiny periscope into the parrot and look for certain identifying structures."

I asked the smuggler why parrots are so popular. "They're the only bird that will accept a human," he explained. "People raise doves but you can't get a dove to crawl on your finger or hop on your head. The parrot alone will tolerate human companionship. People are infatuated with them because they take on human characteristics. You can teach them what to say if you get them young enough. I sold one bird to a woman who had a vocabulary of two hundred words—the bird, not the woman—and it could sing three songs: two operatic arias, plus 'La Cucaracha.' It had perfect pitch.

"I feed my birds twice daily. At first I only fed them masa harina, but as I smuggled more and more of them I learned they needed a more nutritionally balanced diet. Now I dice up carrots and apples and lettuce and throw it all in a blender with a big scoop of peanut butter. I make a batter out of it and feed them straight from a cup.

"In the beginning, I bought parrots in groups of ten. Business became so good a friend of mine started selling them for me. At the time I was paying twenty dollars apiece for them, and he paid me a hundred thirty dollars for each one. Anything he could sell them for over that was his to keep. I know he made a killing on them, and some months, well, I was making a thousand dollars a week bringing them in.

"Crossing the birds at Laredo was different from crossing them at Amistad," the birdman related. "We developed a good working relationship with our supplier in Nuevo Laredo. As soon as we'd pick up the birds at his house we'd go to a Pemex gas station and my partner would inflate our inner tube. Then we'd drive over to the east end of town and walk down to the river with the tube and a full cage. We'd lay the cage on top of the tube and my sneakers on top of the cage. I'm not sure how deep the river was there, but I could walk across a quarter of the way. When the water level got up to my chest the undercurrent was so great that it'd throw my feet out from under me, so I'd swim the rest of the way holding the tube in front of me. The first time we crossed I ended up a hundred twenty yards downriver from where I expected to. We solved that problem, and I've used the same spot dozens of times since."

Soon the smuggler was selling his birds through franchise outlets. "I had a Houston salesman. He'd buy some birds from me, go back home, sell them, and come back for more. Then I had a guy work San Antonio. Our deal was that he'd pay me a hundred forty dollars for each bird and sell them for a hundred seventy-five dollars. He made more money on a weekend working for me than all week at construction. I had a third guy take Austin and another fellow cover Dallas for me. I ended up taking orders from my salesmen. They'd tell me how many they could unload and I'd pick them up in Mexico and bring them back north.

"Running parrots has been good money. I earned a vacation in San Francisco and I went to Cozumel, too. I bought a whole new wardrobe and made all the payments on my car.

"Last year I got a new partner. He's the type who doesn't like to fool around. He said, 'Look, we need to design a cage that will hold *fifty* birds. If you're going to smuggle, why risk only ten at a time? The more times you cross the river, the more chance there is of getting caught. Just make fewer trips but bring fifty at a time.'

"That made sense to me. So we came up with a cage which wasn't very high but it was almost five feet long. My partner drove the car and I did the crossing. We started using walkie-talkies. He was Parrot Trooper II and I was Parrot Trooper I.

"I persuaded my banker to loan me the money to help finance the first big load—I told him the money was for a vacation, which in a way it was. I paid him back the first week. Word got around about all the available birds and people were buying like crazy. Some guy offered to take them east to sell. I could make even more money doing that, except parrots are very temperamental. If the birds get in a draft they'll catch pneumonia. If an air conditioner or heater is blowing they'll catch cold and die faster 'n hell. There's also a slim chance of parrot fever, but they can only get that from the filthiest food, the dirtiest water, and the most intolerable living conditions. Still, I always medicate my birds with streptomycin and tetracycline to make sure. I may send some east yet."

"I've got another year left of college and I'm starting to think—with the size of my operation, if I get caught I'd probably get a felony rap. But it'd be a first offense so I'd likely get five years probation. Also, my parents have been giving me a lot of flak. They know what I'm doing and they don't like it at all. I tell them, 'Look, when I worked for an oil company I was making three dollars an hour. I'd get my paycheck, go out one night, blow fifteen to twenty dollars and just sit figuring it took me seven hours working my butt off to go out at night. That just wasn't worth it. That's why I started doing parrots.'"

Parrot Trooper's father pleaded with him to forgo smuggling, even offering to give him money. "I said, 'Dad, it's a challenge. I know what I'm doing.' Running birds has been a high-adrenaline rush. It's the most euphoric sensation you could ever experience—something you want to tell your grandkids: I swam *the Rio Grande with fifty parrots*."

JAN REID

"Busting Out of Mexico," from *Close Calls* (2000)

IN 1976 THE WAR ON DRUGS was undeclared—at least the term had not gained popular usage—but it was being strenuously fought. Many Mexican smugglers, who were
called *fayuqueros* and *contrabandistas*, turned to drugs. Mexican heroin was said to be of
inferior and unprofitable grade, and cocaine (always and naively blamed on Colom-
bians) was just beginning to regain its historic popularity in the United States. The
drug in greatest demand was marijuana. American hippies, thrill seekers, and quick-
buck artists often blundered into the trade with a nonchalance that rose up and bit
them like a diamondback. Ever since Richard Nixon created the Drug Enforcement
Administration (DEA), El Paso had been the front line and command central. At the
same time, draconian penalties for possession of pot had been lightened in Texas, a
reflection of whose sons and daughters were getting high and busted. Mexican officials
had another obsession about contraband; they feared American guns as much as the
American establishment feared drugs. But it was in their interest to limit the drug

traffic, and Mexican cops often worked directly with the DEA. There might be a climate of leniency in the States, but if Americans trying to run drugs out of Mexico got caught down there, *pues, buena suerte.*

Conditions in Mexican jails and prisons were no surprise to Mexicans, but Americans exposed to them were aghast. Protests were being lodged at the diplomatic level. One night in March 1976 two Texans took the matter into their own hands. With ski masks and shotguns they ran in the city jail of Piedras Negras, the border town across from Eagle Pass. They grabbed two gringo marijuana smugglers and set all the prisoners free. The commandos were across the bridge and gone before the Mexicans could react, and over several months the jailbreak mushroomed into an international incident. I had a magazine assignment to write about the episode, and if I delivered it would get me out of a monetary bind. But except for radical groups in the States that claimed responsibility, thinking it would give them credibility, no one was talking. The rumors led to Dallas, where I camped on a friend's sofa as the days passed and cursed my lack of leads and luck.

Then an unemployed truck driver and badly wounded Vietnam ex-Marine named Don Fielden consented to a *Dallas Times Herald* interview set up by his lawyer. Fielden was dark-haired and thickset and had a dark gap under his lip where his front teeth had been knocked out. He said had been hired to do it by a psychologist and former pro wrestler named Sterling Davis. The old man was on federal probation for fraud, he had a serious heart condition, and his problematic son Cooter had been caught red-handed with 175 pounds of pot near Saltillo. The American youth got his throat cut in Mexican prison, and now he was doing his years in a cramped and suffocating municipal jail. The father appealed to the State Department, threw away money trying to bribe Mexican officials, and in desperation, he finally advertised for jailbreakers in Dallas truck stops, bars, and drive-ins. Fielden, who was looking at jail time now but envisioned a movie star playing his role in a big box office action film, referred contemptuously to his assistant as "the backup man."

Mike Hill towed away cars for a living and was often chauffeured by cops to Dallas jail, then released, among the usual suspects. One night a driver employed by Hill hauled off the car of a Dallas city council member, which irked her enough that Hill was arrested, his own vehicle towed to the city pound. In the truck, police said, were a loaded derringer and revolver, an unloaded shotgun, and two baseball bats. Hill cracked jokes and wore cowboy hats, and he walked with an odd slouching stride. He was a familiar Texas character—the tough guy good old boy. One night he had been rolling through the lot of a favorite Dallas hangout when a friend stuck his head in the van and grinned.

"Hey, boy. You wanta go to Mexico?"

Christ, we never learn.

Hill knew the fun was over, that he was in trouble now, and after reading the newspaper he saw that he was being dealt out of even the credit for their derring-do. So he asked someone how to call a press conference and booked a room one morning in the downtown Press Club. A few reporters showed up to hear him out; I was among them. After he spoke the reporters packed up their tablets and tape recorders and circled past him warily, leaving him blue and twitching for a cigarette. I talked to Hill and asked if he had any immediate plans. He told me nervously that he was supposed to be arraigned the next morning in the federal courthouse in Del Rio, and his truck was broke down—he didn't know how he was going to get down there. I blinked and said I'd take him. Within two hours we were speeding toward the Rio Grande, the air inside my little car thick with the smoke of this urban Marlboro man. Over the next two days he told me an amazing story in exchange for a ride and "a big old steak," as he put it. Fielden eventually talked to me, too, as well as one of the prisoners they had set free, and testimony at Hill's federal trial indicated that what they had told me was largely true. Fielden, who testified against him as part of a plea bargain, had to do his time, but Hill never spent a day in jail for his reckless behavior. His six-year sentence for "gunrunning" was overturned on appeal. Mike became my friend in those months, and we stayed in touch for many years.

~

HILL SAID HE HAD NEEDED money badly, and an expense-paid trip to Mexico sounded like a vacation to him. He and Fielden arranged to meet on one Saturday night at a Denny's in Dallas. By this time Fielden was desperate for a partner. Few men had been interested in the deal: the risks were mortal and the take-home pay was only $2,500. That night Hill listened to Fielden's story and studied his plans for the breakout while Fielden drew pencil sketches on paper napkins. Fielden kept saying, "It's not against the law, as long as you don't hurt anybody it's not against the law." Hill avoided making a commitment for a while, but when Fielden said he wanted to leave on Monday, Hill replied, "What's wrong with tonight?" Fielden said he had to get some traveling money together and agreed to leave the next day.

Driving south in Fielden's Ford, they quickly got on each other's nerves. Hill went through coffee like it was tobacco, so every few miles Fielden had to stop at a cafe. Hill's legs were numb from the frigid gale of Fielden's air conditioner. Fielden wanted to talk about the jailbreak; Hill wanted to watch the passing countryside and think about getting laid in Mexico. Hill asked Fielden how much money he had raised, and his partner muttered, "A hundred dollars." Hill thought: a hundred dollars? I thought I was getting in on a big-time deal.

In the car were Fielden's sawed-off shotgun and Hill's twelve-gauge pump. As they drove farther south it became more apparent that Fielden intended to stage the raid without any further delay. "Uh," Hill said. "I thought we were just gonna go down there and kinda look at it."

The next morning, Fielden and Hill paid nickel tolls at Eagle Pass and walked the International Bridge across the Rio Grande, on that day a shallow, muddy stream that swirled against the steep bank on the Mexican side. Hill had always been enchanted by the idea of Mexico. He liked the food, the music, the raven-haired women. Hill was excited as he passed the Mexican customs inspector. He knew no Spanish, and was not aware of the extreme importance Mexican officials attached to that sign of warning: *Terminantemente Prohibida: La importación de armas y cartuchos . . .* The importation of guns and bullets . . .

Hill's stomach convulsed when he saw the Piedras Negras jail. It was too well guarded, too far back from the street. Back in the Eagle Pass motel room, they considered diverting the Mexican cops' attention with fires or explosions, but whenever Fielden started talking too intently about the break, Hill rolled a joint and smoked it. The next day, they watched the jail from a tamale stand and inspected the streets in the vicinity, attracting a following of shine-boys, pimps, and guides. Everything about it looked wrong to Hill. The street in front of the jail ran one way toward the border and bridge, but it was extremely narrow. Cops stood in front of the jail. Hill and Fielden weren't even sure Cooter Davis was still in the Piedras Negras jail.

Upon returning to the motel, Hill talked by phone to the father Sterling Davis for the first time. The psychologist in Dallas "sounded real positive about not sending anybody any money," Hill said, and he only presumed that his son had not been moved. Fielden wanted to stage the break while he still had money to pay the motel bill. At midnight Hill put on his gloves and drove the Ford across the bridge, but as Fielden inspected the sawed-off double-barrel, Hill continued to argue against going through with it. Hill said he didn't even know what Cooter Davis looked like. If Fielden got killed, was Hill supposed to run in the jail yelling, which one of you guys did we come after?

The argument was interrupted when a Piedras Negras patrol unit pulled up behind the Ford and turned its flashing lights on. Twisting around to see if the cops got out with pistols drawn, Fielden reached for the door handle and growled, "We're gonna have to take 'em out . . ."

"Wait a minute," Hill cried, grabbing for Fielden's arm as one of the cops got out of the car. "Let's see what he wants, and then we'll kill him."

As the Mexican cop approached, Hill extended a hand toward him and said, "Señor, which way to Boys' Town?"

The cop's gaze focused with curiosity on Hill's grimy glove. But he said, "Ah, señor. Follow me."

Trailing the patrol unit, Hill fell far enough back so that Fielden was able to ditch the guns in some bushes. In the red-light district Hill and Fielden thanked the cops and went into one of the bars. Hill only had twenty dollars, but he was so happy he bought one of the whores several drinks.

The next day was visitors' day at the Piedras Negras jail. A guard frisked Fielden and Hill and unlocked the door that led back to the prisoners. A stocky man with curly hair greeted Fielden from the first cell. Fielden stood shoulder-to-shoulder with other visitors outside the bars as he whispered instructions to Cooter Davis. Hoping to gain some insight into the man he was going to rescue, Hill spoke briefly with Davis, but he wanted badly to get out of that jail. Hill was convinced that the purpose of their visit was transparently obvious to the guards; compared to the other visitors, they looked like gangsters. And Hill had spent enough time in American jails to react emotionally to the horror of this one. The odor in the jail was appalling. The visitors were panting and drenched with sweat. Recalling the expressions on the prisoners' faces, Hill later remarked, "Have you ever seen a drowning dog?"

In the motel room Hill and Fielden argued again. Hill wanted a third man in the car with a walkie-talkie. "I've got to get this deal done," Fielden finally exploded. "I never took a deal that I didn't do. All I want is somebody to watch my back. I'll do it."

"Your back!" Hill cried. "I'm thinking about my butt, I'm thinking about my whole damn body!"

Fielden drove when they crossed the bridge after midnight. As they headed for the brush where they had stashed the guns, Hill was talking fast and furiously. They'd been hanging around the jail for three days; the Mexican cops had to know something was up. They didn't have enough gasoline money to get back to Dallas. "I don't want to do it tonight," Hill said. "My karma's not right."

Fielden was disgusted, but their lack of money worried him. Fielden knew from his combat experience that in an operation like this, both men needed conviction, if not total confidence. Hill's reluctance could get them both killed. After they retrieved the guns they came upon the same cops who had stopped them the night before. This time Fielden got out of the car. "Well, we're through in Boys' Town," he told the cops. "How do we get out of here?"

~

THE NEXT MORNING a friend wired Fielden $50. They paid the motel bill, gassed up the Ford, and headed back to Dallas. On the way they had a flat. Fielden was uncertain he could ever count on Hill. But he had no other partner in mind; in hiring Hill he felt he'd already scraped the bottom of the barrel. Hill told Fielden he would proceed with the breakout only if they could recruit a third man and if they had enough money for their expenses. Fielden assigned Hill the task of finding the third man. As a token of good faith, Hill said he could probably raise the money if Fielden could not.

That Saturday Hill met Sterling Davis for the first time in the office on Northwest Highway. Hill was impressed by the verbal assurance of the craggy-faced man, but something about the office made Hill think the doctor "hadn't been there too long." Davis showed Hill a photocopy of a check for $5,000, but again refused to advance them any expense money.

Hill proceeded with marked ambivalence. In the presence of Fielden, he offered the lookout job to a hulking friend. But something—perhaps affection, perhaps doubts about the man's reliability—made Hill ask his friend after Fielden was gone: "You remember those wetbacks you took on with a ball bat? They paid me two thousand dollars to get you across the border."

The friend quickly withdrew. Hill next offered the job to Billy Blackwell, a stocky eighteen-year-old with shoulder-length hair who had previously worked for him in the wrecker business. Blackwell now mowed lawns for a living; he lived with a teen-aged brother but ran with a tough older crowd. To Billy Blackwell, Mike Hill was a figure to emulate. Hill often teased his young protégé. "Stick with me, Billy, and we'll go places," he joked. "Let's you and me rob a bank."

Billy laughed at the banter and always tagged along; Mike hadn't gotten him in trouble yet. Hill was willing to trust his life to the eighteen-year-old. He knew that Billy Blackwell's loyalty was absolute.

But Hill again stalled. By now both men had begun to feel some sense of personal obligation to Cooter Davis, but Hill would have welcomed a development that took him off the hook. "I was trying to stay alive as long as I could," he later explained. He called Fielden and asked if he had been able to raise the money. Sounding dejected, Fielden said he had exhausted all his possibilities. Hill regretted his offer to raise the money himself. He considered telling Fielden that his monetary well had dried up, too, but he hated to lie his way out of it. He kept remembering his visit to the jail— the stench and the drowning-dog expression on the prisoners' faces. So instead Hill lied to raise the money.

He told a business creditor that repossession of a tractor-trailer rig in Mexico was worth $10,000 to himself and another man. With considerable misgivings, the creditor loaned Hill $1,000, using the silver van for collateral, and said he was also willing to extend enough money on a separate loan to put Hill back in the used-car business. The offer provided Hill with a monetary out; he could pay his bills now without Sterling

Davis' money. But Hill had become intrigued by another possibility. A frizzy-haired American in the cell next to Blake's had gotten word to Fielden that he would pay equal money if he came out, too. Fielden at first intended to bring out only those two men. Hill wanted to free all the prisoners. If every freed American voluntarily came up with $5,000, they were talking about a potential haul of more than fifty grand.

Though Hill was more cautious than Fielden, he craved adventure, too. All those factors tipped the balance in favor of Hill's participation. He borrowed a spare for Fielden's Ford, walkie-talkies, new gloves, and blue ski masks with red insets on the faces. Hill was not an educated man, but he understood guerrilla psychology. They would go across in dark clothing, relying on the element of surprise. Mexican cops did not often encounter men with shotguns and ski masks.

The next morning Hill phoned Blackwell and said, "Get your clothes together, Billy. We're going."

~

HILL SMOKED A JOINT as he waited for his partners, and when Fielden's Ford pulled up outside the metal prefab apartment Hill looked out and saw a man with sandy razor-cut hair. That's not Billy, he thought, then remembered that the youth had been instructed to wear a short-hair wig.

Hill had described the project to Billy in extremely vague terms. He suspected that his young friend thought they were actually going down to repossess a truck. As they drove south, Hill tried to impress Blackwell with the seriousness of the situation. "Billy, what it boils down to is we're going to war down there, actually."

Billy swallowed hard. "Well, Mike, don't you think I need a gun?"

In Waco Fielden bought a bottle of scotch. Hill knew he had to be straight when he crossed the Rio Grande, but in the meantime he and Billy were passing joints. As darkness fell and they passed through San Antonio, tension in the Ford began to build. "Why don't you quit smoking?" Fielden finally said.

Hill thought about it for a minute and said, "Well, hell, you're drinking."

They checked into a motel in Eagle Pass and watched TV until it went off. Billy got extremely quiet when Hill and Fielden pulled out the guns and ski masks. Fielden briefed Blackwell on each of the five checkpoints, and shortly after 2 a.m., Billy wrapped his jacket around the walkie-talkie and began his lonely walk across the International Bridge.

Hill and Fielden gassed up the Ford and returned to the motel, where Hill stashed the rest of his money, about $400, in his shaving kit. He didn't want the Mexican cops to enjoy it. Near the bridge again they tried to raise Billy, but a Mexican CB operator broke in over them. Finally Billy called from the vicinity of the jail: "Ringo, this is Sam. There's a bunch of activity over here now. Cars coming in and out."

"Okay. We'll call you back in ten minutes."

Waiting at the border, Hill took a couple of swallows from Fielden's bottle of scotch. A few yards away two Eagle Pass patrolmen were conducting some kind of investigation. Hill and Fielden pretended to study a map, and the cops drove away after giving them a long look. The cops circled the block, then circled it again. Hill got out and went over to the patrol car. "We've been trying to read that map for an hour," he told the cops. "How do you get to Boys' Town?"

The cops laughed, gave Hill directions, and drove away. In the car Hill and Fielden were unable to raise Blackwell. "They must've got Billy," Hill said. "Let's go on across." Crossing the bridge, Hill swallowed a tablet of speed.

Fielden's intelligence report anticipated three Mexican cops at the border, one in the small park behind the tollgates and three at the jail. At the border they saw at least six uniformed officers, all impressively armed with chromed sidepieces. After clearing Mexican customs, Hill turned off the plaza and tried to circle through the maze of narrow streets to the jail. Very quickly they were lost. A carload of Mexican youths pulled up beside them. Hill and Fielden knew that the street in front of the jail led to the bordello. "Pinoche, pinoche," Hill cried. The Mexican youths laughed and motioned for the Ford to follow.

After tipping their guides a dollar, Hill and Fielden at last raised Billy. "Six of the cops just left," he radioed. "There shouldn't be but three in there now."

They picked up Billy a block from the jail, and Hill parked the Ford one parking space away from the jail lot. Fielden began: "If you have any second thoughts, if your karma's not right . . ." But Hill was pulling on his ski mask, too.

On the sidewalk Hill did a double take as he passed the car parked in front of the Ford. "Don't freak out," he whispered to Fielden, "but there's a cop asleep in that car."

Fielden froze. "*What*? Where?"

Headlights fell upon them from behind. Fielden concealed the sawed-off with his bulk and turned his face away; Hill stuffed his pump in a long flower pot on a wall, ripped his mask off, and turned to face the approaching motorists. Just some horny American boys. He put his ski mask back on and stared across the street. In the police auto pound he saw cars with all the doors flung open. Paranoid flash: they'd been set up, cops were lying down behind the seats! Fielden forged ahead with the tense determination of a Marine about to plant the flag at Iwo Jima. Hill followed at a trotting walk, searching the rooftops for soldiers with rifles. When Fielden grabbed the handle of the jail door, for the first time Hill was absolutely certain this deal was going down.

Fielden had been studying a Spanish dictionary, but he was not certain how to say, "Get your hands up." He yelled, "Palmo asente!" as he burst through the door. When he saw the inside of the jail, he thought god *damn*, we're gonna have to teach that boy how to count. Through Hill's mind sped an image from a favorite movie: Paul Newman and Robert Redford, Cassidy and Sundance, running toward a lethal hail.

Behind two counters five guards and five police officers were interrogating an eighteen-year-old Mexican girl who'd been jailed on drug charges but claimed membership in a cop-killing terrorist organization in the Sierra Madres. When Fielden and Hill ran through the door the disbelieving cops froze for an instant, then scattered in ten directions.

"*Freeze!*" Fielden bellowed, and gave one cop a whack with the shotgun when he proved reluctant to surrender his pistol. Hill vaulted across the counter, and the Mexican stenographer fell out of his chair in front of him. Fielden looked up after relieving the first cop of his gun and saw that two more had their pistols drawn and aimed. "Huh uh," Fielden warned, and the force of the sawed-off twin barrels won out: two more pistols dropped to the floor.

Staring at the bore of Hill's twelve-gauge, two cops raised their hands. As if he were bailing water, a third tried to dislodge his pistol from his holster. Then Hill saw the M-1 propped against the wall. Easing toward the rifle, Hill glimpsed the toe of a man's shoe just behind him. He yelled and wheeled his twelve-gauge around. The cop reeled back in terrified surrender. Hill had come very, very close to committing murder.

But the element of surprise had worked. They had subdued the cops without firing a shot. Fielden hurried to the barred door that led back to the cells and popped the chain with the bolt cutters. While Hill watched the cops, Fielden encountered the unarmed guard who tended the cells and a Mexican prisoner who was outside his cell when the shouting started. Fielden ran to the first cell and weighed down on the handles of the bolt cutters. But this chain broke the jaws of the bolt cutters. Fielden looked helplessly through the bars at Cooter Davis. Davis groaned, "Oh, shit."

"Get the key," one of the inmates recommended.

"How do you say keys in Spanish?" Fielden snapped.

"Llave," the inmates clamored. "La llave."

What were they saying? Yobby? The Mexican inmate lashed the unarmed guard with the broken chain. The guard finally got the message when Fielden held the sawed-off to his head. Fielden walked the guard to a desk in the front office, then came back and unlocked Cooter Davis's cell.

Hill started herding the cops down the corridor toward the cells. The eighteen-year-old girl and confessed guerrilla looked at Hill and said, "Me too?"

"You too, baby. You better move."

"Me too?" the girl said again.

Hill raised the shotgun to the girl's eye level; she scampered after the cops down the hall. Cooter Davis came out front and Hill handed him the Mexican M-1. While Cooter watched the cops, Fielden unlocked the two remaining cells containing American men. One imprisoned Frenchman opted for the security of his cell, but the Mexican nationals were extremely willing to share the fruits of American labor. One of the American inmates ran around to the back and pried a weakened bar until the women were able to wriggle free. At least two dozen inmates were soon milling the corridor, shushing each other and trying to contain their excitement. "Nobody goes out before us," Fielden ordered. "There's a man out there who'll cut you in two."

The Mexican who had attacked the guard broke for the front. Davis shouted a warning and leveled the M-1, but the Mexican reached Hill, who'd been pacing nervously and exhorting Fielden to hurry up. The Mexican asked Hill if he had any more guns. Hill noticed the man had blood on his head. He handed over a cop's pistol, and the Mexican kicked open an office door, revealing two *federales* who had been interrogating the man's wife before the jailbreak started. Since then they had been hiding quietly. The Mexican proceeded to pistol whip the *federales* noisily.

"Who was that?" Hill asked Davis, who had followed the Mexican up the hall.

"He's all right," Cooter replied, then returned to the back. Suddenly Billy's voice came from the walkie-talkie: "Mike, you got two coming through the door."

Heart pounding, Hill crouched behind the counter and waited. The Mexican cops never arrived; opening the door they'd seen an American inmate carrying a carbine. "Billy, where are they?" Hill finally blurted into his walkie-talkie.

"I don't know, man. They left."

Inside, Fielden herded the cops into a rear corridor but he couldn't get the deadbolt lock to slide. He rounded up Davis and his frizzy-haired friend who had promised money and led the procession out of the office. One of the American men asked Fielden to take the women but Fielden shook his head. Fielden told the Americans to turn right at the sidewalk, right again at the first corner. "When you hit water you know you're at the Rio Grande."

Hill was jumping up and down, trying to let Fielden know he was caught up in the crowd. One of the American girls grabbed Hill's arm but he pried her fingers loose and joined Fielden, Cooter, and his hairy monied friend in the front ranks. They ran to the Ford as the escapees sprinted. As the five men pulled away from the curb, the Mexican cops were already filtering back into the front office of the jail, and in the excitement Hill had forgotten to cut the telephone line. The driver of a garbage truck pulled out in front of them. "Punch it!" Fielden yelled. "They're trying to block us in."

"Calm down!" Hill yelled. "That guy's just trying to turn around."

Hill had been in Mexico eight minutes, and the rush of his amphetamine was really coming on. After what seemed like an eternity, they circled the plaza and reached the tollgate. Hill groaned and kept his foot away from the accelerator as the driver of a red station wagon chatted amiably with the customs toll taker. Finally the station wagon rolled away from the gate. Hill grinned at the Mexican official and handed him a quarter. Twelve cents would have sufficed.

As they crossed the bridge Fielden leaned forward and Cooter started heaving incriminating evidence toward the river. Hill saw one of the guns bounce off the bridge, and Fielden looked back and saw one of the ski masks lying on the walkway. Everybody in the car was jabbering. Looming above the roof of the U.S. customs station was the neon sign of Texaco, and beyond that, Sears.

"We're home," Hill was saying. "We're clean, just stay calm, we're gonna make it, we're doing it, god damn, we're home . . ."

The U.S. customs inspector was an old man. "Are you all American citizens?" he asked routinely. "Did you bring anything back from Mexico?"

JOHN DAVIDSON

from *The Long Road North* (1978)

THE NUEVO LAREDO-BOUND BUS slowed to a halt on the last descent into the desert. "Hay muertos?" a passenger asked in the dark. "Are there dead?" Out the window to his left Javier could see the waiting headlights of a long line of cars. "Es otro camion," a man commented. Javier couldn't see the wrecked bus and was too tired to stand up and look. He leaned his head back and closed his eyes. After a while, he sensed the bus moving into the line of white headlights, then a flashing red light, and finally darkness.

When Javier woke again, the bus was splashing slowly through water. A wake angled out until it lapped at the house fronts along the street, and stranded cars rocked gently as the bus proceeded into deeper water. "Esta hundido Nuevo Laredo," a voice in the dark softly exclaimed the obvious. Looking at the flooded streets, Javier thought of the river. If it was flooded, they couldn't swim. A smuggler would have to take them across. Too tired to worry about it, Javier leaned his head against the window and closed his eyes.

When the bus pulled into the Nuevo Laredo terminal it was 3 A.M. Javier shook Juan awake, the Anglo stood, and they gathered their belongings to get off. Downtown, the water had run off into the river, and the streets were deserted. Momentarily lost, the two brothers stood in the milky neon glow in front of the bus station until Javier asked the driver about a place to stay. Directed toward a cheap hotel, they started down the empty street, Juan carrying his cardboard box tied with a string and Javier his orange and black flight bag.

At the hotel, they got a small windowless room for four dollars. Without bothering to remove his clothes or black boots, Juan pulled the green bedspread back on the double bed and lay down on the spotted gray sheets. Javier took off his shirt and then his cowboy boots, which, to discourage scorpions, he propped upside down in the corner before switching off the bare bulb in the ceiling and lying down next to Juan.

They were all tired after the fifteen-hour bus ride from Jalisco and slept late the next morning. As they checked out, the woman at the desk showed them newspaper headlines that read *"Cyclone!"* The storm killed three people and injured fifteen in Nuevo Laredo. Another twenty-eight people died when a bus crashed north of Monterrey. It had been the worst storm in years.

Outside it was hot, and the humidity rose off the damp ground and pavement. Javier and Juan walked directly to the bridge, then followed a chain-link fence west along the riverbank. At the railroad tracks that lead to the train bridge, Javier scrambled up the embankment, and Juan followed. On the other side, they dropped down into knee-high grass and mesquite and pushed through till hitting a trail. Garbage thrown from houses on the riverbank above was scattered along the trail, and there was the sweet smell of putrefaction. At the river's edge they could see the water, dense brown and pocked by whirling eddies, and farther out, rafts of river trash and the stately progression of floating tree trunks that marked the current's velocity.

"Can you swim?" Javier asked.

"Some," Juan answered.

"But not in this," Javier said and smiled. "You would get caught in the trash or a log would hit you. Then you would drown." He squatted on his heels to watch the river. "I wonder how many have drowned in this?"

Juan looked at him.

"No one knows what happens to the ones trying to cross. In the river, we're neither here nor there, so no one counts."

Juan shrugged indifferently and settled on his heels to watch the river. They turned in unison as a man came around a bend in the trail. His pant legs were rolled above the knee, and his bare feet stuck in an old pair of unlaced shoes. He was carrying his shirt in his hand. "Lots of water," Javier greeted him.

"Enough," the man agreed.

"How long will the river be up?"

"Who knows," the man answered as he passed. "A week. Maybe more."

They watched the man till he disappeared around the next bend, then turned back to the river. "What do you think?" Javier asked. "Will we make it or not?"

"Pues, sí," Juan shrugged noncommittally.

"We'll see," Javier said and stood up.

Climbing out of the river bottom, Javier indicated what appeared to be an impenetrable thicket of mesquite. Grass rose a foot and a half to an intricate crisscross of mesquite limbs that formed a green wall. "The first fifty miles," he said, "it's like this. Only worse." He turned and climbed the bank to the railroad tracks.

In town, they waded through the jam of American tourists and Mexican vendors on the narrow sidewalks. Away from the bridge and past the market and curio shops, they found an inexpensive restaurant where each ordered carne guisada, tortillas, frijoles, and Pepsi-Cola. They ate slowly, using pieces of tortilla to tear the stewed meat into delicate shreds, which they rolled with beans and salsa into small tacos. When he finished, Javier cleaned his teeth with a napkin and got out his cigarettes.

From the restaurant, they walked to a small corner grocery store. Javier selected two plastic net shopping bags: one blue and green plaid, and the other orange and yellow. He asked the woman behind the counter for six cans of refried beans, six cans of large sardines, a small bottle of salsa picante, two loaves of Bimbo white bread, five packages of crackers, four packages of Parade cigarettes, several boxes of matches, and a bottle of rubbing alcohol. After paying the woman, Javier distributed the purchases between the two plastic bags, tied the strap of his canvas bag to the plastic handles of one shopping bag, and draped them both over his right shoulder like saddlebags. Juan transferred the shirt and pair of pants from his cardboard box into his shopping bag and they stepped back into the street.

At a hardware store, Javier bought a compass for himself and a white straw hat for Juan, which, on closer inspection, turned out to be plastic. So equipped, they retraced their steps down Avenida Guerrero toward the bridge, turned west, and in the early-afternoon sun, walked out past the railroad station, the cemetery, and into the slums of Nuevo Laredo.

On the low side of the streets, the soggy contents of houses were draped on fences and shrubs or stacked on any dry surface to catch the sun. Block after block, the houses became poorer until the town finally petered out with one last corner grocery. Squatting in the shade against the wall, a man watched them approach. "Hey!" he called when they got closer. "Where you going?"

"Más allá," Javier evaded. Farther on.

"Toward Carrizo?" The man stood to face them. Beneath his straw hat, he had yellow eyes and a three-day growth of beard. "A truck is coming that will take you."

"We'll see," Javier answered, and they walked into the store. Inside, he asked the *señora* for an empty half-gallon plastic milk bottle and bought himself and Juan a Pepsi. When they walked back out, a man was sitting in an old red pickup parked in the shade of the building next to the man with yellow eyes. The driver looked up from his friend and took in Juan and Javier with their boots, hats, and plastic net shopping bags. He made nothing of the Anglo. "I imagine you want to cross the river," he said.

"It's a possibility," Javier admitted.

"I can take you toward Carrizo where a man has a boat. Thirty dollars."

"Ten each?" Javier asked.

"That's right. Ten each."

Javier took out a ten and collected another from the Anglo. He handed the man the twenty dollars and put his bags in the back of the truck. "What about your friend?" the man asked.

Javier looked at Juan and shrugged. "He doesn't have any money."

"You could loan it to him," the man suggested.

"Not when I have barely enough to cross the river," Javier answered and started climbing in.

"Fifteen for both," the man offered.

"Leave him here," Javier said coldly and sat down in the back of the truck to indicate he was ready to leave. The driver looked down at his friend with yellow eyes, both shrugged, and he started the engine. As the truck drove away from the store, Juan and Javier looked at each other but made no sign. As they pulled on to the road, the driver glanced into the mirror and saw Juan standing forlornly with his shopping bag. He stepped on the clutch and the brake, leaned out the window, and shouted angrily, "All right. Get in!"

The truck ran west along the gravel road a mile south of and parallel to the river. Where the land was low and flat, standing water came up to the truck's axle and the flooded mesquite flats looked like swamps shimmering with heat, reflecting the blue sky with its stray white clouds. Speaking above the sound of crunching gravel and the partially submerged muffler, Javier touched Juan's arm and said, "We may have to walk all of tonight in water."

Impassive, Juan finished tearing a rind of thumbnail with his teeth. "We cross tonight?"

"At sunset. If we can get away from the river at night, the airplane won't see us."

"Airplane?"

"From immigración. They patrol with the airplane and in jeeps and trucks." Then, pointing at the submerged pasture, "Do you think you can sleep in water?"

"I'd rather walk in it."

"Walk enough, and you can sleep anywhere," Javier assured him.

The truck faltered twice before reaching dry land and going on toward Carrizo. After half an hour on the road, they approached a small cluster of shacks where the driver brought his pickup to a halt in the middle of the road. Letting the motor idle, he opened the door and stood on the running board. "Here there is a man with a boat," he said.

Javier looked at the shacks and back toward Nuevo Laredo. "No, señor, too close. Here la immigración would catch us for sure. Farther on." The driver started to argue, but got back in the truck. Twenty minutes and two ephemeral swamps later, they came to a large white warehouse, closed and overgrown with weeds and sunflowers. On the far side of the building the driver stopped the truck in front of a solitary shack. "For ten dollars," he complained when he got out of the truck, "this is as far as I take you."

Javier and Juan climbed down with their belongings. An undernourished adolescent in a large cowboy hat and black jeans tucked into cowboy boots loped out from the shack and stopped before them. "You want to cross the river," he said, his pale eyes tracking independently across them. Not knowing which eye focused and which stared into space, Javier hesitated and the driver said, "Héctor, where's Rodrigo?"

"He's coming now. Any minute," the boy promised. He was so thin—a backbone inside a ragged white T-shirt—it appeared unlikely that he could propel the cowboy boots. "Three others are already waiting. We'll take them all today."

"Then I'll leave these two with you," the driver said and got back in his truck. As he drove away, Juan and Javier followed Héctor to the shack, which was circumscribed by a ring of trash as far as the arm could throw. Away from the road, the tin shack, its roof weighted down with worn-out tires, had been expanded by a makeshift awning covered with huisache branches and a lean-to kitchen. An old Formica-and-chrome kitchen table and chairs sat in the shade of the awning.

"If you have food you want to heat," Héctor offered.

"Not now," Javier thanked him.

"Perhaps you have a cigarette you can give me?"

Javier took out his pack, gave Héctor and Juan each a cigarette, and took one himself. Javier started to sit down at the table beneath the awning after they had lighted the cigarettes. "Not here," Héctor stopped him. "Sometimes the federales come; you had better hide in the bushes." He led them out of the radius of trash and into the mesquite, where three men sat at the edge of a clearing around a washed-out campfire. Two of the men had paper bags at their sides and the third a black plastic shaving kit. "They're going too," Héctor said by way of introduction, and the three men nodded. Javier and Juan dropped their bags in the ring of ashes and sat down on the ground in the long shadows of the mesquite trees. Héctor squatted down beside them to finish the cigarette he was smoking. "Güero," he said after studying the Anglo for a moment. "Why don't you just walk across the bridge?"

"Pues, no tengo documentos," the Anglo said and looked nervously at Javier.

"But you would only have to say you were American. If they even asked."

"But I don't speak English."

One of Héctor's two eyes focused on him. "Where are you from? Not Mexico."

"El Salvador. Soy de allá."

"Don't the people speak Spanish there?" He swayed on his haunches. "I hear an accent."

"Yes, but my family speaks German. My parents came from Germany. That's the language I spoke first."

Héctor rocked slightly forward, dropped the cigarette, and stood. "Very soon Rodrigo will be here," he assured them one last time and started back to the shack.

They watched Héctor leave, then Javier asked the men where they come from. "Veracruz, donde no vale la vida," the round-faced man sitting in the middle answered for the three. "And you?"

"Jalisco," Javier echoed. "Where life has no value." Javier stretched out on the ground, put his canvas bag beneath his head, and pulled a weed to chew on. "How long have you been waiting here?"

"Since midday," the same man answered. "What time is it now?"

Javier looked at his wristwatch. "Four o'clock." To the west he could see cumulus clouds building as if for the sunset.

"Rodrigo is probably getting drunk somewhere," the man speculated. "The skinny one with the eyes said they took nine this morning."

"Nine," Javier repeated. "That's a good business."

"Yes, but it's not a regular harvest."

"It never is," Javier agreed. "You've been before?"

"Yes, but not the others," the man answered.

"Then you're the one who knows the way?"

"I know which way is north."

"That's good," Javier said and pulled the long stem of the weed through his teeth to shred it. "The first time I went, one of us had a compass. We walked for three days and came to a big river. At last we thought we were getting out of the brush. We spent most of a morning looking for a place to cross before we realized it was the Rio Grande."

"You walked in a circle," the man said.

"That's right," Javier smiled. "The one with the compass didn't know how to read it. Like idiots, we almost crossed back into Mexico."

"But you made it."

"Barely." Javier sat up, stretched, and then propped up on one elbow. "Just barely."

"How many days did it take?"

"Eleven to San Antonio. We almost starved in the brush before we got to Carrizo and had to stop at a ranch and work for food. They gave us each two dollars for three days of cutting mesquite posts and said if we didn't leave they would call la migra."

"Be glad they didn't need more posts. You would have worked more days for the same amount of money."

"True," Javier said and sat up farther. Gazing toward the man, he had noticed that beneath the cuffs of his green polyester trousers hung a set of plaid polyester cuffs. The other two men also had double sets of cuffs hanging above their boots. "You're wearing two pairs of pants," Javier pointed out.

In unison the three men looked down at their cuffs and then up. "For the snakes," the man in the middle explained.

"They must be bad now."

"Perhaps the rain makes them crawl up in the trees to stay dry."

Javier studied the mesquite around them to imagine the outcome of crawling snakes. "That way they would strike us in the face or on the arms, rather than on our boots." Juan shifted uneasily, attracting Javier's attention. "Snakes scare you?" Javier asked.

"Psssh," Juan exhaled disgust and turned away.

"The last time," the man in the middle went on, "we found a corpse. Snakebite, we decided."

"Many say they've seen bodies. Thank God, I never have."

"Not a pleasant thing," the man assured Javier.

One of the men who hadn't spoken got up and walked out into the brush. When he returned, he was carrying a milk container like Javier's except that it was partially caved in and dirty from months on the ground. He hit it against his leg to knock the dent out and the dirt off.

"Does it leak?" one of them asked.

The man held it to his mouth and blew till it was full and he could blow no more. "No leaks," he announced and sat back down. "Good," the man in the middle said. "We can cut a stick for a plug."

"Or make a knot of grass," Javier suggested.

Héctor reappeared to ask for another cigarette and to say that Rodrigo would be there any minute. Reminded that they had been waiting most of the afternoon, the man in the middle got up and said he thought they would walk farther up the river to see if anyone else had a boat. "No more boats," Héctor warned. "Rodrigo comes and you're not here, he won't wait for you. He'll be angry that you left." The man shrugged; they picked up their belongings and started for the road. Héctor followed behind, cajoling and threatening.

Javier watched them go, then lay back down, resting his head on the canvas bag. "If we cross by sunset," he said, "that's soon enough." He pulled the brim of his baseball cap over his eyes and drifted off to sleep.

It was dusk when they heard the pickup. There was honking, then shouting and drunken laughter. Confident it was not federales, Javier and Juan picked up their bags and walked out toward the road. In the half light, they could see a blur of activity between the shack and an old truck. A radio was snapped on to jar the evening quiet, children ran, a flame jumped before an old woman in the lean-to kitchen, and an old man staggered at the side of the truck. Héctor, when he saw the two brothers, brought Rodrigo out to talk. Powerfully built, dressed completely in black, Rodrigo acted as surly as he looked. "You want to cross," he said and hitched his pants tighter. Splayed, tusklike teeth sprouted from his upper gum when he opened his mouth.

Yes, they wanted to cross, Javier answered politely.

"You can pay?" He looked them over as if it might be by the pound.

Yes, Javier answered, they could pay. Without a word, Rodrigo turned, walked to the shack, and dug in an ice chest for a beer. He tilted the bottle back and drained it. A woman in bulging red stretch pants came up and applied herself to Rodrigo as if she in turn intended to drain him of some vital force. Watching the galvanic weld, Héctor commented with approval. "Married last month."

Rodrigo disengaged, walked back, and hitched his pants. "Tomorrow morning when it gets light, I'll take you across. You can sleep tonight behind the warehouse."

Javier and Juan sat on the warehouse loading dock and ate a can of refried beans. Above them they could hear bats swoop, and before them the tops of six-foot-tall sunflowers swayed at the edge of the dock. Juan coughed dryly on the first wad of beans spread thick on a soda cracker. He reached for the empty milk container and started to get up. "Where are you going?" Javier asked.

"To ask for water."

"Don't ask them for anything. If they don't rob us we'll be lucky." He spread a cracker with beans, shook some of the red sauce on top, and handed it to Juan. "Let them forget we're here."

After eating, they smoked a cigarette, then lay down on the dock with their heads next to the wall. The night air was cool, but the raw concrete beneath them was still warm from the sun. At the edge of sleep, Javier heard someone on the steps to the dock. Héctor came toward them carrying a large bundle. "You want these?" he said and dropped a couple of blankets. They spread one blanket beneath them and pulled the other over, "Tonight," Javier said happily as dirt sprinkled onto them from the blanket, "we sleep like the President."

Javier woke with the first gray light. He sat on the dock and watched the shack. Above, a skim of clouds sped east across the sky, a rooster crowed, but the shack remained silent while the protective dark slipped away. The sun was almost up when the door opened and a little girl ran out. She pulled down her panties, squatted at the edge of the mesquite, then ran back to the shack. The sun rose and Javier lay back down to wait. When he woke again, it was full day and Rodrigo was in front of the shack washing his face in a dishpan. Still dripping, he climbed the steps to the dock and squatted down in a friendly way at the end of their blankets. "How much money do you have?" he asked.

"Twenty."

"Each?" he said and sucked his upper lip down over his teeth.

"Together," Javier answered.

Annoyed, Rodrigo ran a hand through his still-moist, wavy hair. "You think I can take you for that?"

"It's all we have," Javier replied.

"You'll have to give me more, a wristwatch or something of value," Rodrigo said and left the dock without waiting for a response.

Thirty minutes later, Héctor appeared and said they should follow him. Carrying their plastic shopping bags, Javier and Juan trotted behind him across the road and through a cornfield toward the river. Overhead, the sun had broken through the morning haze. The damp ground was steaming. They came out of the field onto a road that twisted and turned toward the river. From behind, they heard horses and saw Rodrigo approaching in an old wagon hitched to two red nags. The old man and another man they hadn't seen before were chasing the wagon, and Rodrigo was beating the horses with a heavy knotted rope. The wagon, a wooden relic adapted with automobile tires, was too large for the horses, but bolting, eyes rolling, they caught up with Javier and Juan and forced them off the road. As it passed, they could see the boat—two automobile hoods welded together—bumping up and down in the wagon bed.

At the mouth of a ravine, the horses and wagon stood beneath a stand of large pecan trees. Héctor led the brothers down a path into the ravine. At the end, they could see Rodrigo and the two men waiting on a small knoll above the river, the boat floating below in the water. As if barring the way, Rodrigo stood to face them. "How much can you pay me?" he started over.

"Twenty dollars," Javier repeated.

"That's not enough," Rodrigo said angrily. "I take la raza across; I help la raza. It's a good thing I do, but I must be paid. If caught, I go to prison and my family starves."

"It's all I have."

"What about your wristwatch? What kind is it?"

Javier looked at the dial. "Timex. It's old but I need it. I can't give it to you."

Rodrigo scowled at the Anglo. "What about you?"

"Nada," he said and showed empty hands.

Rodrigo turned his back on them. Héctor and the two men looked from Javier to Rodrigo and back to see who would give. The tension mounted until Javier repeated. "It's all I have."

"Then give me the money," Rodrigo relented.

They slid slowly down the bank on their heels to the boat, which had three crossboards for seats. Rodrigo stationed Juan and the Anglo in back, Javier in front, and climbed into the middle. Before telling Héctor to push them out, he studied the dense trees and brush on the opposite bank for movement. The mile of river they could see from bend to bend was clear, and the silence revealed no warning hum of a Border Patrol surveillance plane. Héctor shoved the boat into the swirling brown water, and Rodrigo dug in with oars made of plywood squares nailed to long sticks. With each heavy stroke, the two ends of the boat twisted at the welded seam, but by keeping within shelter of the bank, Rodrigo managed to row against the current without the two hoods splitting apart. The boat moved laboriously upstream until Rodrigo lifted the left oar and dug hard with the right to swing the boat into the current, then dug with both oars to propel them across the forty yards of river before it could sweep them too far downstream. Midway, a mat of trash caught and passed them, the individual sticks ticking against the tin hoods. Javier started to speak, but Rodrigo hushed him—a voice carries too far on water—and there was only the steady thunk of the oars in the notches cut into the side of the boat.

~

THE PROW OF THE BOAT hit bank at the edge of a canebrake, and the passengers scrambled out into ankle-deep mud. Rodrigo handed up their bags and Juan shoved the boat back into the current. Staggering from the weight of the mud on their boots, they crashed through the cane and pushed their way up an overgrown ravine to a dry bank, where Javier sat down to slice thick wedges of mud off the bottom of his boots with a stick. He handed the stick to Juan and, breathing hard, whispered, "We have to get away from the river fast. No more noise." He stood, swung the plastic shopping bag counterbalanced by the weight of the canvas bag over his shoulder, and started north.

The heat of the river bottom was oppressive. Rather than shade, the trees and brush gave off humidity, and the lack of breeze was claustrophobic. Following behind, Juan could see Javier's dark brown shirt beginning to soak black and the empty water container bouncing loose in the plastic shopping bag.

Without slowing, they climbed a steep dirt bluff given to cave-in that marked an earlier meander of the Rio Grande and the outer edge of the river bottom. At the top, beyond a barbed-wire fence and dirt road that ran along the rim, they could see flat pastureland; below, a curving sweep of river and the lower Mexican bank. Javier stepped on a wire next to the fence post and jumped over. Juan followed and they sprinted across the road and through the open part of the pasture to the cover of a clump of mesquite trees. The ground was clear, and they wove quickly through the mesquite until they came to another fence that separated the pasture from a field of corn. Again they jumped the fence and, crouched over, ran between two rows of corn to the next fence. The midday sun was fierce in the open field, and they were stung with sweat and panting for breath. The next pasture, where they spooked a small herd of cows, brought them uncomfortably near a farmhouse. They circled away through the mesquite, crossed another fence, and kept going until they heard the clear whine of pickup tires on hot asphalt. The tires thumped rhythmically across a bridge and whined away.

Breathing hard, Javier came to a halt beneath a large mesquite tree where he dropped his bags and sprawled on the ground. "Carretera," he rasped and nodded toward the highway when Juan dropped beside him; he was so dry, the cotton was edging out in gray flecks at the corner of his mouth. Juan sat fanning himself with his white hat and staring as Javier rummaged in his canvas bag and took out the compass to check directions. Sure they were going north, Javier climbed the mesquite as high as the limbs would take him and looked out toward the road. A car whined past, and when it disappeared, he dropped back to the ground. "We have to cross a bridge," he said and swung his bags over his shoulder.

Through the tops of the mesquite they could see a taller line of cottonwood and sycamore indicating a creek. Thick brush protected their approach to the bridge, and from its base they saw the water still running muddy from the storm. Javier dropped his bags at the foot of a concrete rampart and took the water bottle. "Stay here," he whispered when Juan started to follow him down to the creek. Juan sat down on the rampart and watched Javier crouch beyond a clump of willows to fill the container. From above, he could see a large black water moccasin uncoil in the willow and slide into the water.

"Did you see the snake?" Juan asked when Javier handed up the jug.

"I wish it was the last," he answered. His baseball cap was tilted back, his face was wet, and drops of water hung in the sparse hairs of his mustache and goatee. He watched with interest as Juan drank from the jug. Through the translucent plastic, the water showed brown. When Juan finished, Javier refilled the jug and put it in his shopping bag. "One at a time, we cross the bridge," he instructed. "Wait till I'm across and hidden, then you come. Listen for cars." He put his bags over his shoulders, and on all fours crawled up the rampart to the bridge. As he was about to haul himself over the concrete railing, they heard a diesel semitrailer, and he squatted down and waited for the truck to swoop thunderously past and drone on into the distance. Grinning at Juan, he pulled the baseball cap snug, climbed over the railing, and ran across the bridge. Juan could see him crouching and the plastic bag bouncing on his shoulder. In turn, he climbed the rampart, waited a moment, and ran across.

On the far side of the bridge, Javier was waiting out of sight at the bottom of the road's embankment. Juan waded down through knee-deep grass. They crossed the fence and started through a new pasture. The grass gave way to a hard, sandy crust shaded by mesquite trees, where they picked up the parallel tracks of a road. Javier looked back and stopped when he noticed Juan walking in one of the sandy tracks. "Step on the grass," he said. "You won't leave footprints." He turned and walked on.

The terrain began to change to hard rocky ground cut with shallow gullies and covered with low-lying scrub brush. Without the cover of mesquite trees, they were exposed to the hot sky and could see the land ahead begin to roll. Near what appeared to be a small abandoned feedlot, Javier cut away from the road through the thickest stand of brush until he came to an eroded ditch. At a clump of scrub oak that spanned the ditch, he dropped in and crawled into the shade. Juan crawled in behind, and, sitting on either side of the ditch, they passed the water jug back and forth. "What do you think?" Javier asked.

"It's not so bad," Juan answered.

"We haven't begun."

MARÍA EUGENIA GUERRA

"Nothing to Declare" (1994)

In the early 1950s, the International Boundary and Water Commission and the governments of the United States and Mexico condemned 113,000 acres of productive farm and ranch land along the middle basin of the Rio Grande to build the Falcón Reservoir. Also condemned along the waterway were a handful of Spanish colonial land grant settlements that pre-date Jamestown, settlements that disappeared beneath the reservoir waters.*

Though it was predicted that the filling of the reservoir would span several years, a Gulf hurricane and sudden upriver rains precipitated a rapid rise in the new reservoir. Residents of those condemned historical towns learned quickly they would not have the time to move methodically and with closure from their ancestral homes. Refugees in their own land, they fled to higher ground. Taken by surprise, many of them left without treasured family documents and photographs, the firearms of their revolutionary ancestors, the antique furniture and implements of their households and ranches, and their dead.

---

* Many towns in Mexico, as in the United States, have the same or similar names. Guerrero, Coahuila, mentioned earlier as a gateway to a noted crossing of the Rio Grande, is upriver from Guerrero, Tamaulipas, a community displaced by the Falcón Reservoir.

October 31, 1953

I will try to tell you this in English.

That's my mother in the bag, what's left of her—some bones, dust, and hair, a bit of the flowered silk dress we buried her in, the *medalla* of the Virgin de Guadalupe, a few beads of the silver and pearl rosary.

When the government finished the dam and before the reservoir filled, they told us to sign papers for exhumations and documents so that the remains of our dead could come legally from Mexico to the United States. It didn't cost anything, but it took time to get the paperwork in order, which I didn't have, considering my job and the children and the elections. So I dug her up myself without the *permisos*, put her in the grain sacks that I tied securely with soft baling wire under the frame of the truck, and drove her over the bridge like it was nothing.

The Customs gringo at the *puente* at Roma asked me all *chulo*—¡*hijo de puta*!— "Anything to declare?" And then he walked off to answer the phone, leaving me to wait.

Well, I declare, Goddam, it was work to dig her up, and it was work to endure the misery of losing our land along this river so that Eloy Bentsen could water his cucumbers in the Emerald Valley. I declare, Ike Eisenhower, Mr. Shiny Whitehouse Whitehead, that I will never eat fish from your lake, nor will my children, grandchildren, and great-grandchildren. We will never enjoy the water paradise you dynamited from the ranchland floor to fill with the snow melts of Colorado and New Mexico and the rains of Mexico and west Texas.

And I declare, Mr. President, that though you have inundated the dreams of centuries, that in time, those who come after you will realize that you and the deluvial silts were the executioners of this great river, this Río Grande, this *Río Bravo del Norte*.

The dreams did not drown here, no señor. It may take entire lifetimes, but the dreams will resurface from the murky reservoir floor to take life in the hearts of the children and those who loved this land. Fish swim where we drew our first breaths and suckled at our mothers' breasts.

And I declare, *Mr. Hijo de la Chingada*, that this river that has been the lifeblood of these lands will become a cesspool.

You told us that it would be years before the waters rose and there would be time to move the graves, the households, and the livestock. You condemned our property and the appraiser from Laredo said you owed us a nickel on the dollar for our houses that were built a hundred years ago of squared sandstone block. He made the appraisals without so much as looking, for he was busy buying up resort acreage on the new lakefront. You acted like you were giving us something, and you hoped we wouldn't notice how little it was.

I waited until the moon was full to dig her up, the last full moon before the water crested. I left my tools just inside the cemetery walls and I walked a last time down the cobbled streets of stones pulled from the river, allowing myself once more to feel the pride of this beautiful city where for two centuries our people made their lives, buried their dead, and invented and exported to you the *vaquero*, and his romance and his tools.

There was a ceremony here last week. It was the last day this was an official town. Church bells summoned us one last time to the plaza. The clock was removed quietly from the tower, as well as the church bells, and everything that day was part of the ritual for closing the life of this place. The city archives, the histories of 250 years of marriages, births, and deaths had been carefully packed in boxes to go to the new town that is built from cinder blocks on the raw, defoliated shore of the new lake.

A governmental decree read in a voice that cracked with desperate passion pronounced that on that day the town ceased officially to exist. The consecrated relics of the church and altar were removed. The Mexican flag was lowered for the last time while the band played the *himno nacional*.

We embraced and wept—sisters and brothers, cousins, aunts, mothers, children, uncles, and grandparents. Some of us lingered to kiss the doors of our old homes, to hug the stucco and carved relief corners of the houses of the grandfathers. It was hardest to explain to the old people. How were they to comprehend that hydro-electricity and water conservation could be more important, sir, than our land and our homes?

Con Jesús en la boca I stayed back to watch the immense dignity of the long, sad parade of automobiles and trucks, wagons, and horseback riders, dropping a million tears along the dusty road out of our town and into the *carretera* to the new city.

Mr. President, our hearts were great vessels of sorrow, for we never really believed you would do this to us or that this day would arrive. We had in the election prior delivered our votes like good people, and we believed that in return you would care for us. We believed at some point that you would change the direction of the waters, but the waters have continued to rise and soon we must all leave.

So much heartbreak to favor one man's onion fields and citrus groves. You are claiming the cotton and vegetable fields and grazing lands of a hundred farmers and ranchers so that Eloy can water his crops. Piss on Eloy's crops, and piss on you, sir.

It was rage I felt, and an infinite sadness, Mr. President, in the hours before the sun set one last time on our town, and I walked to the cemetery to make the tidy bundle of my mother's bones.

The cemetery was empty, for most of the dead had been moved. I stepped carefully so as not to fall into one of the open graves. I felt my resolve to begin and finish as I reached for the *talache* and dug. My rage turned into a sadness that gave way to the keen longing for some other outcome. It was here that I felt the injustice I knew would fit me like a skin for the rest of my life.

I dug, sir, into the damp earth, and I felt my heart quiver with a pain that tore to a depth then unknown to me. I felt the back-flip, the arch of my soul, as it tried to know for the first time what it would mean never to walk here again. I wept and I wailed while the sun dropped behind the sierra and the vultures came to roost on the high, dry-stacked stones of the cemetery walls. I clung to the marker of my mother's grave, a simple white marble angel with outstretched wings. I wept into those hard stone wings, wishing they might embrace me, and I tasted the salt of my tears and the dust of centuries.

My hands shook as I rolled a cigarette to calm myself before I lifted my mother's remains a bit at a time into one of the carded cotton quilts she and I had made with my grandmother.

That's right, Mr. President, it was not your idea to do this and the *guerra mundial* was not your war, and it was the president before you, a Democrat, who summoned us to this sacrifice, this particularly cruel aberrance of justice. But why have you come here and expected us to act like this is a celebration? Why do you insult us like this? Why do you insist we line the roads to wave at you in your great camelhair overcoat or that we join you in your parade of black Chryslers to the top of the dam where you will pronounce your platitudes for progress? As you drive to the dam, will you see from your motorcade the city of tents at the roadside and the displaced souls who wait for the government to honor their property values for replacement homes?

It is nearly winter, and the wind howls through those tents, lifting the flaps and blowing sand throughout the day in a bitter contrast to the genteel lives we lived in the elegant, quarried stone homes of our small towns on this river. Our lives had order and respect. We cooked in hearths and drew *agua dulce* from our wells and cisterns. Does anything, Mr. President, tell you this may not have been the best decision? Does anything about this make your conscience twist just a bit in your chest?

Progress will elude the new replacement towns you build on this river until we remember how to dream again, until we forget even for a moment what you have taken from us in the mirror image flourish of the pen-strokes of the bureaucrats of two governments who determined the greatest good for the most.

¡Hijos de la chingada! ¡Desgraciados! I will never think of that massive concrete dam you have built as anything more than the tomb that marks the place where you stopped our dreams and the great river from its flow to the Gulf.

Mr. President, I dug late that afternoon with a fury into the loam of our lives until I came to the place where my mother has slept in peace for two decades. Now I, Chabela Vistamonte, have disturbed the eternal rest of the dead.

It was enough to lose her, sir, and to bury her, but I could not endure thoughts of her slumber under a hundred thousand acres of water, and that is what prompted me

RUSSELL LEE

to this desperate act in the company of vultures spitting up carrion on the cemetery walls.

Though you, Mr. President, figure largely into a thousand questions about our fates, you are no part of the answer, and you will never be as we attempt to understand this government-invented injustice against the peoples of two countries along this waterway. Of what scope and finality is this measure that the living have come here to fetch the dead?

Waiting for that government monkey on the bridge to come back here so he can wave me through officially from one country to the next, I recall that last drive out of the old town, the parade of those with broken hearts as big as bricks. The vista of the town in the rear-view mirrors did not grow smaller, and it never will. That vista will—I promise you on the archangel that watched over the grave of my blessed mother—in memory over the years grow larger, more lovely, the trees greener, the children more beautiful, the livestock fatter, the ranchers more pleased over the recent rains, the plenty of the onion and cotton harvests greater than any in all time.

"No, nothing to declare," I answered that *pelado* when he came back to his station.

ELENA PONIATOWSKA

from *Guerrero Viejo* (1997)

On a sunny white morning, Eulogio opens the door for Doña Julia's herd of goats. There are thirty-seven, and a small calf hardly taller than the goats. Valdéz, a little black dog of insignificant appearance, watches them; however, that little dog is a memorable character. At the time of my death, I would like to think about Valdéz. "Yes," says Eulogio, "he's named Valdéz." Eulogio Medeles Hernández has a dog of his own that is much bigger and more important than Valdéz, a Lassie type, but ever since Eulogio sold his own herd of forty-three goats, the dog has taken refuge along with his sadness in the shade of a broken-down and abandoned automobile, and has not moved from here except to bark without conviction at the few strangers that venture in this direction, inebriated by the sun. Here they call automobiles "muebles" (furniture) and most of the cars on the roads are "trocas" (pick-up trucks). Eulogio tells us: "When I sold the herd of forty-three goats, the dog began to howl. He missed them.

He cried for a short time. I would just ring the bells that goats wear around their necks and the dog would stop, happy to go and meet them, and I said, I'm just upsetting the poor animal. Since the dog was raised with the goats, they would chew the rope to set him free when I tied him up and he would jump just like the goats."

Doña Julia's goats set out in a storm of hooves down the path and Valdéz guides them, taking them at seven and bringing them back at five in the evening when the sun sets. The hooves resonate on the limey ground, dry and stretched like a drum. Valdéz's steps cannot be heard and leave no tracks. Valdéz receives almost nothing in exchange for his services, hard tortillas soaked in water and a bone every once in a while. Every morning he throws himself through the door of the shack where he sleeps with the goats, with a contagious happiness that perfumes the air, and leaves joyfully with his flock. One would expect to find soft pastures, green grass kept level by pruning teeth, but no, the landscape is desolate, severe, thorny, and the goats with their Picasso-like frames, dash, their muscles tensed and long, their knife-like leanness, between the rocks and the thorns. It is painful to think those dancing and skillful legs are not touched by anything sweet.

The mesquite is also stone and the goats are stone; they eat anything, staining their muzzles with blood. They even eat empty Campbell soup cans. The desert plants are weapons: the saguaro cacti raise their guns, the yucca, the edge of their knives, the prickly pears their thorns. For the goats everything that glitters is gold and they chew it. There go the goats on top of the prickly pears and it doesn't matter to them that their tongues are torn apart, as long as they eat a prickly pear fruit. Eulogio says who knows what kind of magnet those red prickly pears have that so attracts the goats, that they climb right on top of them. This herd is as obsessive as the cacti that persist in spite of the lack of water, in spite of the dry land, in spite of the harshness and the loneliness. Such caprine grace for such hostility! If any animal is graceful and moves with ease, it is precisely a goat with its head alert, its white beard, and its infallible movements. If anyone knows where to step, it is, without a doubt, a goat.

Perhaps the stones of Guerrero Viejo are so imposing, so tremendously strong because everything that happened on the border (and still happens) was transitory, vanishing, temporary. As a result the houses could be blown away by the wind. The word "duration" didn't exist on the northern border, so no one came ready to stay; everyone, men and women, whole families arrived with one sole purpose: to risk their lives in order to cross to the other side. Those who were unsuccessful settled their failures on the Mexican side of the river and lived poorly, without seeing the horizon, and there is nothing worse in life than to live without seeing the horizon.

In the midst of all those flights, those river crossings, that anxiety, and that quest, Guerrero Viejo dropped an anchor and stayed. Its fortitude makes it so special be-

RICHARD PAYNE

cause on a strip of land where everything moves to "the other side," the stones settle and even their shadows turn to stone.

What the people of Guerrero Viejo never expected as a reward for their tenacity was the final sinking, the disappearance they now fight against. If they hadn't chosen to leave, they certainly didn't want the river to take them. Theirs is a mortar of loyalties. Here I stay, here I stay, here I stay and will remain and not even the river will be able to move me from here. Nevertheless, only the water can wear them down, dampen them, rot them because each person of Guerrero Viejo seems to say, I am not moving from here, on the dry plain, in the hostility of the sticky air. I will remain here, I will stay.

Except for Doña Julia and Eulogio, no one lives in Guerrero Viejo any longer. From time to time fishermen abandon their clothes to rot in the sun in one of the roofless houses, waiting to be devoured by some crazy goat. The fishermen enter the water at the dried-up river bed to see if they can get lucky, but since the drought the last few years has been terrible, they leave, never to come back, and the only things left in Guerrero Viejo are the whispers.

"I was named Julia Zamora Villareal by my parents. From my husband, I am the Widow González. Listen, I live in Guerrero Viejo because I was raised here, you hear? And because to me it is a good town and I'm not going to leave it, I raise my animals here; my middle child of the six children I have lives with me, and as long as I live I want to be near their warmth; it doesn't matter if they are married, you know what I mean?

"I take care of my fifty animals in Guerrero Viejo. I have goats, yearling sheep, a bull calf, and my five hogs. I sell sodas, bread, chips, cigarettes, rice, matches, sweets, and things like that that make life better, from my house, you know what I mean? I also sell my little goats and lambs. I'm sixty-four years old now, but I became ill with diabetes and they lopped off a toe on this foot so that my blood wouldn't get gangrenous and the pus wouldn't go to my heart. The house I live in is from 1875; before, I lived next to where it flooded, a little ways over there, but this house on the corner was left empty and I have lived in it for twenty-five years. It has two rooms, a kitchen and a huge room like an enormous ballroom, you know what I mean?

"I get up at six, and open the door for my animals, no I don't feel bad I'm living in a ghost town, I have never been afraid, never. Not even a little, not even when I was young was I afraid. Well, after all, I know how to shoot; anyone who approaches me without warning I'll shoot dead. I like to have weapons or a dog to warn me. As a child I taught myself to shoot really well. Once the soldiers asked me what I wanted a weapon for:

Well, to shoot.

It doesn't even have a cartridge.

Well, I ran out but soon I can get some.

"Sometimes they might be good people, but sometimes bad people might come, and I'd shoot at them even if it's at their feet, yes, well yes.

"Years ago six or seven families still came to Guerrero Viejo to fish, but the river dried up and now only Eulogio and I are left. Sunday the priest came to see the church. I'm the only one that takes care of the church. I'm the one that takes care of the church and reports how things are; that the mosaics are cracking a lot, that people take the stones, that people should control themselves and not crush them but they break them! You figure out what they break them with. They write their first name and last name in letters all over the walls—I say, if it isn't a barracks why are they doing that—and they even put where they're from and that's how they vandalize the walls with their spelling.

"They have even come from the other side with cranes to take the stones, the iron works, the headstones from the graveyard, you hear? Well, what's the matter with them? They take everything, and my eyes will never see them again. I'm the only one that takes care of the Virgin in the church."

Doña Julia is right. When the sun sets, the light of two oil lamps flashes on the bank of the river. It reflects in the water where there is any. And if the curious were to go into the church they would see toward the back "undercover and where the rain cannot reach it," a little homemade altar in front of the image of the Virgen del Refugio. "I lit the lamps to ask the Virgin to help us and send us water. I sweep the church floor and everything. I take away all the refuse that people leave, tourists from Mexico, because the people from the United States are cleaner, they are exquisite in everything they do, they do pick up their garbage while Mexicans throw theirs all over the place.

"They come on Saturdays and Sundays, do you know what I mean? When there was water, entire families of forty, fifty boats came to spend the day, to eat and take pictures, and it was nice to see how they arrived by water. Others came from inland to get to know the area because their parents were from Guerrero and they wanted to find out what their house looked like and where they were. So I tell them: well, just tell me your name and I'll show you your house. Look, this is where the González house was, here the Zamoras built their house but the river never took it away. Now only that pile of stones is left.

"People have been gone from here since 1953, forty-three years ago. Others that come start to cry just remembering how hard it was for them to leave the town, but anyway, that's how life is. The boats don't come anymore, but there isn't any water any longer. I can say that the people should not have left; the water even if it comes, only rises to the corner of the Hotel Flores. All the empty houses are there just waiting for the townspeople to return. They are good houses that can be just like before in a short time because they are solid. The only one that the water has worn away is the church, and in spite of that it endures, it doesn't allow itself to fall. It is a courageous church, it is brave, it has a good foundation.

"I walk alone through the streets like a queen. I can walk now. Before I couldn't because of the cropped toe on my left foot, but that's over and I walk, although with much sadness, because I think that in a short while I will be even more alone because Eulogio Medeles Hernández has told me that he is going to go home to Reynosa with his children. Last year in April there was still a little water, but now the river has receded a lot. Before there was good fishing at the Falcón Dam, but now with the drought there are very few fishing and things are not going well for those few.

"I don't like to be sick, I want to be well so I can work. I milk goats and make a little goat cheese with the goat milk curd, and my cheeses are delicious. I sell them. I have light because I bought a car battery, and at night I turn on the light and an oil lamp for my little saints, and with those I live quite well."

Both Doña Elisa Valadez (who lives in the replacement town, built thirty miles away when river was dammed) and Doña Julia feel the same way about Guerrero Nuevo: "I don't like it even as a place to die," says Doña Elisa.

"I ask only one favor of my children when I die. That they just put a cross on me, but I don't want a colored one, I want it to be black because I have suffered a lot since I was a kid because in the past parents were very tough. I never went to a dance, and now it's a blessing to have such good children. Yes, and it has been eight days since I've seen them, I'm drowning. I hug them, I kiss them, and I want to take my heart out to give to them. I insist: leave me on this land, next to the river, put me in my coffin, and don't forget that I want a black cross."

PART 6

Frontera

WHEN THE FIRST SPANIARDS IN TEXAS took refuge around the mouth of the River of Palms, a people called Borrados observed them from the thickets of the mainland and the dunes along the beach. They spoke Coahuiltecan and subsisted largely on plants; game was scarce and elusive, and they were not exceptional hunters or fishermen. They ate roasted bulb roots of maguey, prickly pear tunas, and mesquite beans smashed and stirred with dirt—to their palates a tasty flour. The Franciscan missionaries were among them by 1700, and in another hundred years, the Borrados were extinct—killed off by Comanche and Apache raiders but in the main by smallpox and other European maladies. Survivors were absorbed into the new Spanish-speaking culture, mestizos.

The Valley was not a defining battleground of the Texas Revolution. Santa Anna and his Mexican army crossed the river upstream and believed the war was essentially won when they overwhelmed the freebooters and traitors at the Alamo and took back San Antonio de Bexar. But a dozen years later, the buildup and face-off of the U.S.-Mexican War pressed close on both sides of the lower river. For a while more insults and taunts carried across the Rio Grande than musket balls. In those days the chaparral north of the river was marked on many Texas maps as the Wild Horse Desert. Mustangs and longhorns proliferated in the brush. After the war and the U.S. annexation of Texas, Spanish land grants and water rights that had been good for centuries were cast aside in the new dominion. Steamboats chugged upriver with passengers and freight and made a thriving and handsome port town of Roma. One of the South Texas river captains was Richard King, who with partners and minions and by writ, intimidation, and violence chased Mexican landowners south of the river and consolidated the endless King Ranch. Aggrieved men raided north of the Rio Grande, and the Texas Rangers retaliated with maximum force. To many South Texans of Mexican heritage, the rangers, *los rinches*, were hated thugs and enforcers.

Born in a Mexican border town, Juan Cortina was one of those men who believed the Valley had become a world warped by gringo injustice, and he inflicted more terror on the border than Pancho Villa ever would. In 1859 Cortina's riders sacked Brownsville, slept in U.S. army barracks at Fort Brown, and stormed the town jail and set its prisoners free.

To Robert E. Lee, the U.S. army colonel sent to restore order on the Texas border, Cortina was just a bandit. Texans called him "the red robber of the Rio Grande." But to Mexicans, he was a patriot who would later serve with distinction as the duly elected governor of Tamaulipas. Brownsville boomed and frolicked during the U.S. Civil War, moving Confederate cotton across the river to English buyers in Matamoros. A month after the now-Confederate general Lee surrendered his army and sword to Ulysses S. Grant at Appomattox Courthouse, the Civil War's last battle raged through the Valley's river bottomland. Rip Ford, the famed Indian fighter and Texas Ranger, led a Confederate cavalry charge that overwhelmed black Union soldiers at Palmito Hill. But men in both uniforms were looking over their shoulders for the guerrillas of Juan Cortina. In 1871 Cortina, by then a Mexican general, swore off hostilities against the United States; a bill to pardon him actually passed the senate of the Texas legislature. But the empires, egos, and grudges were too large. Cortina spent the rest of his life locked in a vendetta with his nemesis and rival, the onetime Rio Grande boat captain Richard King.

The frontier's tradition of isolation, mistrust, and violence lies near the surface; the seminal work of Chicano literature in Texas, written by the folklorist and stylist Américo Paredes in 1958, is *"With His Pistol in His Hand": A Border Ballad and Its Hero*. Paredes was fascinated throughout his long academic career by the *corrido*, a form of folksong, usually accompanied by guitars and accordion, that is unique to the borderlands and fashions a kind of instant pop history. The *corrido* he chose as a metaphor for the culture was a celebration of Gregorio Cortez, a South Texan who avenges his brother's murder by a gringo sheriff then leads *los rinches* on a chase toward the river and safety on the Mexican side.

Of course, the vast majority of people in the Valley today are just trying to provide for their families and make a living. The region's underlying rocks and fissures didn't possess the oil and gas that transformed Texas in the twentieth century, but entrepreneurs in the Valley have always been inventive—no other part of the state could make an industry out of orange and grapefruit trees. Highways on the Texas side of the Valley are crowded with the neon clutter of fast-food America, the motor homes of "snowbird" retirees giving themselves a break from winters up north, and the astonishing volume of trucks and tractor-trailers set loose by NAFTA. But then you see a reminder, an old pickup with an exhaust problem and a bed full of fresh-picked okra. Life in the Valley always comes back to plants that people eat—and water. The narrow, murky green river. The only source.

~

ON THE TEXAS SIDE of the lower Rio Grande Valley, about 1,700 farmers rely on their irrigation rights. At an average 26.5 inches a year, the rainfall is too meager and erratic to support commercial production. Joe Aguilar farmed 3,000 acres of vegetables, cotton, corn, and grain at Peñitas, near Mission—he irrigated about 1,000 acres. Aguilar worked the land his dad had cultivated. He hoped his daughter would continue to work the farm but wondered if one would exist. "I got out of citrus several years ago," he told me. "Think about an orange—it's all water."

Aguilar was a reserve constable in his community and an elected school board member. He was no firebrand. In April 2002 he and a few other growers got to meet President Bush at his ranch in Crawford. Aguilar informed the president that he was going to take part in a tractor blockade of bridges over the Rio Grande to protest the water issue. The president wished the men his best and said he was trying to help.

The four-hour shutdown of three international bridges that spring was peaceful; cops stood aside. The Texas farmers had hoped they would be met by growers in Tamaulipas who had also been left dry by the watermasters in Chihuahua. But the Texans' hope for a united front in both valleys would not be rewarded. Tamaulipas farmers later blockaded the bridges with their own tractors, but the Mexican farmers were protesting to keep the water, not give it to Texas.

Efforts by farmers on both sides to get their governments to act in the water fight continued to have little effect. Politicians seemed more inclined to dance around the issue. At the start of the summer in 2002 Mexican president Vicente Fox planned to visit Texas, meet with Texas governor Rick Perry and President Bush, and address the legislature in Austin. The Mexican congress, which was aggravated by the water conflict and the rhetoric of some U.S. officials, and which had purse control over presidential trips abroad, vetoed the trip. Then the IBWC signed Minute 308, an agreement with the agency's counterpart in Mexico, CILA, in which the Mexicans agreed to release 90,000 acre-feet of water into the stream. But the agreement was more about posturing than about taking real action; it referred to water that was already stored in the Rio Grande's border reservoirs, Amistad and Falcón. The order required no more release downstream from the Conchos reservoirs, and it could be rescinded at Mexico's request if drought on the Conchos worsened. U.S. Secretary of State Colin Powell received a letter from Texas growers calling Minute 308 a "colossal failure" and an embarrassment for the United States.

Trying to ease the tension, the State Department sent Dennis Linskey, its director for U.S.-Mexico border affairs, to the Valley. Joe Aguilar told me that he spoke up at the meeting: "I asked him, 'Have we been sold to Mexico, and if we have, for how much?' It was a serious question. He thought I was being sarcastic."

ROBERT RUNYON

~

LATER THAT MONTH Carlos Ramirez, a former mayor of El Paso and head of the U.S. section of the IBWC, was being excoriated in a Washington meeting by Texas congressmen and their aides. Exasperated, Ramirez blurted that President Bush had called him directly and ordered him to sign Minute 308. Ramirez hung on to his job, but administration and State Department officials were clearly displeased. Leaks to the press of Ramirez's remark further convinced the farmers that their interests were not a particularly high priority of Bush's. Then that August, Fox canceled another planned visit to Texas. He attributed the cancellation to Texas's execution of a Mexican national despite international protests and an appeal by the Pope, but Aguilar and other Valley farmers were planning a public protest against Fox and Bush at Crawford. Such a thing would not make good television for either man.

With more success than Bush and a red-faced governor Perry—who had promised the farmers relief that failed to materialize—Susan Combs had positioned herself as the Valley growers' champion. In her fifties, the agriculture commissioner was a skillful politician, and in a state controlled by Republicans, she was expected to run for higher office sooner than later. "If the Mexicans are not going to give us the water," she told me, "then by God we ought to ante up and help our people in the Valley. How about the filling stations? How about the grocery stores? How about the guys who fix the trucks? How about all the collateral damage? We really could turn the Valley into a parking lot."

Combs's attitude toward Mexico's politicians was undisguised contempt: "From everything I'm hearing, their position is, 'We're not going to let the gringos have it.' They've got a governor in Chihuahua who says, 'If the rain falls here, it's mine.' He does not believe he has to be a partner in the treaty. What kind of neighbor is that? All we hear from them is 'Gimme water, gimme money. Gimme gimme gimme.' They're like irresponsible toddlers."

"So you stick by your statement that Chihuahua is a rogue state?" I remarked.

"Sure. Yesterday I called them renegade. Whatever. Starts with an *r*."

~

IN OCTOBER 2002 Mexico officially defaulted on a Rio Grande water debt of almost 1.5 million acre-feet. A week later, Combs released new satellite photographs which showed, she claimed, that a tropical storm had increased Mexico's storage to 2.5 million acre-feet. Vicente Fox's point man on the water dispute was Alberto Szekely, an urbane Mexico City diplomat. "Talk to the author of that study, at the Center for Space Studies," Szekely told me in response to Combs's new pronouncements. "He will tell you those figures refer to our total storage capacity, and don't allow for silt. Our storage in the reservoirs is exactly what we say it is."

"What is the solution to Mexico's water debt?" I asked him.

"The solution," he answered lightly, "is that Mexico will work out a schedule of repayment over the amount of time allotted by the treaty, which is five years."

Bush and Fox finally met for 45 minutes at an Asian Cooperation summit in Baja California. Bush expected Fox's support for the UN Security Council vote on the war against Iraq. Fox wanted Bush to make some concessions on immigration. Neither leader yielded on those issues; relations between the two countries were suddenly at their frostiest point in years. And to the amazement of Valley agriculture figures, the Rio Grande and the water debt were not prominently mentioned as items on the presidents' agenda for discussion.

"Look," said Jo Jo White, the manager of the Mercedes irrigation district. "We realize that with trade, immigration, drugs, terrorism, and the rest, the concerns of Rio Grande Valley farmers are a pretty small piece of the equation. But we really do feel like we've been abandoned by our government. We're at our wits' end. This situation with the Conchos has been going on six years, and the worst could be yet to come. We really could lose our citrus and sugar-cane production down here."

White was a prominent member of an organization called Texans for Treaty Compliance. For some years they had been tossing around a plan for scrapping the 1944 treaty. Let Mexico keep the Conchos water, their argument ran. Under the treaty, the U.S. released about 1.5 million acre-feet, or a tenth of the flow of the western Colorado (the river of the Grand Canyon), to Mexico. The Texas farmers proposed cutting the Mexicans off and building a pipeline from Hoover Dam across the desert and Rockies to the Rio Grande, at a pipeline construction cost of a million dollars per mile. The desperate idea was predicated on the notion that Arizona and California, which had tremendous water problems of their own, were going to give up supply in order to help farmers in South Texas. Drought had set in all over the West. Mexico protested that the water released from the Colorado was so salty it was destroying agriculture between the Arizona border and the Gulf of California. And even Combs predicted that because of the lack of snowmelt in the southern Colorado Rockies, the United States would soon incur its own water debt to Mexico.

At his farm near Mission, Joe Aguilar told me that he believed the presidents of both countries had good intentions, but he feared their hands were tied by their allegiance to multinational produce companies. Aguilar had been trying to sell acreage and was buying trucks to start a small transport firm, hoping to diversify. Like most area farmers, he was beginning to understand that the governments could dodge this issue for years, and there was no relief in sight.

Ironically, in their fight over the Rio Grande, the Texas farmer and the Chihuahua governor, Patricio Martínez, wound up sounding alike. "If we're ever going to get any help," said Aguilar, "it's going to have to come out of the sky."

ROBERT RUNYON

But then it seemed to happen. The powers of nature intervened. A week after Mexico defaulted on its water debt, rain poured all along the Rio Grande. The whitewater recreation companies were busy again in Big Bend. Residents of Laredo were evacuated. Many streets of Brownsville flooded. Water stood everywhere in the lower Valley. But Aguilar told me wearily that the six inches that fell on his place only had him slogging in mud. "We were out of water," he said of his irrigation allotment, "so we didn't plant fall onions. We got rain, but now it's too late. Melon farmers down here have cantaloupes and watermelons starting to rot, because it's so wet. That's the catch with irrigation," he said. "It's not just having the water—it is the *timing* of the water."

RICHARD PAYNE

ROLANDO HINOJOSA

from "A Sense of Place" (1983)

I BEGIN WITH A QUOTE from a man imprisoned for his participation in the Texas–Santa Fe Expedition of 1841; while in his cell in Mexico City, he spurned Santa Anna's offer of freedom in exchange for renouncing the Republic of Texas. Those words of 1842 were said by a man who had signed the Texas Declaration of Independence and who had served in the Congress of the Republic. Later on, he was to cast a delegate vote for annexation and contributed to the writing of the first state constitution. He would win election to the state legislature and still later he would support secession.

And this is what he said: "I have sworn to be a good Texan; and that I will not forswear. I will die for that which I firmly believe, for I know it is just and right. One life is a small price for a cause so great. As I fought, so shall I be willing to die. I will never forsake Texas and her cause. I am her son."

The words were written by José Antonio Navarro. A Texas historian named James

Wilson once wrote that Navarro's name is virtually unknown to Texas school children and, for the most part, unknown to their teachers as well. A lifetime of living in my native land leads me to believe that Professor Wilson is correct in his assessment of the lack of knowledge of this place in which we were born and in which some of us still live.

The year 1983 marks the one hundredth anniversary of the birth of my father, Manuel Guzman Hinojosa, in the Campacuas Ranch, some three miles north of Mercedes, down in the Valley; his father was born on that ranch as was his father's father. On the maternal side, my mother arrived in the Valley at the age of six weeks in the year 1887 along with one of the first Anglo settlers enticed to the mid-Valley by Jim Wells, one of the early developers on the northern bank. As you may already know, it's no accident that Jim Wells County in South Texas is named for him.

One of the earliest stories I heard about Grandfather Smith was a supposed conversation he held with Lawyer Wells. You are being asked to imagine the month of July in the Valley with no air conditioning in 1887; Wells was extolling the Valley and he said that all it needed was a little water and a few good people. My grandfather replied, "Well, that's all Hell needs, too." The story is apocryphal; it has to be. But living in the Valley and hearing that type of story laid the foundation for what I later learned was to give me a sense of place. By that I do not mean that I had a feel for the place; no, not at all. I had a sense of it, and by that I mean that I was not learning about the culture of the Valley, but living it, forming part of it, and thus, contributing to it.

But a place is merely that until it is populated, and once populated, the histories of the place and its people begin. For me and mine, history began in 1749 when the first colonists began moving into the southern and northern banks of the Rio Grande. That river was not yet a jurisdictional barrier and was not to be until almost one hundred years later; but, by then, the border had its own history, its own culture, and its own sense of place: it was Nuevo Santander, named for old Santander in the Spanish Peninsula.

The last names were similar up and down both banks of the river, and as second and third cousins were allowed to marry, this further promulgated and propagated blood relationships and that sense of belonging that led the Borderers to label their fellow Mexicans who came from the interior, as *fuereños*, or outsiders; and later, when the people from the North started coming to the Border, these were labeled *gringos*, a word for foreigner, and nothing else, until the *gringo* himself, from all evidence, took the term as a pejorative label.

For me, then, part of a sense of the Border came from sharing: the sharing of names, of places, of a common history, and of belonging to the place; one attended funerals, was taken to cemeteries, and one saw names that corresponded to one's own or to one's friends and neighbors and relatives.

When I first started to write, and being what we call "empado," which translates as drenched, imbibed, soaked, or drunk with the place, I had to eschew the romanticism and the sentimentalism that tend to blind the unwary, that get in the way of truth. It's no great revelation when I say that romanticism and sentimentalism tend to corrupt clear thinking as well. The Border wasn't paradise, and it didn't have to be; but it was more than paradise, it was home (and as Frost once wrote, home, when you have to go there, is the place where they have to take you in).

And the Border was home; and it was also the home of the petty officeholder elected by an uninformed citizenry; a home for bossism, and for old-time smuggling as a way of life for some. But, it also maintained the remains of a social democracy that cried out for independence, for a desire to be left alone, and for the continuance of a sense of community.

The history one learned there was an oral one and somewhat akin to the oral religion brought by the original colonials. Many of my generation were raised with the music written and composed by Valley people, and we learned the ballads of the Border little knowing that it was a true native art form. And one was also raised and steeped in the stories and exploits of Juan Nepomuceno Cortina, in the nineteenth century, and with stories of the Texas Rangers in that century and of other Ranger stories in this century and then, as always, names, familiar patronymics: Jacinto Treviño, Aniceto Pizaña, the Seditionists of 1915 who had camped in Mercedes, and where my father would take me and show and mark for me the spot where the Seditionists had camped and barbecued their meat half a generation before. These were men of flesh and bone who lived and died there in Mercedes, in the Valley. And then there were the stories of the Revolution of 1910, and of the participation in it for the next ten years off and on by Valley *mexicanos* who fought alongside their south bank relatives, and the stories told to me and to those of my generation by exiles, men and women from Mexico, who earned a living by teaching us school on the northern bank while they bided their time to return to Mexico.

But we didn't return to Mexico; we didn't have to; we were Borderers with a living and unifying culture born of conflict with another culture and this, too, helped to cement further still the knowing exactly where one came from and from whom one was descended.

The language, too, was a unifier and as strong an element as there is in fixing one's sense of place; the language of the Border is a derivative of the Spanish language of Northern Mexico, a language wherein some nouns and other grammatical complements were no longer used in the Spanish Peninsula, but which persisted there; and the more the linguistically uninformed went out of their way to denigrate the language, the stiffer the resistance to maintain it and to nurture it on the northern bank. And the uninformed failed, of course, for theirs was a momentary diversion while one was committed to its preservation; the price that many Texas Mexicans paid for keeping the language and the sense of place has been exorbitant.

ROBERT MENDOZA

"A Piece of Land" (1997)

THE VOLUMINOUS ABSTRACT OF TITLE (prepared by the Henry Abstract Company in 1958) has been in my possession since the spring of 1991 when I assumed responsibility for the administration of my mother's estate. The four-inch-thick mass of court documents is a sort of *bildungsroman* (if you accept my conceit of the land as the developing central character). And I have, on a long winter's night in Laredo, fortified by duty-free cognac, read it straight through *as* a novel.

The story opens grandly in the tradition of the historical romance, but inevitably, as the scores of decades pass and the petty litigants crowd the stage, the narrative descends into a genre more akin to the dirty realism of Raymond Carver.

On August 11, 1797 (almost 200 years to the day before I felt compelled to tell this story, having just signed an earnest-money contract for the sale of our ranch), Charles IV of Spain rewarded the loyalty of a group of his soldiers with what would later come to be known as *Porcion 5*, the Manuel Gonzalez grant. The land constituted an enormous rectangle jutting northwards from the banks of the Rio Grande (30,610,000 square *varas;* 5,318 acres). For the 30 years remaining in the Vice-Regency of Nuevo Santander, seven families managed not only to endure but to prosper in their harsh exile. In the bad years, when every thorn seemed a cross in a galaxy of losses, they became inured to the vengeful rage of the Coahuiltecan indigenes who not only carried off livestock but also relatives and retainers, never to be seen again. They learned to abandon their mesquite *jacales* and construct sturdy limestone or adobe bunkers (*casas fuertes,* prototypes of the fortress domiciles that epitomize early Texas architecture.)

In 1827, Cristobal Benavides petitioned the fledgling Republic of Mexico for recognition of his title to *Rancho de San Cristobal de Xaquima* (as the land grant was then known). The Benavides clan and their descendants would remain figures in the harsh arid landscape for many years. The vast tract would be partitioned many times into as many diverse configurations. At the close of the American Civil War, the holdings along the riverbank were the site of prosperous dairy farms, while the rich alluvial *vega* yielded bumper crops of vegetables and fruits.

As the 19th century waned, irrigation schemes forced an advancing verdant front northwards to what would become the right-of-way of the Rio Grande and Eagle Pass Railway and the Webb County Mines Road (stygian arteries linking the coal boom communities of Dolores and Minera to Laredo). Bright barbed-wire fence lines isolated melon and onion fields from the fat glossy cattle (the mongrel long-horns having been supplanted by the spawn of calculated scientific couplings). Bankers looked upon the land and saw that it was good. Bleak estate inventories (wherein an eldest son was bequested three cows and a nickel-plated watch) seemed to be figments of a forgotten past as dim as the oval portraits of the steel-eyed forebears consigned to attic trunks.

However, for some families, the bounty was often tainted. From the 1890s onwards, Dickensian melodramas were played out, featuring probate-maddened brothers at each other's throats, with trial lawyers as their sinister seconds. Barren landowning couples expediently adopted orphans (who arrived via oxcart from beyond the Sierra de Bustamante) to participate in elaborate schemes designed to deny the *gobierno bolio* survivorships over their beloved *ranchito.* All the elements of telenovelas are in evidence: vitriolic divorces, bank foreclosures, *criadas* taken in adultery (later surfacing as legatees), sheriff's sales, Abuelito (a Lear of the brushland) declared *non compos mentis* for refusing night after night to come in from the front porch (where he rocked raptly attending to the keening counsel of an owl—a pitch pregnant with the immensity of the Chihuahuan desert whose distant mountain ridges were the same hue as his cataract-wracked orbs).

The faded blue covers of the Abstract also contain a roll call, a veritable wax museum of Laredo and Webb County's civil *nomenklatura* since the demise of the Republic of the Rio Grande: Santos Benavides, John Z. Leyendecker, Sam Jarvis, Justo Penn, Ed Mann, A. M. Bruni, Porfirio Flores, Honore Ligarde (*père*), Martin (*père et fils et oncle et cetera*). It's a magic realism lantern of border politics. I open a page of the abstract at random, carefully noting the name of a fledgling notary, then rapidly flip pages forward until he is a newly-installed County Clerk or Tax-Assessor. Moving right along into the bureaucratic future, another sheaf of documents reveals his transmutation into a jowly County Judge. (On closer examination, I note that this last document was filed by the Judge's namesake and scion, the new County Clerk.) It's all so Garcia Marquez: gesture, gestation, party affiliation, reincarnation.

Late one night last year, I was wandering about downtown, trying to summon the Laredo of 1922, a somnambulist amidst the vestiges, when I stumbled upon Bruni Plaza. Its bronze dedicatory plaque (grouted into the same Deco green tile that cloaks the Plaza Theatre) quoted Commendatore Bruni: "God has given us political power to serve the people." Alas, no one can assert that Laredo was blessed with a soil fertile to irony.

My own family name does not appear in the Abstract until 1956, the year my father bought some 300 acres from J. H. Cardilli. Our ranch, like others in *Porcion 5*, forms a strait triangle. It is a long narrow sleeve entered from the narrow cuff, which opens onto the Mines Road and extends directly northwest past the ragged selvage of Santa Isabel Creek. Our exiguous tract is bolstered by the more substantial domains of Servando Benavides and Max Mandel to the west and east, respectively. The ranch land that lies to the south of the Mines Road and extends to the banks of the Rio Grande was also once owned by the Cardilli clan (who sold it to A. M. Bruni several decades ago).

I was 13 years old in 1958, a good age to begin a relationship with the land. Ranch work requires strength, stamina, and a certain type of idealism. I possessed a modicum of the first two qualities and an adolescent's boundless reserve of the third. My age promised that every year I would become more of an asset and less of a liability (though unlike a child born to the ranch, I had everything to learn). The experience was, I believe, profoundly positive (a judgment made from the perspective of my late middle age and residence hundreds of miles distant). I acquired certain specialized skills (such as learning to rope and ride, to quote the hackneyed lyric) that I've never had occasion to exercise since those days. More importantly, however, I had the opportunity to come into contact with the magic and multifariousness of nature. I was privileged to enjoy the company of people who were passionate about the land (committed to any sacrifice in order to wrest the potential immanent within a harsh terrain).

In 1958, the ranch was unimproved land, with the exception of a single silted-in stock tank and a half-mile of washed-out caliche road. We soon were busy buying up pasture fences (fashioned from ax-hewn mesquite posts harvested during brush clearing), while a bulldozer noisily scooped out a new stock tank. Soon, an old one-bedroom shack was transported from the banks of Laredo's Zacate Creek and set up to catch the breeze from the original willow-wreathed stock tank. The Cardilli-era structures had collapsed long ago and were reduced to shambles of sun-bleached lumber that harbored colonies of enormous field rats. The old ranch house's tin roof sheets had been wind-cast into impenetrable huisache thickets (where they would moan eerily on moonless nights). The ranch was bereft of electricity until the mid-1960s. Night emergencies, and there were many, were illuminated by kerosene or automobile headlamps. (The searchlights that accessorized many 1950s cars proved indispensable in that time and place.)

My family aspired to be cattle raisers, albeit on a very modest scale. The decision to concentrate on bovine husbandry was decided by failure analyzing a process of cruel elimination. Our attempt to grow a mixed crop of squash and onions (the plow was a railroad tie bristling with spikes and dragged by our army surplus jeep) was a dismal failure. The harsh unblinking sun and the wind bearing the exhalations of the Chihuahuan desert shriveled the tender sprouts. Also, we never exercised our easement which entitled us to Rio Grande irrigation.

Our next initiative involved goats, but the ones that managed to avoid being devoured by predators ran away. The coyotes also made short work of schemes to mass produce turkeys, guinea hens, or chickens. The serial holocausts spared our 20-odd head of scruffy, mixed-breed cattle. These I herded on foot, since horses proved too high maintenance (someone was always stealing the saddles), and we soon discovered that it took far longer to catch a horse than to round up the cows. I grew nimble at brush walking, or rather bushwhacking, as I ran like hell to head off the one-third-Brahma troublemakers who always managed to surge past the bell cow. Monday mornings in junior high school were always spent surreptitiously plucking out the various spines and thorns I'd harvested over the weekend. Ranching was a real rose garden.

However, it meant always having a place to picnic on Easter (instead of crowding into Lake Casa Blanca or braving the mosquitoes along the riverbank). Besides, real ranchers like us could indulge in contemptuous sneering at the expense of drugstore wannabes who pullulated in downtown Laredo in their spit-polished boots. We also rode herd on the droves of Western-themed TV shows, guffawing triumphantly at their lapses and blunders.

Of course, I did not consider myself an authentic cowboy; these were the men my father hired, as our herd prospered, to carry out the seasonal mass brandings, castrations, horn-lopping, worm-purgings, and pre-auction roundups. From an early age,

I had maintained an avuncular attachment to these taciturn, efficient journeymen. I marveled at their dignity and insouciance as they crouched around the fire where the branding irons were calcinating. They grilled freshly detached calf testicles, which they ate heartily with green-crusted fingers, the result of twisting tails in order to topple a calf into position for whatever ministration was due.

By 1963, my father had managed to upgrade our livestock so that nearly two-thirds of the herd were composed of Santa Gertrudis cattle. This corpulent yet disease-resistant breed, originally developed at the King Ranch, was very popular in Webb County in that era. (Herefords were the other predominant stock, but our range was too rough for that rheumy-eyed denizen of the feedlot.) An enameled Santa Gertrudis Breeders Association sign proudly adorned our front gate. A few yards inside the fence, the powerful, sleek maroon-mahogany creatures themselves could be glimpsed grazing behind a scrim of smoky green mesquite.

Tragically, it was during that most prosperous period the screwworm epizootic erupted in our area. Vector swarms of flies zeroed in on the cattle's most minute cut or abrasion. The flies deposited larvae into the wounds, and the worm voraciously devoured muscle tissue. I have never worked harder or with as much anxiety as during that crisis where we lost some of our most noble animals. For months, we pursued, subdued, and treated the afflicted cattle, cleaning out the gaping, nauseating lesions and swabbing on a black antiseptic paste.

That experience was perhaps partly responsible for my interest in studying veterinary medicine. Unfortunately, Texas A&M was the only university that trained veterinarians. The summer preceding my last year of high school, I accompanied a cousin to help him move into his dorm in College Station. I found the grim campus and its stolid buildings depressing. Also, my cousin's Corps of Cadets cohorts seemed ludicrous—at once ludicrous and priggish.

In retrospect, considering my at-best indifferent scholarship in high school, I would not have gained admission to vet school. Although buoyed by having achieved an A+ in senior-year Anatomy and Physiology, I was severely qualitatively challenged, knowing little math, no chemistry, and less physics. The cognitive skills in my possession were violently skewed towards the verbal end of the spectrum. In my final years of secondary school, I found myself inevitably drawn toward literature.

My reading informed me that I was provincial. I was soon possessed of a desperate urgency to flee a Laredo revealed as a slough of ennui. I went away to university and only returned to the ranch during the odd Christmas holiday. Although the ranch hands were outwardly cordial, I sensed a reproachful distance in their manner. Despite our years of shared labor and strenuous conviviality, a class chill had set in; I had become a college joe, the owner's son. One incident convinced me of this.

One afternoon while we were building a fire for lunch, a large rattlesnake reared up out of the mesquite woodpile. I grabbed a pistol from the table and dispatched the snake with a single shot. Visagras, the eldest of the hands, looked at me with astonishment. His surprise spoke volumes.

After graduating from college in 1968, I did not return to Laredo. My visits became even less frequent after I married. Now and then, I would help out at the ranch, but my presence was somewhat ceremonial. Other hands had taken over my old chores, and I was relieved in more than one sense. I had lost interest in ranching and the sleek, registered Charolais seemed to be doing fine without me.

In 1981, my father died. My mother, who had never shared his passion for the ranch, hastily sold off the Charolais herd he had so painstakingly built up. While my mother was distracted by legal bickering in the wake of probate, the ranch went into precipitous decline. It was no longer a working cattle ranch, but the site of my younger brother's and cousins' *pachangas*.

In 1989, I was living in the noisy, smog-shrouded, crowded center of Barcelona. (A Spanish government survey had recently revealed that the population density of the city's urban core was surpassed only by Calcutta.) At night, I would go out on the west-facing tiny back porch. I had no view, just a patch of sky and the wall of the eighth floor of the apartment building opposite. However, I knew I was gazing westward because Columbus's bronze finger (attached to the rest of his statue atop an enormous column towering over the nearby harbor) indicated the route to America. Ensconced on what I sarcastically called my *azotea*, I would write letters that would take six weeks to reach the states. But often, I would just think about the ranch.

It's April 3, 1991, two weeks since my mother's funeral. I'd arranged to be dropped off at the ranch late in the afternoon. My plan is to camp out overnight and meet the real estate appraiser early in the morning. My campsite is an old favorite on a bald hill overlooking the oldest stock tank on the ranch. When I was 13, a tiny log cabin and a large tin-roofed pavilion were constructed here. The log cabin imploded years ago, its adzed telephone-pole logs, after a quarter century of harsh sunlight, had volatized all trace of creosote and were devoured by termites. Although its tin roof flew away long ago, the pavilion's frame remains intact. The core rectangle of stout railroad-tie stanchions and lintels (notched, fitted, and balanced by a lost generation of skilled carpenters) remains stalwart and dead level. To my eye, it is beautiful, a sort of oaken Stonehenge in its elegant weathered simplicity. The dove-gray, wind-burnished structure frames a view of the Rio Grande in the middle distance and, much further beyond, the mystic intaglio of the Sierra de Lampazos.

Despite all this, friends usually are puzzled by my penchant for camping on this austere windswept place, sleeping on the hard ground, instead of in one of the beds in the ranch house. The house, despite years of often malign neglect, remains structurally sound. The roof doesn't leak. However, most of the windowpanes have been shattered, and wasps have bored through the plywood patching to build mud nests inside. Most disconcerting to my sensibilities is the pervasive odor of field rat bedding.

My reluctance to sleep in the ranch house is also due to the strong likelihood that I could receive unannounced human visitors in the middle of the night. During the last decade and a half, the ramshackle structure has become an Ellis Island of the brushland, a bunkhouse for illegal immigrants riding the roads of the underground railroad to San Antonio. A tall steel television tower ascending from our front pasture replaces the celestial drinking gourd as a reference beacon from across the river.

Also, on many a night, my sleep has been interrupted by a staccato burst of automatic weapons fire from somewhere in the darkness. Those other creatures of the night, the drug runners, have become a ubiquitous and ominous presence in the area. The TV tower is utilized as an azimuth by weary *burros* stumbling northward through the *tasajillo* with their burdens. Last year, the head-shot victim of a settling of accounts blocked the front pasture road while authorities argued and measured to determine whether his pickup truck was on city or county land.

This night will be tranquil; the only mayhem within the pale blue covers of my Flammarion Simenon anthology. Those unfamiliar with my perverse nature might assume that I would be turning the pages of the latest Cormac McCarthy within my candle-lit tent. (My battered UK Picador edition of *All the Pretty Horses* was purchased used at the Tea and Tattered Pages Bookstore in Paris and was read in a seedy hotel in the 20th Arrondissement.) My reading does not go uninterrupted; there is no such thing as a silent night inside the thin walls of a tent. I am serenaded by a pack of demented coyote counter-tenors, the bass line of a Selena *éxito* throbs my way from El Primero's jukebox two miles away, raccoons are washing something for dinner at the stock tank below. All of this, the eternal and the ephemeral, is rendered benign by the vast incandescence of Orion and his retinue.

Early the next morning, after a perfunctory breakfast of La Reynera's gingerbread *marranitos* washed down with a *filtre* of Sumatran coffee, I begin the long walk to the front gate. (The real estate appraiser doesn't have this week's key to the padlock.)

My footsteps on the caliche road startle up sandpipers, cottontails, and memories. I notice that the pasture fence no longer extends into the stock pond. Some 20 feet of fence posts and barbed wire have vanished without a trace. Although the pond has silted dramatically since 1958, I can roughly locate the spot where we once subdued a recalcitrant Brangus in four feet of water. My father, his WWII shipmate Visagras (Hinges, after the crude tattoos that articulated forearms to biceps), and I had pursued the animal into the pool. Finding itself caught between barbed wire and deep water, the Brangus suffered Visagras to rope it. Triumphant and trouserless after the struggle, he hauled the waterlogged yearling ashore while revealing the image of a ship's propeller tattooed on his backside. For days after, my father asserted that Visagras had enjoyed an unfair advantage over the Brangus, for if it had its own propeller, he never would have caught up with it.

I walk past the pond road now narrowed by encroaching *una de gato* underbrush and blocked by fallen willow branches. At the base of the next hill, I note that the corrals and loading chutes are still upright and sound, though choked with tumbleweed and waist-high Johnson grass. This is where Oscar broke his ankle scampering away from an enraged bull. In 1959, my father had picked up Oscar hitchhiking on the Zapata highway. He was about 18 years old and homeless. Oscar became an adopted son, sleeping in a back room in the paint shop on Corpus Christi Street. My father taught him sign painting, a trade Oscar practiced until the ravages of the way he lived made it impossible for him to wield a brush. Oscar and his wife briefly lived in the ranch house until the early 1960s until she ran away, no longer able to bear his moods and the interminable windswept nights. In 1981, during my father's funeral, Oscar went wild with grief and had to be restrained by the solemn blood relations.

The land appraiser is late, which allows me to wander in solitude for a while longer, attending to echoes of vanished voices. This gently rolling front pasture was root-plowed in 1960, clearing away impenetrable *nopal* and huisache thickets, and seeded with buffel grass. There's no traffic on the Mines Road at this hour, and I can discern the rattle-rattle of *guajillo* bean pods and the furtive foraging of a ground squirrel. I lack the discipline to empty my mind; some lines of "Exile's Letter" by the eighth-century Chinese poet Li Po (translated by Ezra Pound in 1915) well up and inform the landscape.

> . . . and all this comes to an end.
> And is not again to be met with.
> . . . and if you ask how I regret that parting:
> It is like the flowers falling at spring's end
> Confused, whirled in a tangle.
> What is the use of talking, and there is no end of talking.
> There is no end of things in the heart.

I look up to notice a pickup has pulled to the front gate. Soon, we are back on the ranch road retracing my early morning footsteps. The man beside me is brightly quoting dollars per acre, comparables. I nod in assent, but my mind is elsewhere. I'm remembering the vanished caretakers and stewards of this land, the characters who populate that *bildungsroman* of a Title Abstract. I remember the words of another Asian poet who wisely noted that all comparisons are odious.

JAMES CARLOS BLAKE

from *In the Rogue Blood* (1997)

ON A WARM FORENOON of pale and cloudless sky they arrived at the Rio Grande, known to the Mexicans as the Río Bravo del Norte. Taylor's scouts had reported that the town of Matamoros, positioned on the south bank of the river and about twenty-five miles inland from its mouth at the Gulf of Mexico, was fortified by a small Mexican garrison. The river along that stretch was eighty yards wide and the Mexicans had confiscated every boat to be found and taken them all to their side and posted sentinels for miles along the riverbank east and west of town.

After sending a detachment to secure Point Isabel on the Gulf as the landing point for his seaborne supplies, General Zachary Taylor chose to give the Mexicans a show. He marched his troops upstream along the north bank and hove into view of Matamoros with regimental bands blaring and colors popping in the breeze. He halted the troops in a wide clearing and rode with his staff officers to the crest of a bluff affording an excellent view of the river in both directions and of Matamoros across the way. The river was the color of buckskin and its banks were lined with cattails except along the Matamoros riverfront and its opposite shore where the ferry had operated before the Mexicans dismantled it on learning of Taylor's approach. There were hardwood stands upriver and down along both banks and cotton fields shone in the distance on the Mexican side.

A crowd of townspeople had assembled on the Matamoros bank to gape at the Americans. In the midst of them was a troop of lancers sitting their handsome mounts and resplendent in green tunics with crimson sashes and tall black shakos with horse-hair plumes. Alongside them an army band played rousing patriotic tunes hard and loud in competition with the strains of the Yankee musicians. Commanding the lancers was a major who now stood in the stirrups and brandished his saber at the invaders and addressed them loudly and at length in eloquent Spanish which Taylor's interpreter translated as a directive to the Yankees to go home or die.

As soon as the major had done with his address, the crowd started in with cursing and shaking their fists and the boys among them threw stones which all fell short in the water. The Americans in the ranks swore back at the Mexicans in explicitly profane terms. The cacophony of martial music and bilingual damnations shook the skies while Taylor conferred with his advisors about defensive positions.

John and Riley had by now been relieved of their gags but they had fourteen days more to carry ball and chain. When Master Sergeant Kaufmann went striding past them Riley called out, "Say now, sergeant, what if that fancy Mex cavalry comes charging across the river, eh? How are me and Johnny here to fight if we're chained down by these damn cannonballs?" Kaufmann gave him the barest glance and went on without a word. Riley looked at John and said, "I have prayed to the good Lord to let me have but five minutes alone with that son of a bitch, just five minutes to set things right with him and I can die a happy man."

"You best pray I dont beat you to him," John said.

The Mexican major now barked orders to his troop and the lancers reined their horses around and the unit trotted off in smart formation down the dusty street and back toward the garrison. The band marched along after, still playing as it went, its volume falling fainter as it moved away from the river. A moment later the only Mexicans still in evidence on the other shore were the sentinels and a few lingering civilians.

While diplomatic efforts to avoid war continued between Washington and Mexico City, Taylor was under orders to stay in place and take no hostile action except in response to Mexican attack. Rumors were rife, the most common of them that the Mexicans across the river were waiting only for the arrival of several more regiments before making their charge. Against that possibility Taylor ordered work to begin immediately on an earthen defensework to be called Fort Texas. It was positioned on the bluff and would have five sides. Its outer walls would be nine feet high and fifteen feet thick. Toward its construction each regiment provided daily labor in the form of rotating fatigue details, and as compensation each man on the detail received a gill of whiskey at the end of the day's work. Required to work with the construction crews every day but denied the whiskey allowance were all men under punishment, including John Little and Jack Riley, who had to labor with ball and chain. They fetched and carried materials and tools, mixed buckets of mud mortar, applied pick and shovel, and all the while cursed the army that treated them less like soldiers than as beasts of burden.

Lucas Malone volunteered for the labor detail at every opportunity and so on most days found himself working in proximity to John and Riley. John introduced Lucas and Handsome Jack to each other one sultry afternoon when they were all shoveling construction debris into wheelbarrows along the fort's south wall. Thunderheads were rising like bloodstained purple towers over the Gulf and the sun gleamed off the whitewashed houses of Matamoros. Riley asked what part of Ireland his family was from. Lucas said County Galway and Riley grinned widely. "But that's me birthplace, man! Some Malones lived a few miles north of us. Could they have been kin?" Lucas said they might have been but he couldn't be sure. They'd had lots of Malone kin in the old country but his granddaddy had fled the sod after killing a man in a donnybrook. He'd kept on running after reaching New York and didn't stop until he made Tennessee.

Riley asked Lucas why he volunteered for the labor gang. "Bad enough to have to do this as punishment," he said.

"Because I'd anytime ruther work like a man," said Lucas, "than march around on a drill field playin at being a soldier. March and drill, drill and march. That's all we do in this fuckin army camp."

"Dont be calling it an army camp," Riley said. "It's a bloody prison is what it is."

Remembering the city prison in New Orleans, John thought Handsome Jack was wrong about that. "Hell Jack, it's only another seven days with these ornaments on our legs," he said.

"Only seven days left this time," Riley said. "Then comes the next time, and maybe we'll wear them sixty days, or ninety. Maybe next time it'll be the fucking yoke for a month or so. Maybe it'll be the bloody lash. These bastards can do any damn . . . hello, what's this?"

Their comrades were flocking to the riverside in high commotion, hollering and cheering and waving their hats. A dozen young women, all of them with long black hair and red laughing mouths, had come to the riverbank and there disrobed completely and entered the river to their brown thighs and now were busily soaping themselves and each other and blowing kisses the while to the cheering Americans across the way. Behind them a squad of Mexican soldiers stood at the water's edge with their rifles unslung and held the girls' clothes and pointed across to the Americans and laughed and said things to the women and quickly backstepped grinning when the girls splashed water at them. Some of the Americans removed their boots and walked partway into the river and called for the women to come over to their side. The women laughed and splashed water in their direction and jumped up and down so that their dark-nippled breasts jounced the more. They soaped each other's gleaming buttocks and threw their heads back and rounded their mouths in mock orgasmic delight as they worked a thick soapy lather into the hairy patches between their legs. The Americans were howling like penned dogs.

"Sweet Jesus," Riley said with a grin, "I been struck mad by the bleeding sun, I have."

Lucas laughed at the happy vision of all that lovely female nakedness in the bright sunlight. He clapped John on the shoulder and pointed to one girl after another. "Look there at *her*, Johnny—right over *there*! Oh, and *that* one, over there, with the bush big as a beaver. You *see* her? God damn!"

Now officers had arrived on the scene with sabers in hand and were shoving their way to the forefront of the crowd of soldiers. The girls were beckoning to the Americans and cupping their pretty breasts to them and calling endearments to them in Spanish. And now some of the Americans had waded out to the river's depths and begun swimming for the other side and the officers ran into the water to their knees and commanded them to turn back immediately. Some of them did but several swam on and midway across the river one of them began to thrash wildly and quite abruptly sank from sight and his body would be found the next day caught against the bank on a tree root at a point more than twenty miles downstream near the mouth of the river.

Three made it across to the shallows opposite and one of them might yet have drowned even then except several of the girls came out and helped him to his feet. The other two Yankees were also helped to wade out onto the bank in their dripping pants. They all three looked back at their cheering comrades and waved and hugged naked girls to them and patted the girls' haunches and buttocks and squeezed their breasts. The girls playfully slapped away their hands and now hurried back into their clothes as the Americans kept at kissing and fondling them the while. The Mexican soldiers laughed and shook the Americans' hands and patted their backs in the manner of old friends. Again dressed in their loose cotton skirts and lowcut sleeveless blouses the girls put their arms around the necks of the American soldiers and the Americans stroked their hips and all of them walked away laughing together down the street and around a corner and out of sight.

A half-dozen officers now stood in the shallows on this side of the river with pistols in hand and commanded the men away from the bank and back to their units. The soldiers were still dazed and breathless from the spectacle of the Mexican girls and were slow to comply, but they did as they were ordered.

All evening the talk around the campfires was of the wonderful exhibition the girls had put on and of the grand time the three who swam across must be having. Bets were made whether they would return, the odds favoring that they would, because the penalty for desertion was far more severe than for simply being absent without leave to have a good time with a girl.

They were struck that night by a violent storm that jarred them awake in fearful certainty that the camp was under artillery attack, so explosive were the thunderclaps. Lightning lit the night with a ghostly incandescence. The wind shook the trees and tore at the tents and carried some away. The river rushed and swelled and overran its banks. It ripped through the brush and made a mire of the lower reaches of the American camp. The storm raged through the night and finally broke just before dawn. The water receded swiftly and the sun rose red as blood over a landscape sodden and fetid with mud and littered with tents and roof straw and river reeds, with uprooted shrubs and drowned dogs and half-plucked chickens caught on driftwood at the river's edge.

That afternoon one of the three who'd crossed the river to be with the girls came back, rowed across by a pair of Mexican soldiers with a white flag attached to the muzzle of a rifle. They let him out of the boat in the shallows and quickly rowed back to their own side.

The soldier, Thomson by name, was brighteyed with excitement and told the men who gathered round him on the bank—John and Lucas and Handsome Jack among that avid audience—what a wonderful and generous people the Mexicans were, how religious, how beautiful and affectionate the women, how delicious the food and delightful the music. Thomson said the other two were not coming back. The only reason he himself had returned was that he did not want to break his mother's heart.

Now a guard detail showed up and the lieutenant in charge placed him under arrest and they took him away. None of them ever saw him again.

The next morning another seven soldiers swam the river, and then five more the day after that. Taylor increased the number of guards along the bank and gave specific orders that nobody was to go in the water except to bathe and then no deeper than his knees. The next day fourteen men swam across. Taylor posted a new directive: Any man seen swimming toward the other side would be warned to turn back and if he did not he would be shot. When one of Taylor's staff officers pointed out that desertion in peacetime was not a capital offense, Taylor responded gruffly: "Disobeying my orders can damn sure be."

The following day four men pretending to bathe in the shallows suddenly began swimming hard for the other shore and ignored the American guards' calls to turn about. In full view of the camp and the Mexicans watching from the other bank the guards opened fire and two of the swimmers spasmed and flailed and bright red billows spread around them in the brown water and they sank from sight. The other two made it across and were hastily hustled away by the Mexican guards.

A week after the exhibition at the river, the sergeant of the guard led John and Riley to the smitty's tent next to the main corral where each was relieved of his ball and chain. As they came out of the tent Riley clicked his heels and John laughed.

That evening dozens of copies of a Mexican handbill were somehow smuggled past the sentries and were soon circulating throughout the camp. They bore the signature of Pedro Ampudia, commanding general of the Mexican Army of the North:

Know ye: that the government of the United States is committing repeated acts of barbarous aggression against the magnanimous Mexican Nation; that the government which exists under "the flag of the stars" is unworthy of the designation of Christian. Recollect now you men born in Great Britain; that the American government looks with coldness upon the powerful flag of St. George, and is provoking to a rupture the warlike people to whom it belongs; President Polk boldly manifests a desire to take possession of Oregon, as he has already done to Texas. Now, then, come with all confidence to the Mexican ranks, and I guarantee to you, upon my honor, good treatment, and that all your expenses shall be defrayed until your arrival in the beautiful capital of Mexico. These words of friendship and honor I offer in Christian brotherhood not only to the good men of Great Britain, but, as well, to all men of Catholic brotherhood presently enslaved in the army of the United States, whatever your nativity, and urge you all to separate yourselves from the Yankees.

"What you make of it, John?" Lucas asked, reading the broadside over one of Riley's shoulders, while John read it over the other.

"The man wants the Brits to quit this army and join his," John said.

"I know *that*," Lucas said. "Do ye reckon he means Americans too?"

"It dont say he'd turn a Yankee down," Riley said. "He's awful shy, though, aint he, about saying just how much he'll pay a man to go over?" They all three looked at one another but none said anymore about it.

All over the camp soldiers were ridiculing the handbill, pretending to wipe themselves with it and putting matches to it and pointing at each other and calling, "Catlike slave! Catlick slave!" But some among the Irish were not laughing, nor some of the Germans. They looked at each other and glanced repeatedly across the river. And each look they gave to the other side was longer than the one before.

That night John dreamt he was running hard through a wide marsh and every time he looked back he saw Daddyjack coming behind him at a walk, following a tracking hound on a leash and steadily gaining ground on John. And then it was no longer a hound on the end of the leash but Maggie, fully naked and moving on all fours as smoothly as a hunting dog, her face close to the ground and hard on his scent, leading Daddyjack on a zigzag course but always toward John, always closing the distance though John was running hard and gasping and felt his heart would burst in his chest. Daddyjack was closing the distance and now yelled, "Blood always finds blood! Always!" And now Maggie was upright and laughing, her pretty breasts jiggling as she trotted ahead of Daddyjack on the leash . . .

And then he was awake, sitting up and gasping and pouring sweat, and Lucas Malone and Jack Riley were sitting up too and staring at him in the moonlit tent and he guessed he must have cried out. But neither said anything to him. After a moment he lay back down and heard them sigh hard and resettle themselves too. And each man of them lay awake late into the night with the rough company of his own thoughts.

One afternoon Colonel Truman Cross, the army's popular quartermaster, went out riding in the chaparral and did not return. There had been reports of Mexican guerrilla bands prowling on the north side of the river and now rumors flew through the camp that they had killed Cross. Some in the local populace told the American authorities that most of these guerrilla troops, whom they called rancheros, were nothing more than savage bandits who had for years terrorized the borderland, gangs of robbers, killers, renegades, rustlers and scalphunters. The two most notorious ranchero bands were led by Ramón Falcón and the infamous Antonio Canales, once president of the short-lived and violent República del Rio Grande. Both men were long-time and bitterly despised enemies of Texans. They had been young officers under Santa Anna at the Alamo and had both been at Mier. Each with his own band had raided Texas throughout its ten years as a republic. The locals warned Taylor that in addition to robbing and killing Mexicans as they always had, the rancheros would now also plunder U.S. supply trains and freely murder Americans in the name of defending the fatherland. Testifying to this view of the rancheros as bloody marauders unworthy of military respect were the Texas Rangers now serving with Taylor. Under command of Colonel Samuel Walker they were the first volunteers Old Zack had accepted into his army, and they had countless tales to tell of ranchero barbarities. Those familiar with the Lone Star way of warfare knew that many such tales could be told about the Texans as well. Indeed, Taylor had accepted the Texas volunteers in the belief that the best way to fight a band of savages was with his own band of savages. Still, some who heard the Texans' stories did not believe the larger portion of them. They attributed the Rangers' gruesome narrative excesses to their well-known hatred of all things Mexican.

And then the ten-man patrol that had been sent out in search of Colonel Cross came back on five foundered beasts and none of their own good horses. Came back two men per horse and every manjack of them naked and tied belly-down over the animal. Two of the corpses were altogether headless and the rest dripping blood and gore from their scalped crowns and the raw wounds between their legs wherefrom the genitals had been severed. Some bore the detached privates in their mouths and some lacked hands and some had been docked of their ears or noses and some were eyeless. Many of the young Americans who looked upon them had never seen such things before except perhaps in nightmares or in imaginings roused by the vile tales of drunken old Indian fighters. And no man among them did now disbelieve the Texans' stories of ranchero cruelty.

Shortly afterward the body of Colonel Cross was found in the chaparral and it too had been mutilated.

The Yankees seethed with yearning for revenge.

The first handbill urging Americans to desert was soon followed by others, each more detailed and explicit in its arguments and inducements than the one before. The fliers pointed out that, unlike the U.S., Mexico was a devoutly Catholic country where slavery was outlawed. They asked why Yankee Catholics or any men who truly believed in liberty and justice for all should make war against one another. They argued that the Irish, especially, had stronger bonds with Mexicans in their common religious faith than they did with American Protestant soldiers. They pledged that any Yankee who chose to fight in defense of Mexico and the Holy Mother Church would be well rewarded for his honorable action. They promised an enlistment bonus to every American who joined the Mexican side. They promised that every man would be given a rank, commensurate with his training and experience but in no case would he hold a rank lower than that which he had in the American army and in all cases he would be better paid. And they promised land. Every man who came over to the Mexican side would receive a minimum of 200 square acres of arable land with at least another 100 acres added for every year of service.

On a clear evening shortly after the most recent bunch of these leaflets had as mysteriously as always found its way across the river and into the Yankee camp, the three friends sat on the bluff and looked across at the brightly lighted town where a fiesta was taking place. Taylor had now posted sentries every few yards along the bank as much to keep his own soldiers from absconding to the other side as to defend against infiltrators. The guards were under order to shoot any man who set foot in the water.

The sounds of music and laughter carried to them from the fiesta. The aromas of spicy Mexican foods mingled with the ripe smells of the surrounding countryside. Fireflies flared greenly yellow on the soft night air.

Lucas Malone was scooping handfuls of dirt and sifting it through his fingers. His gaze was vague and far away.

"I was talking to this Mexie fellow today over by the corral who everybody thinks is a muleskinner but he's not," Riley said, speaking barely above a whisper and looking off across the river. "He's from the other side, dont you know. Name's Mauricio. He speaks good English and he's been talking to lots of the fellas, he has. Other harps mostly, but to the Germans too. Says there's forty or more of us already over there."

John looked at him but said nothing. Lucas looked at the dirt slipping through his fingers.

"He says I'd be made an officer," Riley said, still not looking at them. "Says Ampudia will know me for the soldier I am."

No one spoke. Then Riley said: "How else are you ever to get that piece of land ye claim to want so dearly?"

Lucas looked at him sharply.

"I dont believe they can lose the war," Riley said in a whisper. "There's too many of them. Hell, the country itself will beat this army. Have you seen the maps? It's all mountains from one end to the other."

He turned to them now. "It's not everybody gets a chance for the thing he most wants. It's the chance for me to be the soldier I am, to have the rank I deserve. You, Lucas Malone, I know what ye want. This is your chance too, it is. And you, Johnny, what is it ye be wanting above all else? Is it your own plot of ground, like Lucas here? I've seen the look in your eye when he talks of it, but I've never heard ye say."

John looked from one to the other. What he wanted was unsayable. No way is there for a man to explain what he cannot put in words to himself, what he knows only in the pulsing of his blood. How might he tell that he wanted an end to the dreams of Daddyjack and Maggie? An end to waking in the night with his heart wild in his throat, choking on his own fear, feeling hunted by some dire nemesis drawing closer with every bloody sundown?

"Without a place to call his own," he said, "a man aint but a feather in the wind, now aint he?"

He favored waiting another few days until the moon waned out of sight—or at least until a cloudy night gave them better cover—but Riley and Lucas were set on crossing that very night. And so shortly after midnight they slipped out of the tent and worked their stealthy way through the cottonwood shadows upriver for a quarter-mile and then scanned the near bank from cover of the trees. They spotted a lone sentry singing softly to himself and strolling in the pale light of the crescent moon blazing brightly in a starry sky. No other guard close by. John attracted his attention by lightly rustling the brush and the guard warily approached with his longarm ready at the hip. As the sentry passed by him Riley stepped out from behind a tree and drove the heel of his riflebutt into the back of his head with a wet crunch. He and Lucas quickly relieved him of his rifle and pouch and the few dollars he had in his pocket and then joined John in the riverbrush. John asked if the sentry was killed and Riley whispered that he was not but he might have a bit of trouble walking a straight line ever again.

They stripped naked and bundled their clothes tightly and tied the bundles to their rifle barrels. They eased down the bank which was steeper here than it was down by the town and pushed through reeds that cut them like little razors and slipped into the moonlit water. The river tasted of mud and rot. They held their rifles and bundles above their heads and swam one-handed but the river was running faster and deeper than they had thought and they found themselves being carried swiftly downstream.

"Christ," Lucas gasped as he pulled for the other bank, "we'll be in front of the camp in hardly a damn minute."

But they were all three strong swimmers and made an angled headway across the river. They were within twenty feet of the opposite bank when a voice cried, "You *there*! Turn back *now* or we'll shoot!"

They stroked with desperation now, John in the lead as they reached the cattails and a rifle flashed and cracked on the far bank and the ball smacked the water a foot to his right. He wished the moon would die and go dark. His feet now touched a bottom of soft mud and his breath came hard as he grabbed at the cattails to pull himself to the sloping bank. He felt the reeds cutting his hands but did not feel pain. He flung his rifle and bundle up on the high ground as more rifle shots sounded and a ball buzzed past his ear and smacked the mudbank. He heard Lucas Malone grunt and curse softly behind him and he turned and looked but Lucas was not there. But here came Riley drifting fast alongside and John caught hold of the rifle barrel Handsome Jack extended to him and pulled him into the reeds. Riley slung his sopping things up on the bank and scrambled past him up through the cattails and crawled away into the dark.

As he followed Riley up the bank a half-dozen rifles discharged almost simultaneously and he felt a sharp blow to his lower leg and then a burning and he cursed and squirmed his way up through the reeds. He tumbled up on the bank and pushed his rifle and clothes ahead of him as he crawled into the brush and more shots sounded and rounds hissed through the scrub.

He lay low in the thick scrub brush and looked to his left and saw the pale naked form of Lucas Malone crawling awkwardly into the darkness of a willow stand.

The shots were hitting scattered now and John knew the sentries had lost sight of them. The shooting continued for another minute before it finally ceased. He stayed put in case the shooters were simply waiting for him to give some sign of his position. His lower leg was throbbing and he felt of his shin and sucked a hissing breath when his fingers found the wound. He did not move from his hiding place for some time and then a passing cloud momentarily dimmed and he crawled out of the brush and across an open stretch of ground and into the trees. And there found Riley dressed and waiting for him. Riley helped him to his feet and John quickly put on his muddy clothes. When he pulled on his left boot a white flare of pain behind his eyes made him momentarily dizzy. As they moved downstream through the shadows he felt the inside of his boot slickening with blood.

They came upon Lucas Malone sitting with his back against a tree. He'd been shot in the side and was bleeding freely but he could stand and walk. He'd lost his rifle and his clothes and was naked in the world. John and Riley gave him their shirts and Lucas wore one in the regular manner and the other tied round his waist in the form of a skirt. "You fuckers laugh," he hissed. "I'll put my fist in your goddamned teeth." Riley and John grinned at him and Lucas Malone cursed them softly for sons of bitches.

They made their way through the trees and inland from the river and shortly came upon a sandy trace and followed it through the blue cast of the moonlight to the edge of town. John's boot was now heavy with blood.

A pair of sentries stepped out of the shadows with rifles pointed from the hip and challenged, "Quién vive?"

"Friends," Riley said. "Amigos."

And now an officer and two more soldiers and a man in civilian clothes came rushing down the street and Riley again called out, "Amigos, we're amigos."

The Mexican in civilian dress said, "Está bien, Nachos. Son irlandeses." He pointed at Riley. "Yo conozco este grandote."

"Mauricio!" Riley said. "I didn't recognize ye."

Mauricio laughed and he and Riley hugged and patted each other in a rough abrazo.

The officer put up his pistol and grinned at them and said, "Bienvenidos, amigos. You are welcome."

IRENE BELTRÁN HERNÁNDEZ

from *Across the Great River* (1989)

I WATCH MAMA tie a leather pouch around her waist. She slips a black skirt over it, then turns to fetch her sandals. She bends to tie them on, then moves to the table. She puts bread and a piece of dried meat in a scarf, then she ties the ends of the scarf together into one tight knot. Now, she waits.

"Where are we going, Mama?" I ask.

"On a trip, Kata. Now, dress quickly."

"But Mama, it's still dark outside."

She looks at me sadly. "Kata, I wish we weren't going anywhere, but . . ."

Papa enters the hut. For a moment they stare at each other, but I cannot tell if they are angry. He moves to his cot and picks up his guitar which he slings carefully over his shoulder. "Have you got the pouch?" he asks.

Mama touches her waist. "Yes, but Carlos, it is such a long walk for the children."

She picks up Pablito, my baby brother, and hugs him tightly. I watch as she dries her tears on the baby's shirt. With red eyes she looks around our hut, then she comes over and touches my shoulder. "M'ija, daughter, is there something you would like to take on this trip?"

"Will we be gone long?" I ask.

Again she sobs, then turns her back to me. I hear her blow her nose as I walk over to my cot. I reach under my serape and pull out my cloth doll. "Can I take Anna?"

"Yes, now come. Papa is waiting for us outside." She hands me the scarf. I hurry out the door after her.

The night air wakens me as I follow them. This is strange, I think. Why are we going for a walk in the middle of the night? Papa trudges ahead like a soldier going to battle. He takes such giant steps that it is hard for us to keep up with him. Mama takes two steps for each one of Papa's and I take four and still I fall behind.

Mama runs to catch him. "Carlos, we are leaving the only home we know. In the name of all that is good, please change your mind and let us return to our warm hut." She clings to his arm, but still he walks onward.

"We cannot return! This is a dream that I shall make come true." He walks onward removing himself from her grip.

"Carlos! Some dreams are not meant to be! This dream of yours is wild and very dangerous!" she cries.

"Silence! I will hear no more!" he commands as he walks on even faster.

Mama stops walking and stares at Papa's back. I grab onto her skirt. "Mama, don't cry. See, the stars aren't sad." She hugs me tightly, then takes my bundle. I am glad because the bundle is getting heavy. Besides, I have Anna to carry. I run to catch up with Papa. He is such a tall man, so thin and so brown. I take his free hand and kiss it. He smiles down at me, showing white teeth under a thick mustache.

I glance around. This path is in the middle of nothing but empty land. A tree sprouts up here and there on the desert, and the moonlight is flooding the land as the sun does in the daytime. I keep walking, switching Anna from hand to hand.

"M'ija, daughter, get away from the brush. You might trip on a cactus or uncover a rattler. Stay behind me."

I obey Papa instantly. "Are we going to the river, Papa?" He does not answer, but moves as if he were turning the world under his feet. Walking on, I find myself thirsty. "I want a drink, Papa."

"Soon, daughter, soon," he says, but he does not stop walking.

I look back at Mama, who seems to have slowed down. Her long skirt hugs her thin legs. She puts the scarf with the food on top of her head and balances it. She is small but strong, and her thick black hair is braided in a massive pigtail which swings back and forth with each step she takes. Her face glows in the moonlight, reflecting a quiet sadness.

"We will stop here to wait." Papa points to a spot covered with high brush. Mama sits on a nearby rock and I flop down next to her. Papa then hands her Pablito.

As I rest, I notice they seem frightened. Papa's pacing back and forth worries me. Mama is cradling Pablito. How I envy Pablito, sound asleep like a fat lazy cat on a Sunday afternoon.

"Quiet! We must not make a sound!" warns Papa.

Mama sobs, "Carlos, there is still time for us to turn back. Our family is here in Mexico."

"Woman, I have made up my mind." Papa takes his hat off and rubs his brow, then paces back and forth a few times. "I will return shortly. Remember, stay here and do not move. Do you understand, Kata?"

"Yes, Papa." I touch Mama's calloused hand. Her palm is sweaty. A stray lock of her hair falls forward. She nervously pushes it back in place. Then she bends to kiss Pablito and breaks into heavy sobs. She raises her tear-stained face, then pulls me closer to her side.

I look up into her face. She kisses my forehead, then bends her head in prayer. From between her breasts she pulls out her beads. Mama never goes anywhere without them. Fifty-nine beads in all. Each one represents a prayer. I wonder how Mama remembers all those prayers. She says them nightly.

The night becomes silent. I can no longer hear Papa's footsteps and I can hear Mama's breathing, but not my own. I put my hand to my chest. My heart is pounding away, and I wonder why. Suddenly, a branch breaks. Mama stiffens. I hear him returning, too. Papa is like a big shadow that comes from behind the clouds. "Come," he says, "they are waiting." He takes Pablito from Mama's arms.

"Carlos, I am afraid," Mama mutters.

He turns and faces her, then he gently brushes her hair back. "Do not fear, my love. All is ready and a new life across the border awaits us." He bends and kisses her forehead, then squeezes her shoulder. "Come, we do this for the children's sake."

She takes my hand and picks up the bundle. Then, she bites her lips and rushes along as if she wishes to punish me. We walk downhill. Papa stops. From behind a tree appears another shadow.

"Señor," says the shadow. "We will accept your money, now." Papa turns back to Mama, who lifts her skirt and unties the pouch. I watch as Papa takes the pouch over to where the man stands and pours the entire contents onto the sand.

The shadow bends on his knees next to Papa. I listen while Papa counts the paper money out loud, then hands it to the man whose arm is eagerly outstretched. The moonlight shines upon a large tattoo that is imprinted on the man's right arm. I walk over to his arm and take a closer look. It is the picture of a woman with some kind of rope around her waist. No, I decide. It is not a rope. The woman holds a snake in her hand. The snake's body is curled around her waist. I step away from the man at once.

"Ah!" says the shadow. "What is this shiny stone that winks at me from within the sand?"

I look to where he points, and there, within the sand, I see a golden yellow glow that seems to be a stone of some kind. Papa hurriedly takes the stone and some other coins and puts them back into the pouch. Then, he rises and straightens the guitar upon his back. "Let's get on with this, man!" demands Papa sternly.

The shadow rises, too. He has large teeth that sparkle white in the moonlight. "When you hear the call of the doves, proceed downhill to the river bank." Then, the shadow disappears into the high brush much like a cloud that is hidden within a dark sky.

Papa and I walk back to Mama. She says, "Carlos, I did not like that strange man."

"Nor did I, but it is too late. The money is gone and we must go on." He takes Pablito from her. We hear the cry of the doves and Papa moves ahead at a fast pace.

It is downhill all the way. We run, dodging rocks and cactus. In the moonlight, I can see that Pablito is no longer asleep. He bobs up and down on Papa's shoulder, crying in discomfort. Papa hushes Pablito, but the guitar strings play by themselves.

Papa and Pablito are way ahead of us. My legs spin as fast as a weaver's wheel. Without warning my feet go out from under me and I fall, causing Mama to lose her balance. She falls and we both roll and roll as a wheel rolls downhill. Then, she pushes me aside in one big thrust. "Carlos!" she screams. She stops abruptly against a cactus plant and screams as the thorns tear into the soft flesh of her arm. I sit up stunned with the taste of sand caked on my tongue.

Papa reaches us in one giant stride. He stands me up and checks my arms and legs. Then, he hands me the baby. He rushes back to Mama and stares down at the wound. He quickly examines her arm, then looks up to search the path. "Beloved, we shall remove the thorns later. Now, we must hurry because your screams might have alarmed them."

Mama nods that she understands and shakes the tears from her face. Papa takes Pablito and clutches my arm. We are off, running downhill like the wind.

I glance back at Mama who follows. Her arm must feel like burning fire, but still she is able to keep up with us. I see a visible cloud of dust rising rapidly behind her.

"Where are the clouds!" Papa snaps as if he is angry with them.

Papa's grip is like an iron bracelet choking my wrist. I want to tell him to let go, but I dare not, for I can see that he is very angry. Instead, I hold tightly to Anna.

Again, I hear the cry of the doves as it echoes out from the darkness. We run faster and soon strange voices become louder. The high weeds snap at my face and arms and the mud covers my feet. We approach the river bank where Papa stops. Still carrying Pablito, he wades out waist-deep to a boat where a man sits waiting. Papa hands him Pablito, then dashes back for me.

Papa carries me into the water, which feels cold against my legs. He loses his footing and we go under. The cold water surrounds me and chokes me. I hold tightly to Papa and to Anna and when we finally come up, I gasp. Papa lifts me onto the boat, then he turns to help Mama, who now waits on the river bank.

In the distance, I hear a motor as if a truck is coming our way full speed. I glance up, and there on top of the hill I see two lights that zigzag downhill. Then, I hear voices that echo four or five times. They say, "Alto! Stop! We will shoot!"

I hear a loud cracking pop, which seems to come from out of the heavens. Mama screams and I turn to see her fall into the water with a big splash. Mama and Papa go under, leaving nothing but circles of water floating everywhere.

Suddenly, two large lights beam upon the water. The man that sits in the boat moves quickly and shoves us down into the bottom of his raft. Pablito starts crying, and with his hand, the man signals me to quiet him. I hug Pablito, hoping to warm him, but my dress is wet and he pulls away. I hear whizzing sounds all around us. It sounds as though God has sent bolts of lightning to strike us, but soon they stop.

I peep into the water around me, searching for Mama and Papa. Then, I glance up at the huge man in the boat. He crouches low, letting the boat drift, rocking itself back and forth. Suddenly, they pop up beside us, and Papa shoves Mama into the boat.

"Go! Man, go quickly!" Papa yells.

The man shakes his head. "No, it's too far for you to swim. Come with us."

Small splashes of water again sprinkle around us and the whizzing noises start again. "Go! I will swim!" Papa demands before he goes under.

The boat lurches forward. I look to see that the river is now carrying Papa further away, but our boat moves in the opposite direction with greater speed. Soon, I cannot see Papa at all.

Once in a while a moan escapes from Mama's lips and she stirs. I look up at the big man with the gleaming eyes. He is sweating and the muscles on his arm jump as he rows. As the time passes, I grow tired of searching for Papa and I sigh, feeling very lost without him. I glance down at Pablito, who is sleeping against my arm. I wish I were he. He doesn't worry. He just sleeps and eats.

The man stops rowing and sits. Soon the rocking of the boat hushes me into drowsiness, but I force myself to stay awake as the boat glides through the water like a floating log. It soon stops against some tall brush sticking out of the water, and there we wait.

After some time, a voice from the river bank breaks the silence that surrounds us. "Chente," it says, "it is clear now."

The man in the boat pulls out the oars and rows, guiding the craft through high brush which gives way to land. He pulls in the oars and says, "Compadre, we had trouble this time. The woman is hurt and the children are wet and cold. Their man went under, trying to swim the river."

"Rotten luck!" answers the man on the bank who emerges from the shadows of a tree. He catches the rope that is thrown to him, then pulls in the boat and ties the rope around the tree. The man called Chente jumps out of the boat into the water. It comes to his waist. He turns and holds out his arms for the baby. "Pass him to me so that I may take him ashore."

I give him Pablito and he wades ashore and hands him to the other man. Then, he returns for me. He is strong and lifts me easily, then he carries me to the shore.

Mama moans loudly as he picks her up in his arms. It seems that they will fall into the cold water, but the man holds fast. When he reaches the bank of the river, he gently lays her on the ground. "She's in bad condition. We must get her to Doña Anita's right away." He lifts his head from Mama's chest. "Are you children okay?" he asks.

I nod yes.

"Bueno. Good. We must be on our way to get help for your mother." He lifts Mama into his arms and motions for me to follow with Pablito. When I do not, he turns back. "Come!" he commands.

I cross my arms and stand frozen. "Papa is still out there!" I shout as I point back to the river we have just crossed.

"My friend will wait for your Papa. We must get help for your mother or she will die." He hurries up the steep path, and I follow him carrying Pablito. I catch him on top of the hill and I ask, "Where are we?"

He keeps walking, but answers, "No longer in Mexico, niña." His breathing is heavy. "You are in the land of good opportunity."

"But, what does that mean?" I ask, very puzzled.

He chuckles, "You are in the United States of America. The river we just crossed is called the Rio Grande. You are now in Texas."

"Is that good?" I ask, still curious.

"Sí, yes. It is very good. You shall see."

AMÉRICO PAREDES

from *George Washington Gómez* (1990)

THERE WERE YEARS when spring came early to the Golden Delta of the Rio Grande, and this was one of those years. The morning sun, shining from a clear-blue sky, gave a warm, pleasant tang to the cool breeze that still smelled of winter. Already was the sour-orange tree by the fence putting out its delicate shoots that soon would become white perfume. This was the time of year when the chaparral for a brief time became a kind of fairyland. When the little dew-covered plots of grass that grew between each thorny tree were carpeted with pink primroses, and the patches of open field were purple with the wild violet that Mexicans call *alfombrilla*, little carpet. The thorny trees of the chaparral—the mesquite, the ebony, the huisache—were covered with their fluffy flowers, the first in pastel shades, the second an ivory white, the third an old-gold yellow, all three of a delicate, almost imperceptible fragrance that purified more than perfumed the air. The yucca shot out its wax-like blossoms like a white-robed sentinel of the woods, until Lent arrived and people would harvest the white leaves and boil them into a salad that tasted very much like the meat they abstained from during the Lenten period. Spiders spread out their webs from one branch to another, and in the early morning sun their dew-covered strands shone like jewels set on lace. The mockingbird sang in the thickets all through the sunny day and on into the moonlit night. It was such a morning in late February, and Doña Domitila walked into the yard back of the house, where María was washing. Doña Domitila was the spinster sister of Doña Teodora Gracia and lived with the Gracia family across the street. Two sisters never looked so unlike each other as Doña Teodora and Doña Domitila. When Doña Teodora walked into a house the floorboards creaked. She was big, fat, and aggressive. Doña Domitila was spare and self-effacing, inquisitive and gossipy. But she also was a learned woman by community standards; she read a lot of novels. And she was helping María teach Guálinto to read in Spanish.

"Ave María Purísima," Doña Domitila said in the sing-songy manner the phrase required.

"Buenos días de Dios," María replied, turning from the soapy tub beneath the willow. "Doña Domitila!" she continued as she wiped her reddened hands on her apron. "The shots, did you hear them? What was it? Do you know?"

"Know! Goodness, yes! It was horrible! Oh, Doña María, it was horrible!"

"Who? What?"

"It was Filomeno Menchaca."

"Oh," María said shortly. Then with something of compassion, "Poor Filomeno. But he was bound to end that way, may God forgive him." She crossed herself.

"Hmph," said Domitila with a toss of her head. "He's probably roasting in the Fifth Hell by now. After all the men *he* killed. I'd swear the law themselves had him killed. He knew too much about a lot of things."

"You shouldn't talk about such things," María said. "It could be dangerous, you know."

"Perhaps you're right. But it was horrible."

"Did you see it?"

"Mercy no. Not the incident." Domitila mouthed the word with relish. It was a popular word these days in the papers: international incidents all over the world. "Not the incident, Doña María, but I saw the body. Then the law came and made us go away. Oh, but it was horrible. Have you ever seen a dead man all torn up by bullets, Doña María?"

María shuddered. "No," she said in a small voice. "No. Never."

"Don Feliciano must have." Domitila gave María a shrewd look. "Some people say he was in the Revolution."

"He may have been," said María with a frown.

"By the way, was he home during the shooting? Isn't today his day off?"

"He went to Morelos. On an errand."

"Still in politics. That man is going to be rich someday, Doña María."

María frowned. "Sometimes I wish he wasn't in politics."

Domitila sighed. "Oh, he's a wonderful man, your brother Feliciano. He wasn't made to stay in the country pulling up stumps like so many other men. I wonder why he's never married. Is it true that he's thinking of running for sheriff?"

"Absolutely not," María said quickly. "On the contrary, he hopes to rent some land and grow his own vegetables for the new store."

"A farm owner too! How wonderful! When is he starting, Doña María?"

"It's just in his mind," replied María, sorry she had said anything about it.

Guálinto's head appeared beside the trunk of the willow. He remained half-hidden as if reluctant to be seen. That was not peculiar in itself, he was still somewhat shy before Doña Domitila. But there was more than shyness in his appearance. His lips were pale and he was shaking. His mother's casual glance became a sharp look.

"What's the matter with you?" she demanded. "Where have you been?"

Guálinto tried to slow his heavy breathing. He swallowed hard. "Nothing," he mumbled. "Nowhere."

"It was probably the shooting, poor little dear," said Doña Domitila. Guálinto shot her a look of startled hostility.

"That was it," María agreed. "It must have frightened him. But it's silly to get so worked up over the sound of a few shots. Why, he's almost dead of fright."

Guálinto hung his head and lost some of his tenseness. "Look at Doña Domitila," his mother said. "She *saw* the dead man. Is she scared like you?"

Guálinto remained silent, his eyes on the ground. "Go into the house, you coward," his mother ordered. "In a little while I'll go and make you some tea."

He walked off docilely toward the house. As he moved away he heard his mother say to Doña Domitila, "He scares so easily."

Doña Domitila said something he could not catch. But he breathed a bit easier. It had come out all right, his mother did not suspect. But he felt a hot lump in his throat. He was no coward. Someday he would show them, his mother and all the rest. Someday he would grow up and then he would go out and kill five or six Gringos like Gregorio Cortez and Cheno Cortinas. But now he had to be a coward to all the world. He climbed into bed and relaxed his tense little limbs. But though he buried his face in the pillow, he could still see it, everything.

Doña Domitila, she *saw* the body. He snorted into the pillow in spite of the hot throbbing at his temples. His mother had told him many times not to play with the

Vera boys at their house. If they wanted to play with him they should come to Guálinto's yard and play there. It wasn't because of Mrs. Vera, she said; she was a nice lady. She just didn't like for Guálinto to play on that street. But the Vera boys were such wonderful guys. Chicho, who was seven, was a regular fellow. You could suggest any old game and Chicho would play it with you. And he would let you win too. He was always smiling with those big white teeth of his. And nine-year-old Poncho was Guálinto's hero. He walked with a self-confident swagger and laughed in a way that made you laugh too. Nothing was too difficult for Poncho. He could climb the highest trees, going out over the intertwining branches from one tree to another like Tarzan. He knew where the birds' nests were, and he could make the best slingshots and bows and arrows you ever saw. And though he never looked for a fight, there were few boys in the *barrio* Poncho couldn't lick.

So Guálinto liked to play with the Vera boys over at their house, and he did so whenever he had a chance, though his mother always scolded him if she found out. That morning Guálinto was playing with Chicho out on the sidewalk in front of the Veras. The sun shone on their unheeding heads as they bent over a captive red ant. The man next door had been splitting wood. He stopped now and came over to the fence to watch, his silk shirt wet with sweat. "That ant is going to sting you," he said.

"Oh, no," answered Guálinto. "We're good ant-catchers. We've caught hundreds and millions of them, haven't we, Chicho?"

Chicho giggled and nodded and the man chuckled. "You don't even know how much a million is," he said.

Chicho looked up admiringly. "You know how much a million is, Meno?"

Meno scratched his head. "Can't say that I do exactly. But it's more than a thousand."

"More than a hundred even?" persisted Chicho.

"Sure, sure. A thousand's more than a hundred." Meno looked up the street where two men were walking toward them. "Some friends of mine," he said and moved down along the fence to meet them at the gate. "Qui'ubo, muchachos," he said with a grin.

One of the pair smiled a frank, engaging smile. "Nothing new, Filomeno. How's things with you?" Still smiling he pulled a gun from under his coat and fired.

Filomeno clutched at his shirtfront. His mouth tightened and his eyes grew big with surprise. For a dull, heavy moment he swayed drunkenly, one hand shielding his breast and the other pawing at his empty belt. Then the other man shot him—once, twice. Filomeno gave two short grunts as the bullets thudded into him, blasting the fabric of his shirt into little bits that flew in all directions like paper from a firecracker. He stumbled backward and fell heavily over the wood he had been splitting.

The two opened the gate and walked in. Filomeno was twisting and thrashing in the dirt, making choking piglike noises. Once his fingers closed over a stick of wood. He turned over and managed to sit up against the wood-pile, his silk shirt sticky and dark with blood, his face distorted and set like the flattened face of a wax figure. The two men watched him in silence. Then the first one shot him in the face. The bullet made a splattering sound and Meno pitched forward and didn't move any more. The two men walked out, carefully shutting the gate behind them.

Guálinto had stood watching it all, his hands tightly clenched around the pickets of the fence, his face pressed against them. He wanted to run when he saw the men walking out but he could not, anymore than he could take his eyes off the stained carcass sprawled on the woodpile. After the killers closed the gate they came toward him. He clung to the fence, and as the men came closer he shut his eyes. A hand touched his head and a voice said, "Better go home, boy." And the killers' measured steps died away.

When Guálinto opened his eyes at last, the men were a half-block away in the direction of the brush and the river. They walked leisurely, without a seeming care in the world. People were beginning to gather, all kinds of people. They seemed to spring out of nowhere and everywhere with the suddenness of apparitions. A big boy

ROBERT RUNYON

on a bicycle carrying some packages. Another on foot, in overalls, with a bag of groceries. Pale-faced and frightened. Then a fat red-faced man in a dimity undershirt, a portly woman wearing a dirty apron. They were quickly engulfed by a sea of faces that heaved and moved about in confusion. Dark faces, red faces, white pasty ones. Bearded faces and faces clean-shaven, thin ones, round ones. Men, women, hair top-knots, mustaches, shawls, hats. Faces high on tall men, faces closer to the ground. Faces with open, breathless mouths. Faces with lips tight and twisted as if their own-ers were holding back the need to vomit. Grim-looking faces, morbid strained faces with hungry probing eyes. A little girl's eyes peering from behind a skirt. The serious, puzzled face of a baby in a man's arms.

They had no eyes for Guálinto, those hungry searching faces. But he shrank from them, along the fence to a clump of *quelite* weeds growing by the fence post where Filomeno's yard bordered on that of the Veras. Here he crouched, darting looks in every direction through the maze of thick purple stalks. There was no sign of Chicho. He had vanished with the first shot. Some people opened the gate and went in, where they milled and pushed around the body till Guálinto could no longer see it. Everybody was speaking at once, softly as if in church, creating with their combined voices a deep, buzzing sound. Now and then a louder voice rose sharp and discordant above the hum of the crowd. Then the voice of an old man, dry and shallow like the twang of a cheap guitar. But commanding. The murmur of voices stopped.

"Don't touch him," the old man said. "We must leave everything as it is for the law. You over there, don't kick up the dirt. The law won't like it if you rub out any signs."

The law! The words pulsed in Guálinto's head. Half-pronounced, they set his throat throbbing. The law. He pushed himself deeper into the clump of weeds. They would come. They would take him away, pushing him along in front of them and cursing him. Then they would beat him to make him tell all he knew. They would make him a witness. The horror of the word struck him like a blow. Witness, in-former, pariah. He had to escape before the police came. If only his legs would carry him. But they were limp like wet rags. He pleaded with himself for just a little strength and courage. Now . . . One effort only . . .

The murmur of the crowd took on a new sound and out of it leaped the words, "Ahi viene la ley!" Guálinto sank back against the fence. The law had come.

The gray touring automobile creaked to a stop by the sloping sidewalk amid an eddy of dust, and out of it stepped some men in Sunday suits and big hats. They walked casually up to the gate. Two were soft-looking, middle-aged men, one red-faced and clean-shaven, the older one a bit grizzled. The third was a pale slender young man. He was not wearing boots or a hat. He carried a pencil and a pad in one hand. The young man looked all around him with quick, curious eyes. He stared for a moment at the clump of weeds, and Guálinto quaked. But no. He was not looking at Guálinto. He was looking down the road. Stealthily Guálinto turned his head to look also and his heart beat faster. The men who had killed Filomeno were still in plain sight.

The young man with the pad and pencil pointed at the two men in the distance. The policemen glanced idly in that direction and turned to enter the gate. Again the young one pointed, and he said something Guálinto did not understand. The older of the other two answered, and he sounded annoyed. By now the crowd had begun to gather around the policemen. Their faces were animated, expectant. Even professional killers can be likable, and Filomeno Menchaca had many friends in the *barrio*. With a kind of repressed excitement the crowd glanced now at the officers, now at the distant figures. Men began telling each other just loud enough so the law could hear, "Esos son. That's them. They can still catch them." The killers were growing smaller and smaller in the distance.

The elder of the two policemen was annoyed. It was more than apparent in his voice when he addressed the young man. The young man talked back and the policeman spoke sharply and with finality. Then he turned to the crowd, "Vamoose," he shouted. "Vamoose pa' la casa."

The law opened the gate and walked in while the crowd dispersed slowly and with many backward looks. Little groups of three or four straggled off in different directions, muttering and glancing at the officers and at the empty distance into which the two killers had disappeared. Angry, accusing looks were directed at the men of the law, who either did not notice them or did not care. After the crowd was gone they just stood around. They did not look for signs or anything like the old man had said they would. They just looked at the body. The oldest stepped over and stirred the body with the toe of his boot. He gave it a little kick and said something which made the red-faced one laugh. The young one did not laugh. After a while they moved away from the body and started talking to each other. They passed cigarettes around and smoked. Even the young one was laughing by this time.

"Now!" Guálinto said to himself, trembling. He crawled out of the weeds and stood up. To get home he would have to pass in front of the gate, but he would do it slowly as if he were just walking by. He started on shaky legs, his eyes studying the ground in front of him. When he reached the gate, one of the men inside turned toward him and yelled. Guálinto froze. Out of the car came a fourth man carrying a black bag. He staggered up the grassy slope to the sidewalk and stood before Guálinto, breathing heavily. There was a strong smell of liquor on his breath. Then he pushed the boy aside and went in through the gate. Guálinto ran all the way home.

GARY CARTWRIGHT

"Border Towns," from
Confessions of a Washed-Up Sportswriter (1982)

IT HAS BEEN A LONG, HOT, very dry drive from Austin and I am in no mood for restraint or the preachings of the chickenhearted. For the last hour or more, as we dropped like doughballs into the sizzling delta of the Lower Rio Grande Valley where the great sky is master, I have been listening to Billy Joe Shaver singing "Ain't No God in Mexico," contemplating how that border-crossing feeling does for sure make a fool out of a man. What can I say? It makes you want to whistle. To understand, you have to feel twenty years old, and a ten-dollar bill has to feel like a hundred. You have to crave cheap liquor, cheap sex, and cheap thrills, and you need a passion for anarchy and a blind spot for trouble. An international bridge is always an invitation to fantasy—that is why, on the American edge of every bridge, there is a discount store where poor Mexicans can glut themselves on plastic and polyester, and on the Mexican side there is a money exchange where Americans can make believe that pesos come from orchards. Soon, my bridge and I will be reunited.

I am drinking at the well-padded bar of Brownsville's Fort Brown Inn, overlooking the *resaca* that centuries ago was the riverbed of the Rio Grande, waiting while my traveling companion, M.S., showers and changes into something that will make her look like a Mexican field hand.

While I wait, I peruse the day's headlines. A captain in the Mexican army has been arrested for attempting to smuggle ten thousand rounds of ammunition into his own country. And Henry the Peacemaker Kissinger is, they say, negotiating a deal for the exchange of prisoners with Mexico. Also, Mexico has discovered giant oil reserves.

"Something is afoot," I observe as my traveling companion joins me.

"Something always is on the border," M.S. replies.

Yes, but it takes the hard practiced eye and hedonistic perception of an old river-runner to know just what. Like the river, political power is mindless and arbitrary. Take, for example, the case of the unfortunate Matamoros army officer. In other times, he would be a hero, a subject for monuments—he may be yet. Smuggling can be the ultimate heroic act when committed in the name of a cause, in his case the continuation of the Mexican revolution, which has been maintained in varying degrees against a succession of tyrants ever since the 1790s when the Holy Office de-

288   nounced Father Hidalgo for reading forbidden books. An honorable profession, smuggling. It is only when politics shift that it gets a bad name. Or take the case of the miserable wretches that Henry the Peacemaker is attempting to spring from the dungeons of Mexico: most of them were put there with the aid and insistence of the drug enforcement agencies of the United States government. Yesterday's refuse is today's humanitarian pursuit.

Even the oil discoveries have the thoughtless ring of history. It was right here at Fort Brown, maybe on the banks of this very *resaca*, maybe under this very table, that the expeditionary army of General Zachary Taylor camped, foreshadowing the Treaty of Guadalupe Hidalgo, by which the U.S. grabbed for herself half of the territory of Mexico, thus fulfilling Manifest Destiny and grinding the Mexican nation forever under the boot heels of Uncle Sam. Or so it was written. Maybe all that will change. Maybe in fifty or one hundred years, wetbacks will have blue eyes and wear Willie Nelson T-shirts.

Brownsville, and its larger, more sinister sister city, Matamoros, are the southernmost points in the twelve-hundred-mile river border separating the two countries. A perfect place to begin our personal exploration of border towns. So it is that I now feel the exhilaration. We are traveling in M.S.'s brand-new Buick with the air conditioner and tape deck; I have three hundred U.S. dollars in my jeans, a good map, some books, some names and addresses, and time enough to kill four men my size. What is more, M.S., my comely, enterprising research assistant, is a woman who never backs away from a dare or underestimates the therapy of a cheap thrill. On the first page of my notebook, under the notation about the great sky, the sea meadows, the endless fields of okra, onions, fruit and grain, and the very tall, very slender palms that stand like formations of dark flamingos, I record the words of some old river desperado whose name is long forgotten: "We love living more than we love life."

~

TRAVEL EDITORS and border samplers will tell you that the best place in Matamoros to eat and drink is a spot called the Drive-Inn. They will tell you about the elegant dining room with chairs that make you disappear, and about waiters in tuxedos, linen table cloths, wild-game dinners and flaming desserts, about the dance floor with revolving lights where coiffured women outfit their young sons in blazers and white shoes and make them lead while a Mexican orchestra very heavy on violins and organ renders such traditional numbers as "Baby Face" and "I Left My Heart in San Francisco." All I can tell you is, the joint is phony and ridiculously overpriced, the drinks are watered, and the waiters resemble something Mexico might manufacture and export to France.

The Texas Bar on the *zócolo* (central square) is a moderately good spot—at least the waiters ignore you. You can get cheap tequila and a good shrimp cocktail down the street at the Moctezuma, a gay hangout. By far the best place we found in Matamoros was Los Portales on the Victoria Highway, a few miles from the center of town. Los Portales specializes in *carnes al carbon* (charcoal-broiled meats), and on a warm evening you sit on the patio under willows and blooming oleanders, enjoying good mariachis. The clientele is mostly Mexican families. The family unit hasn't yet dissolved in Mexico and you can frequently see three or even four generations knocking down beer and *cabrito* while little kids in Zorro masks scramble at their feet.

Owner Everardo M. Gonzalez, a courtly old caballero, retains the trappings of his Indian ancestry: authentic oxcarts, Mexican charro saddles of hand-tooled leather and cured mesquite core, and a large black-and-white portrait of Zapata. Any taxi driver can find Los Portales, or for a couple of pesos you can grab a maxi-taxi (VW bus) out south Sixth Street. Just watch for the oxcart, or the maddening smell of charcoal-broiled meats.

There was a wedding reception going on at the pavilion next door, so after dinner we wandered over and joined the fun. The bride wore one of those storybook gowns you see in the shop windows of Mexico—Mexicans are very big on weddings and funerals. Mexicans are also excessively generous, and those who have tasted upward mobility are ludicrously class-conscious.

"Did I ever tell you the story of the portrait of the wife of the Telephone Pole King of Durango?" I ask M.S. as we drink tequila and watch the bride and groom pose for pictures. "I never actually met the lady, of course, but I attended a Christmas party at her home a few years ago. Crazy Dennis Hopper was in Durango making a film and he had rented out the mansion of the Telephone Pole King."

"How did he get appointed Telephone Pole King?" M.S. asks.

"I'm coming to that. It was a very grand home. It was like a time warp—something out of the fifties, a grand piano, and gardenias floating in the swimming pool. You really expected to see Esther Williams and Ricardo Montalban waltzing across the patio. Anyway, the portrait. It hung in the most prominent spot on a prominent wall of bad paintings. The dear lady was portrayed as a veritable madre de Mexico, a heroine of epic stature, superimposed over Aztec pyramids, the eagle and the serpent, Father Hidalgo, Benito Juárez, every legend and symbol of the country's struggle. That was how the wife of the Telephone Pole King chose to have herself portrayed.

"The so-called Telephone Pole King made his fortune planting telephone poles along the mountain highways outside of Durango. Of course there were no telephones way out there, and there was no wire between the poles. But if the government ever got around to it, the poles were waiting."

"What did the Telephone Pole King do before he sold telephone poles?"

"Sold shoes," I tell her. "Mexicans are very big on shoes. The two most prominent buildings in any Mexican town are likely to be the cathedral and the Canada Shoe Store."

We were the only two people in the pavilion wearing Mexican sandals. But it was okay. We were from *el otro lado*—the other side.

On the *zócolo*, near a Mexican discount store called Mas Mas Mas, we run across Tim Perez. Or rather he runs across us and refuses to go away. Tim Perez is a professional tour guide and insists on taking us to some overpriced rock joints in the Zona Rosa—pink zone. Tim is a pleasant, gregarious man in his late sixties. He speaks good English and claims to have friends in all fifty states.

Tim tells us that he has never met a man he doesn't like. He also tells us: "You must understand, women are the true heroes of Mexico—of the revolution." Tim says we should relax, have some fun. M.S. says she thinks it would be fun to dance with that slender Mexican boy with the turquoise necklace and the shirt unbuttoned to his waist. Tim has a brief coughing fit. He takes off his service hat and fans himself.

"Don't worry," he tells me as we watch M.S. approach the soon-to-be-amazed young Mexican. "He's . . . how do you say . . . queer."

While M.S. is showing her partner around the dance floor, Perez tells me his life story. He was born in Guadalajara, which he constantly refers to as "the second-largest city in Mexico," as though its size is one of the largest factors of his life. "My mother was the greatest person who ever lived," he says. His oldest brother was a conscript in the army of Carranza, a onetime sidekick of Pancho Villa who lost his revolutionary zeal once he got to the palace in Mexico City. Perez doesn't remember his father too well because he was still a baby when his mama gathered up her cooking pot and children and followed the older brother to war. "That was the custom of that time," Perez tells me. "We lived some in Veracruz, but mostly we traveled with the army, chasing Villa and the revolutionaries." When Carranza was murdered in bed by one of his own officers, Mother Perez took her brood to Matamoros where there was work harvesting. She died 26 years, 10 months, and 8 days ago, Perez says sadly. She is buried next to his oldest brother. Perez visits the graves every single day, sometimes bringing fresh plastic flowers.

"Your revolutions," I tell him, "are infamous for their irresolution."

"The revolution was like the children's game—king of the mountaintop," Perez tells me. "Whoever is on top makes the rules. Somebody has got to make the rules. What's the difference?"

"It was a helluva problem for the United States, your revolution. We never knew which side to back."

"It was like your Vietnam," Perez observes.

"It still is," I tell him.

"I am old now," he says. "I don't want another revolution. Revolution is murder. Many men die, and nothing changes so much. We should all be friends. We should all love each other."

"Mexican guys are the greatest dancers in the world," M.S. says as she rejoins the table. "That's about all they are."

Perez presents us with a bill of twenty dollars for his services, which I calculate have cost us twice that much again in bad drinks and cover charges. Perez insists on seeing us to a taxi. He gives the driver a tongue-lashing in Spanish, then tells us: "He will take care of you, don't worry."

I wake with a boss stud-bull monster Mexican tequila hangover and wonder where went the boy I once knew? Border-town Mexico is like I remember. Only it's not. Or I'm not. Something has changed. I prefer to think it's Mexico.

M.S. is already poolside, boiling under a sun that may be great for cotton and citrus but is intolerable when applied to the human body. I take a quick look around the Fort Brown Inn, which is billed as "21 acres of Tropical Paradise." In my notebook I write: "Pestilence . . . floods . . . famine . . . fine, pale sand that sticks to your teeth . . . inhuman heat . . . giant killer shrimp." In Paul Horgan's monumental two-volume history of the Rio Grande, *Great River*, there's a marvelous exchange between one of General Zachary Taylor's bedraggled officers and a fresh replacement just shipped down from the East. The replacement asks the veteran if those could possibly be fleas crawling through his hair, and the old officer replies indignantly: "Fleas! Do you think we are dogs who go about infested with fleas? These are lice!" I ask the woman desk clerk in the inn lobby to direct me to the ruins of old Fort Brown, and she says I'm standing on them.

There are, I learn later, several existing buildings from the old fort across the *resaca* on the campus of Texas Southmost College. Citizens on both sides of the river have a passion for recycling history. There is, for example, a little locomotive repainted red, white, and blue in honor of the Bicentennial in a small park near the hotel. A Chamber of Commerce sign explains that this is Old Number 1, the very locomotive that made its first international run in 1873. A trademark still visible on the belly of the old puffer claims it was built in Philadelphia in 1877. History has been economized. History has been reduced to black and silver markers telling you that under this tree General Zachary Taylor encamped. There is nothing about the true settlers of the Lower Rio Grande—the bankrupts, the bandits, the escaped criminals, the army deserters, the gamblers, swindlers, exploiters, and armies of occupation.

Across the shallow, muddy river, I retrace my wayward steps, dodging the demolition derby traffic along the narrow streets of Matamoros. It is Saturday afternoon and the streets swarm with *campesinos* (farmers or country people) and their families. The heat has driven most of the gringos indoors, on their own side of the river. I observe the curious mixture of 1950s modern and colonial architecture, the beautiful tiled sidewalks, the surprising number of handsome wood frame buildings, the hustlers and beggars and thieves. Pat Crowe, a friend who grew up in Brownsville, had told us, "The attitude toward property is completely different here. If you need something, or even if you don't need it but would like to have it, it is socially acceptable to steal it." Ford pickup trucks are a popular item among thieves. This is not because of some intrinsic quality developed in Detroit, but because Ford ignitions are quickly and easily interchanged. Old Henry sure knew what he was doing when he invented "a car for the people." The police department of Matamoros fences the hot pickups, or that's the story that goes around. Another local scam, Pat told us, is spare parts. Mexico literally runs on spare parts. Having miraculously avoided the disgrace of a junkyard along some U.S. interstate, the expatriate vehicles of America find long and useful service in Mexico, where a piece of baling wire is worth ten trips to the dealer. Mexicans like anything loud and faster than a burro, but they especially love trucks. They decorate their scabby trucks like they decorate their homes and churches and graveyards with fringe, ornaments, and holy objects.

Of course the two biggest scams anyplace on the river are guns (going south) and dope (going north). The products are endemic and interchangeable. A Browning automatic rifle is worth a pound of cocaine. Several times each week the river spits up the body of a poor smuggler or unscrupulous dealer, gunned down in an unexpected moonlight encounter.

Munching a slice of fresh watermelon purchased from a sidewalk vendor who also played marching songs on a portable handcrank organ, I find my way back to the Teatro Reforma, an old theater building that Perez had pointed out. The wonderful old building was supposed to be the city's tribute to the emperor Maximilian and his power-mad wife, Carlota, but the royal couple never showed. That would have been about 1865, I calculate. What a fiasco. On one side of the river, the Union was chasing the Confederacy, and on the other side Maximilian's fancy-pants French army was chasing the roving government-in-exile of Benito Juárez. Caught in the middle of this insanity was the port city of Matamoros. Matamoros is known as thrice heroic, having been burned by three different invading armies.

As I cross the bridge again, I am aware of the enormous amount of cargo being moved at a given moment. In the exact middle of the bridge a Mexican boy sells American cigarettes for two bucks a carton. An old Mexican woman has stopped to rearrange some articles in her American grocery sack.

My God, is that Alpo dog food I see? For her *esposo*, perhaps.

SUNDAY . . . EN ROUTE TO REYNOSA

I'll tell you up front about getting busted. It happened at the American customs station on the International Bridge at Progresso, a hot, dusty town of no distinction halfway between Matamoros and Reynosa.

There is only one reason an American would stop in Progresso, and that's to eat at Arturo's. Arturo's is what the Drive-Inn is cracked up to be, a really first-class family-style restaurant, featuring a wild-game dinner and *carne al carbon*. Prices are high, but prices are high everywhere. Kiss good-bye to the myth of the cheap Mexican border town.

Inspector Reynaldo of U.S. Customs must have spotted us fifty yards away. Two smiling gringos in a new Buick. No liquor to declare. No Mexican pottery. Just taking in the sights, heh? He had us open the trunk and he went straight for the only suitcase with a lock. It was uncanny: it was like he had built-in radar. Inspector Reynaldo rammed his fist straight through M.S.'s carefully folded lingerie to a cardboard box clearly labeled backgammon.

"Mother of Christ!" I said as he opened the box. "Where did that come from!"

I could see from his expression that Inspector Reynaldo was wondering the same thing.

The inspector treated us with the cordiality reserved for truly master criminals. He took a long time to weigh the marijuana. It came to forty-eight grams, less than two ounces. That puzzled him. He telephoned for a female customs agent, then they gave us both an amazingly thorough body search. They went through every piece of luggage as though they were inventorying the estate of Howard Hughes, then they started on the car. Finally, Inspector Reynaldo stepped back, shaking his head.

"I don't understand," he said. "Where is the rest of it?"

"There ain't no rest of it," I told him. For the better part of an hour M.S. and I had been sitting in the customs office looking at a portrait of Gerald Ford with his arms crossed resolutely and that dumb cartoonist's grin on his face, wondering why God made some of us more stupid than others.

"This is all too simple," Inspector Reynaldo said, pacing about like Peter Sellers in *The Pink Panther*. "You have less than two ounces of marijuana . . . I don't understand. Why? It's too simple. What are you trying to pull on me? I want an explanation."

"Gringo estupido," I said. "Who else would smuggle Austin grass into Mexico, eat lunch, then smuggle it back?" If I hadn't been so busy feeling sorry for myself, I would have felt sorry for Inspector Reynaldo. You could read his mind. *Duped again.* Here he was, the scourge of the Progresso bridge, squandering his time with two five-and-dimers while the real load, probably an eighteen-wheeler hauling fifty thousand pounds of high-grade cocaine, slipped through with its terrible cargo.

After checking with the Drug Enforcement Administration in McAllen, which

ascertained that we were indeed small fish not worth frying, the inspector handled it administratively. That is, he seized our marijuana and our brand-new Buick. Then he read us section 618 of the Tariff Act of 1930 and allowed us to reclaim the car for $200 cash, which we had to send for.

But, God, I'd do it all again just to have a snapshot of Inspector Reynaldo's face when M.S. finally handed him the money and asked could she please have her favorite roach clip back. That of course was out of the question, but the propriety of the question greatly disturbed Inspector Reynaldo.

It was late that afternoon when we again crossed the bridge, this time at Reynosa, the most Mexican of border towns, owing to the fact that the only thing on the Texas side is the discount store crossroads called Hidalgo. We purchased a cheap bottle of palm rum and checked into the Hotel Amelia to wash away our despair. The Amelia is your traditional Mexican hotel, which is to say the toilets don't flush and the showers are carefully engineered to flood the bathroom.

"How do you feel about your goddamn border now?" M.S. asked. I ignored the question. I was trying to work the air conditioner, but the knob fell off in my hand.

"Did you know that in Mexico they train engineers to design things that don't work?" I said, drinking palm rum from the bottle. "It's a fact. The economy of Mexico is totally dependent on repairmen. It would therefore be catastrophic if anything worked."

"Yes," she sighed. "It would be a miracle."

After a delicious meal of tacos purchased (eight for one dollar) from an ingenious street vendor of gourmet stature, we decided to take in the *zona roja*—the red-light district. In larger cities like Matamoros and Nuevo Laredo, the *zona roja* (AKA Boys' Town) is located in walled fortresses four or five miles from the center of town. The difficulty in escorting an American woman to the *zona roja*, aside from the obvious, is that taxi drivers absolutely refuse to be a part of such foolishness. Reynosa's red-light district, however, is located near the *zócolo*, and with some instructions from our friend the gourmet taco vendor we found it on our own.

There is a sinister low-life aura about any Mexican whore district—again, there is that time warp, only now you're in the thirties, you're in the Foreign Legion and cutthroat Arabs are bellying across every rooftop. But the *zona roja* in Reynosa is Mexican Dogpatch, the flash of a twisted libido swooping low, devouring sweet children in choir robes. We walk along a cratered, flea-bitten street of neon bars with names like Chinese Palace, ignoring indifferent glances of taxi drivers, pimps, shoeshine boys, and hookers in blonde wigs and tight dresses who mingle on the sidewalk against the oppressive heat inside. This is the main street, the showcase. The low-rent street, which intersects it, is pure Swine Alley—the central feature being rows of barracks-like rooms where ratty old hookers sit in open doors framed against naked light bulbs and lumpy beds and pathetic personal garnishings such as teddy bears and pinups of Mexican movie stars and radios with broken plastic cases. A brightly lighted club called Ciro's reminds M.S. of where they used to hold FFA dances in Oklahoma, so we stop in for a couple of beers.

"It's like an FFA dance," M.S. says. "Look, the girls sit with their backs to the walls, waiting for the men to ask them to dance. That poor fat girl. I'll bet no one ever asks her to dance. All the men look like farmers and cowboys. Look how they hold the women almost at arm's length."

The *campesinos* drinking beer at rough wooden tables pay us no attention: whatever we are up to, it is none of their affair. I am concerned that maybe the hookers will consider M.S. a threat, but that is not the case. A nice-looking young woman even asks her to dance.

At the Chinese Palace, we meet a bright young Mexican pimp named Pancho, who speaks good English and tells us that he is from a prominent family of Mexico City drug dealers. By now we feel comfortable, even euphoric. Pancho tells the girls that I am a writer, and soon they are clustered at our table, writing their names in my notebook.

M.S. shares the popular assumption that most Mexican whores are poor farm girls kidnapped and forced into a life of slavery, but Pancho tells her that is not necessarily correct.

"They are not slaves," he says. "They can go away. Only they don't have no place to go. It is not a bad life for a young girl. They make sixty, seventy dollars a week, sometimes more, and they are protected."

"What happens when they get old?"

"What happens when any of us get old?" Pancho asks rhetorically.

MONDAY . . . LAREDO–NUEVO LAREDO

Feels like the first day of summer. Driving north on Highway 83, paralleling the river, the terrain changes from tropical to shimmering desert. White Brahmas stand motionless among mesquite and chaparral.

We stop at the old river port of Roma, once a haven for smugglers and bandits. Here the river is wider, cleaner, better defined. I am interested in tales of an infamous outlaw of the 1860s, one Abram Garcia, AKA the White Cavalier, but nobody in town ever heard of him. I'll bet their great-great-granddaddies did. Garcia rode a snow-white stallion, dressed in tight velvet trousers and short jackets of gold and silver thread, and carried enough weaponry to pulverize a mountain. It was the White Cavalier's pleasure to watch grown men dance. He encouraged them by shooting at their feet, and when the dance had ended he ordered them stripped and whipped to death.

With the exception of an old (1840) Oblate Fathers mission now occupied by a small museum, the citizens of Roma fairly well ignore the ruins of their hot little village. But you can walk along the north bank of the river and get an idea how it was. Pulques Cantina still exists, after a fashion. I bet the White Cavalier had some big times in there. The store of Manuel Guerra stands, its ancient hand-cast brick walls, great hand-carved, weathered doors, and weed-choked courtyard preserved by the Texas Society. The descendants of Manuel Guerra now operate an export-import business from a modern, aluminum-sided office and warehouse across from the old store.

An item in the museum catches my eye. It appears to be the ammunition belt of a dead-solid drinker—three holsters shaped like whiskey bottles hanging from a broad leather strap. No one in the museum can account for its purpose. I'll bet the White Cavalier could figure it out.

We stop south of Laredo to inspect the well-preserved ruins at San Ygnacio, and an hour later we are secure in the arms of the twentieth century, in a large, cool, elegant room at La Posada Motor Hotel, overlooking the river and Mexico. La Posada is a hotel for your low-range fat cats from both sides of the river. I mean, Laredo ain't Cozumel or even Acapulco, but layouts such as La Posada do offer maximum creature comforts for what M.S. calls "your basic trader class." In the bars, and at poolside, Mexican and American wives practice their bilingual proclivities ("Que niños usted?") while their husbands make deals. The corner of the hotel behind the swimming pool was for a brief time in 1840 the capital of the Republic of the Rio Grande, a breakaway confederation of federalists opposed to the despotic rule of Santa Anna. There were *seven* flags over this part of Texas.

Because its streets are narrow and loud and smell like motor fuel, Nuevo Laredo is considered by purists as your most faithful border town. It is busy in that maniac, turbine, move-your-ass-outta-my-way fashion that Juárez, Durango, Monterrey, and other much larger Mexican cities are busy, yet it is small enough to cover on foot. With the exception of the *zona roja* and several good restaurants, any place worth visiting is within walking distance of the bridge. The Cadillac Bar, where the Ramos gin fizz is a tradition worth sampling. The *zócolo*, where horse-drawn carriages wait to show tourists the sights. The market.

The Plaza de Toros has, unfortunately, been closed; the nearest bullfighting plaza is in Monterrey, a two-hour drive into the interior.

The best eating place in Nuevo Laredo (maybe the best in Mexico) is Jorge 'n' Charlie's Laredo Grill, a couple of miles out the Monterrey highway. It's a modern place, but the walls are plastered with old photographs and newspaper reproductions illustrating the history of Mexico—six revolutionaries hanging from a single tree, Villa puffing a joint, Villa and Zapata posing like Aggies in the National Palace, an unidentified man in a black suit grinning and having a smoke in preparation for his final performance before a firing squad. Everything on the menu is worthy of attention. Only an idiot would fail to sample the oysters *diablo, madranzo,* and *Cardenas.* Order oysters 4-4-4. The lime-butter steak or garlic-battered shrimp with mustard sauce will reduce the most jaded connoisseur to a slobbering swine. The waiters are attentive and have a sense of humor. After dinner they serve a complimentary white russian and a dish of lollipops. There is also a wheelchair, in the event you have difficulty returning to your car.

In the heat of the afternoon we escape the insanity by retreating to the bar of the Hotel Reforma. Until recently the Reforma bar was a place of quiet dignity where old waiters with limps recalled the days of the quick getaway and young matadors talked of going in high and clean over the horns. It is still a good place to watch the traffic along Avenida Guerrero, but the linen tablecloths have been replaced by textured vinyl ones, the lighting is fluorescent, and the old ceiling fans have given way to central air conditioning. The waiters skip lively now, and the only customer who could possibly be a matador wears a baseball cap turned sideways. On the avenue there is a monster traffic jam as an eighteen-wheeler that has made an illegal turn attempts to back up against the flow of traffic. Another eighteen-wheeler that is pinned up in traffic blocks the way. Soon the two drivers are on the sidewalk, shouting and waving their fists. A thousand horns blast a raucous concert.

"What do you suppose are in all those trucks?" M.S. asks wistfully.

"Mexico," I tell her. "They are hauling it away."

"I'll bet they can sell it in the U.S.," she speculates.

"I'll bet you're right," I say.

Sometime after midnight, when M.S. is sleeping, I walk back across the bridge and take a five-dollar taxi ride to the *zona roja*—Boys' Town. I have a tequila in all the old places. Papgoyas, the Savoy, the Club Miramar, the Marabu. But the thrills are not cheap.

They're not even thrills. In one final foolish gesture I trade my watch for a hooker's black lace bra. In my present condition, it seems like the perfect gift. But halfway across the bridge, returning to the hotel, I throw it into the Rio Grande and watch it float toward the sea.

TUESDAY . . . EAGLE PASS–PIEDRAS NEGRAS

Sixty miles north of here, in the Del Rio–Acuña–Amistad Lake region, the highway will desert the river, leaving it to its wild, reckless meanderings down through the Big Bend, then north again along the Chihuahua wasteland all the way to El Paso and Juárez. It's almost a symbolic gesture, an act of ultimate revulsion, as though the course of civilization was not yet prepared for such hostile terrain or arbitrary tricks of nature.

There are still a few small falling-off places where a visitor can stand on sheer cliffs and look across into the wilderness of a foreign land. One of these is the Texas ghost town of Langtry, Judge Roy Bean's old hangout, inhabited mainly by rattlesnakes and vinegarroons. There are, of course, the spectacular canyons of the Big Bend, which a motorist can reach by zigging and zagging among mountain peaks and through moonscape gaps that make the planet Mars look like Sunday at Fair Park. And there is the hellhole of Presidio-Ojinaga, best viewed on the TV weather map.

But it is hundreds of miles now before the highway and river make their peace just south of El Paso.

Since I have been to Juárez many times, and have no intention of going again just now, I will offer two suggestions: (1) stay out of the *zona roja*, unless your pleasure is getting robbed and/or beaten about the head; (2) eat at least one meal at Julio's Cafe Corona, where the *caldillo* (a fiery Mexican stew) is unexcelled. With its purple mountains and thin desert air, El Paso–Juárez is the most scenic of the river border towns, and almost the most sinister. This is a land and a law unto itself. Until the Mexican government cracked down, Juárez was a popular spot for quicky gringo divorces. Now it's a popular spot for contacting hit men or big-league drug czars. If I had to pick just one border town for those hedonistic qualities mentioned at the beginning, I would pick Juárez. If I had to pick five, it wouldn't even be on the list.

Five days into our adventure along the river of latent desire, I feel this ambivalence: my soul cries *more*, but my head answers *never*.

Where the highway from Laredo to Eagle Pass–Piedras Negras bends away from

the river, we are stopped by U.S. immigration officers searching for aliens. They are attempting to break the back of a smuggling ring specializing in human cargo.

"What they do," an officer tells us, "is lower them with ropes from the old bridge to a place where they can wade ashore and cut through the U.S. customs lot without going through immigration. They charge the Mexicans about three hundred pesos each [twenty-four dollars]. We figure sixty-five or seventy make it across each week."

"Why can't they just walk across the bridge like everyone else?" M.S. asks.

"Some of them are either too poor or too disreputable to get a bridge crossing card," he explains.

"We must have crossed a dozen bridges," M.S. says, "and we didn't have any kind of card. It doesn't seem fair."

I implore the immigration officer to ignore this last demented remark, explaining that my traveling companion has a fever but will no doubt be all right as soon as I can get her to a Dairy Queen. The officer understands. His quarry would not be dressed like Mexican field hands, driving a new Buick. We thank him and are quickly on our way, but I am still wondering about those aliens out there in the brush, alone in hundreds of square miles of desolation. I don't know where they think they are going, but they won't like it when they get there. Could it be that they are going nowhere, that the adventure is the trip itself?

As we pass through Carrizo Springs and the road bends back toward the river, I write in my notebook: " . . . beautiful desolation of the great ranches . . . except for the highlines and fences, the land is much like the Comanches found it centuries ago when they first crossed the river just south of Eagle Pass."

After the bedlam of Laredo, there is a healing tranquillity about Piedras Negras. The north bank of the river was the site of Fort Duncan, one of the chain of river forts established to ward off smugglers, bandits, and bad Indians, but the only "battle" that Paul Horgan records in his history of the river took place in the 1850's when an American hoodlum named Callahan crossed the Rio Grande in pursuit of some Seminole Negro slaves who had escaped. Callahan and his raiders never recovered the slaves, but they did pause long enough to loot Piedras Negras, and the soldiers at Fort Duncan covered Callahan's retreat.

Perhaps the serenity that we feel now can be attributed to the easy, laid-back, compromising attitude of the early settlers. Although the citizens of the Texas side had little sympathy for the Confederacy (they voted overwhelmingly against secession), immense shipments of Confederate cotton crossed here and were transported by land to the Mexican seaports of Matamoros and Bagdad. When word reached the river that the emperor Maximilian had been captured and executed by firing squad, they threw a memorable party in the customs house at Piedras Negras.

In the late-afternoon shadows we stroll the narrow, pastel streets, eating ears of buttered corn. Lovers, drunks, and loafers share the concrete benches of the zócalo. The local movie house, Cine Rodriguez, is featuring a film about a mad professor who gets his jollies bolting naked blondes into chastity belts. An ancient campesino with a silver-and-velvet-trimmed carriage and a horse that may have been left here by Cabeza de Vaca tips his hat and offers us a ride. There is a sign on the side of the carriage. It says, in English: "Back From Moon—Welcome." A boy is selling tickets to the bullfight in Piedras Negras.

We wander through the cluttered, low-key back streets of the market, pausing to inspect an amazing variety of medicinal herbs.

"If we could only read Spanish," I tell M.S., "we would realize that we have landed in a veritable dope fiends' Garden of Eden. I've read that there are something like forty-seven hallucinogenic plants growing wild in this part of Mexico."

"Para la mala digestión?" M.S. says, reading the labels. "Gripe . . . hemorragia . . . rastornos . . . mestruales . . . devildad sexual? What does it mean?"

"I'm just guessing," I tell her, "but it probably means it will get you high or kill you."

We had already determined to do a quiet dinner and early bed, but now we're chasing tequila with *sangrita* (a flavorful nonalcoholic drink composed chiefly of hot chilies and orange, lime, and tomato juices; not to be confused with wine-and-brandy-based *sangría*) at a fancy joint called Las Roches, overlooking the river.

A number of drinks later we are dining and dancing at the Moderno Restaurant, an authentic fantasy land of leaded onyx tables, plastic zebra-striped seats and genuine American toilet paper. The owner, Raul de los Santos V, a splendid figure with a Gable moustache and a loud sport coat, tells us that he can supply anything our hearts desire.

"I have many friends," Raul says. "Not just in Mexico. On both sides. You tell me your troubles, I will take care of them."

In the company of Raul de los Santos V and Manuel D. Sanchez, owner of the A-1 Plumbing Service in Uvalde, Texas, we hit every bar in Piedras Negras. Sanchez' wife carries a sack of coconut shells in which bartenders can prepare her favorite drink of rum and fruit juice. Sanchez tells us proudly that though he has only a third-grade education, he is the plumber that Governor Dolph Briscoe normally calls in an emergency. Sanchez and his wife drive to Piedras Negras about once a week, "to get away from the kids and the telephone and have a damn good time." And by God we are, we are having a good time.

"I ain't no Meskin," Sanchez proclaims at one point.

"I'm an Arapaho. You call me a Meskin again, I'm gonna pick up my hoe and . . ."

We are laughing and falling out of chairs. Me and Sanchez take an oath of blood brotherhood. We even attempt to cut our wrists with a kitchen knife. Fortunately, we are too drunk.

"I don't know about you," I blather as they pour us out in front of our motel just before dawn, "but I ain't ever had a better time."

"I can always tell," M.S. says. "About midnight you get that wild look and start talking like the Frito Bandito."

WEDNESDAY . . . GARNER STATE PARK

Spent the entire afternoon on the banks of the Rio Frio, in the shade of a granddaddy cypress. There is no word in any language for this kind of sick. I am shivering and sweating like a pig, and my hand is shaking so badly that I am having to dictate these notes. I have a terminal overdose of Mexican border towns. I will die here, and now.

"What shall I write?" M.S. asks.

"Just repeat the first line," I say, shutting my eyes. "Tell them we love living more than life. Only make it past tense. *Loved.*"

"Are you sure?" she asks softly, tenderly.

"Just as sure as I'm gonna die."

EARL NOTTINGHAM

OSCAR CASARES

"Domingo," from *Brownsville* (2003)

THIS MORNING AFTER THE STORM, the edge of the alley was the only dry place a man could wait for a ride. Water filled the gutter and spilled over into large puddles. A toad had been squashed in the middle of the street; its guts trailed down toward the curb. Tree branches leaned against power lines. Domingo squatted on his haunches, far enough away from the smell of wet trash and a dead tacuache that lay stiff in the middle of the alley. He tilted back his straw cowboy hat. His machete hung off the side of his belt. He had been waiting over half an hour for la señora Ross. If she did not come soon, he would have to start working after the sun had already made the day hot. He was not afraid of hard work, but at seventy-three years of age he knew it was important to work slowly and be sure the job was done well. As he waited for la señora, he tried to distract himself with different thoughts of how his day would go, but his mind drifted back to the same thought he had woken up with that morning:

today was the birthday of his Sara. She would have been twenty-one years old on this day, a woman with her own family by now. He knew his wife was back home doing something to remember their daughter, to remember the one year she was with them. Like so many times before, Domingo tried to imagine what Sara might look like as a grown woman, but he saw her only as a little girl and this brought back some old feelings he had worked hard to silence. He was thankful when he saw that la señora had finally arrived.

Domingo opened the car door and la señora's little dog barked and barked. The dog had long brown hair and little black eyes that seemed to pop out of its head.

"Bueno días," la señora said.

"Buenos días, señora," Domingo said.

"Mucho trabajo at la casa," she said.

These were the same words they said every Saturday morning when she arrived for him. La señora spoke very little Spanish and Domingo even less English. They had learned to communicate with their own sign language, which was made up of the physical motions of what they were trying to say. There was a sign for Domingo to sweep the grass off the sidewalk and driveway. A sign told him exactly how to trim the bushes. Another sign let la señora know that the lawn mower needed more gasoline. The sign they used the most was the one to say that it was very hot. La señora would wipe her brow with the back of her hand. "Mucho calor," Domingo would say. "Mucho, mucho calor," la señora said. "Sí, hace mucho calor," Domingo said. If there was something they couldn't figure out a sign for, la señora would go next door and ask for help from the girl who cleaned her neighbor's house.

This Saturday, la señora stopped on the way to her house. She motioned for Domingo to wait in the car. She left the air conditioner on the High setting and turned the radio dial to a Tejano station, smiling as she did this. He understood that she had adjusted the radio for him, but he had never cared for that type of music and the disturbing sound created with so many instruments. In any case, it was difficult to hear anything because the little dog would not stop barking. Where he came from, someone would have beaten the dog by now. Domingo tried to ignore the animal and enjoy the cold air. He put his face up to the vent and felt the air blow through his eyebrows.

When they finally arrived at the house, la señora showed him the area of the backyard where several branches had broken off the ebony tree and fallen over the patio area. Two smaller branches were floating in the light blue water of the swimming pool. He used his machete to cut the pieces so he could stuff them into the plastic trash cans. Later, la señora asked him to use a long pole with a net at the end to scoop out the tiny leaves in the pool. Domingo liked working for her because he knew he was guaranteed work for the entire day. Her property was much larger than those in the neighborhood where he usually worked. She also owned a new lawn mower that was more powerful than any he had ever used. La señora was very particular about her yard and how she wanted it maintained. The grass along the sidewalk needed to be trimmed a certain way so that it met up with the pavement but did not hang over the edge. Domingo took pride in his work and wanted la señora to be pleased with the way her yard looked.

At lunchtime, la señora's daughter brought out two ham and cheese sandwiches for him to eat. The young lady had a pleasant smile, and it was hard for him not to wonder how beautiful his own daughter might have been, but he knew these feelings would not do him any good and he tried his best to distract himself with other thoughts. He was hungry by this hour of the day, so he ate everything she brought out to him. He sat in a lawn chair under the patio umbrella, imagining this was how people of money ate when they stayed in hotels. The sandwiches were filling, but at his age the spicy mustard upset his stomach. He would have mentioned this to la señora, except he didn't have the words to say it, and even if he did, he didn't want to seem unappreciative.

He was finishing his lunch when la señora came out to show him what she wanted him to do next. She made a hacking sign to tell Domingo that he needed to cut some more broken branches left from last night's storm. The tallest limbs were cracked and hanging on to the house. He nodded and made a motion as if he were climbing a tall ladder. La señora walked with him to the garage, where she kept the larger tools.

Domingo gazed up at the sky as he climbed the aluminum ladder, stepping lightly on each rung. The white clouds floating over the Rio Grande Valley appeared close enough for a man to reach out and touch with his hand. Sweat was streaming down his face, and the band of his hat was drenched. His machete hung off the back of his belt. The ladder wobbled slightly as he hacked at broken branches, and he thought he might have been more secure on the rungs if he had climbed barefoot. He would have done this, but he was embarrassed to show his tired, cracked feet in front of la señora. They were the feet of an old man who had worked his whole life like a mule. Some of the jobs he took paid very little, but he felt fortunate to still be working. No one could say he had ever backed down from a day's work.

He had to climb onto the roof to reach some branches that were near the antenna. Domingo looked down and saw la señora watching him. The roof was over thirty feet high, and it occurred to him that this was the highest place he had ever worked. La señora owned a two-story house that was bigger than most of the houses on her street. From where he was perched, he could see the red arch on the Matamoros side of the bridge. If he stood on his toes, he could barely make out the tops of the billboards that invited tourists to drink more rum and eat dinner at restaurants across the river. Seeing this little bit of his country made him think of his home. It also made him think of Sara.

La señora was yelling something up to him, but he couldn't understand what she was trying to say.

"¿Mande, señora?"

She jerked her hands up as if she were being shocked, and Domingo understood he wasn't supposed to touch the antenna. He waved back to let her know that he understood.

One by one, he cut the branches loose and let them fall to the ground, making sure they landed a good distance from where la señora was standing. As he worked, his memory took him back home. He could see the baby walking the way she did, like a little drunk man. She crawled faster than this, but she was determined to walk on her own. Sara was always learning new things, which made Domingo and his wife believe God had blessed them with an intelligent child. He thought now that if he had stopped her from trying to walk and made her crawl, maybe she would not have been so curious to see what was down in the pit. His wife had asked him to build a fire so she could heat water to wash clothes. He turned around for a second. Even now he had trouble understanding why his wife had left him with the baby. They took her to a woman who knew how to heal, but she offered them only prayers. They borrowed money from their family to take her to a clinic, but there they told them her brain had been damaged by the fire in the pit and the best they could do was keep her comfortable. They asked God for a miracle. The women of the family prayed a Rosary over the little girl every day. Domingo and his wife made a promesa that if their baby were to get better, they would walk the ten or twelve days it took them to get from where they lived outside of Ciudad Mante to Mexico City, in order to visit the Basilica, and, on their knees, give thanks to the Virgen de Guadalupe. And still the child suffered for a month until the night she died. After they buried her, Domingo told himself he would never enter another church unless he was carried through the doors in a wooden box. But he knew this was wrong, and for a long time he had wanted to make peace with these bitter feelings. As he looked toward the river, he thought that today, on Sara's birthday, might be a good time to speak to God. He wished he could go back and be with his wife, cross the bridge and buy a ticket for the next bus headed south. But he had to remind himself that he had been home less than a month earlier and getting back across was becoming more difficult with the immigration authorities stationed along the river. He concentrated on the work he was doing, letting the machete fall harder on the broken branches, but the need to find peace in his heart would not leave him.

The sun was lowering itself by the time Domingo returned to the little room where he slept. The room belonged to the Ramirez brothers and was attached to their tire shop. They allowed him to stay there for free, with the understanding that he would watch over the repair shop at night. Since the brothers also stored tires in the

RUSSELL LEE

room, the space for his cot was limited. He was grateful to them for offering him a place to sleep, but he never stayed in bed too long, because of the loneliness it brought him and the fact that the smell of so much rubber gave him a headache. His clothes were stored in a cardboard box under the cot. The only other belongings he placed inside the box were a photo of his wife with the baby and a tattered envelope with the directions for where to send his money back home.

After he washed his hands and face at the sink inside the garage, he put on a pair of jeans and a green shirt la señora had given him. The jeans fit a little big in the waist, but that was what belts were for. He used a rag to clean the dust off his black shoes until they looked presentable. Then he grabbed his hat and locked up the little room.

Holy Family Church was a short walk from where Domingo lived. He had passed by the church many times but had never considered attending the Spanish mass they offered Saturday evenings. By this hour, the services had ended and he was hoping to have a moment alone before the altar. He had always considered the church small compared with most churches he knew in Mexico, but now as he walked toward the entrance, he felt as if he were approaching a very large mountain. The saints on the stained-glass windows looked like images he had seen once in a long, fitful dream. Domingo pulled on the large wooden doors, but they were locked. He peered through the window and saw a single light shining down on the altar. He walked around to the side of the building, but the doors were locked there as well. In all his years, he had never seen a church with its doors locked. Perhaps his imagination, or even God himself, was playing tricks on him for having stayed away so long. But the doors were just as locked the second time he tried.

Domingo was heading back to his room when he saw a couple, an older man and woman, walking with a small gray and white dog. The man used a cane and looked at least ten years older than Domingo. The woman was younger than her husband and she held the dog's leash. Domingo greeted the couple and asked them if they knew why the church doors were locked. The old man said he truthfully did not know the answer to this question, but perhaps it had something to do with the priest not wanting to work late. The man's wife shook her head and said the real reason was that the church had been broken in to too many times, and once, it had even caught on fire accidentally. She doubted whether he would find any church in town open at this hour. Domingo thanked them and kept walking.

When he arrived back at his room, he lay on the cot and rested. Sometimes he bought beer and drank outside the room on a wooden stool. But he tried not to do that anymore, because it was difficult for him to stop after two or three beers and then he would miss work because he overslept. All he wanted now was to fall asleep and forget his failed trip to the church. The room was dark except for a ray of light that leaked in through a corner of the ceiling. He wondered if there was some way of entering another church, at least to light a candle and say a short prayer. So much time had passed, and now waiting another night felt like an eternity, the same eternity he and his wife had endured while they waited for God to bless them with a child. For years, he had felt cursed because his woman had not become pregnant. She was younger and healthier than he was. There was no reason for them not to share in this blessing. And finally, when they had lost all hope of bringing a child into the world, Sara was born. How then could the child have been taken from them so quickly? Domingo blamed himself for not having kept her away from the pit. He carried the guilt on his back as if it were a load of firewood that was added to with each passing year. It was impossible for him to make sense of the tragedy. How could God have permitted it to happen? And then Domingo remembered something he had seen not so long ago. He was riding in la señora's car when they drove by a house where people were standing on the street praying. Someone had discovered the image of the Virgin Mary in the trunk of an alamo tree. The shape of the Virgin Mother's face and arms were formed into the bark. People were staring up at the image from both sides of the street, and the group closest to the tree was praying a Rosary. A slender woman with short hair was pushing a young boy in a wheelchair. The boy's spine was arched as if he were trying to reach a knife stuck in his back. He wore a large bib and his head was swollen to the size of a pumpkin. Next to the tree, an older woman with a long braid knelt at an altar. A man leaned against a fence with his one leg, while his right pant leg, folded in half and sewn up underneath him, flapped in the wind like a small brown flag. Domingo remembered that la señora honked her car horn at a woman standing in the middle of the street with her head bowed and her arms reaching toward the Virgin Mary. He didn't understand what la señora had said, but he knew it had something to do with all the people in the street.

Domingo put on his clothes and locked the door to his room again. As much as he wanted to do something to remember Sara's birthday, he could not escape the question of whether the image was truly the Virgin, though he reasoned that so many people could not be wrong. After all, they were people who possessed much more faith than he had in the past twenty years. What right did he have to question their beliefs?

The road leading to the bridge was backed up with cars for several blocks. There seemed to be as many headlights as there were flashing lights announcing the rate of the peso at the various money-exchange houses. Domingo could see young people laughing and having a good time as they waited in traffic. There was one car full of young women and they all waved at Domingo as if they knew him. The light turned green and he crossed the busy street near the college and the McDonald's restaurant. He loved the hamburgers they served and eating lunch there on Sunday, his day off, was one of the few pleasures he allowed himself. He had to admit that the Americans made very good hamburgers, which was another reason to admire how advanced this country was.

He was a block away from the center of town when he saw the cathedral. Before he could check to see if the doors were open, he noticed that the steel gates were locked. The lights in the courtyard were on and he stopped to look up at the towers stretching into the night sky. He imagined that if a man could stand on top of one of these towers he might be able to reach heaven, maybe even see an angel.

Half a block from the cathedral, someone whistled out to him. Two women were standing near the entrance of El Economico Hotel. The taller one had broad shoulders and wore a sequined tube top with a tight miniskirt. Her companion had long blond hair that stood out against her dark skin.

"Venga pa'ca, papacito."

"¿Por qué andas con tanta prisa?"

Domingo might have stopped if he were a younger man and it were a different night, but only until he realized they were actually men dressed as women. The shorter one called out to him to slow down, that they didn't bite, not very hard anyway. Domingo looked at the different storefronts as he walked away. One store had piles and piles of used clothing covering the floor like giant anthills. At the next corner, he heard norteño music coming from down the street. Men and women were laughing and stumbling out of a cantina. He had never entered these places near the center of town, thinking that no one wanted to see an old man drinking and feeling sorry for himself.

The bus station was a plain white building that would have gone unnoticed by most people if it were not for the buses heading to the North every hour. Taxis were lined up in front of the terminal, waiting for the passengers that had arrived. The station faced the levee and the International Bridge. Domingo recognized the sounds of the nightlife coming from across the river, but he continued to walk as though he had not heard anything.

He turned the corner in front of the station and walked two blocks before he saw the tree. A man was kneeling at the altar. His wife stood trembling next to him, one hand on her husband's shoulder and the other hand on an aluminum walker. As the husband prayed beneath the tree, Domingo could see the image of the Virgin Mary with her arms wide open.

Now that he was finally looking at the tree up close, he didn't know if he could pray beneath it, if he could see it as more than just a tree. He wanted to believe this was the work of God. It was God who had made the tree, so He must have also created the image of the Virgin Mary. Domingo remembered the famous story of Juan Diego and how the image of the Virgen de Guadalupe appeared before him in the hills of Tepeyac and how at first nobody believed him. Domingo wondered how one man could have so much faith in his beliefs. He felt a deep sorrow for having turned his back on God because of the misfortunes in his life.

When the man finished praying at the altar, he wiped away his tears and helped his wife into their car. Saliva ran off her chin and onto her T-shirt. The husband placed the walker inside the trunk and drove away.

Domingo removed his hat and made the sign of the cross as he knelt at the altar. A chain-link fence stood between him and the image. Next to the tree was a white house with its lights off. As much as he wanted to make peace with God, he felt strange kneeling beneath the tree. The truth was, he wanted to leave and wait until the morning when the churches would open, but he couldn't allow this day to pass him by. People had left dozens of photos tacked onto a large piece of plywood leaning against the fence. He looked at the pictures—three men standing next to an elderly woman sitting in a rocking chair, a young soldier back from the war, an older woman wearing a graduation gown, a wrecked car, a retarded woman sitting next to a giant teddy bear, a newborn baby with tubes connected to his mouth and belly— and tried to set aside his doubts. Domingo bowed his head and prayed to the Virgin Mary to please send a message to his Sara. He wanted her to know that her father had kept her memory alive and that he always would as long as God gave him air to breathe. He had not forgotten what day this was, and if she were here, he himself would sing "Las Mañanitas" to her, the same way her mother had done on her first birthday. He explained to the Virgin how much he wanted to be on a bus headed home so he could wake up the next morning to the warm touch of his wife. He missed her cooking and being able to share his meals with her. Then he remembered that the reason he had come to the tree was to ask for God's forgiveness. Domingo felt ashamed for having put his desires first. He begged the Virgin to help him ask for mercy. He and his wife had lost their little girl, and he, who had always believed in the hand of God, had turned away when his prayers went unanswered. He pleaded with the Virgin to intervene on his behalf and ask God for another chance to show his devotion and become His most faithful servant once again. He had tried to be a good man all the years God had given him on earth. He had worked hard to provide for his family. Everyone knew this about him. He swore he would have been a good father to Sara if there had been more time. Then he tried to pray an avemaría, except it had been so long since he had prayed that he could not remember more than the first verse. There was a tightness in his chest and he was having trouble breathing. He tried hard to remember another prayer. Domingo begged the Virgin to forgive him, but now he felt as though he were speaking to himself: he was lost beneath the tree.

He stepped back from the altar. The people in the photos seemed to be laughing at him, as if it had been a trick all along. He felt foolish for having believed that he could find the Virgin Mother in the bark of a tree, that he could ask for God's forgiveness by kneeling at an altar on a city street. The tree had no special powers except the ones people placed on it. He was not going to find peace with God here, not any more than he was going find it on la señora's roof or in the little room where he slept every night. Domingo turned his back to the tree and walked away.

People were boarding the same bus that had arrived earlier. He could see a young couple with their arms around each other. The young woman was crying as the man boarded the bus. A mother walked on board holding her little girl by the hand. An older woman wearing a baseball cap carried two large plastic bags filled with grapefruits. A man in short pants held a large radio. The bus driver took each of their tickets. Domingo hesitated on the street corner, asking himself what he should do next. The music was louder from the other side of the river now. All he had to do was walk up the small grassy embankment to see the lights of his country. The thought of going down to the edge of the river entered his mind, but he remembered how dangerous it could be if the authorities spotted him. The bus stopped next to him and waited for the traffic light to turn green. When Domingo looked up, the little girl was looking out the window. Her mother held her in the seat and the little girl stared at Domingo. There was nothing unusual about them, but seeing them pull away, he felt they could've been his own wife and daughter if his life had turned out differently, or if only he would've had more faith. He watched the bus disappear into the center of town, and he walked back to the tree.

Domingo passed the altar and climbed onto the fence. Then he pulled himself up to the first limb. He stood and gently tossed his shoes into the grass, careful not to wake the people who lived in the house next to the tree. The second branch was more difficult, but he strained and pulled until he was standing on it. He slid his feet along so he could get to the final branch. To reach it, he stood on his toes and then swung his right leg over the top. He was thankful that his body did not fail him. He held on to the tree. This last branch was higher than la señora's roof. He could see most of the city and the few cars that were on the street. The wind was strong and he held his hat in one hand. He closed his eyes as the wind blew through his hair. He prayed again, but this time he prayed to God directly. He told God that he was a poor man who had tried to comprehend the mysteries of life. Perhaps this was something no man could comprehend, but in his heart he needed to know why he and his wife had lost their child. And now almost twenty years later, he had discovered there was no answer: it had been the will of God. There was nothing he could do but accept the life he had been given. He asked God for forgiveness and then, for just a second, he let go of the tree in order to make the sign of the cross. In that moment, he felt light enough to blow away like a leaf. It frightened him at first, but he forced himself to let go of the tree again. This time he kept his arms open and waited for his fear to pass. When he opened his eyes, he gazed out toward the horizon, farther than he had ever imagined he could. He looked across the river, past the nightclub lights on Obregón, past the shoeshine stands in Plaza Hidalgo, past the bus station where he caught his long ride home, past all the little towns and ranchitos on the way to Ciudad Victoria, past the Sierra Madre and the endless shrines for people who had died along the road, and even farther, past the loneliness of his little room next to the tire shop, past the reality that he would work the rest of his life and still die poor, and finally, past the years of sorrow he had spent remembering his little girl, past all this, until he clearly saw his wife and then his daughter, Sara, who was now a grown woman.

GLORIA ANZALDÚA

from *Borderlands* (1987)

TIERRA NATAL. This is home, the small towns in the Valley, *los pueblitos* with chicken pens and goats picketed to mesquite shrubs. *En los colonias* on the other side of the tracks, junk cars line the front yards of hot pink and lavender-trimmed houses—Chicano architecture we call it, self-consciously. I have missed the TV shows where hosts speak in half and half, and where awards are given in the category of Tex-Mex music. I have missed the Mexican cemeteries blooming with artificial flowers, the fields of aloe vera and red peppers, rows of sugarcane, of corn hanging on the stalks, the cloud of *polvareda* in the dirt roads behind a speeding pickup truck, *el sabor de tamales de rez y venado.* I have missed *la yegua colorada* gnawing the wooden gate of her stall, the smell of horse flesh from Carito's corrals. *He hecho menos las noches calientes sin aire, noches de linternas y lechuzas* making holes in the night.

I STILL FEEL THE OLD DESPAIR when I look at the unpainted, dilapidated, scrap lumber houses consisting mostly of corrugated aluminum. Some of the poorest people in the U.S. live in the Lower Rio Grande Valley, an arid and semi-arid land of irrigated farming, intense sunlight and heat, citrus groves next to chaparral and cactus. I walk through the elementary school I attended so long ago, that remained segregated until recently. I remember how the white teachers used to punish us for being Mexican.

How I love this tragic valley of South Texas, as Ricardo Sanchéz calls it, this borderland between the Nueces and the Rio Grande. This land has survived possession and ill-use by five countries: Spain, Mexico, the Republic of Texas, the U.S., the Confederacy, and the U.S. again. It has survived Anglo-American blood feuds, lynchings, burnings, rapes, pillage.

Today I see the Valley still struggling to survive. Whether it does or not, it will never be as I remember it. The borderlands depression that was set off by the 1982 peso devaluation in Mexico resulted in the closure of hundreds of Valley businesses. Many people lost their homes, cars, land. Prior to 1982, U.S. store owners thrived on retail sales to Mexicans who came across the border for groceries and clothes and appliances. While goods on the U.S. side have become 10, 100, 1,000 times more expensive for Mexican buyers, goods on the Mexican side have become 10, 100, 1000 times cheaper for Americans. Because the Valley is heavily dependent on agriculture and Mexican retail trade, it has the highest unemployment along the entire border region; it is the Valley that has been hardest hit.

"It's been a bad year for corn," my brother, Nune, says. As he talks, I remember my father scanning the sky for a rain that would end the drought, looking up into the sky, day after day, while the corn withered on its stalk. My father has been dead for 29 years, having worked himself to death. The life span of a Mexican farm laborer is 56—he lived to be 38. It shocks me that I am older than he; I, too, search the sky for rain. Like the ancients, I worship the rain god and the maize goddess, but unlike my father I have recovered their names. Now for rain (irrigation) one offers not a sacrifice of blood, but money.

"Farming is in a bad way," my brother says. "Two to three thousand small and big farmers went bankrupt in this country last year. Six years ago the price of corn was $8.00 per hundred pounds," he goes on. "This year it is $3.90 per hundred pounds." And, I think, after taking inflation into account, not planting anything puts you ahead.

I walk out to the back yard, stare at *los rosales de mamá*. She wants me to help her prune the rose bushes, dig out the carpet grass that is choking them. *Mamagrande Ramona también tenía rosales*. Here every Mexican grows roses. If they don't have a piece of dirt, they use car tires, jars, cans, shoe boxes. Roses are the Mexican's favorite flower, I think, how symbolic—thorns and all.

Yes, the Chicano and the Chicana have always taken care of growing things and the land. Again I see the four of us kids getting off the school bus, changing into our work clothes, walking into the field with Papí and Mamí, all six of us bending to the ground. Below our feet, under the earth lie the watermelon seeds. We cover them with paper plates, putting *terremotes* on top of the plates to keep them from being blown away by the wind. The paper plates help keep the freeze away. Next day or the next, we remove the plates, bare the tiny green shoots to the elements. They survive and grow, give fruit hundreds of times the size of the seed. We water them and hoe them. We harvest them. The vines dry, rot, are plowed under. Growth, death, decay, birth. The soil prepared again and again, impregnated, worked on. *A constant changing of forms, renacamientos de la tierra madre.*

This land was Mexican once
was Indian always
and is.
And will be again.

FRANK ARMSTRONG

EARL NOTTINGHAM

EPILOGUE

THAT DAY GILBERTO RODRIGUEZ took me to Boca Chica, he said that as a boy he could remember a tiny Mexican village beside the river's mouth. His reminiscence made me think of Paul Horgan's masterful book *Great River: The Rio Grande in North American History* and its passages on a similar hamlet, the long-extinct Bagdad. For most of its existence, Bagdad, Mexico, was a cluster of reed huts occupied by contrabandistas and plastered with mud and oyster shells. Like Matamoros, Bagdad enjoyed a heyday during our Civil War—receiving bales of Southern cotton across the river then loading them on European ships that were evading the Union naval blockade. But in 1867, just two years after the war ended and that trade evaporated, the worst hurricane in the Valley's history killed twenty-two people in Bagdad and left just four buildings standing. Like the fishing village that Rodriguez recalled, it was now gone without a trace.

BILL WRIGHT

In his book Horgan wrote about American troops who were stationed beside the Rio Grande during the U.S.-Mexican War. Ordered to stand watch on Bagdad in 1847 was an army lieutenant from Indiana named Lew Wallace. Later in life, as a retired general and governor of New Mexico Territory, he would orchestrate the manhunt for Billy the Kid while writing the novel *Ben-Hur,* which during its day would be exceeded as a best seller only by the Bible. But that posting to a disease-ridden bivouac on the gulf had the young officer wondering if he had any future at all. Wallace described the sight of fresh troops "marching by, flags flying, drums beating, and hurrying toward boats as if they smelled the contagion in our camp or feared an order for them to stop and take our place . . . There was not a soul among us so simple as not to see that we were in limbo."

As Rodriguez and I walked, I looked back at the Border Patrol jeep and the two agents intently watching the gulf and its sand. It struck me that those guardians trying to make Homeland Security work in a place so ill-adapted for its rigors were captives of their own drumbeats and limbo. I was in a meeting once when George W. Bush talked about the unfairness and folly of barricades against Latino immigrants in search of work. "Hell, if they'll walk across Big Bend, we want 'em," he exclaimed, grinning. But he was just a governor then. As everyone keeps saying—it is the cliché of our times—the world has changed.

The fighters of the Rio Grande's water wars are no less in limbo. The river's literature and legend are so full of people swimming, swimming: now I watch the boys wading its mouth with fishing nets, their stomachs barely getting wet. About the time Mexico defaulted on its water debt to the United States and the two presidents chose to ignore the subject, three fed-up Mexicans took matters into their own hands. With shovels they dug a 400-foot-long ditch through the sandbar at Boca Chica, enabling the Rio Grande to run free for the first time in nearly a year. But within a week the tides and currents just laid the sand back in strips. The sand bar was intact. Days later, heavy rains set in again, and muddy floodwater again washed out into the surf. But as the year warmed up, the flow would again grow feeble. We have let the Rio Grande become the river that can no longer find its way to the sea.

ADAMS, ANSEL. Born in San Francisco in 1902, Adams taught himself to play the piano at age twelve and believed music was his calling, but in the 1920s, while hiking in the California highlands, the purity of light and scene before him redirected him to the camera. In addition to photographing nature, he documented the internment of Japanese-Americans in 1943. Photos taken along the upper Rio Grande in the 1940s contain some of his most popular images. President Jimmy Carter awarded Adams the Presidential Medal of Freedom in 1980. He died in 1984.

ANZALDÚA, GLORIA. A Chicana, feminist, poet, prose writer, and cultural critic, Anzaldúa grew up in the Rio Grande Valley. Her *Borderlands / La Frontera* (1987) employs English and Spanish in a variety of forms. She is editor of *Making Face / Making Soul: Haciendo Caras* (1990) and co-editor of *This Bridge Called My Back: Writings by Radical Women of Color* (1983), which won the Before Columbus Foundation American Book Award. Other honors include the 1991 Lesbian Rights Award. Anzaldúa lives, writes, and teaches in northern California.

ARMSTRONG, FRANK. A native of rural East Texas, Armstrong discovered photography while stationed by the Navy in the Aleutian Islands. A protégé of Russell Lee and Garry Winogrand, he has been a Dobie-Paisano fellow, and his work is represented in the permanent collections of the Museum of Modern Art, the National Museum of American Art, the Amon Carter Museum in Fort Worth, and the Harry Ransom Humanities Research Center at the University of Texas at Austin. Armstrong lives and teaches in Massachusetts but for many years has focused on Big Bend and the Rio Grande. His book *Rock, River & Thorn*, was published in 2001.

AULTMAN, OTIS. Born in Missouri in 1874, Aultman moved to El Paso at thirty-five and worked the rest of his life as a commercial photographer. He documented the city's growth from a frontier to a Victorian town, a dramatic counterpoint to the Mexican Revolution. He was initially a favorite of Pancho Villa, who called him "the banty rooster" of the American press. Aultman was the first photographer on the scene at Columbus, New Mexico, after Villa's raid there in 1916, and he followed the retaliatory invasion of Chihuahua by General John Pershing and the U.S. Cavalry. Aultman died in 1943; *Photographs from the Border* was published in 1977.

BALLÍ, CECILIA. A native of Brownsville, Texas, Ballí has reported for the *San Antonio Express-News* and is a writer-at-large for *Texas Monthly*. Her investigation of Juárez, "Ciudad de la Muerte," was chosen, in slightly different form, for the anthology *Best American Crime Writing*. She is finishing a book about the Juárez murders.

BLAKE, JAMES CARLOS. Blake is a writer with roots and footing in two nations. His mother's family had a ranch south of the Rio Grande in Tamaulipas, Mexico, but she attended American schools in the Valley. Blake's father was a Mexican highway engineer who resented how he had been treated in the United States, though professional opportunity prompted him to move to Florida. Blake's novel of the U.S.-Mexican War, *In the Rogue Blood* (1997), won the Los Angeles Times Book Prize for fiction. Set in Florida, *Red Grass River* (1998) won the Chatauqua South Book Award. Blake has written seven novels, as well as *Borderlands* (1999), which contains short stories and a resonant memoir of his upbringing. Blake tends to live where he sets and researches his books. In recent years he has shown up in El Paso and Galveston.

BONAR, AVE. A longtime resident of Austin, Bonar was a University of Texas journalism student when she met her mentor, Russell Lee. One of fourteen photographers named by the Texas Historical Commission to produce *Contemporary Texas* (1986), she took as her assignment the lower Rio Grande Valley. Bonar spent months documenting Ann Richards' winning campaign for governor; her book *With Ann* was published in 1991. Her most recent project explores the Norwegian heritage of Bosque County.

BOSWELL, ROBERT. A prize-winning playwright and author of fiction, Boswell grew up on a tobacco farm in Kentucky, near a part of the Mississippi River that inspired Mark Twain. His novel of born-again Christians, *Mystery Ride*, was a bestseller in 1993. Boswell's honors include Guggenheim and NEA grants and a 1995 PEN Award for a story collection, *Living to Be a Hundred*. His novel *American Owned Love* (1997) grew out of his experience living beside the Rio Grande and teaching at New Mexico State in Las Cruces. He has also guided student writers at the University of Houston.

BOWDEN, CHARLES. A resident of Tucson, Bowden has spent most of his life in the deserts of Arizona. He reports that he writes for magazines to keep the lights on— among them *Esquire*, *Harper's*, and *GQ*—and then takes this loot and scribbles books. His first, *Killing the Hidden Waters* (1977), detailed drought, rationing, pollution, rights wars, and insatiable consumption of water in the West. *Blood Orchid* (1995) and *Blues for Cannibals* (2002) provided searing looks at the underbelly of North American life. Bowden writes with intense emotion and authority about El Paso and Ciudad Juárez, the primary setting of *Down by the River* (2002), an investigation of international drug trafficking and law enforcement.

BRITO, ARISTEO. Construction of the first bridge across the Rio Grande introduced Brito to the notion of "illegal crossings" between his hometowns of Presidio, Texas, and Ojinaga, Chihuahua. His first book of fiction and verse, *Cuentos I poemas*, was published in 1974. Drawing on legend, folklore, and historical archives, he wrote a novel in Spanish, *El Diablo en Texas* (1976). David William Foster translated the work into English, *The Devil in Texas*; it has been hailed as a groundbreaking work of Chicano literature. Brito's novel won the 1990 Western States Book Award for Fiction. He lives in Tucson.

CARTWRIGHT, GARY. A native of Arlington, Texas, Cartwright went to college, joined the army, and then got a job at the talent-rich but impecunious *Fort Worth Press*, where his boss was Blackie Sherrod and his colleagues included Dan Jenkins and Bud Shrake. In the next decade, *Harper's* published his account of a job misadventure in Philadelphia as "Confessions of a Washed-Up Sportswriter," marking a new phase of his career. A novel about pro football, *The Hundred Yard War* (1968), was followed in 1973 by the start of his association with *Texas Monthly*. Cartwright produced exhaustively reported books about murders, *Blood Will Tell* (1979) and *Dirty Dealing* (1984), and an appreciation of people and place, *Galveston* (1991). His other books include a reckoning of mortality, *Heartwise Guy* (1998).

CASARES, OSCAR. Born and raised in Brownsville, Texas, Casares worked for an advertising agency in Austin and wrote stories drawn from memories and tales of his family and community along the Rio Grande. He is a graduate of the Iowa Writers Workshop. His honors include the Dobie-Paisano Fellowship and the James

Michener Award from the Copernicus Society of America. His much-praised story collection *Brownsville* was published in 2003. He teaches writing and Mexican American studies at the University of Texas at Austin.

CESSAC, CHRISTOPHER. A poet whose published credits include the *Antioch Review* and *Cimarron Review*, Cessac works as an attorney and performs as a rock musician, making his home in the Big Bend town of Marfa. His first book, *Republic Sublime*, won the 2002 *Kenyon Review* Prize in Poetry.

DAVIDSON, JOHN. A recipient of Dobie-Paisano and NEA fellowships, Davidson grew up in Fredericksburg, Texas, lives in Austin, and has written for publications including *Texas Monthly* and *Vanity Fair*. His book about undocumented Mexican immigrants, *The Long Road North* (1979), was honored as the nonfiction book of the year by the Texas Institute of Letters. He is currently working on a book about the Mexico City salon and heyday of Leon Trotsky, Frida Kahlo, and Diego Rivera.

DRAPER, ROBERT. The grandson of Watergate special prosecutor Leon Jaworski, Draper came of age in Houston and Austin. His *Rolling Stone Magazine: The Uncensored History* (1990) led to a run as a senior writer for *Texas Monthly*. *Hadrian's Walls* (1999), rooted in his investigations of prison life, won the Texas Institute of Letters award for best first fiction. Draper is writer-at-large for *GQ* and lives in Asheville, North Carolina.

EVANS, JAMES. Knowing nothing of pies, Evans talked his way into a job as a pastry cook in order to move to Marathon, Texas, in 1988. Born in West Virginia, he began taking pictures while following drag racing. Evans has worked throughout the Southwest and in Mexico, but his heart's terrain is the Big Bend; his images of the region and its people have appeared in many national magazines and major museums and galleries. His book *Big Bend Pictures* was published in 2003.

FORD, DON HENRY, JR. A horse breeder and trainer at his home near Seguin, Ford was born to a farming family in West Texas. He risked his life smuggling drugs out of Mexico, spending one year as a fugitive and marijuana grower in the Big Bend. Ford completed a term in a U.S. federal penitentiary and began to write. He has written a memoir of his past as an addict and outlaw along the Rio Grande, *Contrabando* (2004).

GILB, DAGOBERTO. Gilb is the author of *Gritos* (2003), *Woodcuts of Women* (2001), *The Last Known Residence of Mickey Acuña* (1994), and *The Magic of Blood* (1993). The latter collection of stories won the PEN/Hemingway Award and the best fiction prize of the Texas Institute of Letters. Born in Los Angeles, Gilb lived for many years in El Paso. He put in twelve years as a union high-rise carpenter. Gilb won notice with stories of funny, proud people bedeviled by lay-offs, broken-down cars, matters of love, and overdue rent. He has written for the *New Yorker*, *Threepenny*

Review, Harper's, GQ, and *Latina.* His honors include Guggenheim and NEA fellowships. He lives in Austin and teaches at Texas State University in San Marcos.

GILPIN, LAURA. The daughter of a would-be cowboy from Baltimore, Gilpin was born near Colorado Springs in 1891. A student of and admirer of the work of Clarence H. White in New York, she compiled folios and books on Mesa Verde and the Pikes Peak region in 1927. *The Pueblos* (1941) led naturally to *The Rio Grande: River of Destiny* (1949). She was the preeminent photographer of the river from its source to the sea. With a career spanning sixty years, Gilpin died in 1979. Her archives are in the Amon Carter Museum in Fort Worth.

GRAVES, JOHN. The Fort Worth native spent much of his boyhood roaming the bottomlands of the Trinity River. He fought in World War II and afterward spent some years discovering Spain. Graves returned to Texas and embarked with his dog and some tackle on a canoe trip down the Brazos; *Goodbye to a River* (1960) established him as one of the most respected American writers. *Hard Scrabble* (1974) and *From a Limestone Ledge* (1980) were drawn from experiences and neighborly encounters on his small ranch near Glen Rose. His latest book, *Myself and Strangers: A Memoir of Apprenticeship* (2004), recollects his years in Spain following World War II.

GREGG, JOSIAH. A physician, Gregg joined a trader's caravan to Santa Fe in 1831 in hopes of improving his health. He was a Santa Fe merchant and correspondent in the Mexican-American War and died in the California Gold Rush in 1849. His 1844 narrative, *Commerce of the Prairies,* provided countless Americans with their first vivid exposure to the Southwest and West.

GUERRA, MARÍA EUGENIA. The editor and publisher of *LareDOS,* a newspaper that serves both sides of the Rio Grande at Laredo and Nuevo Laredo, Guerra lived in Austin for some years, then returned to her native San Vicente to help her parents on a family ranch. Guerra's short story of Guerrero Viejo and the Falcón Reservoir was drawn from tales told by her family and neighbors and from archival research.

GUTHRIE, WOODY. A native Oklahoman, Guthrie was born in 1912 and lived through the Dust Bowl and "Okie" diaspora to California during the Depression. In 1931, when Guthrie was nineteen, his family set out in fruitless quest of a rumored lost silver mine in the Big Bend. Guthrie's famed body of songwriting includes "So Long, It's Been Good to Know You," "Dust Bowl Blues," and "This Land Is Your Land." His autobiography, *Bound for Glory,* appeared in 1943. Guthrie died in 1967 following a long fight with Huntington's Disease. His novel, *Seeds of Man,* was based on his family's rambles along the Rio Grande and was first published in 1976.

HARRIGAN, STEPHEN. Harrigan is a journalist, essayist, screenwriter, and novelist. A Dobie-Paisano Fellowship produced a highly regarded first novel, *Aransas* (1980), which drew on his youth in Corpus Christi and appreciation of the Gulf of Mexico. An essay in *Texas Monthly* and the collection *Comanche Midnight* (1995) inspired more research and reflection that culminated in his masterpiece novel, *The Gates of the Alamo* (2002). Harrigan is working on a novel about astronauts. He makes his home in Austin.

HERNÁNDEZ, IRENE BELTRÁN. Hernández was a fifteen-year veteran case worker for the Dallas Health and Human Services Department when she decided to try writing books for young adults. *Across the Great River* (1989) was rejected forty-one times, but when finally published, its story of a Mexican girl forced to struggle as an illegal alien helped establish a market for books aimed at young readers who identified with Latino characters and themes. Her subsequent novels include *Heartbeat Drumbeat* (1992), *The Secret of Two Brothers* (1995), and *Woman Soldier / La Soldadera* (2000). She lives in Satin, Texas.

HILL, ROBERT T. An officer of the United States Geological Survey assigned to the Texas-Mexico borderlands, Hill led the first thorough and recorded exploration of the Big Bend canyons of the Rio Grande. With five companions and three boats, Hill's 1899 expedition took to the river at Presidio and emerged many weeks and hardships later at the rail depot and saloon in Langtry run by Judge Roy Bean. His account of the journey was published by *Century Magazine* in 1901.

HILLERMAN, TONY. Born and educated in Oklahoma, where he developed a sustaining interest in Native American life, Hillerman set out on a career as a newspaper reporter in several towns in the West, then taught at the University of New Mexico in Albuquerque. There he launched a series of acclaimed mystery novels set among the Navajo. *Skinwalkers* vaulted Hillerman's books to bestseller lists in 1987. His memoir, *Seldom Disappointed*, won the Agatha Award for Best Nonfiction in 2001.

HINOJOSA, ROLANDO. A pioneering and motivating figure among Chicano writers, Hinojosa grew up in Mercedes, Texas. Following army service in Korea, Hinojosa taught high school English in the Valley. His first novel, *Estampas del Valle* (1982), won a Cuban literary prize, Premio de Las Casas de las Américas, which brought recognition of his talent throughout Latin America. Hinojosa has spent many years writing novels drawn from a complex saga that encompasses sixty years in the Valley. He calls these books "The Klail City Death-Trip Series." Hinojosa writes in English and Spanish. He teaches at the James Michener Writing Center at the University of Texas at Austin.

HORGAN, PAUL. Horgan, who died in 1995 at his home in Connecticut, was a master of both fiction and nonfiction (and was a better than fair watercolorist). Born in 1904, he lived in New Mexico for many years and set most of his books in the Southwest. Horgan's definitive two-volume history, *Great River: The Rio Grande in*

North American History (1955), won the Pulitzer and Bancroft prizes. He won a second Pulitzer in history for *Lamy of Santa Fe* (1975).

IVINS, MOLLY. Ivins was a longtime co–editor, with Kaye Northcott, of the *Texas Observer*. Ivins' career as a reporter led her to the *New York Times*, *Dallas Times-Herald*, *Fort Worth Star-Telegram*, and a nationally syndicated column, which established her as one of America's favorite humorists and political commentators. She broke out as a best-selling author with *Molly Ivins Can't Say That, Can She?* (1991). Co-written with her colleague Lou Dubose, her most recent books, *Shrub* (2000) and *Bushwhacked* (2003), have assessed the politics and presidency of George W. Bush. Ivins lives in Austin.

KELTON, ELMER. Kelton grew up on a ranch in Crane County. Following service in World War II, he took up the newspaper profession. He worked at *Livestock Weekly* from 1968 until his retirement in 1991, but has found time to write more than forty books, most of them novels. Kelton achieved lasting stature with a mid-career burst of inspiration that produced *The Day the Cowboys Quit* (1972), *The Time It Never Rained* (1974), *The Good Old Boys* (1978), and *The Wolf and the Buffalo* (1980). He has won four Western Heritage Awards from the National Cowboy Hall of Fame and seven Spur awards from the Western Writers of America, including one for *The Way of the Coyote* (2002). The Western Writers of America named Kelton the All-Time Best Western Author.

LANGEWIESCHE, WILLIAM. Perhaps more than any major American writer, this Californian has pursued a life without borders. Son of a noted aviator and author on flying, Langewiesche worked his way through Stanford as a pilot and first wrote for flight magazines. He gained the attention of the *Atlantic Monthly* with dispatches from Algeria. His first book, *Cutting for Sign* (1995), explored the U.S.-Mexico border. Other hailed books of reporting include *Sahara Unveiled* (1996) and *American Ground: Unbuilding the World Trade Center* (2002).

LEE, RUSSELL. Lee became one of the star photographers brought by Roy Stryker to a Farm Security Administration project during the 1930s and early 1940s. Born in 1903, Lee studied chemical engineering in college and tried to be a painter. He took his first photographs in the mid-1930s at the Woodstock Art Colony and in New York City. He won work from *Collier's* and *American Magazine* and met Stryker, who put him afield with Walker Evans, Dorothea Lange, Carl Mydans, Gordon Parks, and Arthur Rothstein. Lee found humor, elegance, and dignity in people who withstood the Dust Bowl, racial prejudice, and the Depression. Lee taught at the University of Texas from 1965 to 1973; his protégés included Jim Bones, Rick Williams, and Ave Bonar. He died in 1986.

LIMMER, ARTIE. Limmer is creative director of the office of news and publicity at Texas Tech University in Lubbock. A contributing photographer for *Texas Monthly*,

Limmer pursued the length of the Rio Grande in less than a week, illustrating Jan
Reid's "The End of the River" in 2003.

LOGAN, WILLIAM (BILL). Following a boyhood in Austin and Dallas, Logan survived
intense combat in World War II, graduated from the University of Texas, and worked
most of his life as a newspaperman. For twenty-three years he was the outdoors
editor of the *Rocky Mountain News* in Denver. Logan, who died in 1995, created an
alter-ego who held forth on hunting, fishing, and human nature; *The Old Meat
Hunter*, a collection of those columns, is being edited and illustrated by his son, Bill
Logan.

MCMURTRY, LARRY. The son of a cattle rancher has been the preeminent novelist of
Texas since the publication of his first book, *Horseman, Pass By* (1961). McMurtry's
epic take on a trail drive, *Lonesome Dove* (1985), won the Pulitzer. Throughout his
career McMurtry has inspired moviemakers with story, character, and setting: *Hud*
(adapted from the first novel), *The Last Picture Show* (1966), *Terms of Endearment*
(1975), and *Lonesome Dove* are classics of American film. McMurtry's accomplished
nonfiction includes *In a Narrow Grave* (1968), *Walter Benjamin at the Dairy Queen*
(1999), and *Sacagawea's Nickname* (2001). He is one of the country's premier
bookmen; Booked Up, his store in his hometown of Archer City, is a marvel.

MENDOZA, ROBERTO. A man of diverse and far-reaching interests, Mendoza was born
in California and grew up in Laredo. He holds degrees in English literature and
Latin American studies; he has worked as a house painter and taught in secondary
schools in the United States and Spain. He lives in Austin. Mendoza's reminis-
cences of his family ranch beside the Rio Grande is first published here. He reports that the ranch remains unsold.

MILLER, TOM. Miller lives in Tucson and writes about Cuba, baseball, Panama hats,
Rio Grande smugglers, the heart of Africa—wherever his avid interests lead him,
he seems to find a way. Miller, whose credits include the *New York Times*, *Rolling
Stone*, *Smithsonian*, and *Esquire*, is the author of *Trading with the Enemy* (1996) and
Jack Ruby's Kitchen Sink (2000). The latter won the Lowell Thomas Award for the
year's best travel book. Miller traversed the length of the U.S.-Mexico frontier in
a collection of pieces, *On the Border* (1982), and has edited an anthology of writing
about the border, *Writing on the Edge* (2003).

NICHOLS, JOHN. Born in Berkeley, Nichols has lived and worked in Taos since 1969.
With penetrating wit and style, he has written fiction and nonfiction about water
rights and ethnic conflict in New Mexico and about issues of war, peace, and
injustice throughout the United States and Latin America. His much-praised novels include *The Sterile Cuckoo* (1965) and *The Milagro Beanfield War* (1974), both of
which were made into popular movies.

NOTTINGHAM, EARL. Award-winning chief photographer for the Texas Parks and Wildlife Department, Nottingham has been taking pictures in that capacity since 1996. He has worked for *Smithsonian, Southern Living*, and *National Geographic Traveler*. In 2002, he took the photos selected here for a special report on the Rio Grande by Rod Davis in *Texas Parks & Wildlife Magazine*. His work on the Rio Grande won top photo honors in the 2002 national awards of the Association of Conservation Information. Nottingham lives in Temple.

PAREDES, AMÉRICO. An English professor, anthropologist, and folklorist greatly admired for the flair of his prose, Paredes was born in 1915 and grew up in Brownsville, spending his summers entranced by storytelling performance and tradition in northern Mexico. During World War II he was political editor of the armed forces newspaper, *Stars & Stripes*. After the war, he took degrees from the University of Texas and won a faculty position. *With His Pistol in His Hand: A Border Ballad and Its Hero* (1958) conveyed his enthusiasm for the antiestablishment song form of the border, the *corrido*. *Folktales of Mexico* (1970) was succeeded by his collection of songs, *A Texas-Mexican Cancionero* (1976). Paredes' stylish phrasing and feel for the Rio Grande Valley communities that reared him are on rich display in his novel *George Washington Gómez* (1990), and in a poetry collection, *Between Two Worlds* (1991). In 1989, he became the first Mexican American to receive the prestigious Charles Frankel Prize from the National Endowment for the Humanities. He died in 1999 at age eighty-three.

PAYNE, RICHARD. A registered architect and nationally recognized architectural photographer, Payne lives in Houston and has worked on several books that include *Historic Galveston* (1986) and *The Architecture of Philip Johnson* (2002). *Guerrero Viejo*, with a text by Mexican journalist Elena Poniatowska, was published in 1997 by his company, Anchorage Press.

POGUE, ALAN. Through his Center for Documentary Photography in Austin, Pogue seeks to illumine the displaced and downtrodden. His subjects have included Palestinian refugees, Iraqi war victims, migrant farmworkers, and undocumented immigrants. Pogue contributes often to the *Texas Observer*.

PONIATOWSKA, ELENA. Born in Paris in 1933, she moved to Mexico in 1942 with her mother, whose wealthy family had been uprooted by the Mexican Revolution. She lives in the Federal District and has worked as a journalist since 1954. Literary recognition came with her first novel, *Hasta no verte, Jesús mío* (1969). Next came her investigation of the massacre of students by government troops in Mexico City, *La noche de Tlatelolco* (1971). In 1979 Poniatowska was the first woman to receive the national journalism prize in Mexico. *Nothing, Nobody* (1995) details a calamitous earthquake in Mexico City. She won the esteemed international

Alfaguara Prize for her novel *La piel del cielo* (2001). Poniatowska came to the Mexico-Texas borderlands to write an introduction for the photos of Richard Payne and stayed to produce *Guerrero Viejo* (1997), an elegant book about the half-flooded town and its human holdouts. Laurie Manning translated her text from Spanish.

REAVIS, DICK J. Inclined toward a career in journalism by a father who published a newspaper in the Texas Panhandle, Reavis has roamed and written about Mexico as a correspondent for *Texas Monthly* and the *Dallas Times-Herald* and in his book *Conversations with Moctezuma* (1990). His unflinching investigation shed light on the Branch Davidian tragedy in *The Ashes of Waco* (1995). Reavis is a past Neiman fellow at Harvard and won the 2003 Texas Institute of Letters Award for newspaper writing for a series on homelessness published in the *San Antonio Express-News*. He now teaches at North Carolina State University in Raleigh.

REED, JOHN. A radicalized son of a Portland insurance salesman, in 1914 the Harvard graduate was commissioned by *Metropolitan Magazine* to cover the Mexican Revolution. His dispatches from the camps and battlefields of Pancho Villa established him as a war correspondent and were published as *Insurgent Mexico* that same year. He was in Russia in 1919 when the Bolshevik revolution erupted. He wrote the influential *Ten Days That Shook the World* (1922) and joined that cause, helping found the American Communist Party. Reed died in 1920 at thirty-two; he is the only American buried as a revolutionary hero in the Kremlin.

REID, JAN. Reid grew up in Wichita Falls, Texas, and has made his home in Austin since 1980. He has a career-long freelance affiliation with *Texas Monthly* and has written for *Esquire, GQ, Slate*, and other major magazines. An early article spawned his first book, *The Improbable Rise of Redneck Rock* (1974, with a revised and updated edition published by the University of Texas Press, 2004). Other books include the novel *Deerinwinter* (1985), the collection *Close Calls* (2000), and a memoir, *The Bullet Meant for Me* (2002). Reid's honors include a grant from the National Endowment for the Arts and PEN Texas's award for short nonfiction for an essay about his abduction and near-fatal shooting by Mexico City robbers in 1998. He has continued to work along the Rio Grande and in Mexico: his *Texas Monthly* essay "The End of the River" won the Texas Institute of Letters' award for best magazine writing of 2003.

RUNYON, ROBERT. Born in Kentucky in 1881, Runyon moved to Brownsville in 1909 as a widower looking for a new start. He worked as a commercial photographer until 1926. He documented intensifying fighting and a flood of refugees during the Mexican Revolution. Controversially, he posed Texas Rangers with lariats around corpses of reputed Mexican bandits and circulated the image throughout the United States as a postcard. Though he continued to take pictures of the outdoors and of native plants, he gave up photography as a profession and opened curio stores in Matamoros and Brownsville. Runyon was elected mayor of Brownsville in 1941. He died in 1968.

SMITHERS, W. D. Son of a bookkeeper for a mining company, Smithers was born in San Luis Potosí, Mexico, in 1895. He worked as a teamster for the U.S. cavalry in the Big Bend from 1915 to 1917. He then moved to San Antonio, working as a journalist and commercial photographer. In the early 1930s more unrest on the border prompted him to return to Big Bend. Famous for building a dugout-adobe darkroom that employed sunlight as a light source for his enlarger, Smithers took more than 9,000 photographs. He photographed Pancho Villa, Will Rogers, fur trappers, chino grass merchants, trail drivers, circuit riding preachers, and *curanderos*. After he retired in 1974, he moved to El Paso and wrote an autobiography, *Chronicles of the Big Bend* (1976). He died in 1981.

SPONG, JOHN. A son and nephew of prominent clerics of the Episcopal Church, Spong briefly aspired to be a rodeo clown and bullfighter—it took him one bull to get over it. As an Austin attorney, he held for a time the record as counsel in the largest losing judgment ever rendered by a jury in Travis County. In 2003 *Texas Monthly* sacrificed Spong's talents as a fact-checker and made him a staff writer. He divides his time between Austin and the Big Bend.

WITTLIFF, BILL. Raised in Blanco, Texas, and a longtime resident of Austin, Wittliff is a photographer, writer, publisher, and collector. Wittliff has been honored for his career by the Texas Institute of Letters and is a recipient of the Texas Book Festival Bookend Award. The Encino Press, co-founded with his wife Sally, published works of distinguished literature and history for many years. His screenwriting and film producer credits include *Lonesome Dove*, *The Perfect Storm*, and *The Black Stallion*. His book of photographs, *Vaquero: Genesis of the Texas Cowboy*, was published in 2004. At Texas State University in San Marcos, the Wittliffs have endowed and gathered a treasured archive of writing and photographs of the Southwest and Mexico.

WRIGHT, BILL. A resident of Abilene, Texas, Wright has taken photographs in Antarctica, China, Cuba, Guatemala, Nepal, Mexico, and southern Africa, but he has devoted much of his career to Texas, especially its borderlands. Wright has contributed valuable and critically esteemed books on the Kickapoo and Tigua indigenous tribes; his most recent titles are *Portraits from the Desert: Bill Wright's Big Bend* (1998) and *People's Lives: A Photographic Celebration of the Human Spirit* (2001).

ACKNOWLEDGMENTS AND CREDITS

TWO TRUSTED READERS and good friends played important roles in moving *Rio Grande* from meandering proposals and false starts to the finished book. My agent, David McCormick, suggested an innovative structure—an extensively reported commentary that would be a road map and guide to an anthology of fine writing and photography. Jim Hornfischer began urging me to develop a book about the Rio Grande a decade ago and encouraged me to carry on when its prospects were far from certain.

Ty Fain and his stalwart colleagues at the Rio Grande Institute in Marathon, Texas, and Len Materman of America's River Communities provided moral, material, and creative support. Casey Kittrell was a gifted research assistant, making astute suggestions of content and bringing order to the impossible piles of paper in my office.

Texas Monthly editors Evan Smith and Christopher Keyes and art director Scott Dadich gave the project a large boost at a critical time. Heartfelt thanks to them and to the Texas Institute of Letters for its recognition of the essay "The End of the

River"; and to Theresa May, Dave Hamrick, and all the members of the dedicated staff at the University of Texas Press who worked so hard to make *Rio Grande* a book we are proud to have on our shelves.

And always to my love, wife, and travel companion Dorothy Browne, who pronounced early on that this book was going to be fun and set about delivering on her promise.

CREDITS AND PERMISSIONS TO REPRINT

CESSAC, CHRISTOPHER. "Rio Grande at Noon, Rio Grande at Midnight," from *Republic Sublime*, © 2002 by Christopher Cessac. Used with permission of the author.

DAVIDSON, JOHN. Excerpt from *The Long Road North*, © 1979 by John Davidson. Reprinted by permission of author.

DRAPER, ROBERT. "Soldier of Misfortune," © 1997 by *Texas Monthly*. Reprinted by permission of *Texas Monthly*.

EVANS, JAMES. "Kickapoo Boy Swinging," © 1996, **pg. xxii;** "The Road to Candelaria," © 1997, **pg. 126;** "Boy and Puppy," © 1996, **pg. 135;** "Lajitas Golf Course," © 2002, **pg. 160.** All photographs © by James H. Evans. Used with permission of the photographer.

FORD, DON HENRY, JR. Excerpt from *Contrabando*, ©2004 by Don Henry Ford, Jr., published by Cinco Punto Press. Reprinted with permission of the author.

GILB, DAGOBERTO. Excerpt from *The Last Known Residence of Mickey Acuña*, © 1995 by Dagoberto Gilb. Reprinted with permission of the author.

GILPIN, LAURA. "The Rio Grande Yields Its Surplus to the Sea," **pg. ii–iii;** "The Prospector—Fred Gulzow of Creede," **pg. 3;** "Gorge Below Taos [Midstream Region of the Gorge]," **pg. 18;** "Mexican Irrigator," **pg. 23;** "Elephant Butte Lake," **pg. 40;** "Boy on Donkey, River Background, Near El Paso," **pg. 51;** "Cattle Round Up [Old Timer]," **pg. 194.** Photographs © 1979 Amon Carter Museum, Fort Worth, Texas, Bequest of the Artist. Reprinted with permission of the Amon Carter Museum.

GRAVES, JOHN. "Big River," © 1982 by John Graves, first published in *Texas Monthly*. Reprinted with permission of the author.

GUERRA, MARÍA EUGENIA. "Nothing to Declare," © 1995 by María Eugenia Guerra. Used with permission of the author.

GUTHRIE, WOODY. Excerpt from *Seeds of Man*, © 1976 by Woody Guthrie Publications, Inc. All rights reserved. Reprinted with permission of Woody Guthrie Publications, Inc.

HARRIGAN, STEPHEN. Excerpt from *Comanche Midnight*, © 1995 by Stephen Harrigan. Reprinted with permission of the author.

HERNÁNDEZ, IRENE BELTRÁN. Excerpt from *Across the Great River*, © 1989 by Irene Beltrán Hernández. Reprinted by permission of Arte Público Press—University of Houston.

HILLERMAN, TONY. Excerpted from *New Mexico, Rio Grande and Other Essays*, © 1989 by Tony Hillerman. Reprinted by permission of Graphics Arts Center Publishing.

HINOJOSA, ROLANDO. Excerpt from "A Sense of Place," © 1983 by Rolando Hinojosa. Reprinted by permission of author.

HORGAN, PAUL. Excerpt from *Great River*, © 1955 by the late Paul Horgan. Permission granted by Wesleyan University Press.

336

IVINS, MOLLY. "Mayor of Lajitas Not the Goat He Used to Be," © 2002 by Molly Ivins, from her syndicated newspaper column. Reprinted with permission of the author.

KELTON, ELMER. Excerpt from *The Time It Never Rained*, © 1974 by Elmer Kelton. Reprinted with permission of author.

LANGEWIESCHE, WILLIAM. Excerpt from *Cutting for Sign*, © 1993 by William Langewiesche. Reprinted by permission of Pantheon Books, a division of Random House.

LEE, RUSSELL. "Man on Porch with Family," **pg. 25;** "Home-Building," **pg. 64;** "Girl with Child in Lap," **pg. 235;** "Boy Drinking Water," **pg. 307.** Photographs © 1949 by Russell Lee. Reprinted with permission of Center for American History, The University of Texas at Austin.

LIMMER, ARTIE. "Rio Grande Headwater," **pg. 10;** "Patriotic Bridge," **pg. 54.** Photographs © 2002 by Artie Limmer. Used with permission of the photographer.

LOGAN, WILLIAM (BILL). "The Old Meat Hunter," © 1972 by the *Rocky Mountain News*. Reprinted with permission of the *Rocky Mountain News*.

MCMURTRY, LARRY. Excerpt from *Lonesome Dove*, © 1985 by Larry McMurtry. Reprinted with permission from The Wylie Agency, Inc.

MENDOZA, ROBERTO. "A Piece of Land," © 2003 by Robert Mendoza. Used with permission of the author.

MILLER, TOM. Excerpt from *On the Border*, ©1982 by Tom Miller, published by the University of Arizona Press. Reprinted with permission of the Copyright Clearance Center.

NICHOLS, JOHN. Excerpt from *The Milagro Beanfield War*, © 1974 by John Nichols. Reprinted with permission of author.

NOTTINGHAM, EARL. "River's End," **pg. vi;** "Rio Grande No Más?" **pg. 69;** "Irrigation Pump, Redford," **pg. 88;** "Burned Tamarisk," **pg. 90;** "Herder on Levee, La Junta," **pg. 93;** "Big Bend Baptism," **pg. 302;** "Beached Tree Marking the Border, Boca Chica," **pg. 316.** Photographs © 2002 by Earl Nottingham. Used with permission of the photographer.

PAREDES, AMÉRICO. Excerpt from *George Washington Gómez*, © 1990 by Américo Paredes. Reprinted with permission of Arte Público Press— University of Houston.

PAYNE, RICHARD. Untitled photographs from *Guerrero Viejo*, **pgs. 238, 250.** © 1996 by Richard Payne. Used with permission of the photographer.

POGUE, ALAN. "Illegal Entry," **pg. 60;** "Maquiladora Floor," **pg. 72;** "Mexican Mother and Children in Contaminated Mud," **pg. 273;** "Colonia Beside Stagnant Water," **pg. 287.** Photographs © 2003 by Texas Center for Documentary Photography. Used with permission of the Texas Center for Documentary Photography.

PONIATOWSKA, ELENA. Text of *Guerrero Viejo*, translated by Laurie Mann, © 1997 by Elena Poniatowska. Reprinted with permission of author.

REAVIS, DICK J. "Gateway to Texas," © 2003 by Dick J. Reavis, written on assignment for the *San Antonio Express-News*. Reprinted with permission of the author.

REID, JAN. Portions of the text were published in *Texas Monthly* as "End of the River," © 2003 by Jan Reid; and "The Forgotten River," in *Close Calls*, © 2000 by Jan Reid. The excerpt from "Busting Out of Mexico" is also from *Close Calls*. All rights reserved by the author.

RUNYON, ROBERT. "Soldaderas," **pg. 246;** "Man in Cabbage Patch," **pg. 249;** "Mexican Revolution Refugees," **pg. 262;** "Army Band," **pg. 283.** Reprinted with permission of the Center for American History, The University of Texas at Austin.

SMITHERS, W. D. "El Viejo," **pg. xii;** "Ford on Ferry," **pg. xviii;** "Chino Merchants," **pg. 171;** "Water Boy," **pg. 175;** "Cavalry Commanders," **pg. 183.** Permission granted by the Photography Collection, Harry Ransom Humanities Research Center, The University of Texas at Austin.

SPONG, JOHN. "Sand Trap," © 2002 by *Texas Monthly*. Reprinted by permission of *Texas Monthly*.

WITTLIFF, BILL. "Lonesome Dove, Del Rio, 1988," **cover image.** Courtesy of Southwest Writers Collection, Texas State University, San Marcos.

WRIGHT, BILL. "Early Morning at Paso Lajitas," © 1994, **pg. 156;** "Baby and Horse, Boquillas, Coahuilla, Mexico," © 1985, **pg. 318.** Photographs © Bill Wright. Reprinted with permission of the photographer.

EXCERPTS THAT WERE PUBLIC DOMAIN

GREGG, JOSIAH. Excerpt from *Commerce of the Prairies*, first published in 1844.

HILL, ROBERT T. Excerpt from "Running the Cañons of the Rio Grande," first published in *Century Magazine*, 1901.

REED, JOHN. Excerpt from *Insurgent Mexico*, first published in 1914.